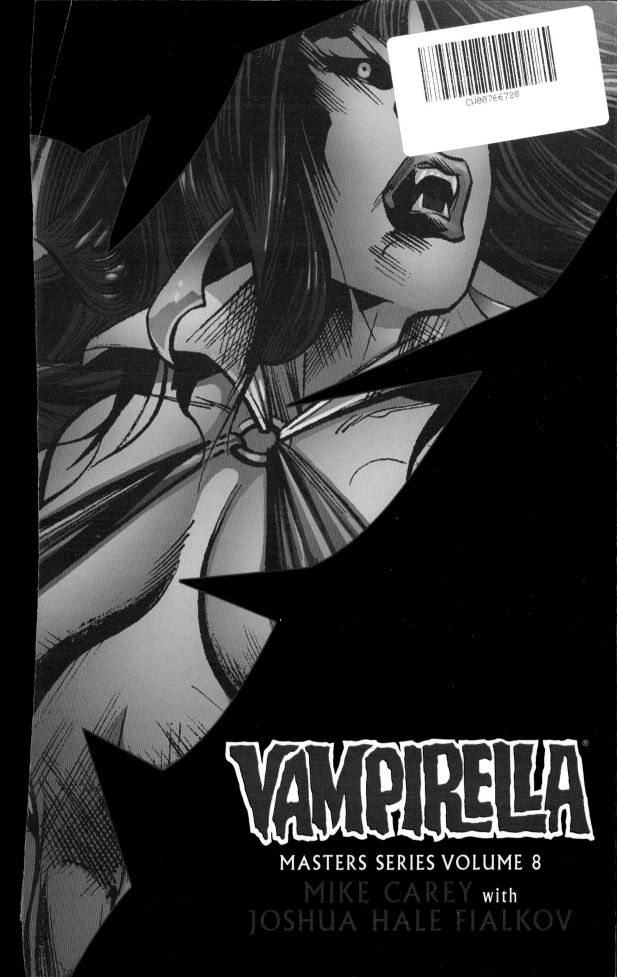

VAMPIRELLA

MASTERS SERIES VOLUME 8

MIKE CAREY with
JOSHUA HALE FIALKOV

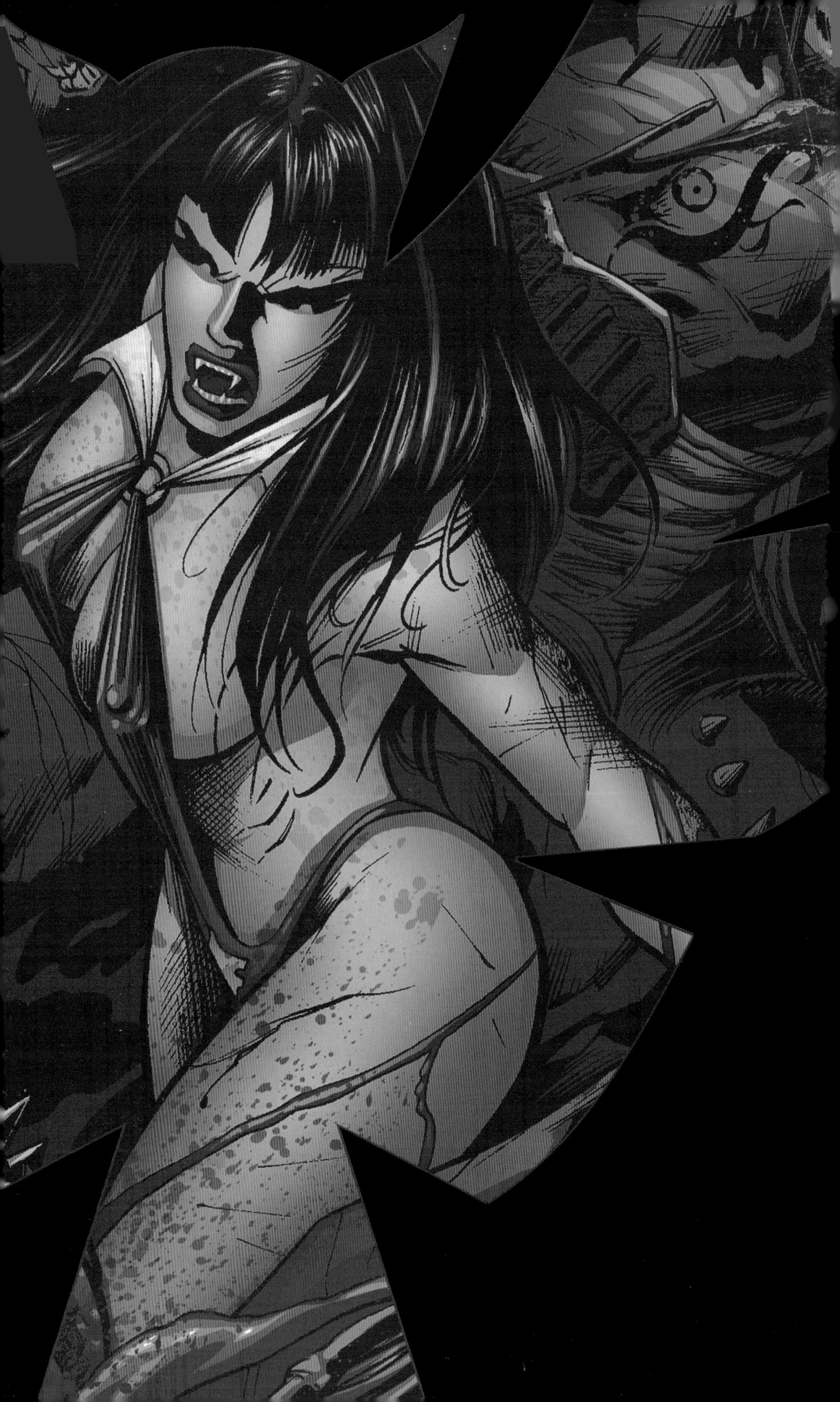

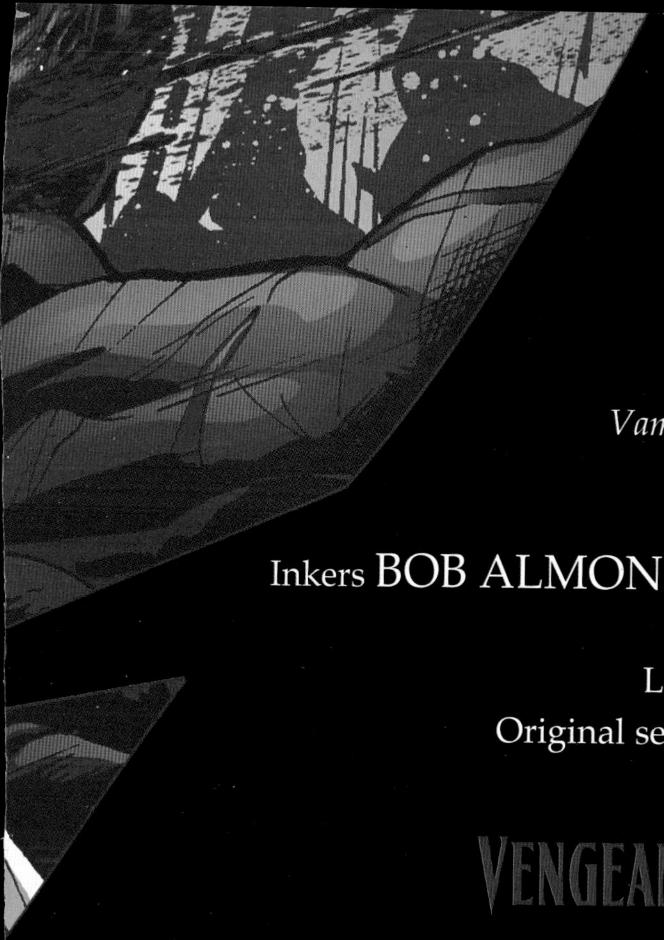

REVELATIONS

Originally published in:
Vampirella: Revelations #0-3 (2005)
Writer MIKE CAREY
Penciler MIKE LILLY
Inkers BOB ALMOND & JOE RUBINSTEIN
Colorist JAY FOTOS
Letterer ED DUKESHIRE
Original series editor BON ALIMAGNO

VENGEANCE OF VAMPIRELLA

Originally published in:
Vampirella Quarterly: Spring 2007 #1
Vampirella Quarterly: Summer 2007 #1
Vampirella Quarterly: Fall 2007 #1
Writer JOSHUA HALE FIALKOV
Artists STEPHEN SEGOVIA & NOAH SALONGA
Colorist JAY DAVID RAMOS
Letterer ED DUKESHIRE
Special thanks to GLASS HOUSE GRAPHICS
Original series editor BON ALIMAGNO

Collection cover artist JOE JUSKO

DYNAMITE®

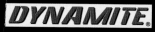

Nick Barrucci, CEO / Publisher
Juan Collado, President / COO
Rich Young, Director Business Development
Keith Davidsen, Marketing Manager

Joe Rybandt, Senior Editor
Sarah Litt, Digital Editor
Josh Green, Traffic Coordinator

Josh Johnson, Art Director
Jason Ullmeyer, Senior Graphic Designer
Chris Caniano, Production Assistant

Visit us online at **www.DYNAMITE.com**
Follow us on Twitter **@dynamitecomics**
Like us on Facebook **/Dynamitecomics**
Watch us on YouTube **/Dynamitecomics**

ISBN-10: 1-60690-432-9
ISBN-13: 978-1-60690-432-9
First Printing
10 9 8 7 6 5 4 3 2 1

VAMPIRELLA® MASTERS SERIES VOL. 8: MIKE CAREY WITH JOSHUA HALE FIALKOV. Contains materials originally published in Vampirella: Revelations #0-3, Vampirella Quarterly: Spring 2007 #1, Vampirella Quarterly: Summer 2007 #1 and Vampirella Quarterly: Fall 2007 #1. Published by Dynamite Entertainment. 113 Gaither Dr., STE 205, Mt. Laurel, NJ 08054.

Printed in China

For information regarding press, media rights, foreign rights, licensing, promotions, and advertising e-mail: marketing@dynamite.com

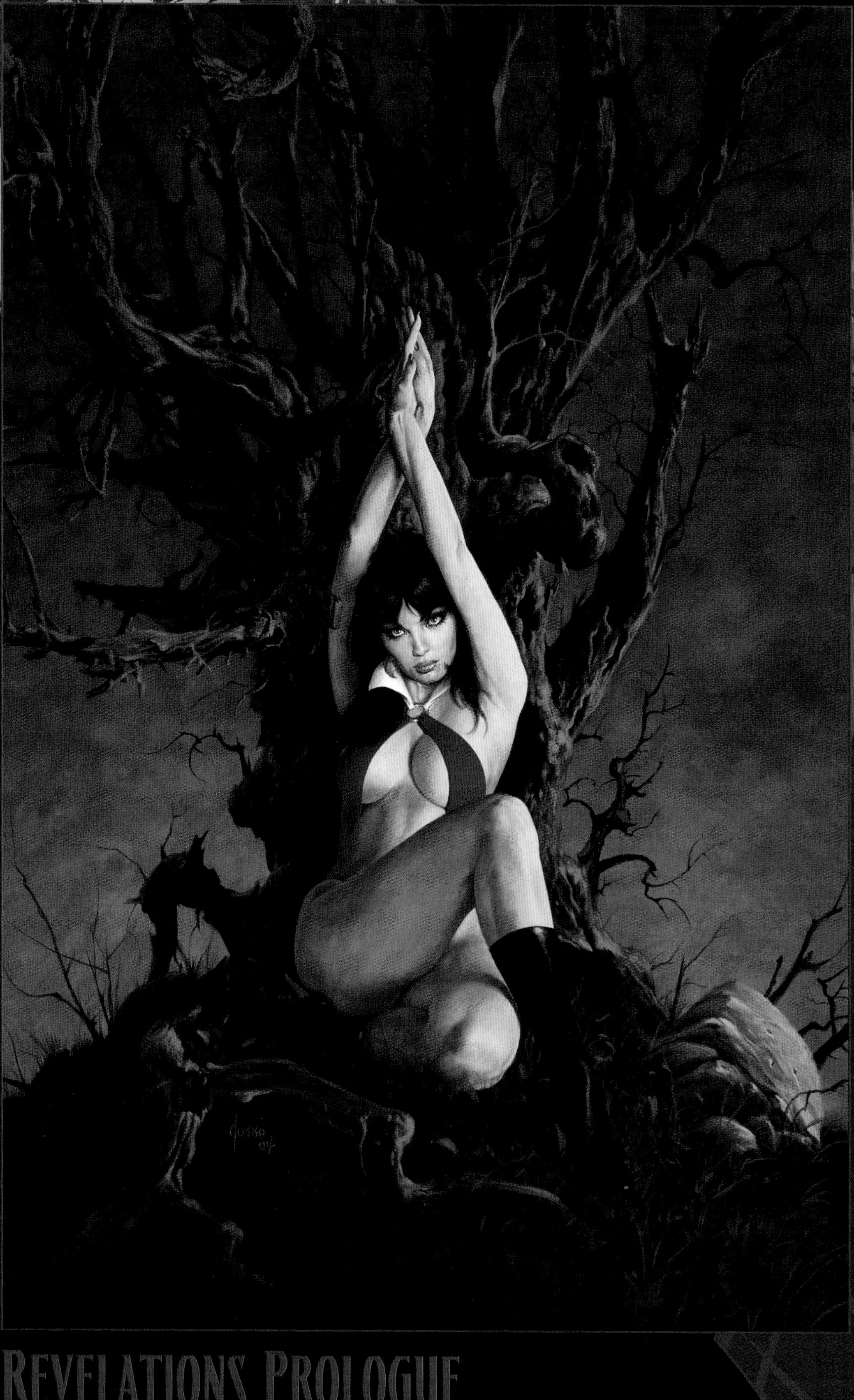

REVELATIONS PROLOGUE

Vampirella: Revelations #0 cover by Joe Jusko

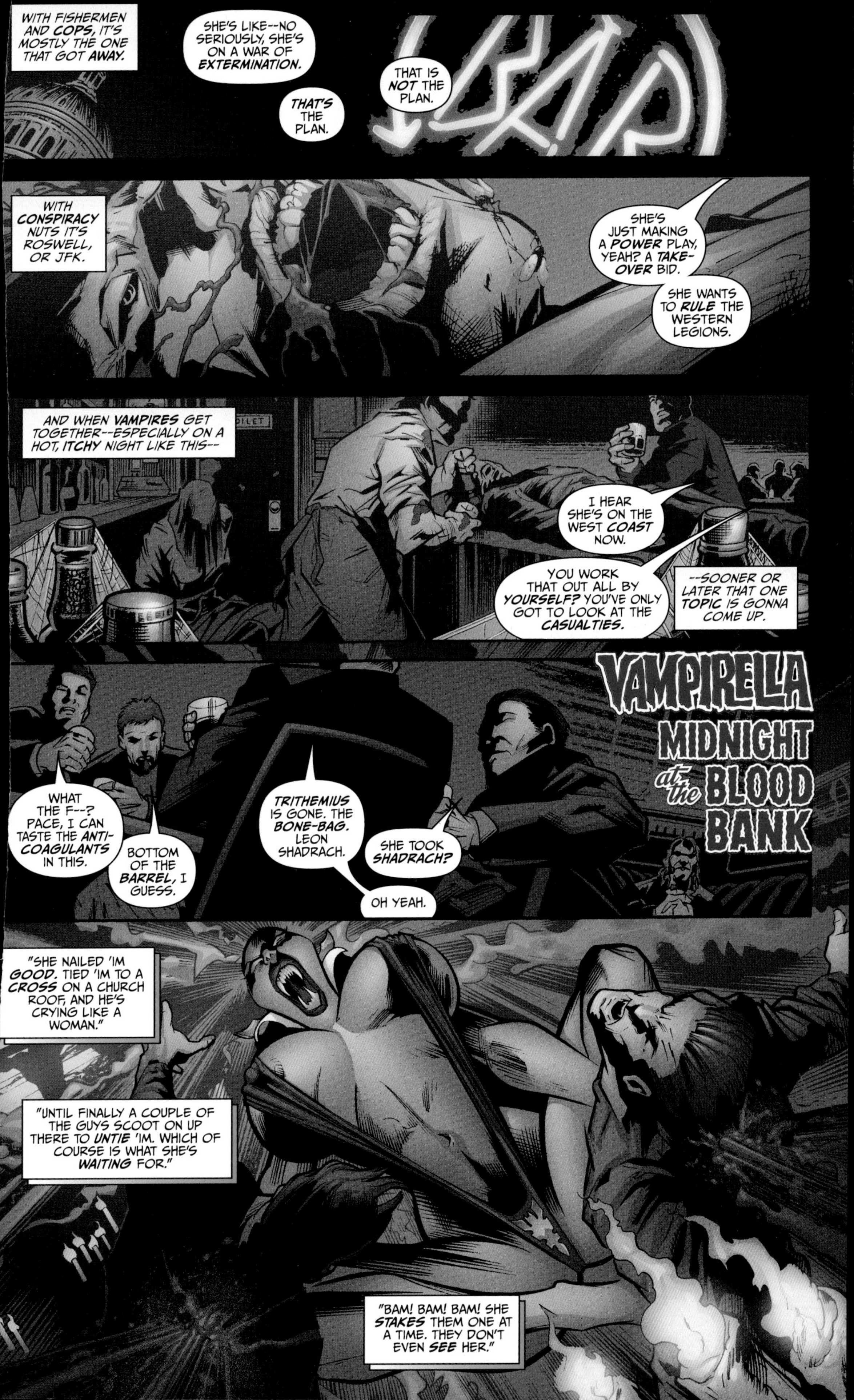
WITH FISHERMEN AND COPS, IT'S MOSTLY THE ONE THAT GOT AWAY.
SHE'S LIKE--NO SERIOUSLY, SHE'S ON A WAR OF EXTERMINATION.
THAT'S THE PLAN.
THAT IS NOT THE PLAN.
BAR
WITH CONSPIRACY NUTS IT'S ROSWELL, OR JFK.
SHE'S JUST MAKING A POWER PLAY, YEAH? A TAKE-OVER BID.
SHE WANTS TO RULE THE WESTERN LEGIONS.
AND WHEN VAMPIRES GET TOGETHER--ESPECIALLY ON A HOT, ITCHY NIGHT LIKE THIS--
I HEAR SHE'S ON THE WEST COAST NOW.
YOU WORK THAT OUT ALL BY YOURSELF? YOU'VE ONLY GOT TO LOOK AT THE CASUALTIES.
--SOONER OR LATER THAT ONE TOPIC IS GONNA COME UP.
VAMPIRELLA
MIDNIGHT at the BLOOD BANK
WHAT THE F--? PACE, I CAN TASTE THE ANTI-COAGULANTS IN THIS.
BOTTOM OF THE BARREL, I GUESS.
TRITHEMIUS IS GONE. THE BONE-BAG. LEON SHADRACH.
SHE TOOK SHADRACH?
OH YEAH.
"SHE NAILED 'IM GOOD. TIED 'IM TO A CROSS ON A CHURCH ROOF, AND HE'S CRYING LIKE A WOMAN."
"UNTIL FINALLY A COUPLE OF THE GUYS SCOOT ON UP THERE TO UNTIE 'IM. WHICH OF COURSE IS WHAT SHE'S WAITING FOR."
"BAM! BAM! BAM! SHE STAKES THEM ONE AT A TIME. THEY DON'T EVEN SEE HER."

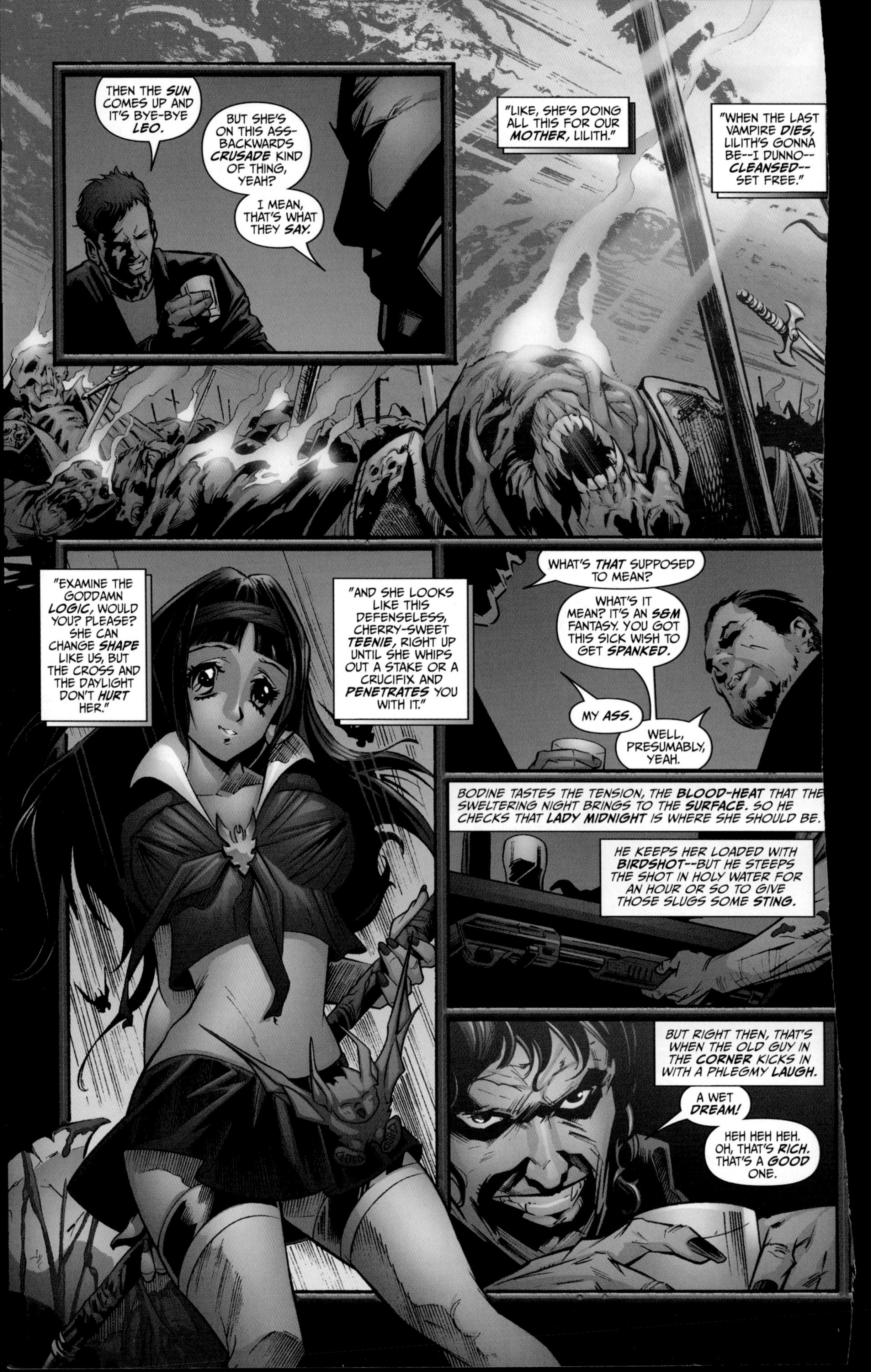
THEN THE SUN COMES UP AND IT'S BYE-BYE LEO.
BUT SHE'S ON THIS ASS-BACKWARDS CRUSADE KIND OF THING, YEAH?
I MEAN, THAT'S WHAT THEY SAY.
"LIKE, SHE'S DOING ALL THIS FOR OUR MOTHER, LILITH."
"WHEN THE LAST VAMPIRE DIES, LILITH'S GONNA BE--I DUNNO--CLEANSED--SET FREE."
"EXAMINE THE GODDAMN LOGIC, WOULD YOU? PLEASE? SHE CAN CHANGE SHAPE LIKE US, BUT THE CROSS AND THE DAYLIGHT DON'T HURT HER."
"AND SHE LOOKS LIKE THIS DEFENSELESS, CHERRY-SWEET TEENIE, RIGHT UP UNTIL SHE WHIPS OUT A STAKE OR A CRUCIFIX AND PENETRATES YOU WITH IT."
WHAT'S THAT SUPPOSED TO MEAN?
WHAT'S IT MEAN? IT'S AN S&M FANTASY. YOU GOT THIS SICK WISH TO GET SPANKED.
MY ASS.
WELL, PRESUMABLY, YEAH.
BODINE TASTES THE TENSION, THE BLOOD-HEAT THAT THE SWELTERING NIGHT BRINGS TO THE SURFACE. SO HE CHECKS THAT LADY MIDNIGHT IS WHERE SHE SHOULD BE.
HE KEEPS HER LOADED WITH BIRDSHOT--BUT HE STEEPS THE SHOT IN HOLY WATER FOR AN HOUR OR SO TO GIVE THOSE SLUGS SOME STING.
BUT RIGHT THEN, THAT'S WHEN THE OLD GUY IN THE CORNER KICKS IN WITH A PHLEGMY LAUGH.
A WET DREAM!
HEH HEH HEH. OH, THAT'S RICH. THAT'S A GOOD ONE.

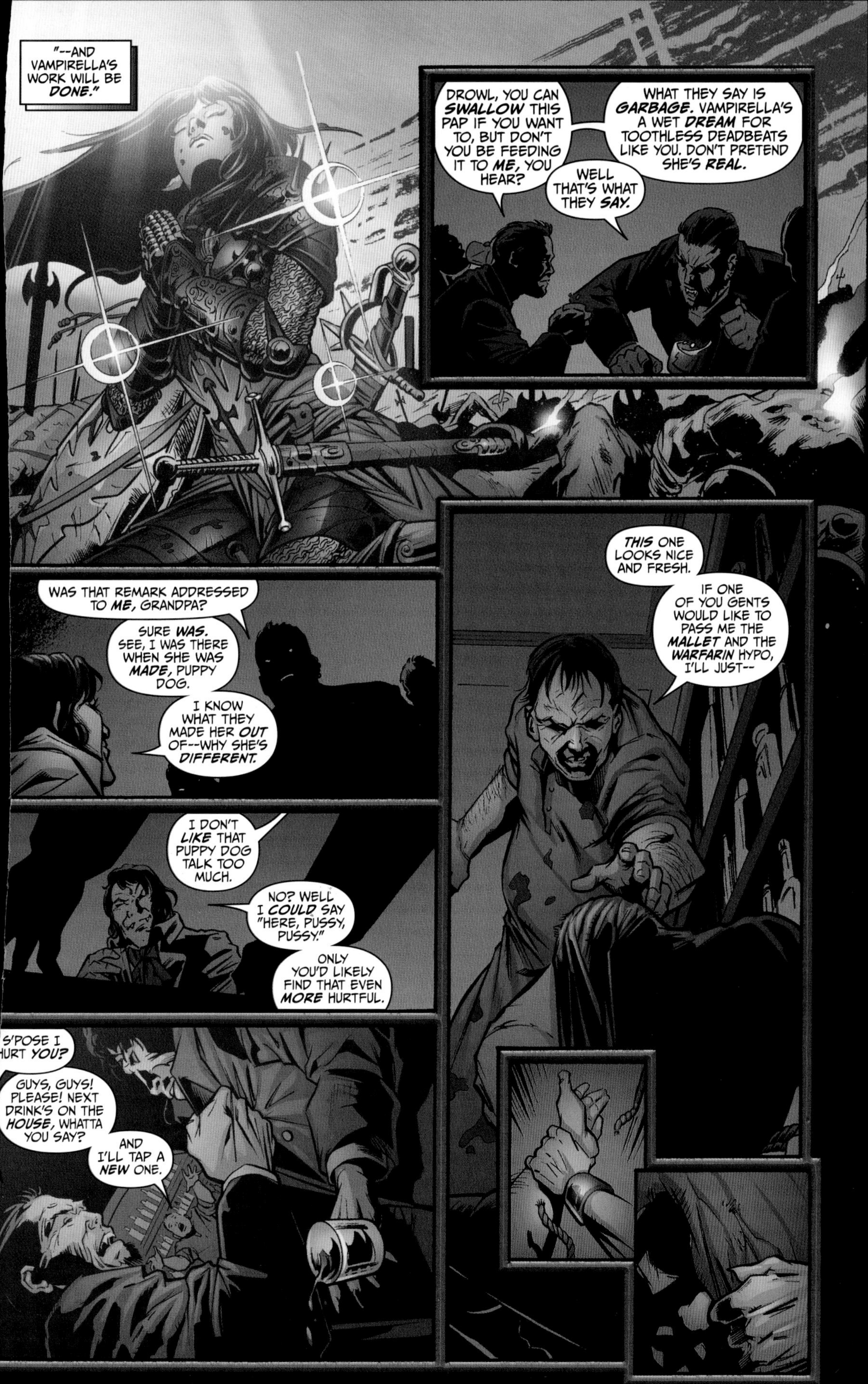
"--AND VAMPIRELLA'S WORK WILL BE DONE."
DROWL, YOU CAN SWALLOW THIS PAP IF YOU WANT TO, BUT DON'T YOU BE FEEDING IT TO ME, YOU HEAR?
WHAT THEY SAY IS GARBAGE. VAMPIRELLA'S A WET DREAM FOR TOOTHLESS DEADBEATS LIKE YOU. DON'T PRETEND SHE'S REAL.
WELL THAT'S WHAT THEY SAY.
WAS THAT REMARK ADDRESSED TO ME, GRANDPA?
SURE WAS. SEE, I WAS THERE WHEN SHE WAS MADE, PUPPY DOG.
I KNOW WHAT THEY MADE HER OUT OF--WHY SHE'S DIFFERENT.
I DON'T LIKE THAT PUPPY DOG TALK TOO MUCH.
NO? WELL I COULD SAY "HERE, PUSSY, PUSSY."
ONLY YOU'D LIKELY FIND THAT EVEN MORE HURTFUL.
S'POSE I HURT YOU?
GUYS, GUYS! PLEASE! NEXT DRINK'S ON THE HOUSE, WHATTA YOU SAY?
AND I'LL TAP A NEW ONE.
THIS ONE LOOKS NICE AND FRESH.
IF ONE OF YOU GENTS WOULD LIKE TO PASS ME THE MALLET AND THE WARFARIN HYPO, I'LL JUST--

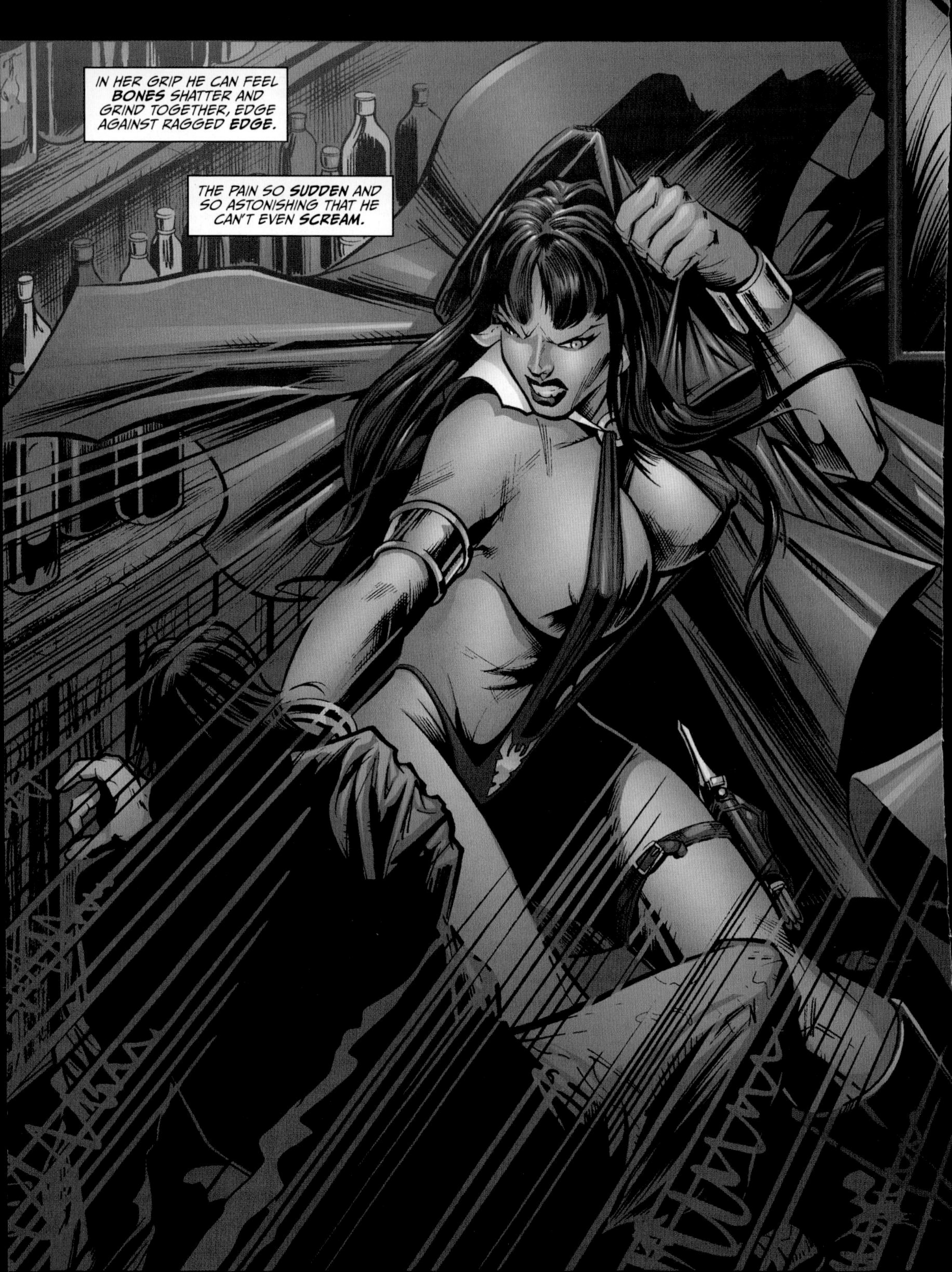
IN HER GRIP HE CAN FEEL BONES SHATTER AND GRIND TOGETHER, EDGE AGAINST RAGGED EDGE.
THE PAIN SO SUDDEN AND SO ASTONISHING THAT HE CAN'T EVEN SCREAM.

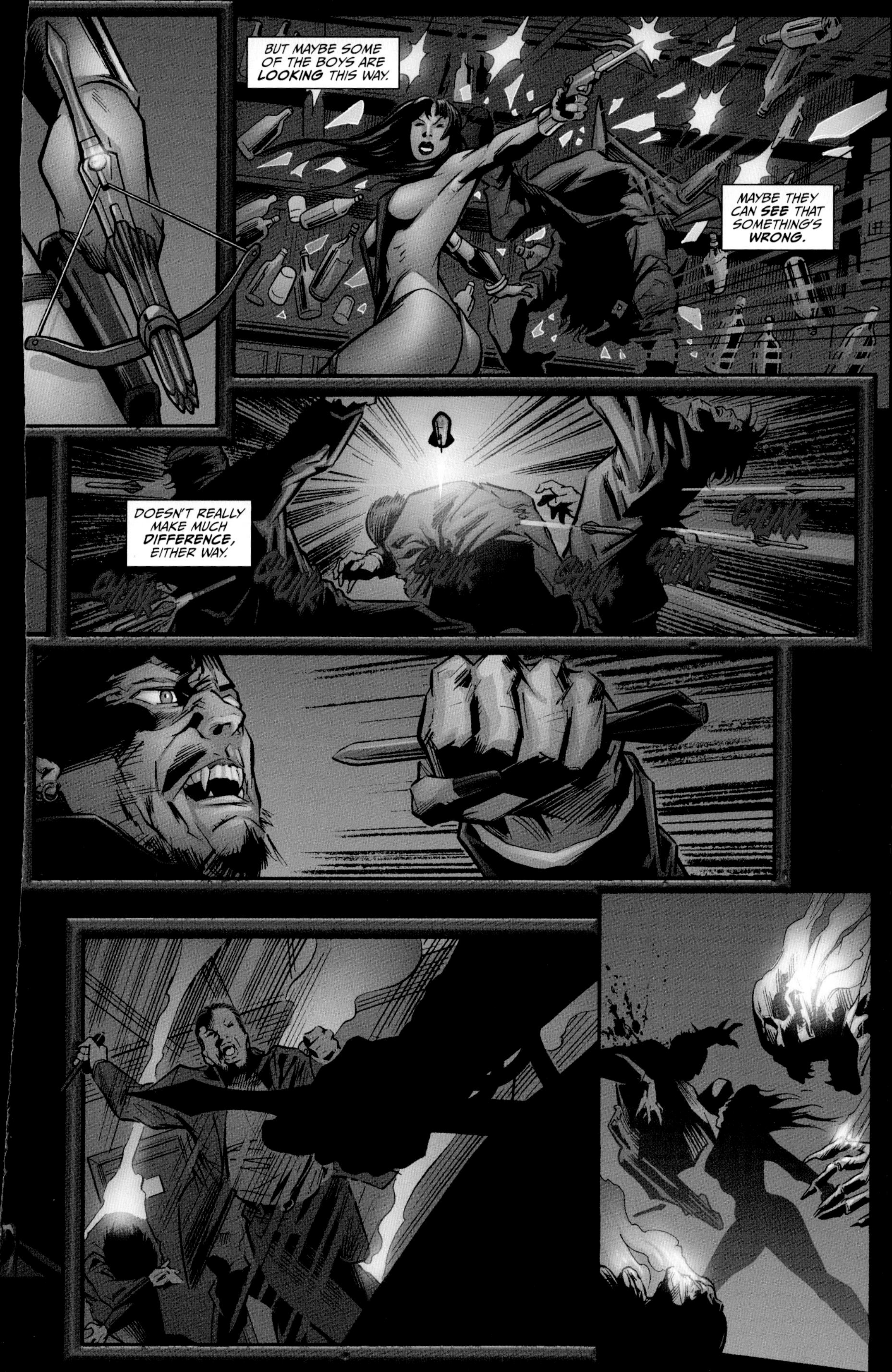
BUT MAYBE SOME OF THE BOYS ARE LOOKING THIS WAY.
MAYBE THEY CAN SEE THAT SOMETHING'S WRONG.
DOESN'T REALLY MAKE MUCH DIFFERENCE, EITHER WAY.
CHUNK
CHUNK
CHUNK
CHUNK
CHUNK

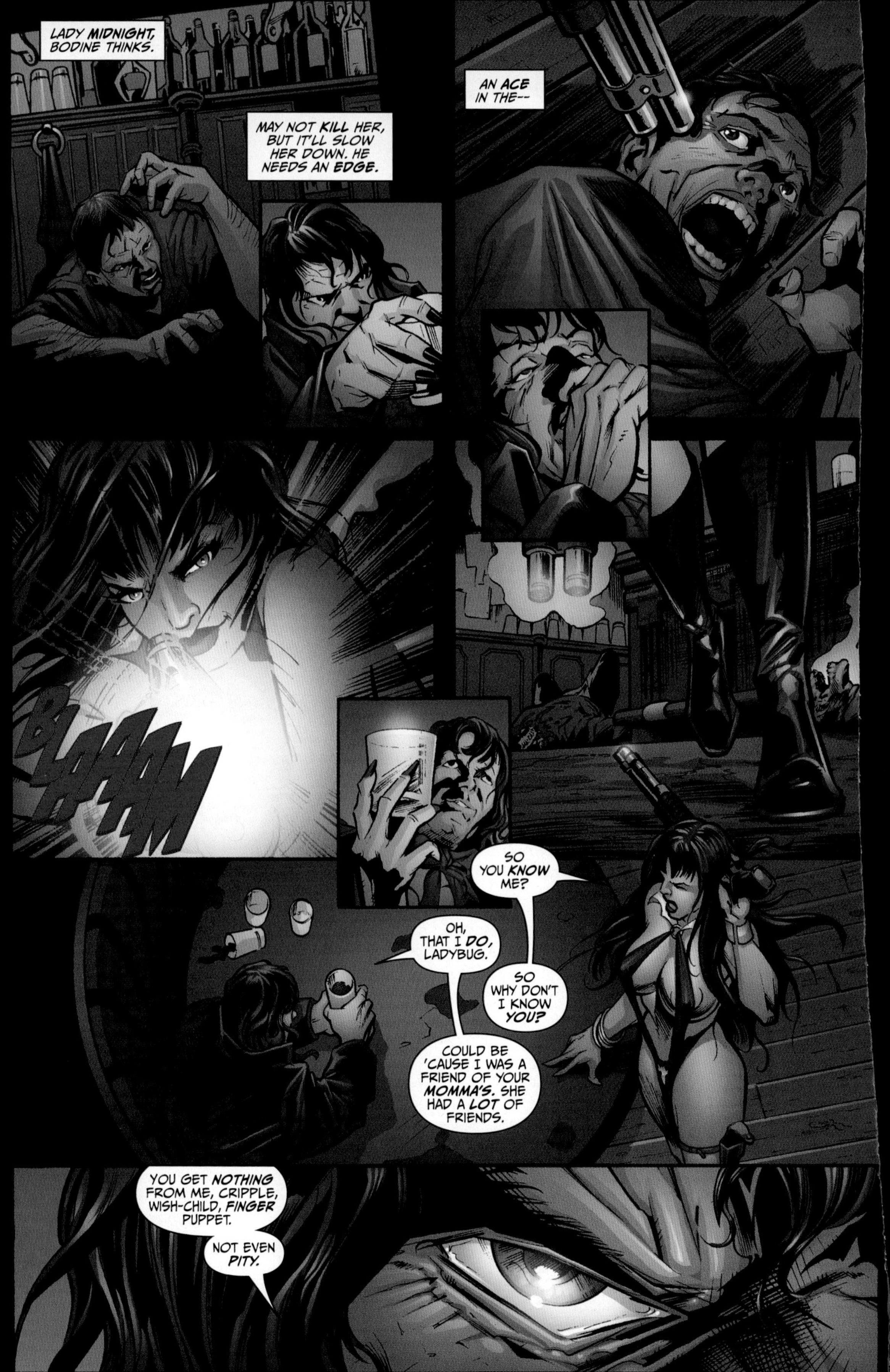

LADY MIDNIGHT, BODINE THINKS.
MAY NOT KILL HER, BUT IT'LL SLOW HER DOWN. HE NEEDS AN EDGE.
AN ACE IN THE--
BLAAAM
SO YOU KNOW ME?
OH, THAT I DO, LADYBUG.
SO WHY DON'T I KNOW YOU?
COULD BE 'CAUSE I WAS A FRIEND OF YOUR MOMMA'S. SHE HAD A LOT OF FRIENDS.
YOU GET NOTHING FROM ME, CRIPPLE, WISH-CHILD, FINGER PUPPET.
NOT EVEN PITY.

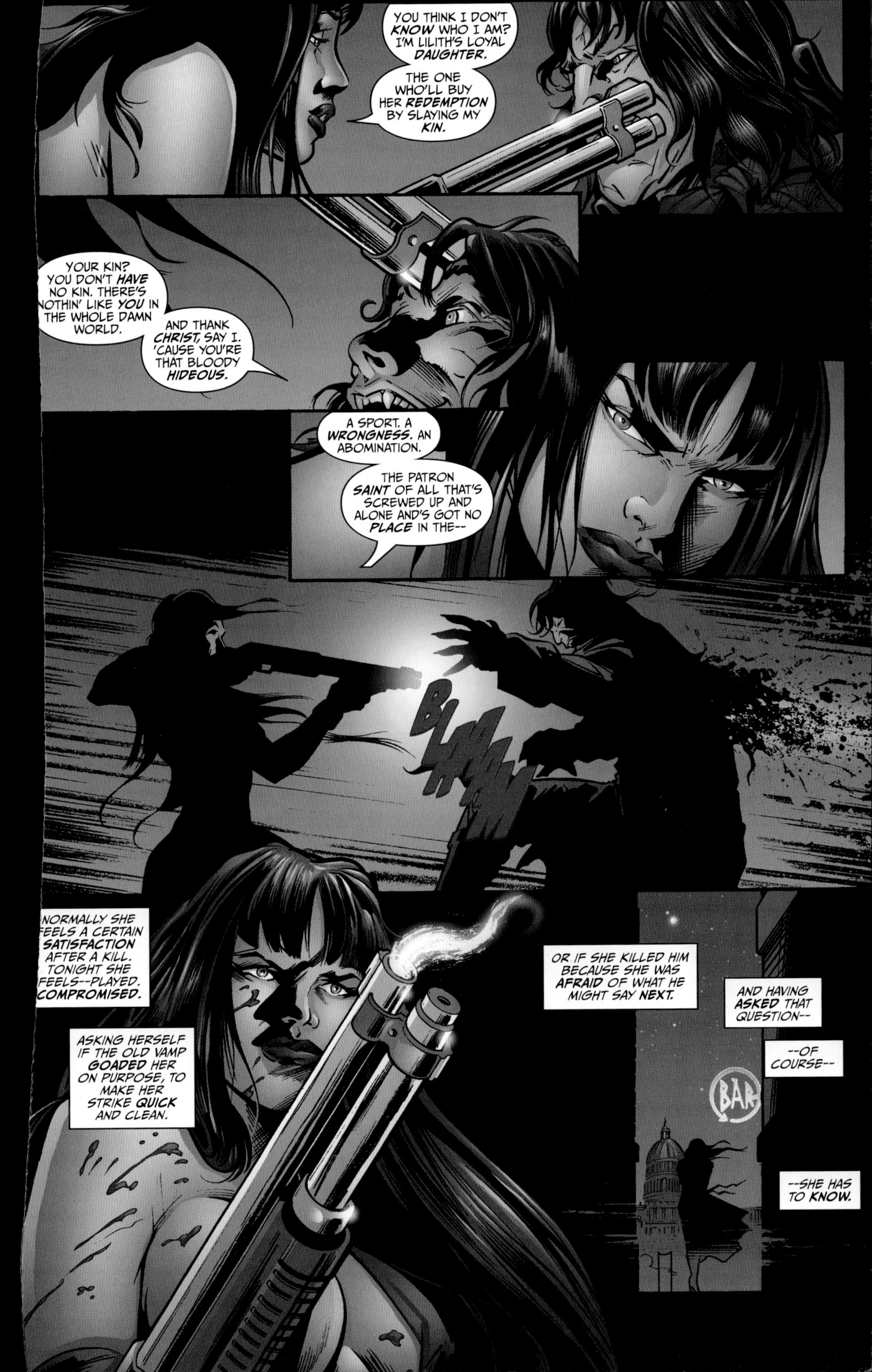
YOU THINK I DON'T KNOW WHO I AM? I'M LILITH'S LOYAL DAUGHTER.
THE ONE WHO'LL BUY HER REDEMPTION BY SLAYING MY KIN.
YOUR KIN? YOU DON'T HAVE NO KIN. THERE'S NOTHIN' LIKE YOU IN THE WHOLE DAMN WORLD.
AND THANK CHRIST, SAY I. 'CAUSE YOU'RE THAT BLOODY HIDEOUS.
A SPORT. A WRONGNESS. AN ABOMINATION.
THE PATRON SAINT OF ALL THAT'S SCREWED UP AND ALONE AND'S GOT NO PLACE IN THE--
BLAAAM
NORMALLY SHE FEELS A CERTAIN SATISFACTION AFTER A KILL. TONIGHT SHE FEELS--PLAYED. COMPROMISED.
ASKING HERSELF IF THE OLD VAMP GOADED HER ON PURPOSE, TO MAKE HER STRIKE QUICK AND CLEAN.
OR IF SHE KILLED HIM BECAUSE SHE WAS AFRAID OF WHAT HE MIGHT SAY NEXT.
AND HAVING ASKED THAT QUESTION--
--OF COURSE--
BAR
--SHE HAS TO KNOW.

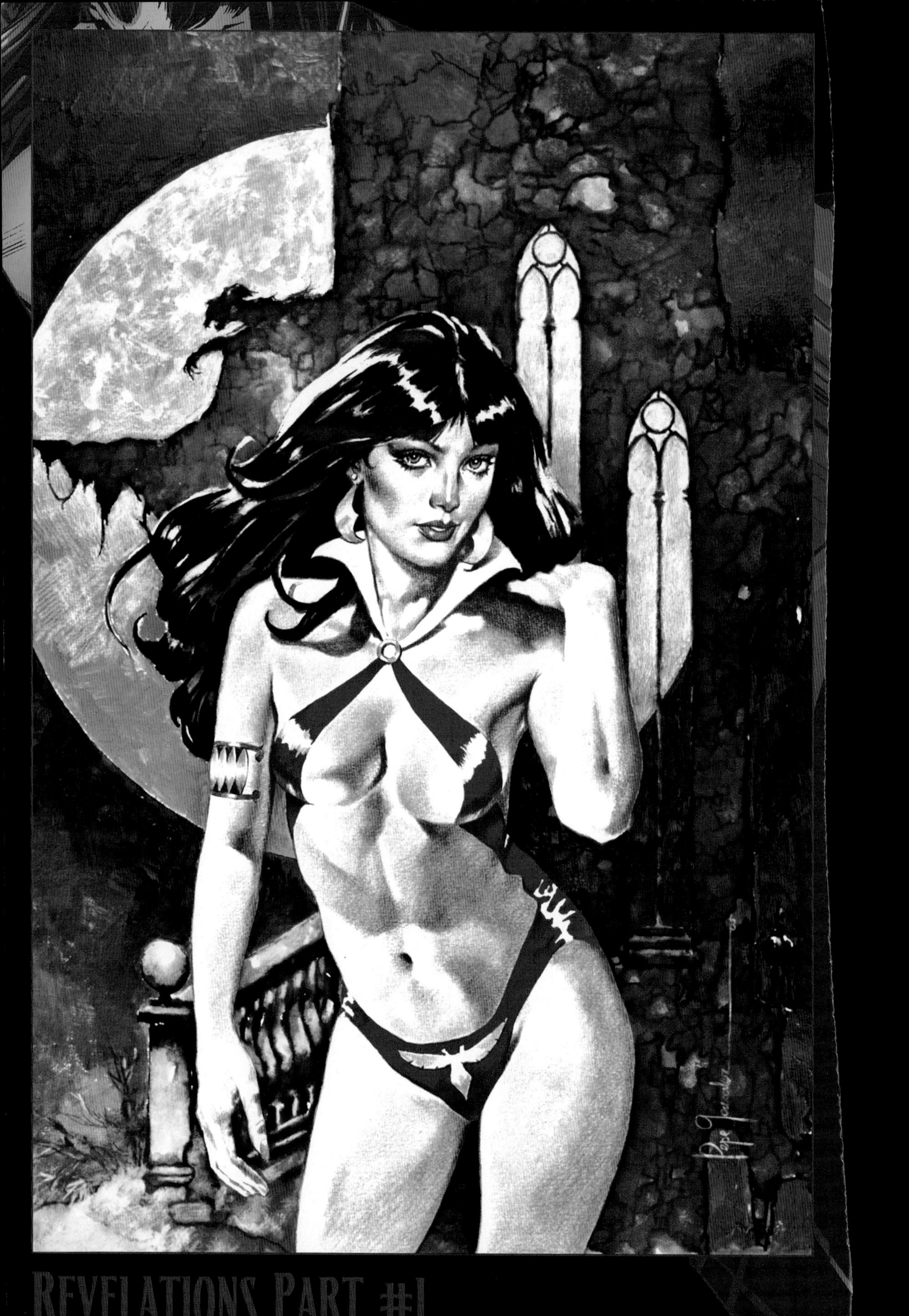

REVELATIONS PART #1

Vampirella: Revelations #1 cover by José Gonzalez

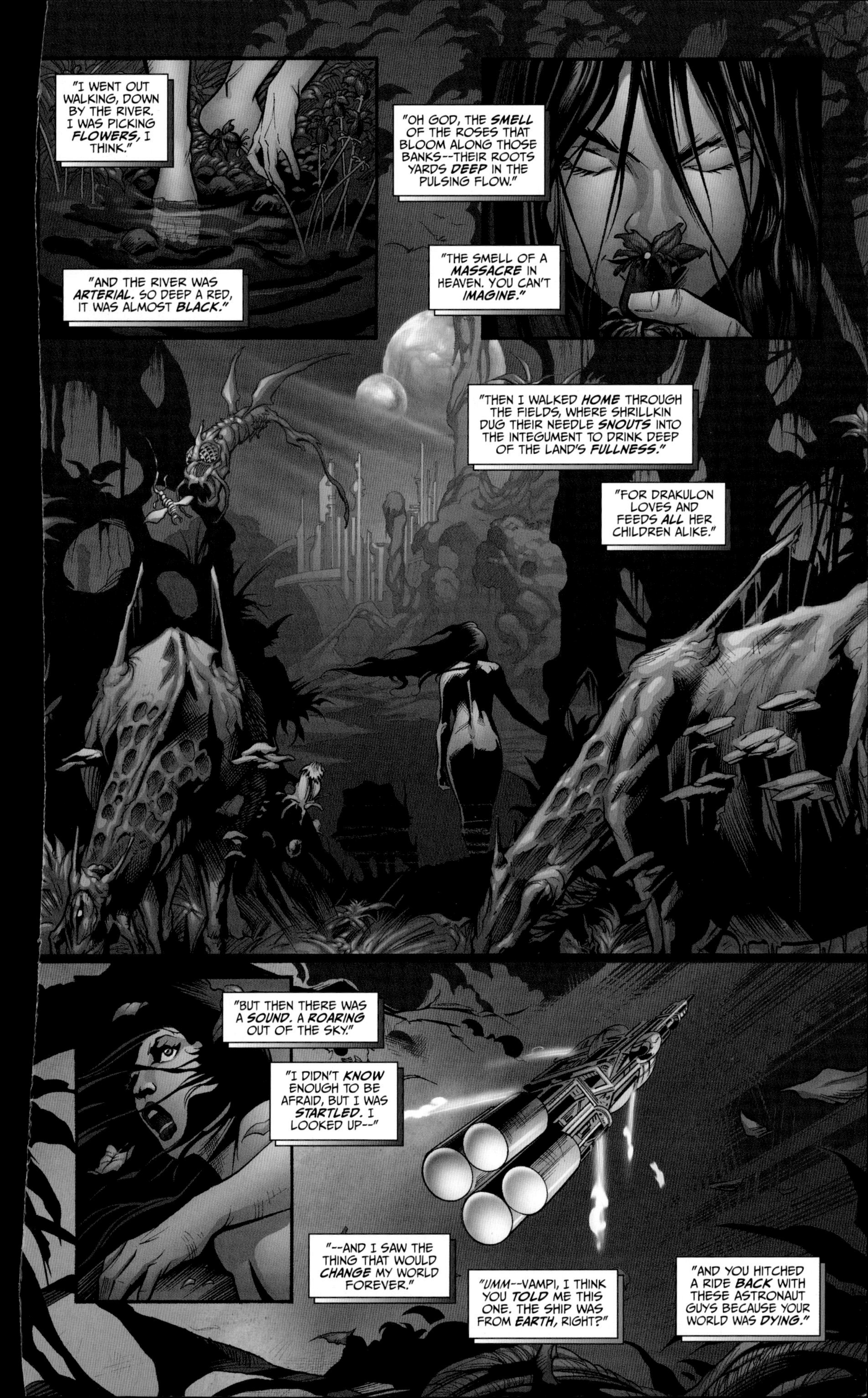
"I WENT OUT WALKING, DOWN BY THE RIVER. I WAS PICKING FLOWERS, I THINK."
"AND THE RIVER WAS ARTERIAL. SO DEEP A RED, IT WAS ALMOST BLACK."
"OH GOD, THE SMELL OF THE ROSES THAT BLOOM ALONG THOSE BANKS--THEIR ROOTS YARDS DEEP IN THE PULSING FLOW."
"THE SMELL OF A MASSACRE IN HEAVEN. YOU CAN'T IMAGINE."
"THEN I WALKED HOME THROUGH THE FIELDS, WHERE SHRILLKIN DUG THEIR NEEDLE SNOUTS INTO THE INTEGUMENT TO DRINK DEEP OF THE LAND'S FULLNESS."
"FOR DRAKULON LOVES AND FEEDS ALL HER CHILDREN ALIKE."
"BUT THEN THERE WAS A SOUND. A ROARING OUT OF THE SKY."
"I DIDN'T KNOW ENOUGH TO BE AFRAID, BUT I WAS STARTLED. I LOOKED UP--"
"--AND I SAW THE THING THAT WOULD CHANGE MY WORLD FOREVER."
"UMM--VAMPI, I THINK YOU TOLD ME THIS ONE. THE SHIP WAS FROM EARTH, RIGHT?"
"AND YOU HITCHED A RIDE BACK WITH THESE ASTRONAUT GUYS BECAUSE YOUR WORLD WAS DYING."

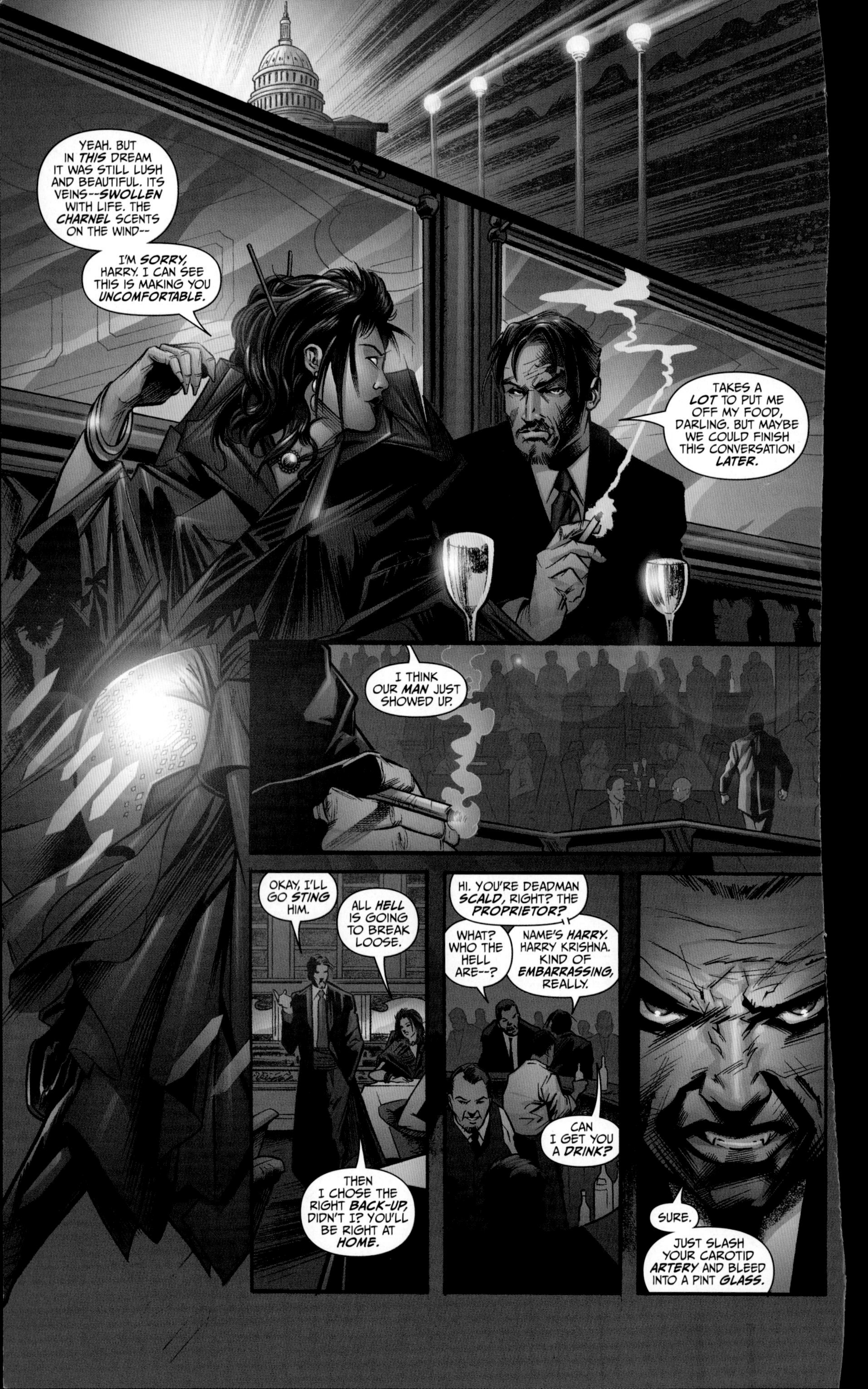
YEAH. BUT IN THIS DREAM IT WAS STILL LUSH AND BEAUTIFUL. ITS VEINS--SWOLLEN WITH LIFE. THE CHARNEL SCENTS ON THE WIND--
I'M SORRY, HARRY. I CAN SEE THIS IS MAKING YOU UNCOMFORTABLE.
TAKES A LOT TO PUT ME OFF MY FOOD, DARLING. BUT MAYBE WE COULD FINISH THIS CONVERSATION LATER.
I THINK OUR MAN JUST SHOWED UP.
OKAY, I'LL GO STING HIM.
ALL HELL IS GOING TO BREAK LOOSE.
THEN I CHOSE THE RIGHT BACK-UP, DIDN'T I? YOU'LL BE RIGHT AT HOME.
HI. YOU'RE DEADMAN SCALD, RIGHT? THE PROPRIETOR?
WHAT? WHO THE HELL ARE--?
NAME'S HARRY. HARRY KRISHNA. KIND OF EMBARRASSING, REALLY.
CAN I GET YOU A DRINK?
SURE.
JUST SLASH YOUR CAROTID ARTERY AND BLEED INTO A PINT GLASS.

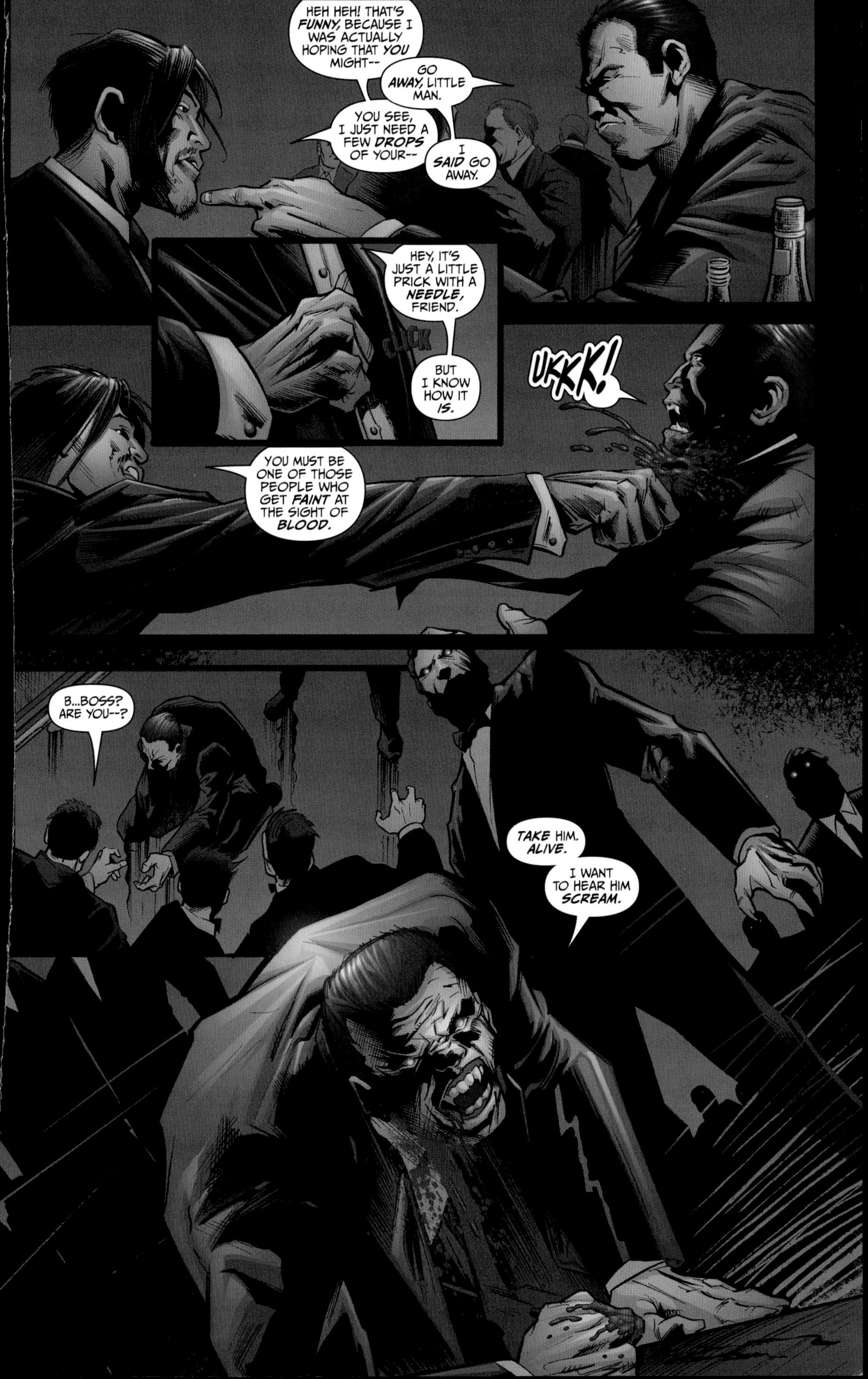
HEH HEH! THAT'S FUNNY, BECAUSE I WAS ACTUALLY HOPING THAT YOU MIGHT--
GO AWAY, LITTLE MAN.
YOU SEE, I JUST NEED A FEW DROPS OF YOUR--
I SAID GO AWAY.
HEY, IT'S JUST A LITTLE PRICK WITH A NEEDLE, FRIEND.
CLICK
BUT I KNOW HOW IT IS.
UKKK!
YOU MUST BE ONE OF THOSE PEOPLE WHO GET FAINT AT THE SIGHT OF BLOOD.
B...BOSS? ARE YOU--?
TAKE HIM. ALIVE.
I WANT TO HEAR HIM SCREAM.

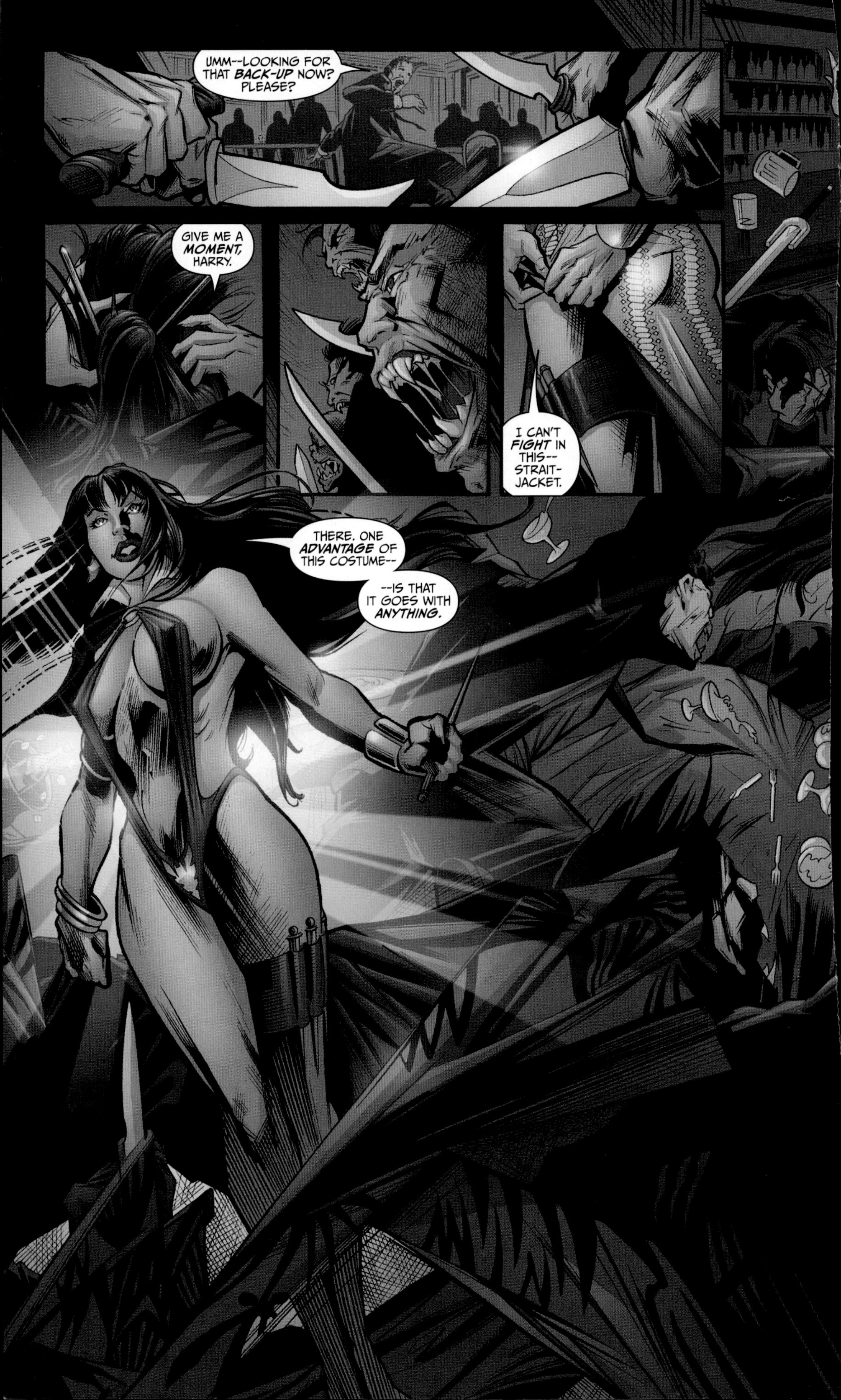
UMM--LOOKING FOR THAT BACK-UP NOW? PLEASE?
GIVE ME A MOMENT, HARRY.
I CAN'T FIGHT IN THIS-- STRAIT-JACKET.
THERE. ONE ADVANTAGE OF THIS COSTUME--
--IS THAT IT GOES WITH ANYTHING.

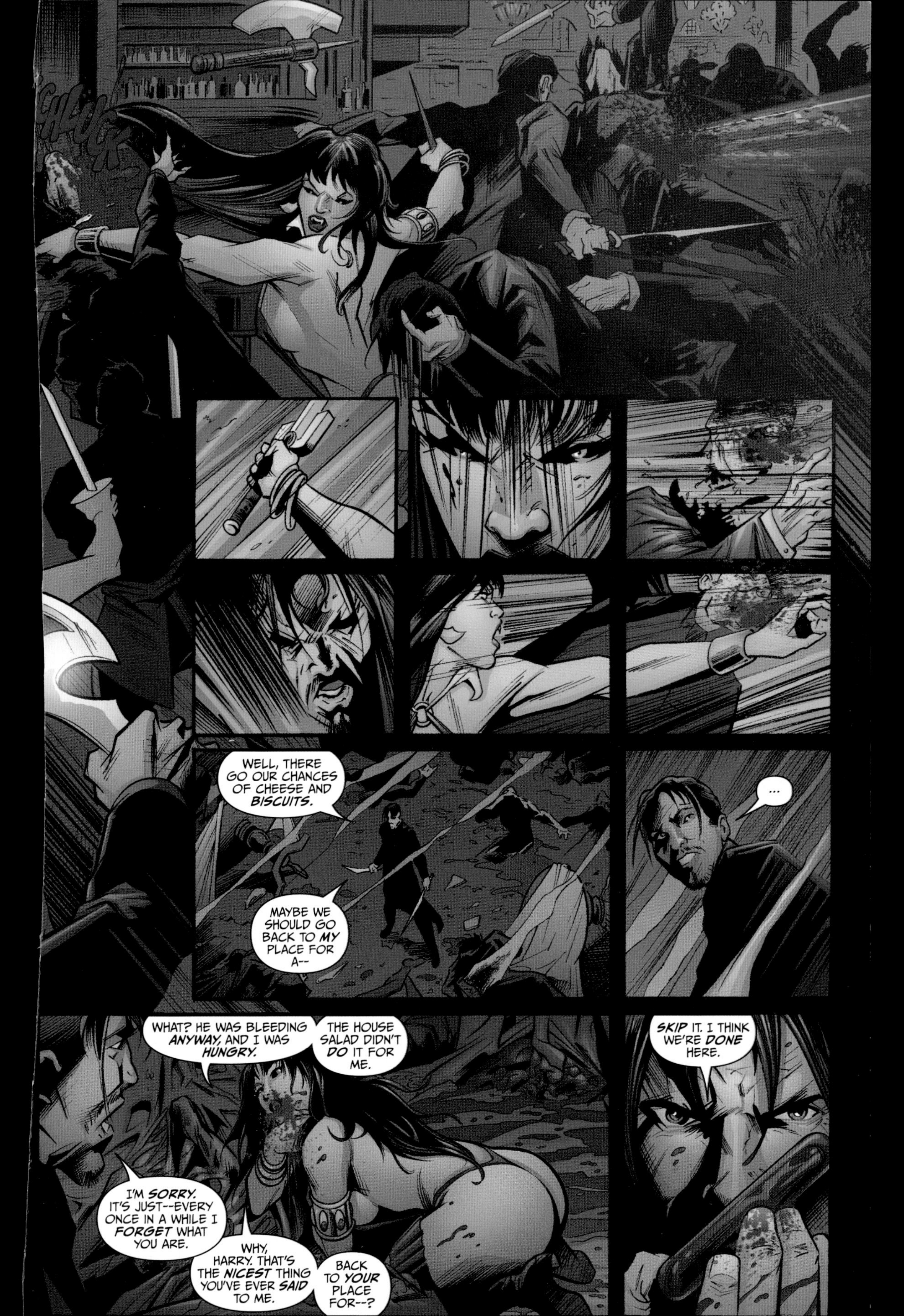
CHUCK
WELL, THERE GO OUR CHANCES OF CHEESE AND *BISCUITS.*
MAYBE WE SHOULD GO BACK TO *MY* PLACE FOR A--
...
WHAT? HE WAS BLEEDING *ANYWAY,* AND I WAS *HUNGRY.*
THE HOUSE SALAD DIDN'T *DO* IT FOR ME.
I'M *SORRY.* IT'S JUST--EVERY ONCE IN A WHILE I *FORGET* WHAT YOU ARE.
WHY, HARRY. THAT'S THE *NICEST* THING YOU'VE EVER *SAID* TO ME.
BACK TO *YOUR* PLACE FOR--?
SKIP IT. I THINK WE'RE *DONE* HERE.

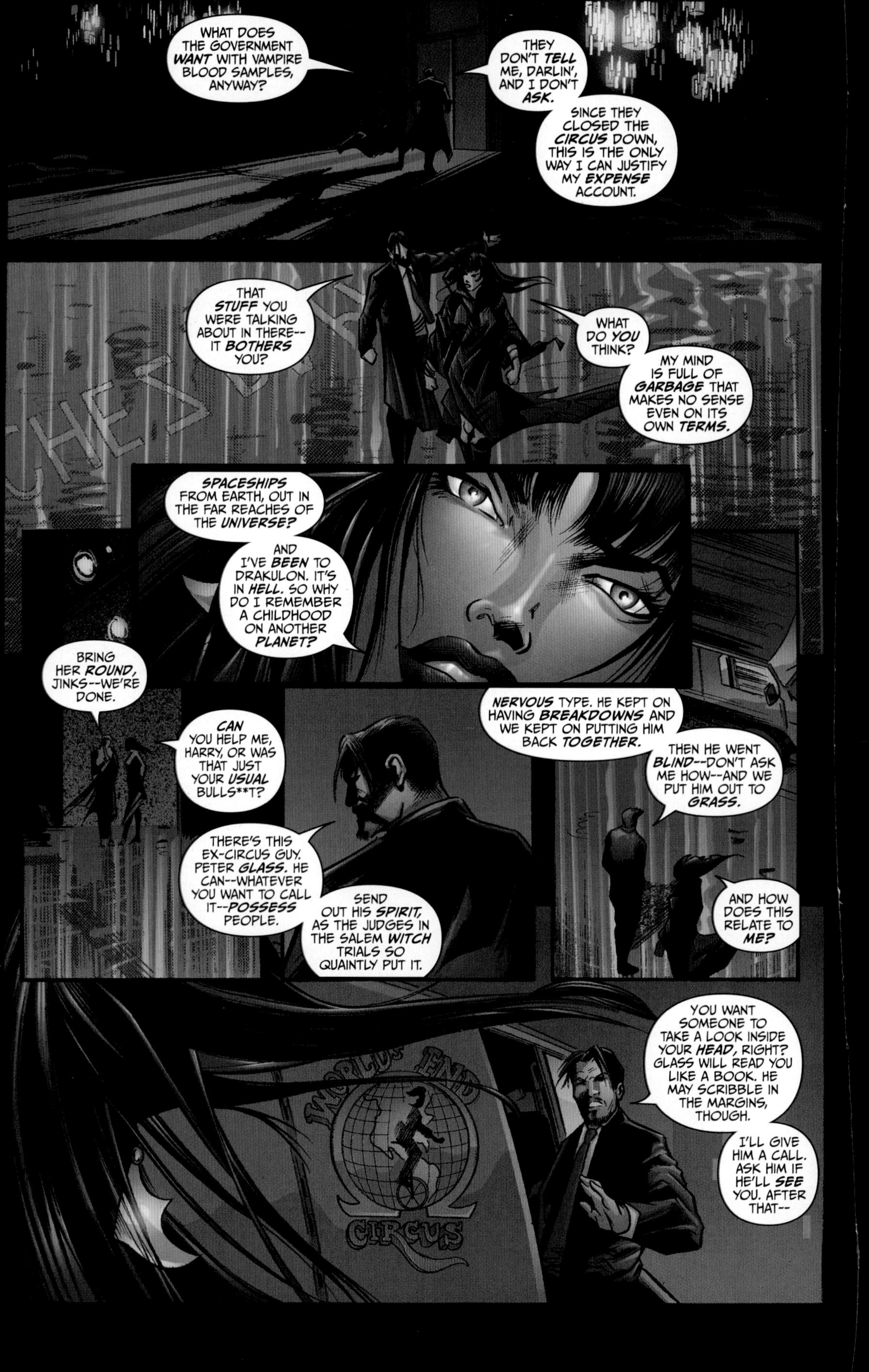
WHAT DOES THE GOVERNMENT WANT WITH VAMPIRE BLOOD SAMPLES, ANYWAY?
THEY DON'T TELL ME, DARLIN', AND I DON'T ASK.
SINCE THEY CLOSED THE CIRCUS DOWN, THIS IS THE ONLY WAY I CAN JUSTIFY MY EXPENSE ACCOUNT.
THAT STUFF YOU WERE TALKING ABOUT IN THERE-- IT BOTHERS YOU?
WHAT DO YOU THINK?
MY MIND IS FULL OF GARBAGE THAT MAKES NO SENSE EVEN ON ITS OWN TERMS.
SPACESHIPS FROM EARTH, OUT IN THE FAR REACHES OF THE UNIVERSE?
AND I'VE BEEN TO DRAKULON. IT'S IN HELL. SO WHY DO I REMEMBER A CHILDHOOD ON ANOTHER PLANET?
BRING HER ROUND, JINKS--WE'RE DONE.
CAN YOU HELP ME, HARRY, OR WAS THAT JUST YOUR USUAL BULLS**T?
THERE'S THIS EX-CIRCUS GUY. PETER GLASS. HE CAN--WHATEVER YOU WANT TO CALL IT--POSSESS PEOPLE.
SEND OUT HIS SPIRIT, AS THE JUDGES IN THE SALEM WITCH TRIALS SO QUAINTLY PUT IT.
NERVOUS TYPE. HE KEPT ON HAVING BREAKDOWNS AND WE KEPT ON PUTTING HIM BACK TOGETHER.
THEN HE WENT BLIND--DON'T ASK ME HOW--AND WE PUT HIM OUT TO GRASS.
AND HOW DOES THIS RELATE TO ME?
WORLD'S END CIRCUS
YOU WANT SOMEONE TO TAKE A LOOK INSIDE YOUR HEAD, RIGHT? GLASS WILL READ YOU LIKE A BOOK. HE MAY SCRIBBLE IN THE MARGINS, THOUGH.
I'LL GIVE HIM A CALL. ASK HIM IF HE'LL SEE YOU. AFTER THAT--

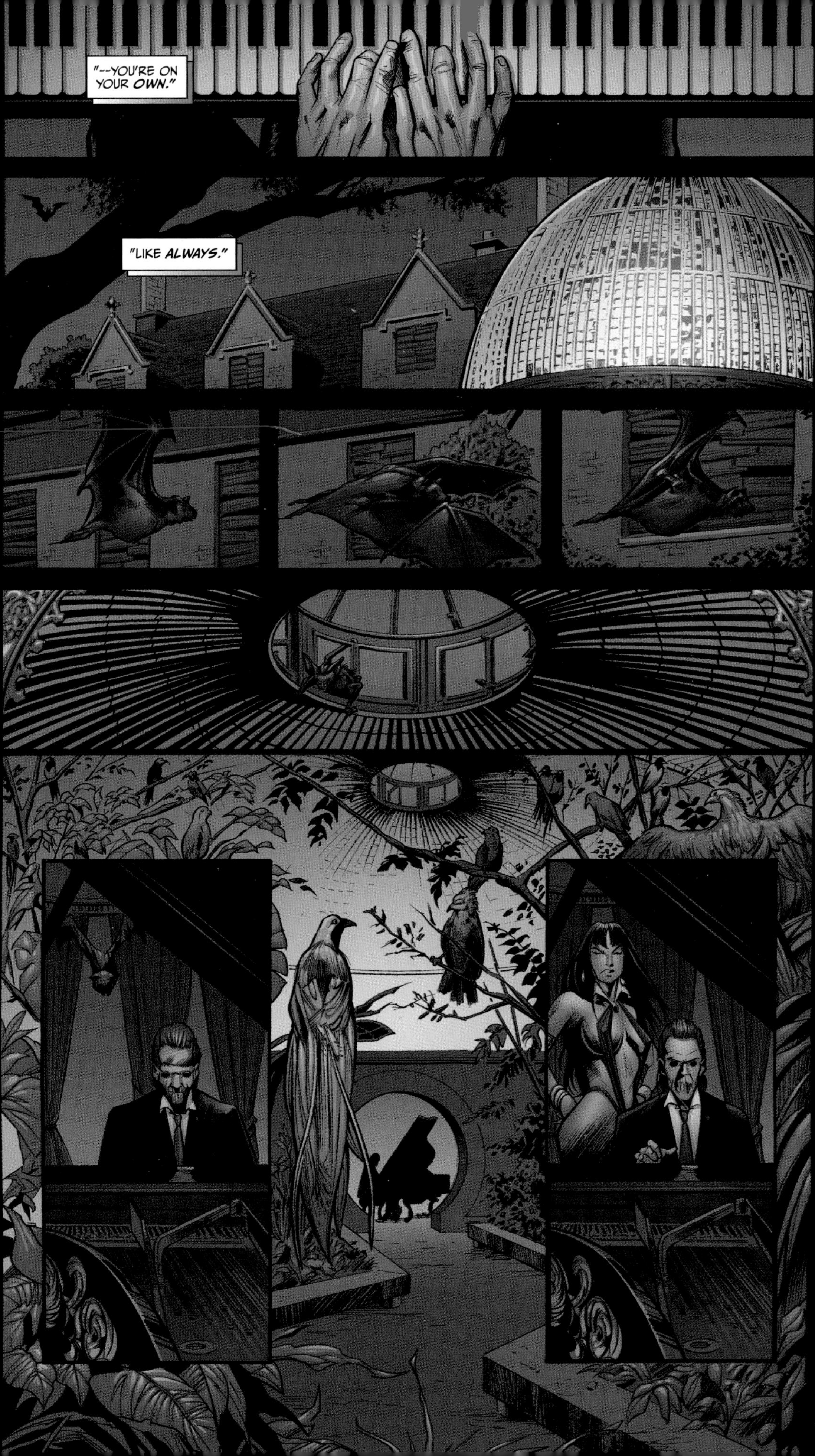
"--YOU'RE ON YOUR OWN."
"LIKE ALWAYS."

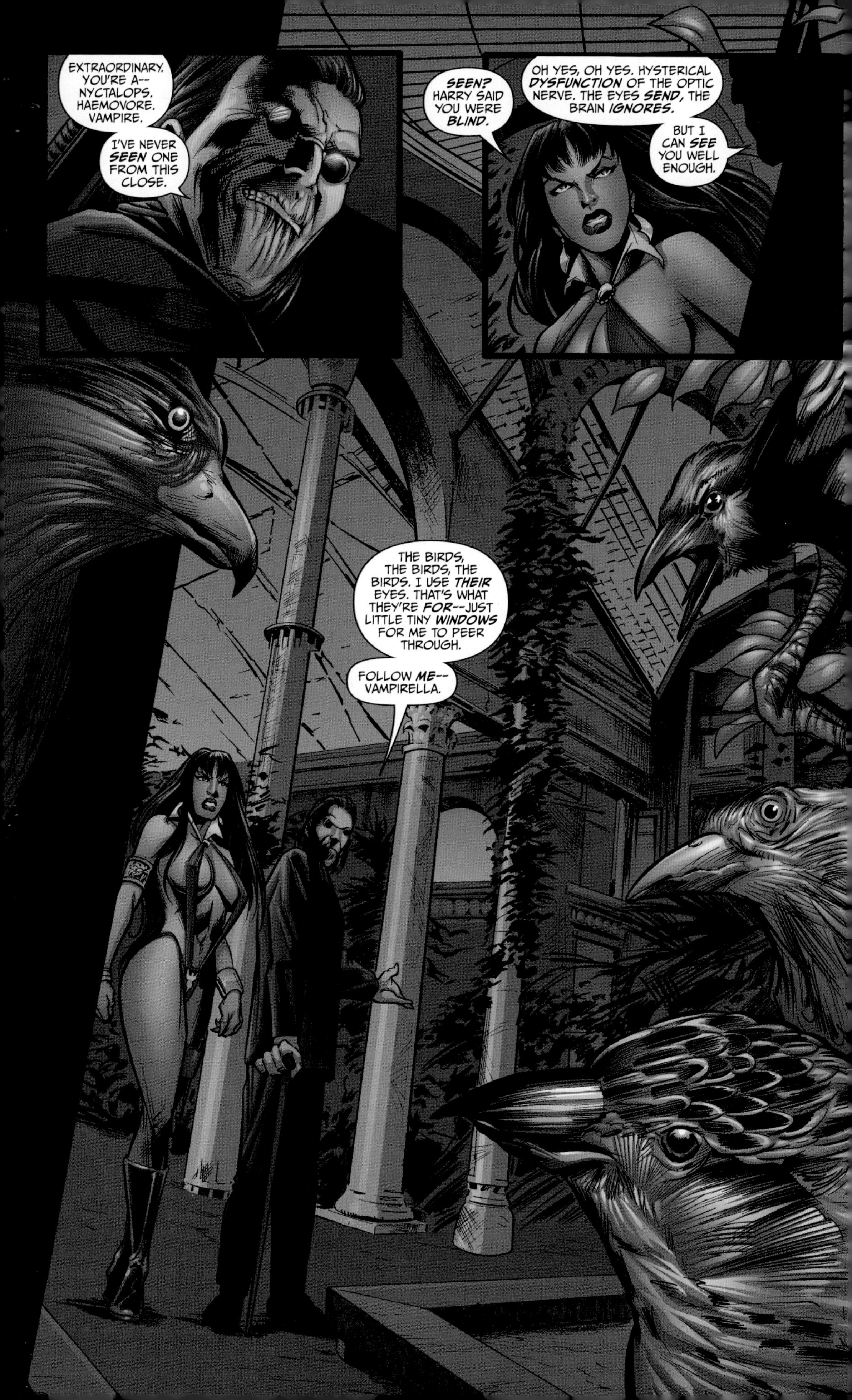
EXTRAORDINARY. YOU'RE A-- NYCTALOPS. HAEMOVORE. VAMPIRE.
I'VE NEVER SEEN ONE FROM THIS CLOSE.
SEEN? HARRY SAID YOU WERE BLIND.
OH YES, OH YES. HYSTERICAL DYSFUNCTION OF THE OPTIC NERVE. THE EYES SEND, THE BRAIN IGNORES.
BUT I CAN SEE YOU WELL ENOUGH.
THE BIRDS, THE BIRDS, THE BIRDS. I USE THEIR EYES. THAT'S WHAT THEY'RE FOR--JUST LITTLE TINY WINDOWS FOR ME TO PEER THROUGH.
FOLLOW ME-- VAMPIRELLA.

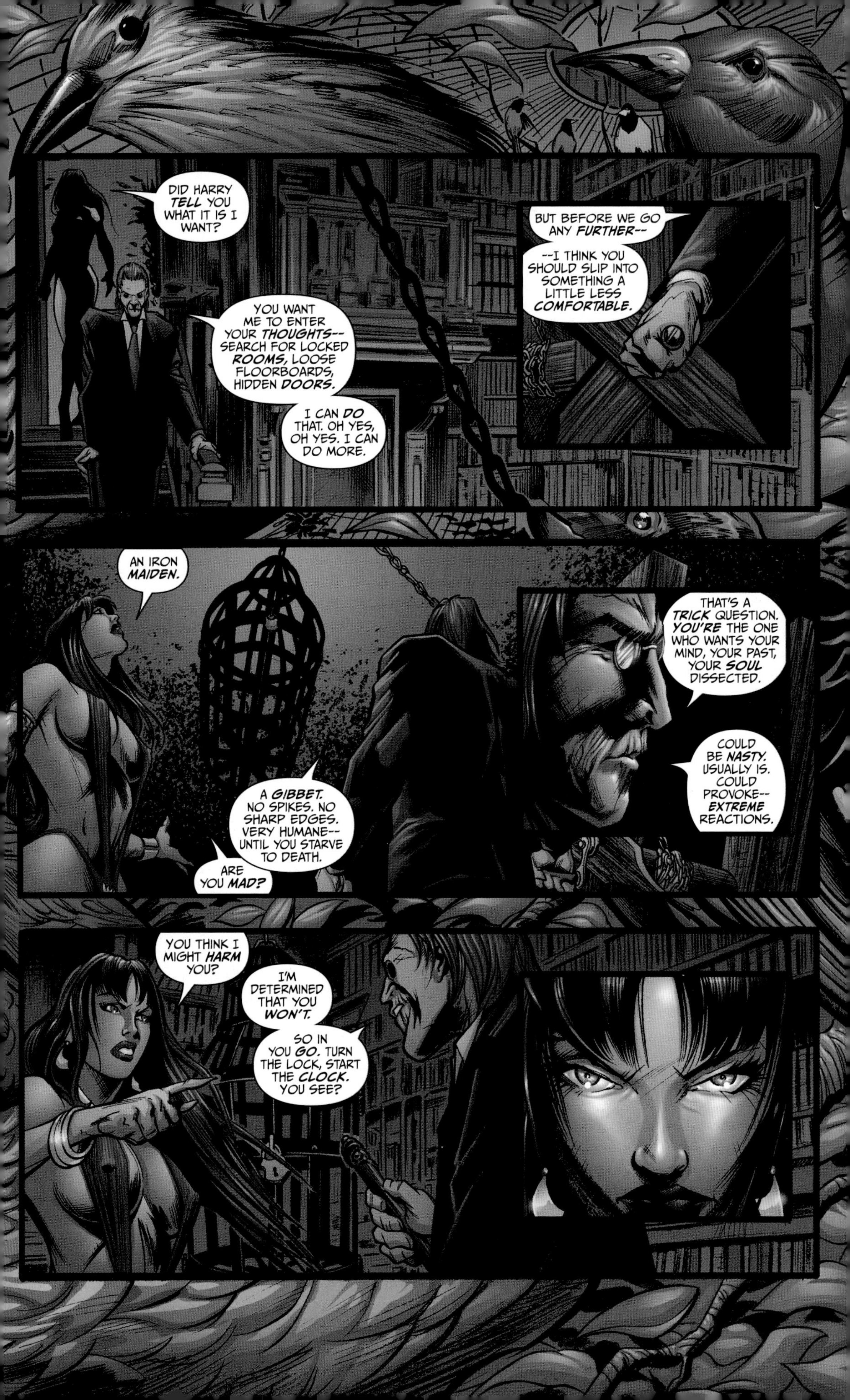

DID HARRY TELL YOU WHAT IT IS I WANT?
YOU WANT ME TO ENTER YOUR THOUGHTS--SEARCH FOR LOCKED ROOMS, LOOSE FLOORBOARDS, HIDDEN DOORS.
I CAN DO THAT. OH YES, OH YES. I CAN DO MORE.
BUT BEFORE WE GO ANY FURTHER--
--I THINK YOU SHOULD SLIP INTO SOMETHING A LITTLE LESS COMFORTABLE.
AN IRON MAIDEN.
A GIBBET. NO SPIKES. NO SHARP EDGES. VERY HUMANE--UNTIL YOU STARVE TO DEATH.
ARE YOU MAD?
THAT'S A TRICK QUESTION. YOU'RE THE ONE WHO WANTS YOUR MIND, YOUR PAST, YOUR SOUL DISSECTED.
COULD BE NASTY. USUALLY IS. COULD PROVOKE--EXTREME REACTIONS.
YOU THINK I MIGHT HARM YOU?
I'M DETERMINED THAT YOU WON'T.
SO IN YOU GO. TURN THE LOCK, START THE CLOCK. YOU SEE?

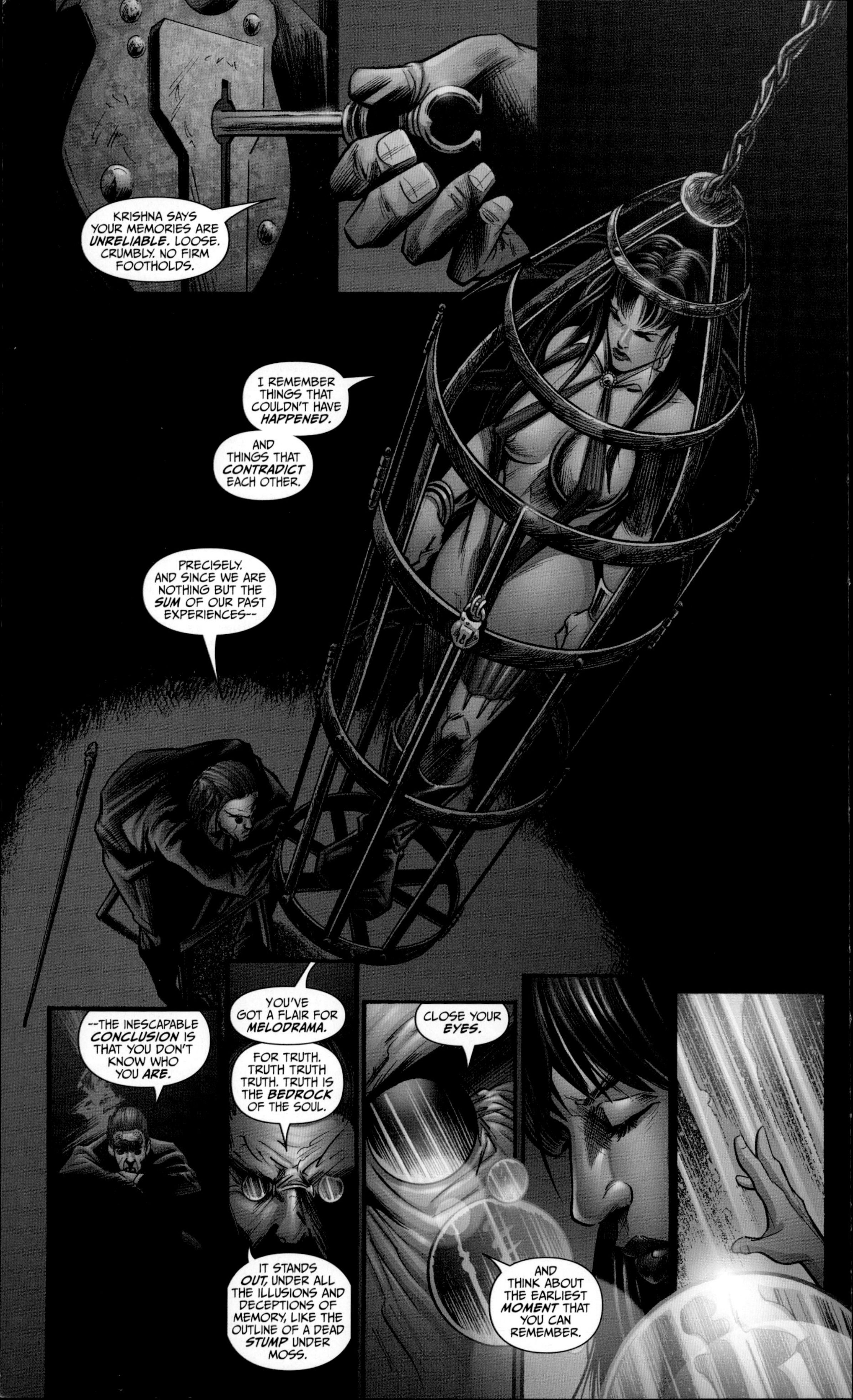
KRISHNA SAYS YOUR MEMORIES ARE UNRELIABLE. LOOSE. CRUMBLY. NO FIRM FOOTHOLDS.
I REMEMBER THINGS THAT COULDN'T HAVE HAPPENED.
AND THINGS THAT CONTRADICT EACH OTHER.
PRECISELY. AND SINCE WE ARE NOTHING BUT THE SUM OF OUR PAST EXPERIENCES--
--THE INESCAPABLE CONCLUSION IS THAT YOU DON'T KNOW WHO YOU ARE.
YOU'VE GOT A FLAIR FOR MELODRAMA.
FOR TRUTH. TRUTH TRUTH TRUTH. TRUTH IS THE BEDROCK OF THE SOUL.
IT STANDS OUT, UNDER ALL THE ILLUSIONS AND DECEPTIONS OF MEMORY, LIKE THE OUTLINE OF A DEAD STUMP UNDER MOSS.
CLOSE YOUR EYES.
AND THINK ABOUT THE EARLIEST MOMENT THAT YOU CAN REMEMBER.

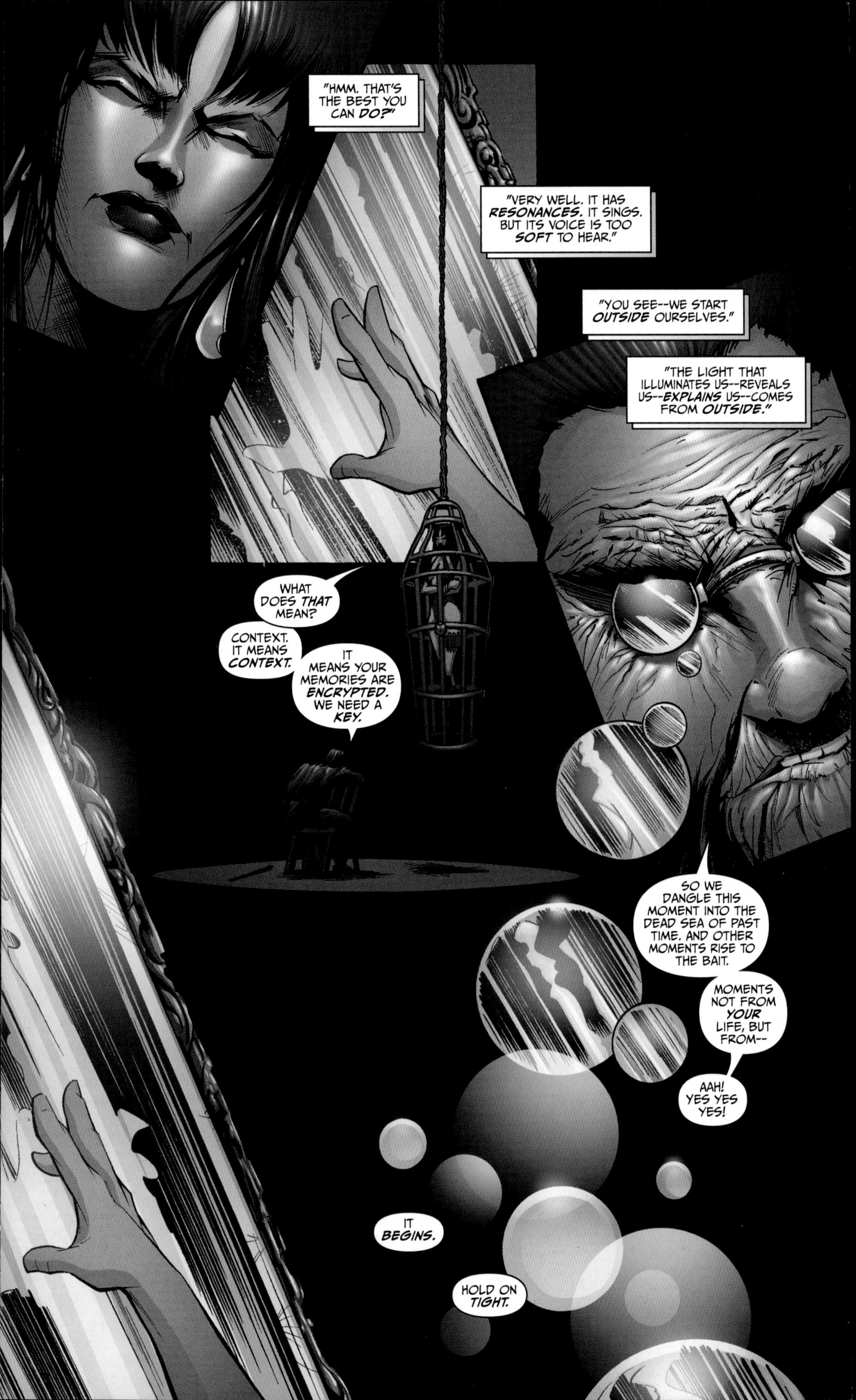
"HMM. THAT'S THE BEST YOU CAN *DO?*"
"VERY WELL. IT HAS *RESONANCES.* IT SINGS. BUT ITS VOICE IS TOO *SOFT* TO HEAR."
"YOU SEE--WE START *OUTSIDE* OURSELVES."
"THE LIGHT THAT ILLUMINATES US--REVEALS US--*EXPLAINS* US--COMES FROM *OUTSIDE.*"
WHAT DOES *THAT* MEAN?
CONTEXT. IT MEANS *CONTEXT.*
IT MEANS YOUR MEMORIES ARE *ENCRYPTED.* WE NEED A *KEY.*
SO WE DANGLE THIS MOMENT INTO THE DEAD SEA OF PAST TIME. AND OTHER MOMENTS RISE TO THE BAIT.
MOMENTS NOT FROM *YOUR* LIFE, BUT FROM--
AAH! YES YES YES!
IT *BEGINS.*
HOLD ON *TIGHT.*

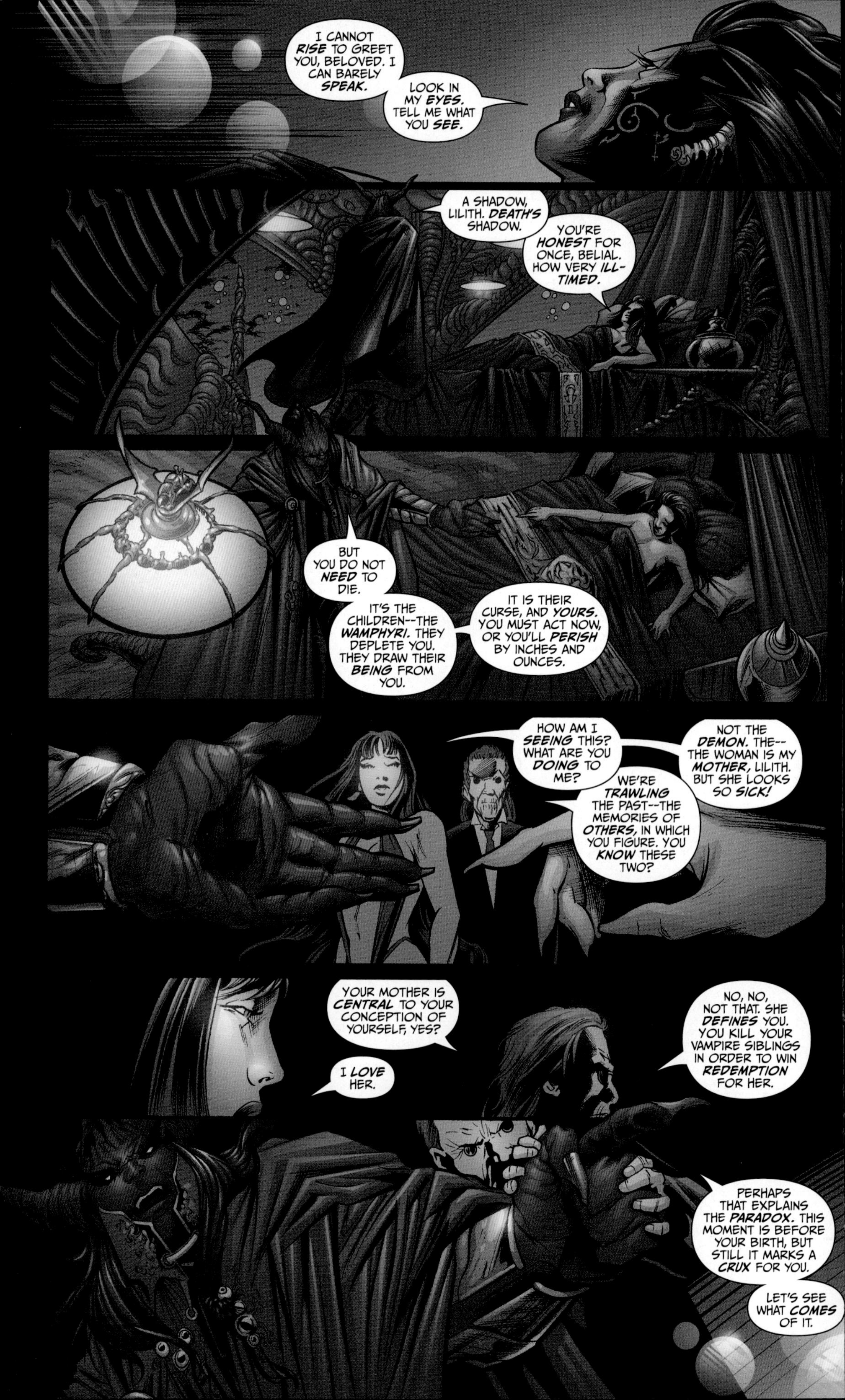

I CANNOT RISE TO GREET YOU, BELOVED. I CAN BARELY SPEAK.
LOOK IN MY EYES. TELL ME WHAT YOU SEE.
A SHADOW, LILITH. DEATH'S SHADOW.
YOU'RE HONEST FOR ONCE, BELIAL. HOW VERY ILL-TIMED.
BUT YOU DO NOT NEED TO DIE.
IT'S THE CHILDREN--THE WAMPHYRI. THEY DEPLETE YOU. THEY DRAW THEIR BEING FROM YOU.
IT IS THEIR CURSE, AND YOURS. YOU MUST ACT NOW, OR YOU'LL PERISH BY INCHES AND OUNCES.
HOW AM I SEEING THIS? WHAT ARE YOU DOING TO ME?
WE'RE TRAWLING THE PAST--THE MEMORIES OF OTHERS, IN WHICH YOU FIGURE. YOU KNOW THESE TWO?
NOT THE DEMON. THE-- THE WOMAN IS MY MOTHER, LILITH. BUT SHE LOOKS SO SICK!
YOUR MOTHER IS CENTRAL TO YOUR CONCEPTION OF YOURSELF, YES?
I LOVE HER.
NO, NO, NOT THAT. SHE DEFINES YOU. YOU KILL YOUR VAMPIRE SIBLINGS IN ORDER TO WIN REDEMPTION FOR HER.
PERHAPS THAT EXPLAINS THE PARADOX. THIS MOMENT IS BEFORE YOUR BIRTH, BUT STILL IT MARKS A CRUX FOR YOU.
LET'S SEE WHAT COMES OF IT.

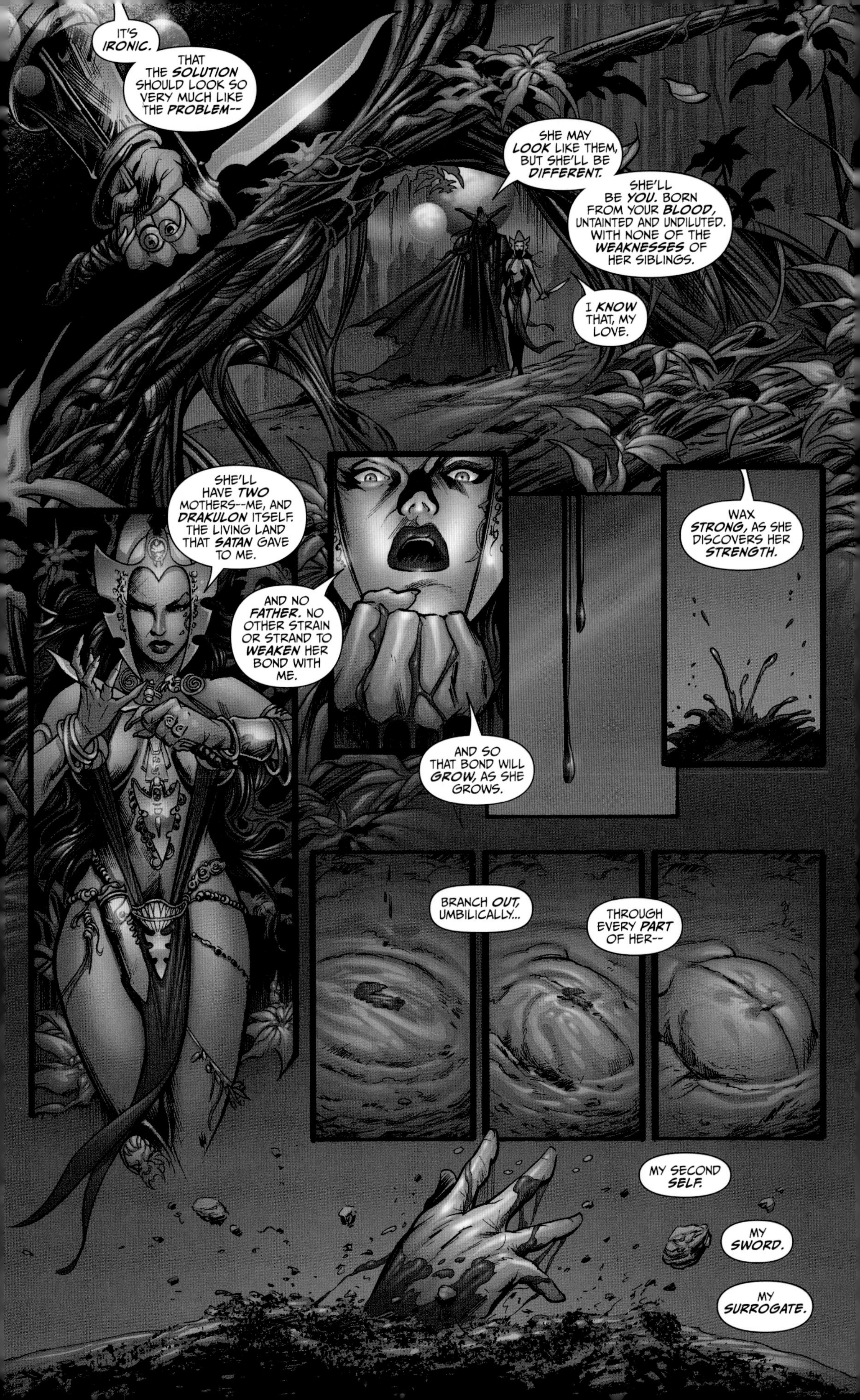
IT'S IRONIC.
THAT THE SOLUTION SHOULD LOOK SO VERY MUCH LIKE THE PROBLEM--
SHE MAY LOOK LIKE THEM, BUT SHE'LL BE DIFFERENT.
SHE'LL BE YOU. BORN FROM YOUR BLOOD, UNTAINTED AND UNDILUTED. WITH NONE OF THE WEAKNESSES OF HER SIBLINGS.
I KNOW THAT, MY LOVE.
SHE'LL HAVE TWO MOTHERS--ME, AND DRAKULON ITSELF. THE LIVING LAND THAT SATAN GAVE TO ME.
AND NO FATHER. NO OTHER STRAIN OR STRAND TO WEAKEN HER BOND WITH ME.
AND SO THAT BOND WILL GROW, AS SHE GROWS.
WAX STRONG, AS SHE DISCOVERS HER STRENGTH.
BRANCH OUT, UMBILICALLY...
THROUGH EVERY PART OF HER--
MY SECOND SELF.
MY SWORD.
MY SURROGATE.

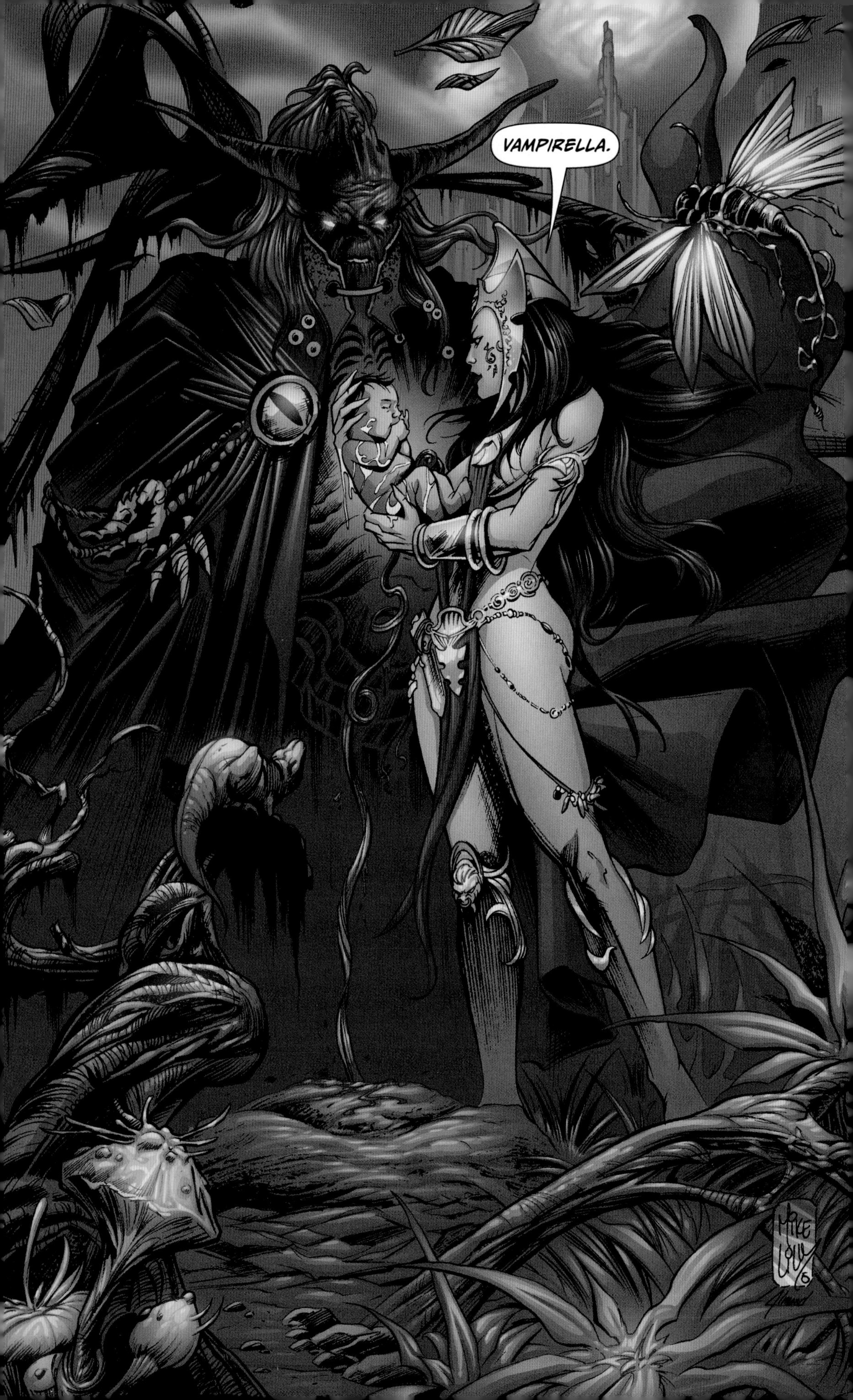
VAMPIRELLA.

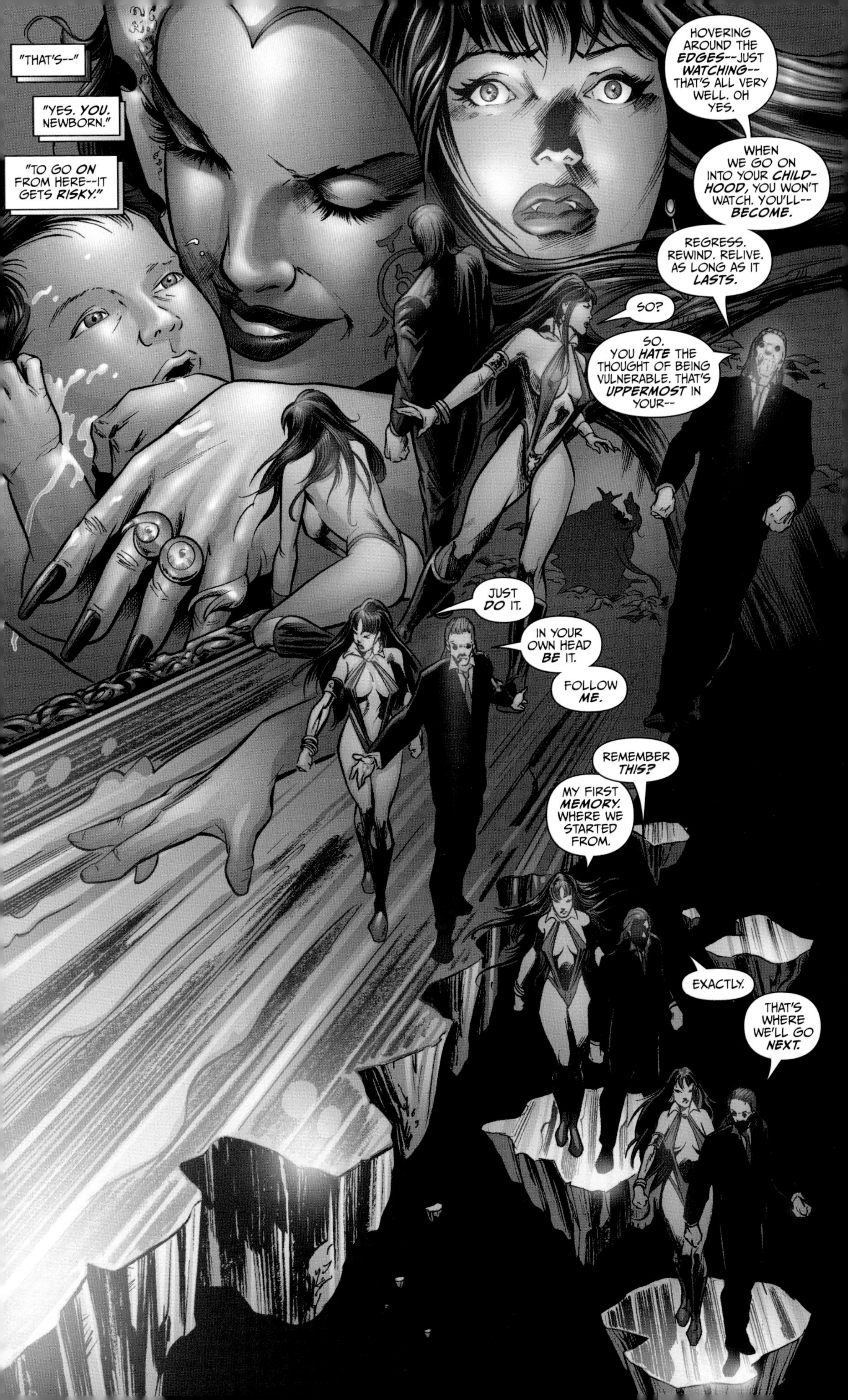
"THAT'S--"
"YES. YOU. NEWBORN."
"TO GO ON FROM HERE--IT GETS RISKY."
HOVERING AROUND THE EDGES--JUST WATCHING--THAT'S ALL VERY WELL. OH YES.
WHEN WE GO ON INTO YOUR CHILDHOOD, YOU WON'T WATCH. YOU'LL--BECOME.
REGRESS. REWIND. RELIVE. AS LONG AS IT LASTS.
SO?
SO. YOU HATE THE THOUGHT OF BEING VULNERABLE. THAT'S UPPERMOST IN YOUR--
JUST DO IT.
IN YOUR OWN HEAD BE IT.
FOLLOW ME.
REMEMBER THIS?
MY FIRST MEMORY. WHERE WE STARTED FROM.
EXACTLY.
THAT'S WHERE WE'LL GO NEXT.

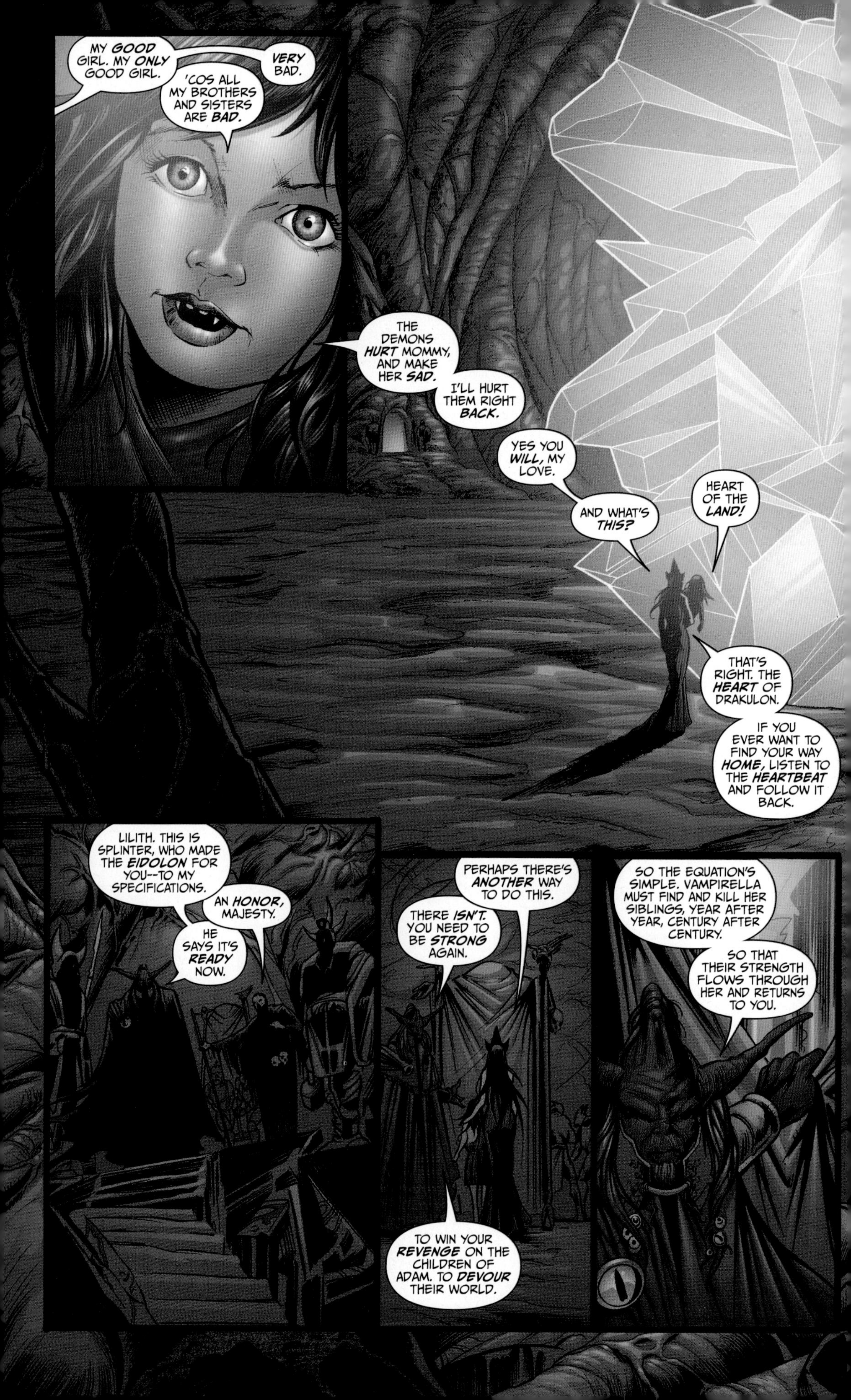
MY GOOD GIRL. MY ONLY GOOD GIRL.
VERY BAD.
'COS ALL MY BROTHERS AND SISTERS ARE BAD.
THE DEMONS HURT MOMMY, AND MAKE HER SAD.
I'LL HURT THEM RIGHT BACK.
YES YOU WILL, MY LOVE.
AND WHAT'S THIS?
HEART OF THE LAND!
THAT'S RIGHT. THE HEART OF DRAKULON.
IF YOU EVER WANT TO FIND YOUR WAY HOME, LISTEN TO THE HEARTBEAT AND FOLLOW IT BACK.
LILITH. THIS IS SPLINTER, WHO MADE THE EIDOLON FOR YOU--TO MY SPECIFICATIONS.
AN HONOR, MAJESTY.
HE SAYS IT'S READY NOW.
PERHAPS THERE'S ANOTHER WAY TO DO THIS.
THERE ISN'T. YOU NEED TO BE STRONG AGAIN.
TO WIN YOUR REVENGE ON THE CHILDREN OF ADAM. TO DEVOUR THEIR WORLD.
SO THE EQUATION'S SIMPLE. VAMPIRELLA MUST FIND AND KILL HER SIBLINGS, YEAR AFTER YEAR, CENTURY AFTER CENTURY.
SO THAT THEIR STRENGTH FLOWS THROUGH HER AND RETURNS TO YOU.

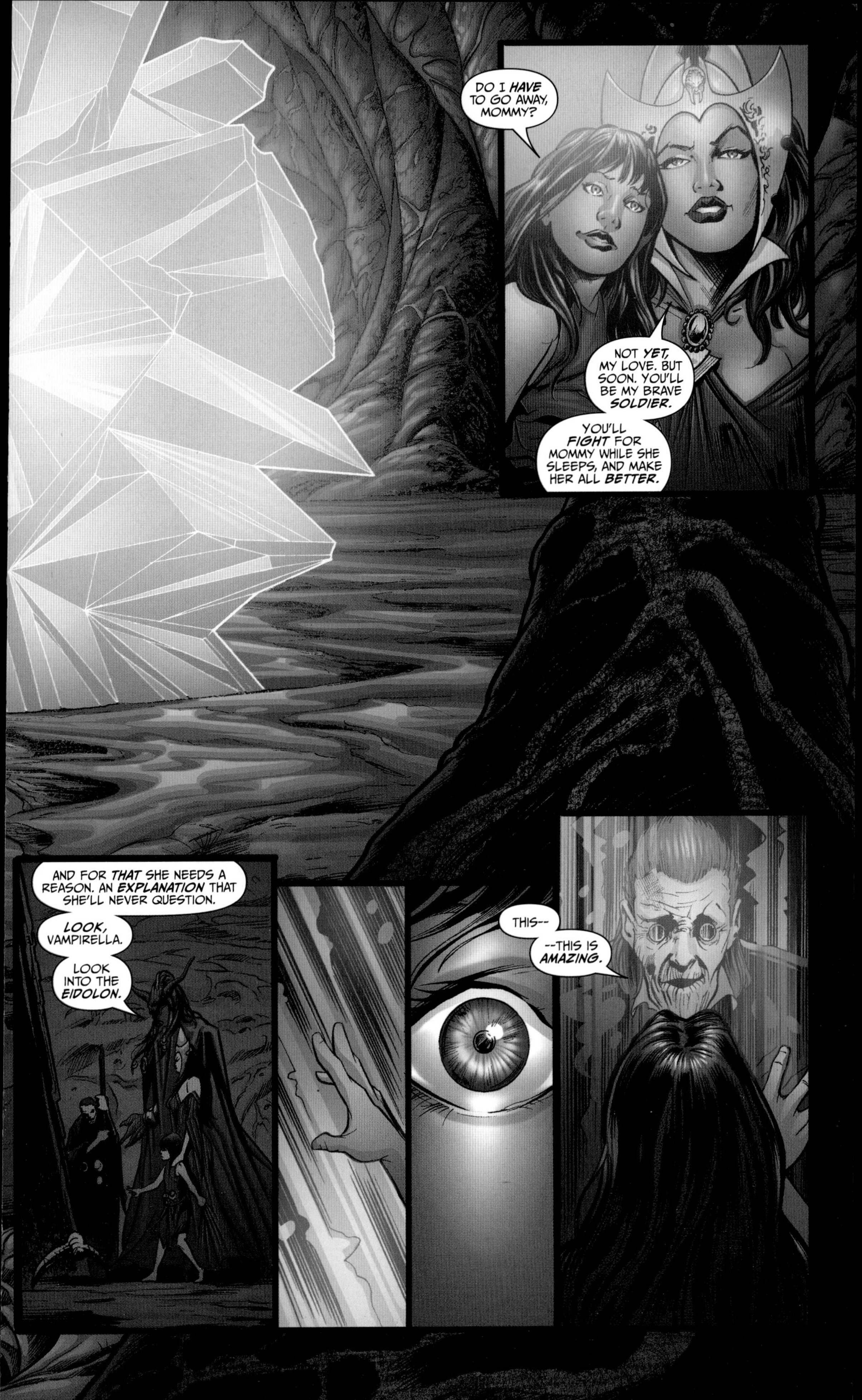

DO I *HAVE* TO GO AWAY, MOMMY?
NOT *YET,* MY LOVE. BUT SOON. YOU'LL BE MY BRAVE *SOLDIER.*
YOU'LL *FIGHT* FOR MOMMY WHILE SHE SLEEPS, AND MAKE HER ALL *BETTER.*
AND FOR *THAT* SHE NEEDS A REASON. AN *EXPLANATION* THAT SHE'LL NEVER QUESTION.
LOOK, VAMPIRELLA.
LOOK INTO THE *EIDOLON.*
THIS--
--THIS IS *AMAZING.*

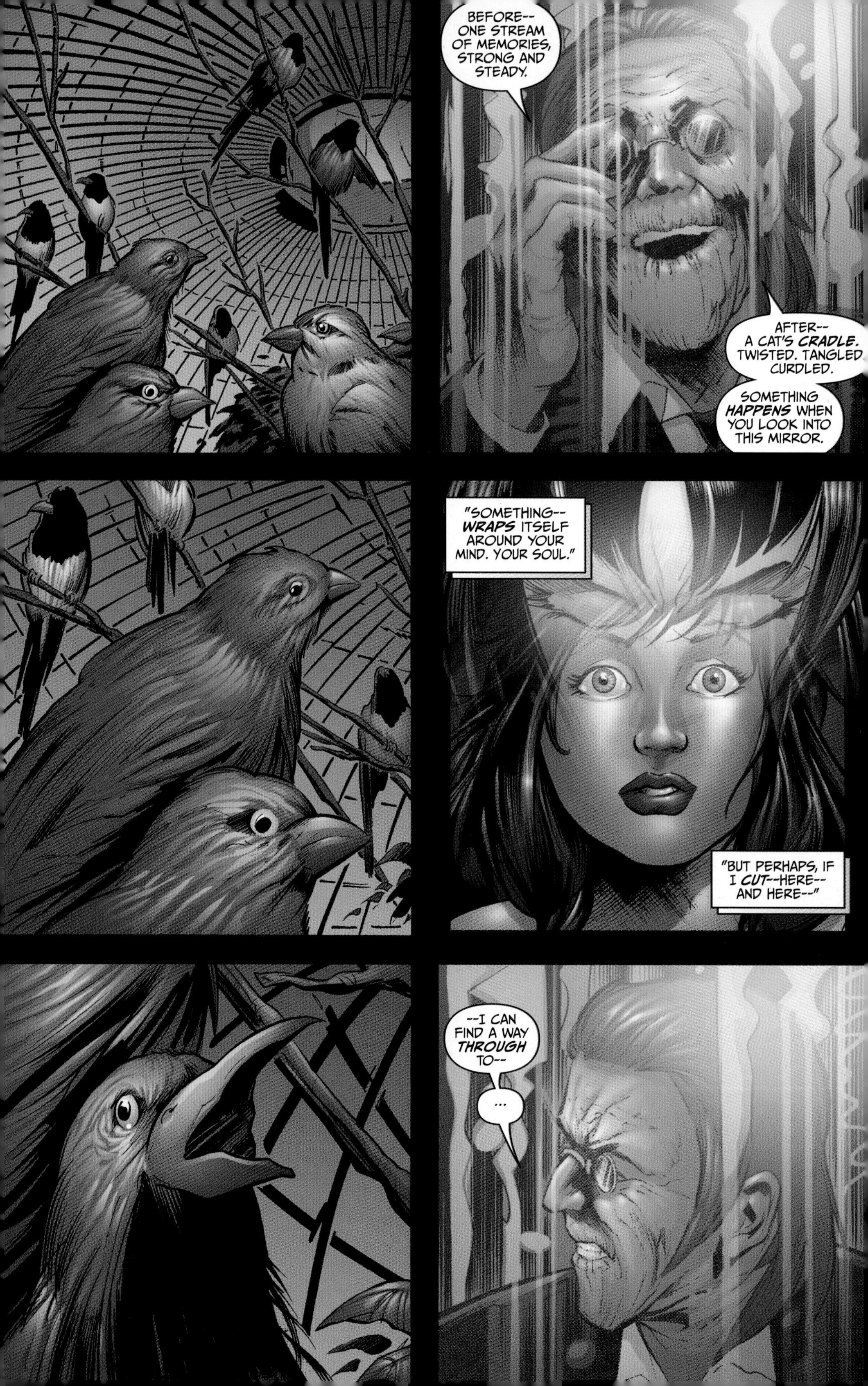
BEFORE-- ONE STREAM OF MEMORIES, STRONG AND STEADY.
AFTER-- A CAT'S CRADLE. TWISTED. TANGLED. CURDLED.
SOMETHING HAPPENS WHEN YOU LOOK INTO THIS MIRROR.
"SOMETHING-- WRAPS ITSELF AROUND YOUR MIND. YOUR SOUL."
"BUT PERHAPS, IF I CUT--HERE-- AND HERE--"
--I CAN FIND A WAY THROUGH TO--
...

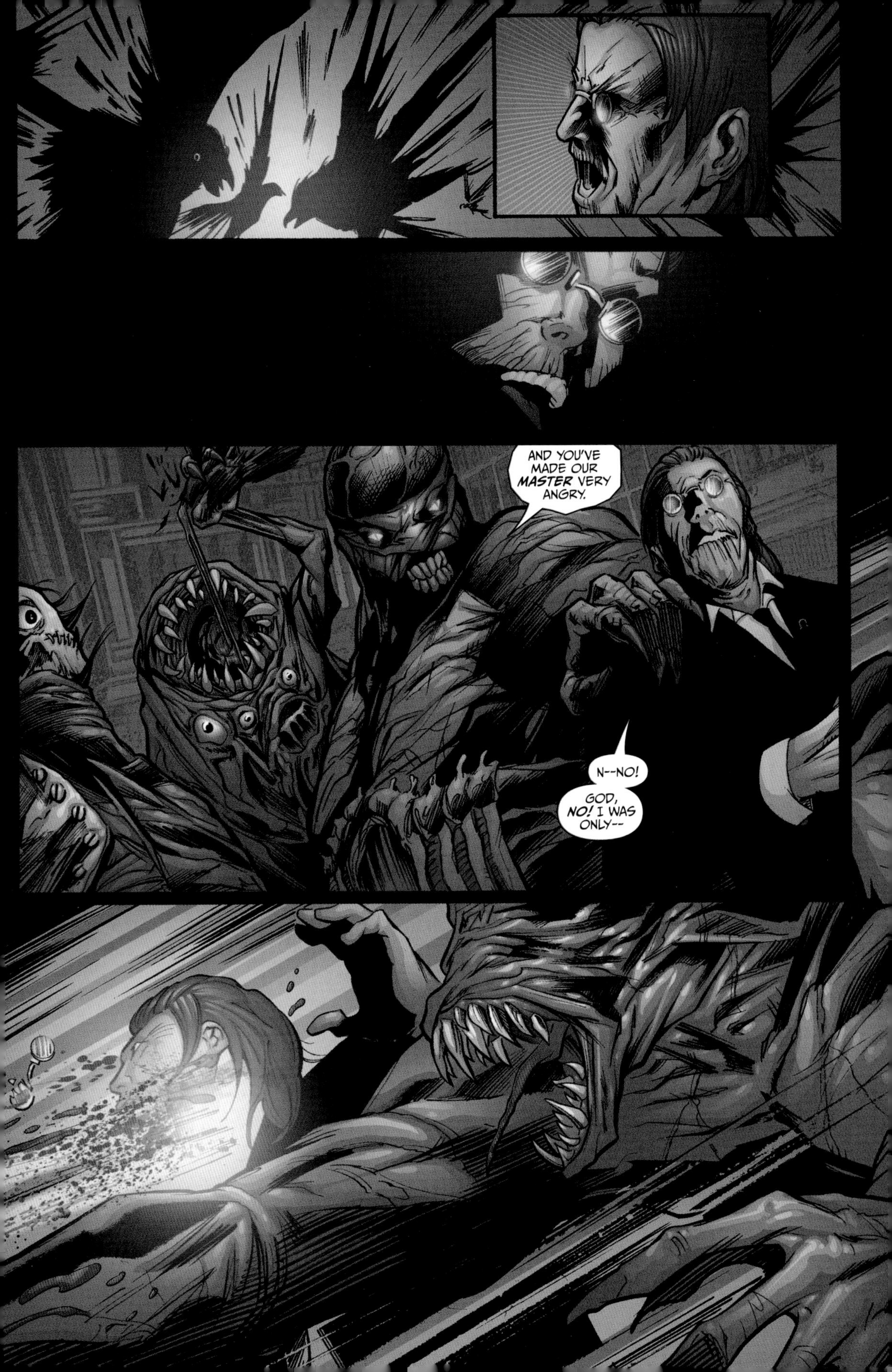
AND YOU'VE MADE OUR MASTER VERY ANGRY.
N--NO!
GOD, NO! I WAS ONLY--

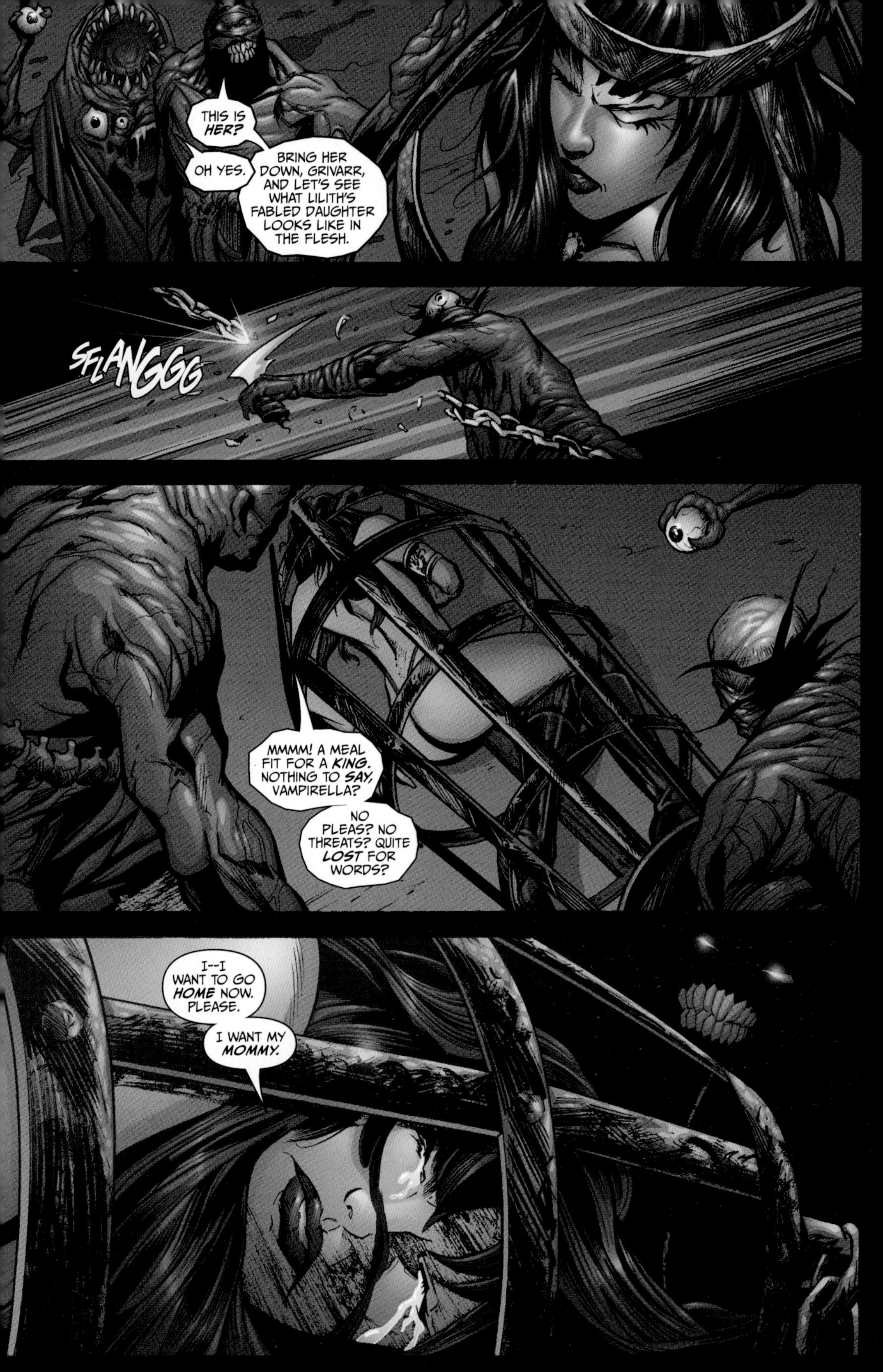
THIS IS HER?
OH YES.
BRING HER DOWN, GRIVARR, AND LET'S SEE WHAT LILITH'S FABLED DAUGHTER LOOKS LIKE IN THE FLESH.
SFLANGGG
MMMM! A MEAL FIT FOR A KING. NOTHING TO SAY, VAMPIRELLA?
NO PLEAS? NO THREATS? QUITE LOST FOR WORDS?
I--I WANT TO GO HOME NOW. PLEASE.
I WANT MY MOMMY.

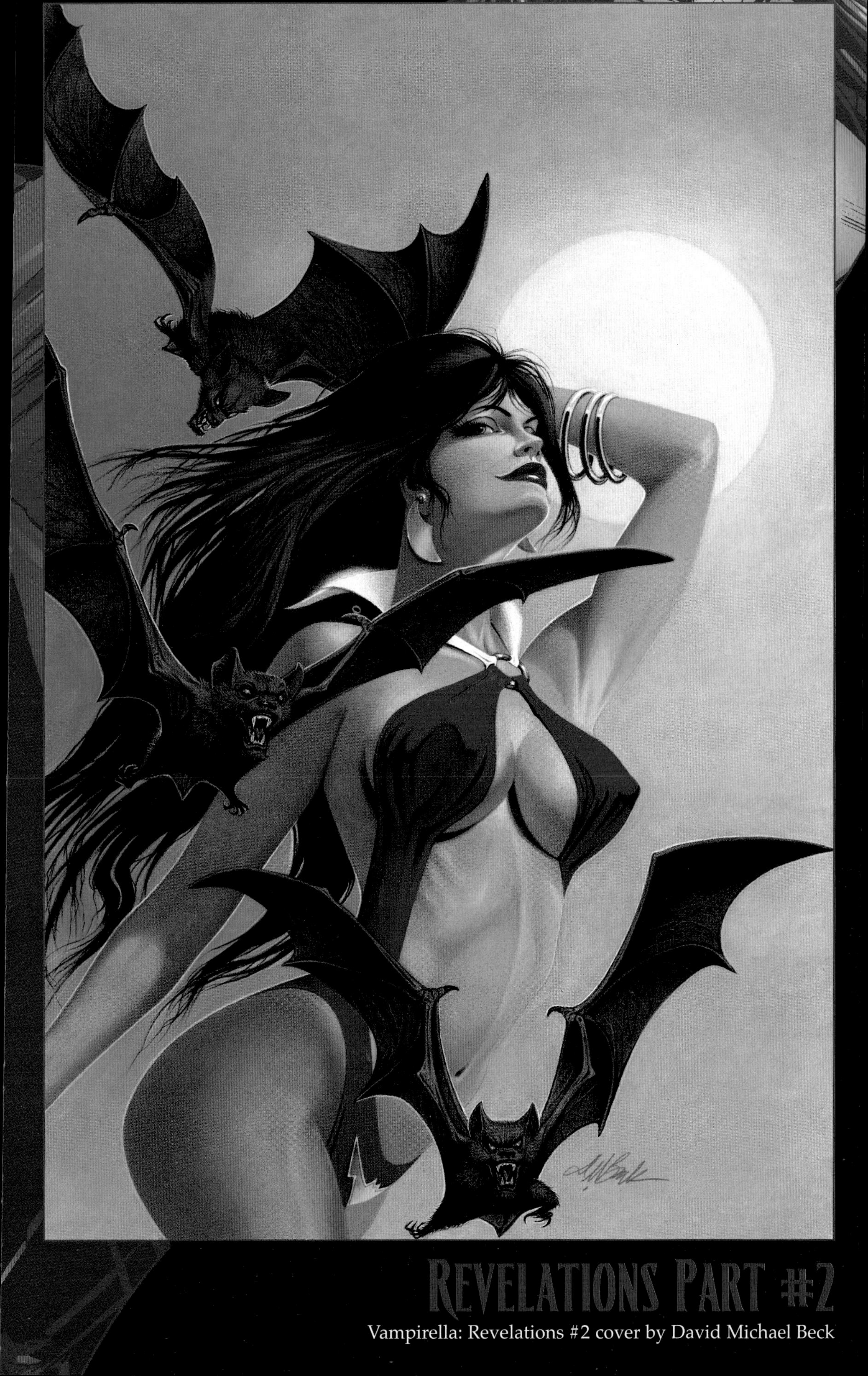

REVELATIONS PART #2

Vampirella: Revelations #2 cover by David Michael Beck

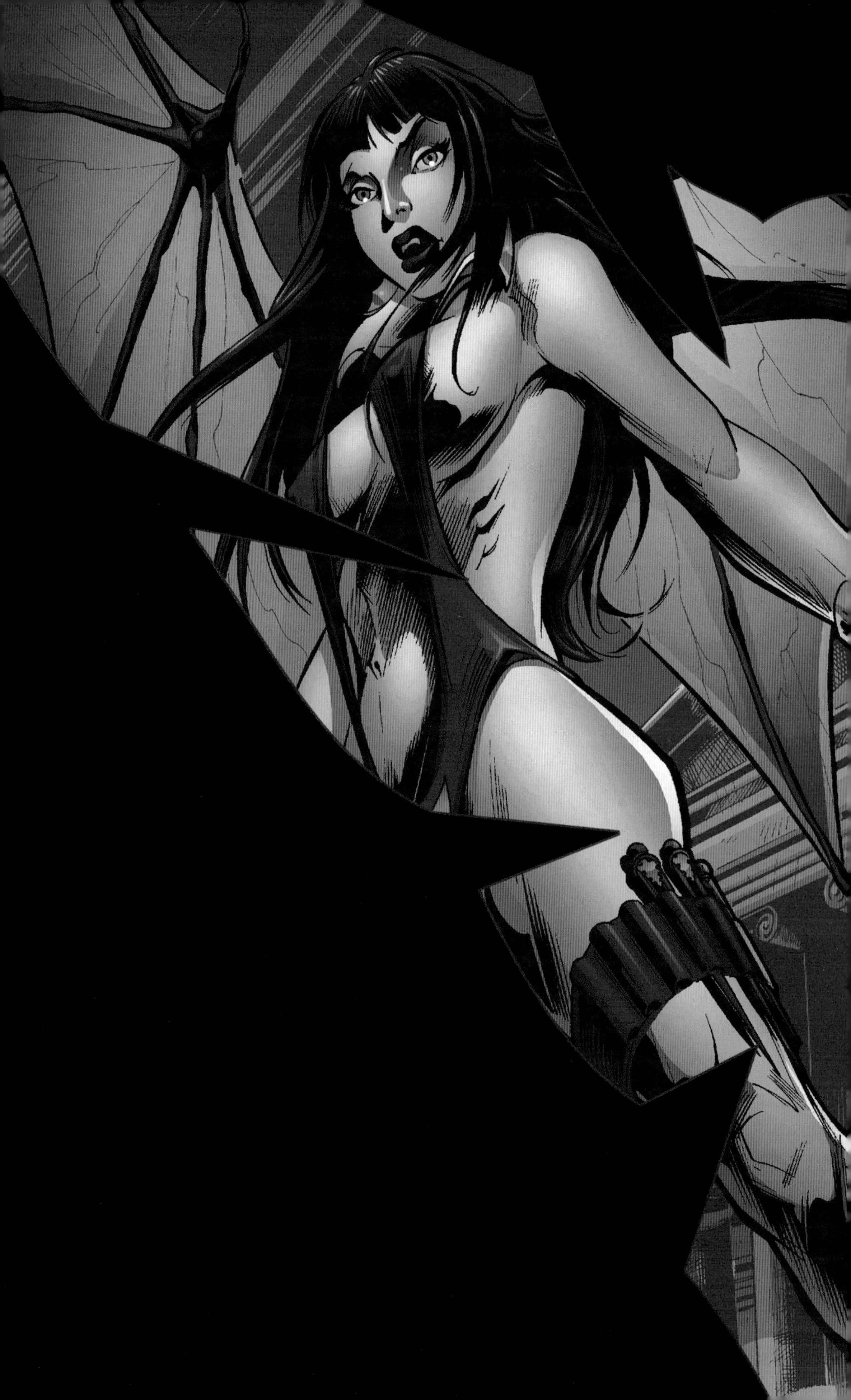

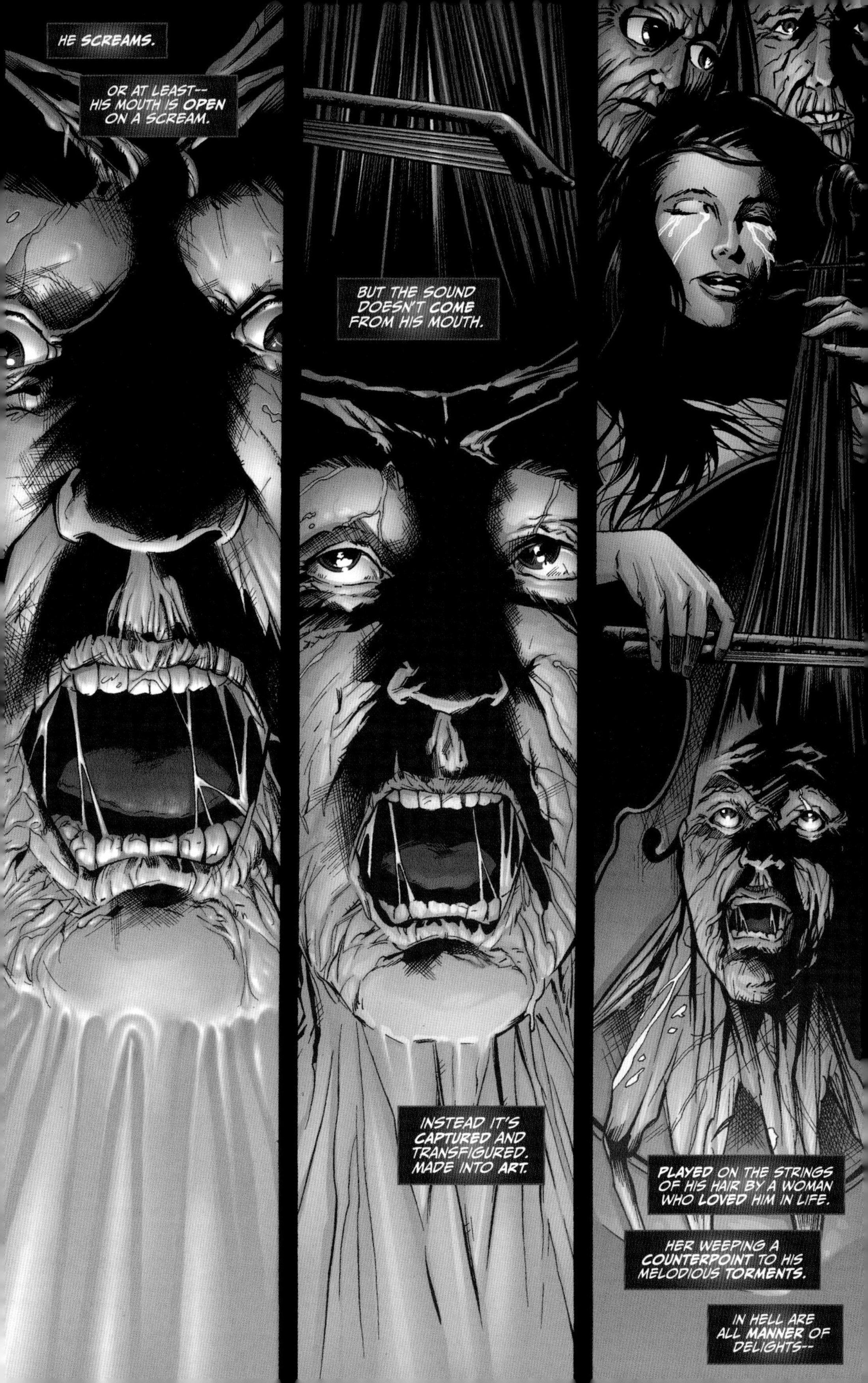
HE SCREAMS.
OR AT LEAST-- HIS MOUTH IS OPEN ON A SCREAM.
BUT THE SOUND DOESN'T COME FROM HIS MOUTH.
INSTEAD IT'S CAPTURED AND TRANSFIGURED. MADE INTO ART.
PLAYED ON THE STRINGS OF HIS HAIR BY A WOMAN WHO LOVED HIM IN LIFE.
HER WEEPING A COUNTERPOINT TO HIS MELODIOUS TORMENTS.
IN HELL ARE ALL MANNER OF DELIGHTS--

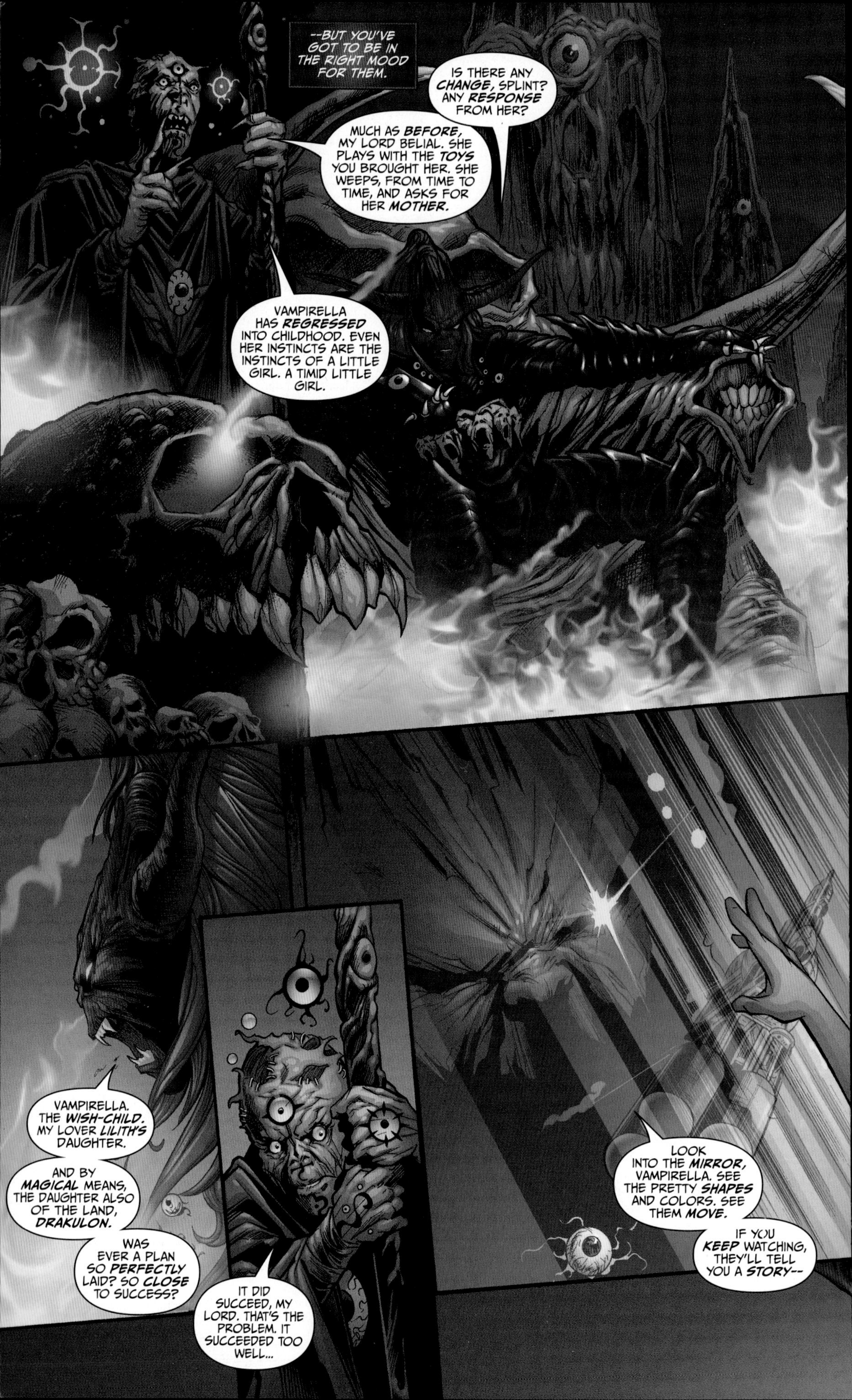
--BUT YOU'VE GOT TO BE IN THE RIGHT MOOD FOR THEM.
IS THERE ANY CHANGE, SPLINT? ANY RESPONSE FROM HER?
MUCH AS BEFORE, MY LORD BELIAL. SHE PLAYS WITH THE TOYS YOU BROUGHT HER. SHE WEEPS, FROM TIME TO TIME, AND ASKS FOR HER MOTHER.
VAMPIRELLA HAS REGRESSED INTO CHILDHOOD. EVEN HER INSTINCTS ARE THE INSTINCTS OF A LITTLE GIRL. A TIMID LITTLE GIRL.
VAMPIRELLA. THE WISH-CHILD. MY LOVER LILITH'S DAUGHTER.
AND BY MAGICAL MEANS, THE DAUGHTER ALSO OF THE LAND, DRAKULON.
WAS EVER A PLAN SO PERFECTLY LAID? SO CLOSE TO SUCCESS?
IT DID SUCCEED, MY LORD. THAT'S THE PROBLEM. IT SUCCEEDED TOO WELL...
LOOK INTO THE MIRROR, VAMPIRELLA. SEE THE PRETTY SHAPES AND COLORS. SEE THEM MOVE.
IF YOU KEEP WATCHING, THEY'LL TELL YOU A STORY--

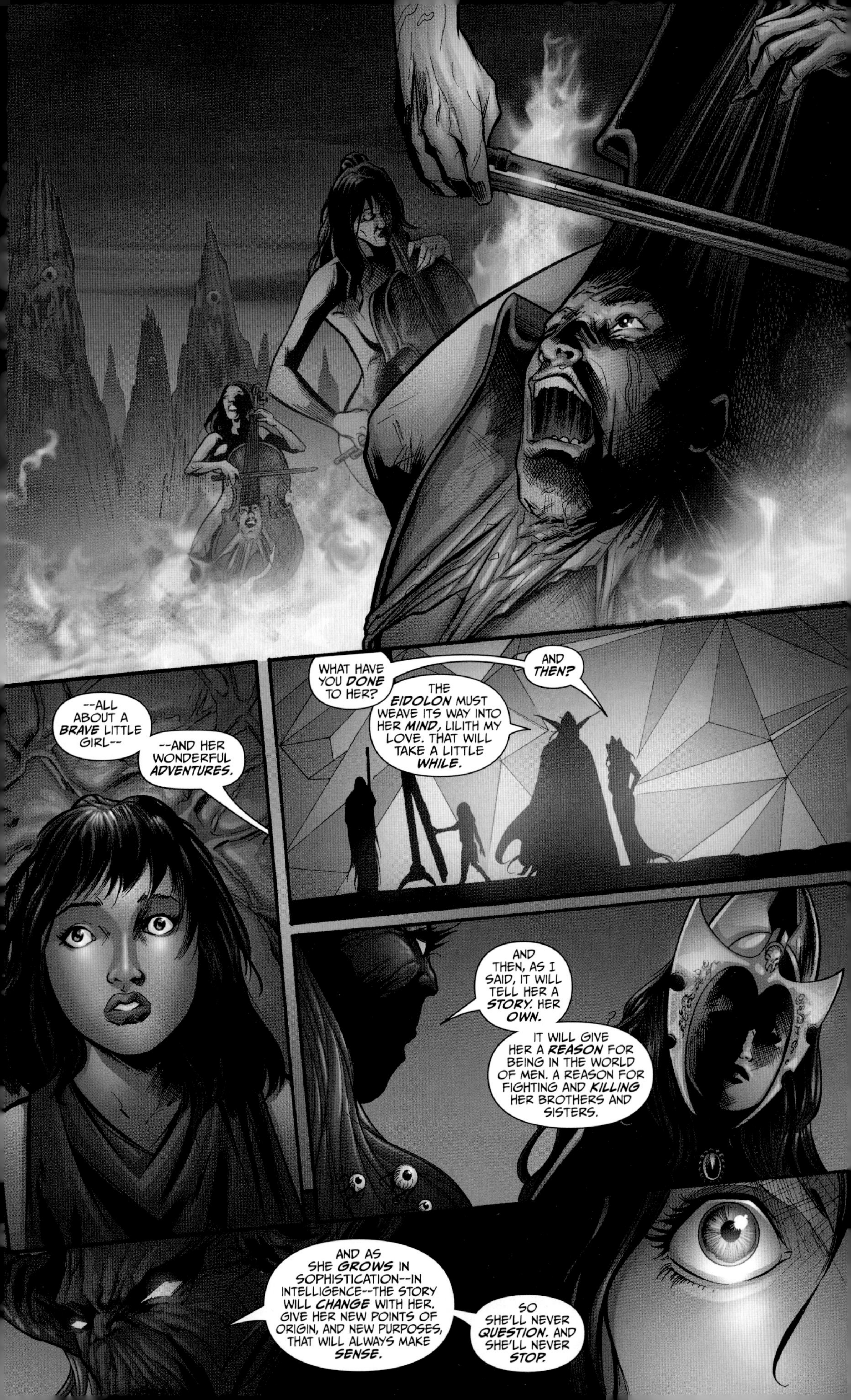
--ALL ABOUT A BRAVE LITTLE GIRL--
--AND HER WONDERFUL ADVENTURES.
WHAT HAVE YOU DONE TO HER?
AND THEN?
THE EIDOLON MUST WEAVE ITS WAY INTO HER MIND, LILITH MY LOVE. THAT WILL TAKE A LITTLE WHILE.
AND THEN, AS I SAID, IT WILL TELL HER A STORY. HER OWN.
IT WILL GIVE HER A REASON FOR BEING IN THE WORLD OF MEN. A REASON FOR FIGHTING AND KILLING HER BROTHERS AND SISTERS.
AND AS SHE GROWS IN SOPHISTICATION--IN INTELLIGENCE--THE STORY WILL CHANGE WITH HER. GIVE HER NEW POINTS OF ORIGIN, AND NEW PURPOSES, THAT WILL ALWAYS MAKE SENSE.
SO SHE'LL NEVER QUESTION. AND SHE'LL NEVER STOP.

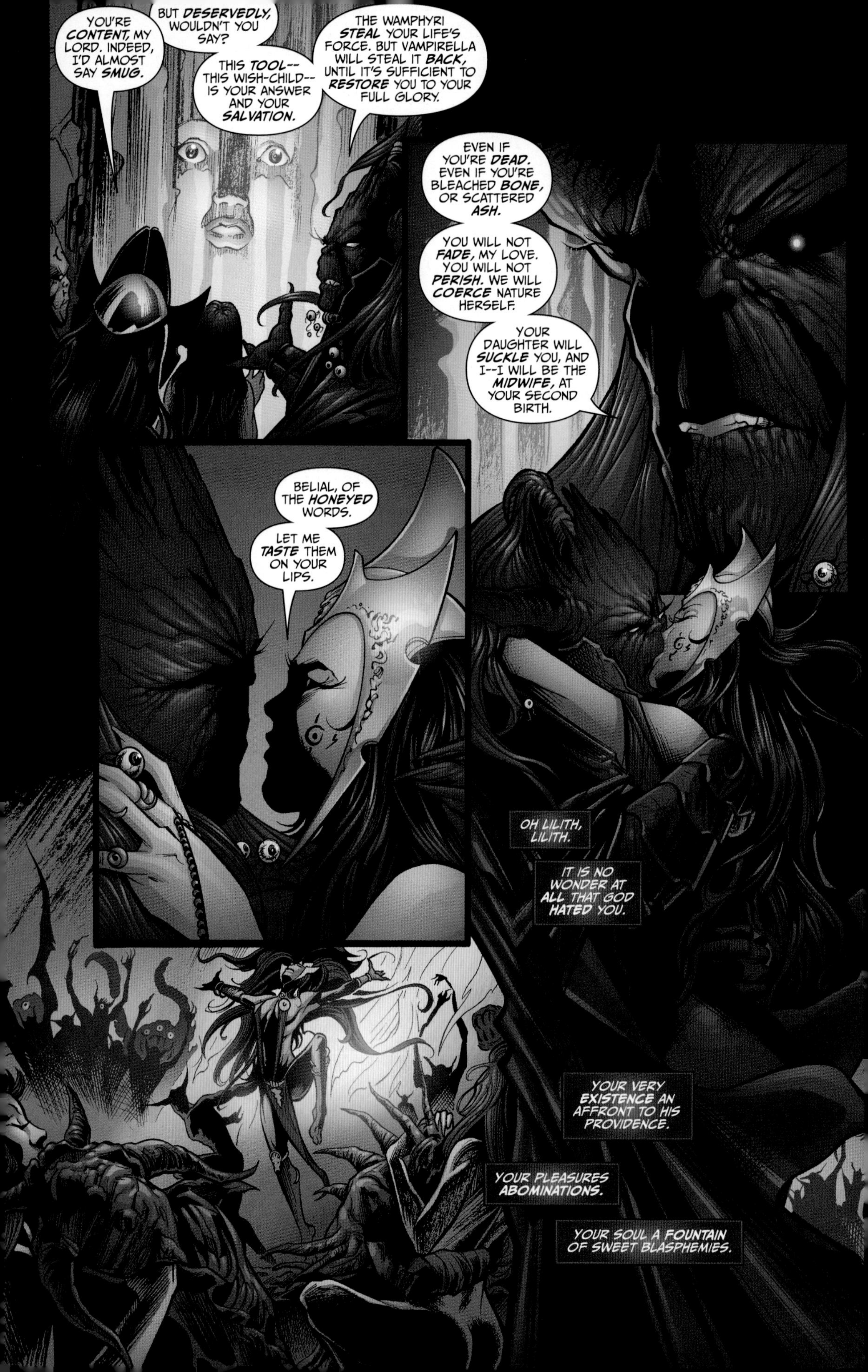
YOU'RE CONTENT, MY LORD. INDEED, I'D ALMOST SAY SMUG.
BUT DESERVEDLY, WOULDN'T YOU SAY?
THIS TOOL-- THIS WISH-CHILD-- IS YOUR ANSWER AND YOUR SALVATION.
THE WAMPHYRI STEAL YOUR LIFE'S FORCE. BUT VAMPIRELLA WILL STEAL IT BACK, UNTIL IT'S SUFFICIENT TO RESTORE YOU TO YOUR FULL GLORY.
EVEN IF YOU'RE DEAD. EVEN IF YOU'RE BLEACHED BONE, OR SCATTERED ASH.
YOU WILL NOT FADE, MY LOVE. YOU WILL NOT PERISH. WE WILL COERCE NATURE HERSELF.
YOUR DAUGHTER WILL SUCKLE YOU, AND I--I WILL BE THE MIDWIFE, AT YOUR SECOND BIRTH.
BELIAL, OF THE HONEYED WORDS.
LET ME TASTE THEM ON YOUR LIPS.
OH LILITH, LILITH.
IT IS NO WONDER AT ALL THAT GOD HATED YOU.
YOUR VERY EXISTENCE AN AFFRONT TO HIS PROVIDENCE.
YOUR PLEASURES ABOMINATIONS.
YOUR SOUL A FOUNTAIN OF SWEET BLASPHEMIES.

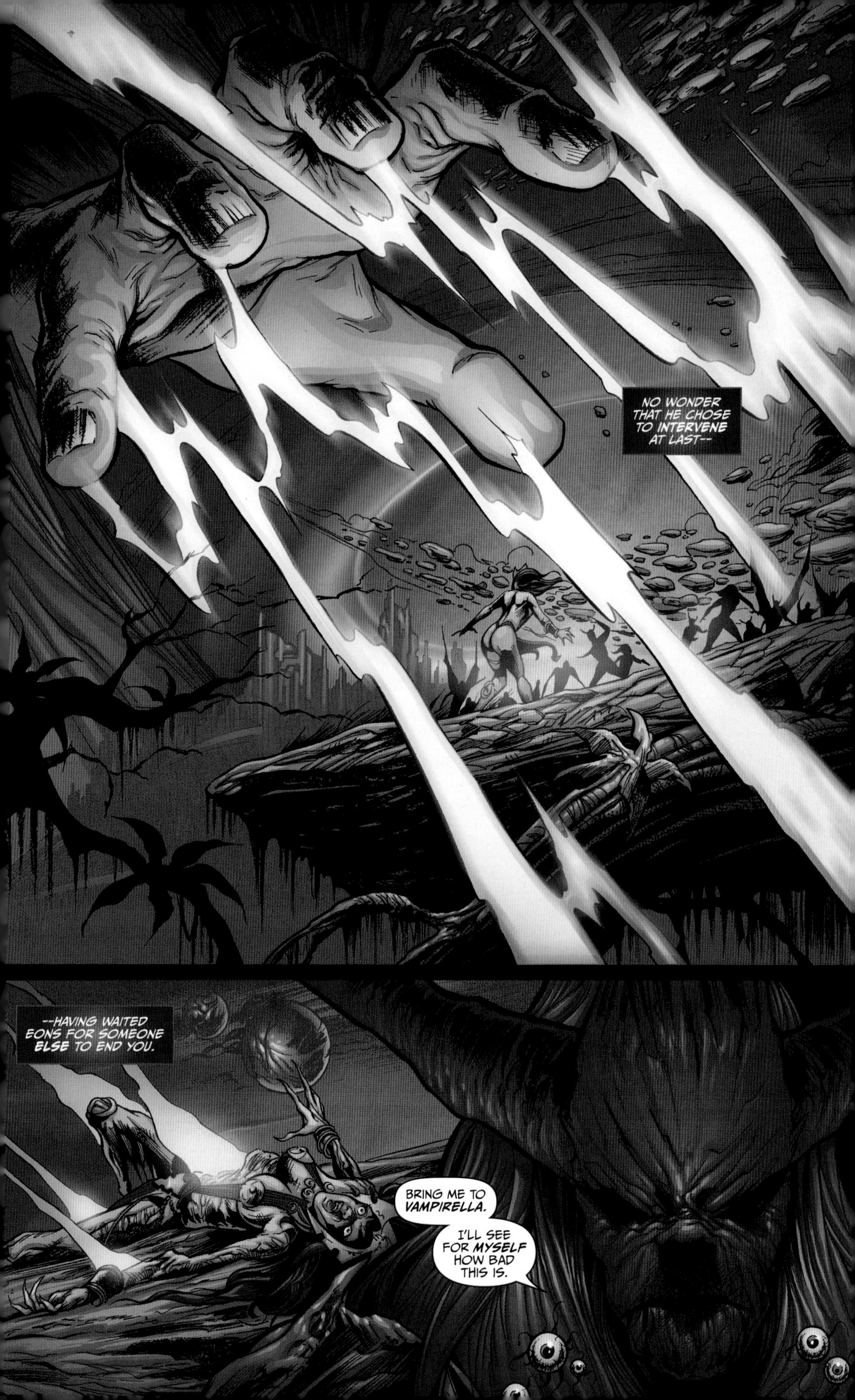
NO WONDER THAT HE CHOSE TO INTERVENE AT LAST--
--HAVING WAITED EONS FOR SOMEONE ELSE TO END YOU.
BRING ME TO VAMPIRELLA.
I'LL SEE FOR MYSELF HOW BAD THIS IS.

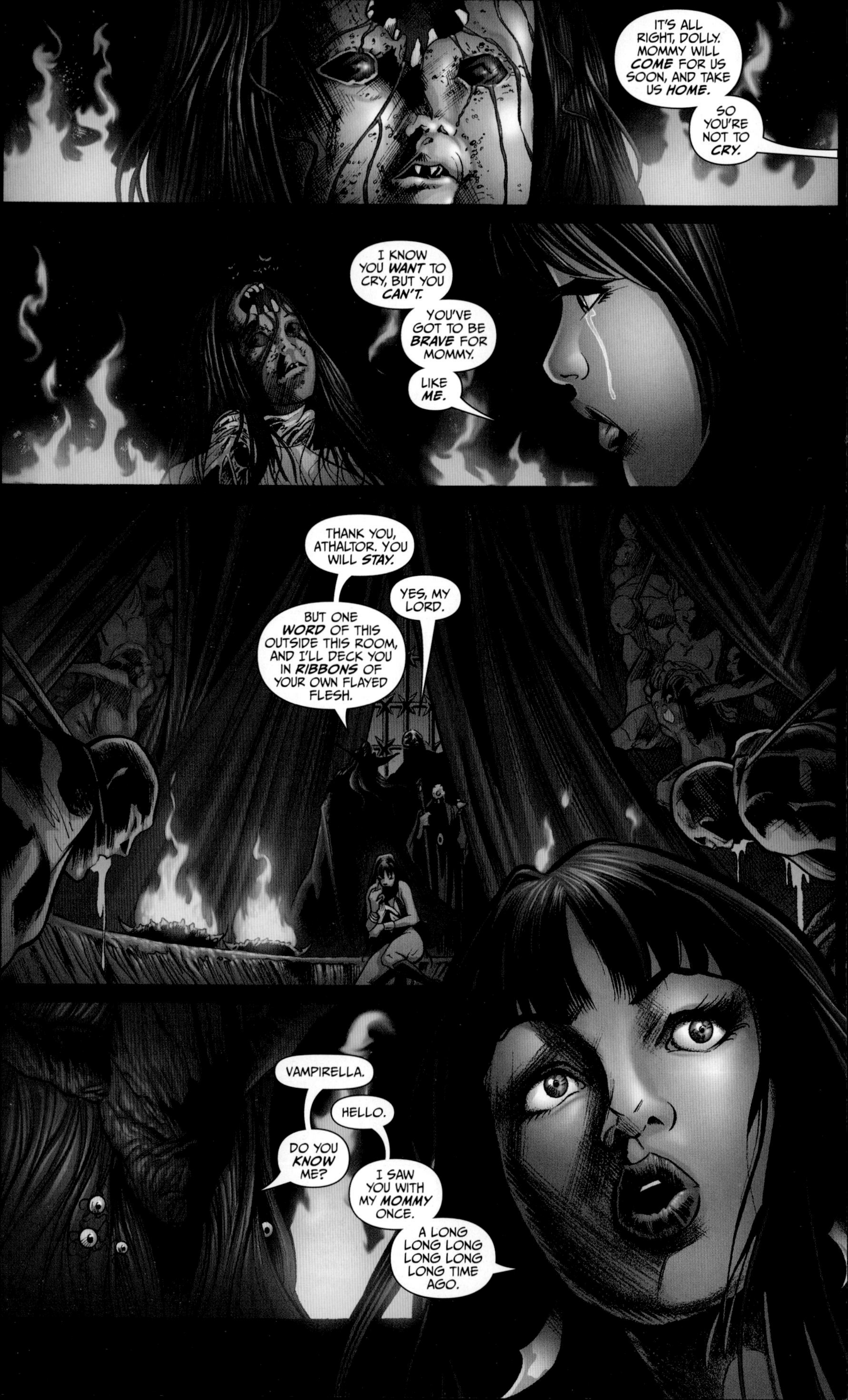
IT'S ALL RIGHT, DOLLY. MOMMY WILL COME FOR US SOON, AND TAKE US HOME.
SO YOU'RE NOT TO CRY.
I KNOW YOU WANT TO CRY, BUT YOU CAN'T.
YOU'VE GOT TO BE BRAVE FOR MOMMY.
LIKE ME.
THANK YOU, ATHALTOR. YOU WILL STAY.
BUT ONE WORD OF THIS OUTSIDE THIS ROOM, AND I'LL DECK YOU IN RIBBONS OF YOUR OWN FLAYED FLESH.
YES, MY LORD.
VAMPIRELLA.
HELLO.
DO YOU KNOW ME?
I SAW YOU WITH MY MOMMY ONCE.
A LONG LONG LONG LONG LONG TIME AGO.

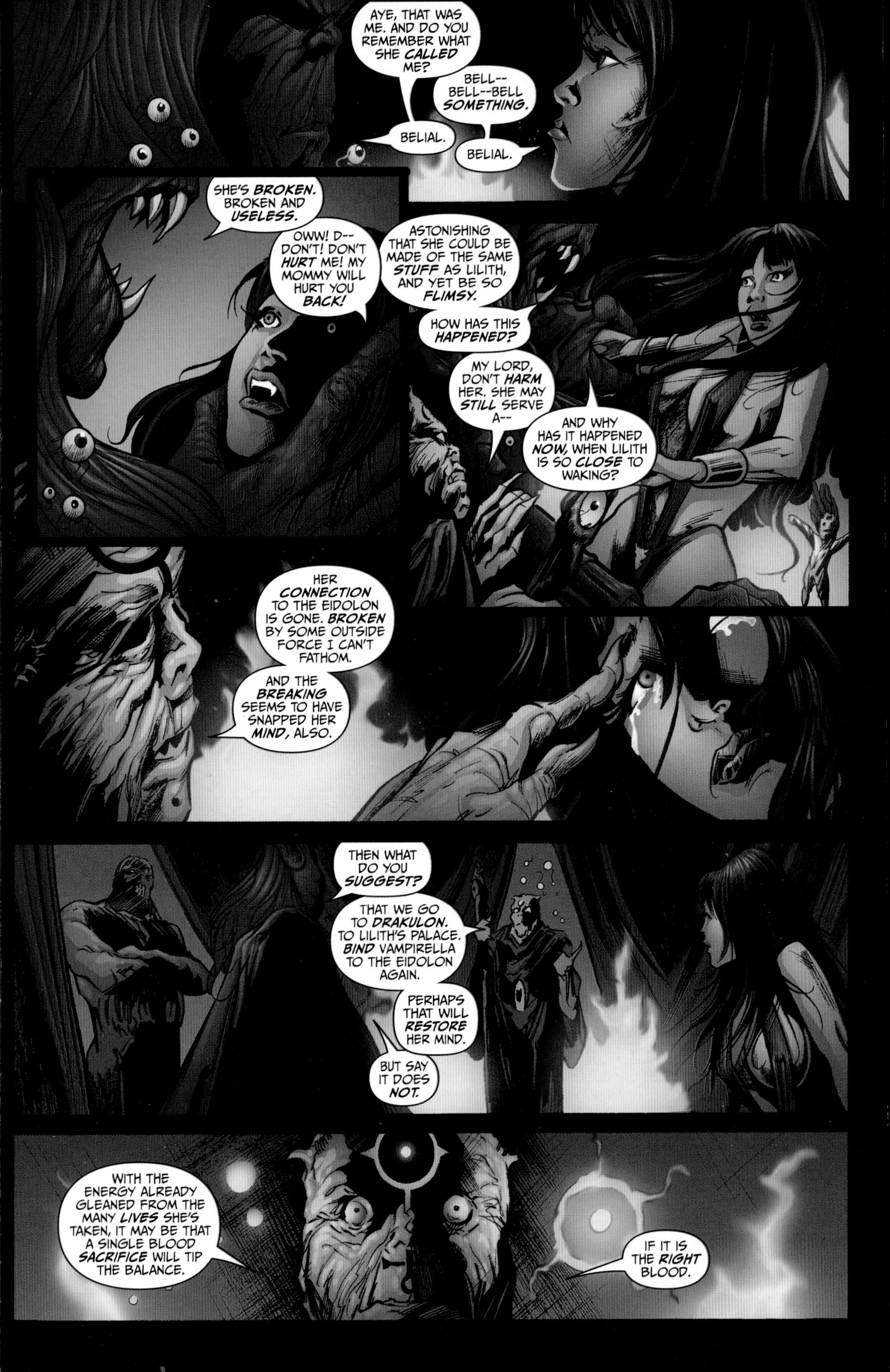

AYE, THAT WAS ME. AND DO YOU REMEMBER WHAT SHE CALLED ME?
BELL-- BELL--BELL SOMETHING.
BELIAL.
BELIAL.
SHE'S BROKEN. BROKEN AND USELESS.
OWW! D-- DON'T! DON'T HURT ME! MY MOMMY WILL HURT YOU BACK!
ASTONISHING THAT SHE COULD BE MADE OF THE SAME STUFF AS LILITH, AND YET BE SO FLIMSY.
HOW HAS THIS HAPPENED?
MY LORD, DON'T HARM HER. SHE MAY STILL SERVE A--
AND WHY HAS IT HAPPENED NOW, WHEN LILITH IS SO CLOSE TO WAKING?
HER CONNECTION TO THE EIDOLON IS GONE. BROKEN BY SOME OUTSIDE FORCE I CAN'T FATHOM.
AND THE BREAKING SEEMS TO HAVE SNAPPED HER MIND, ALSO.
THEN WHAT DO YOU SUGGEST?
THAT WE GO TO DRAKULON. TO LILITH'S PALACE. BIND VAMPIRELLA TO THE EIDOLON AGAIN.
PERHAPS THAT WILL RESTORE HER MIND.
BUT SAY IT DOES NOT.
WITH THE ENERGY ALREADY GLEANED FROM THE MANY LIVES SHE'S TAKEN, IT MAY BE THAT A SINGLE BLOOD SACRIFICE WILL TIP THE BALANCE.
IF IT IS THE RIGHT BLOOD.

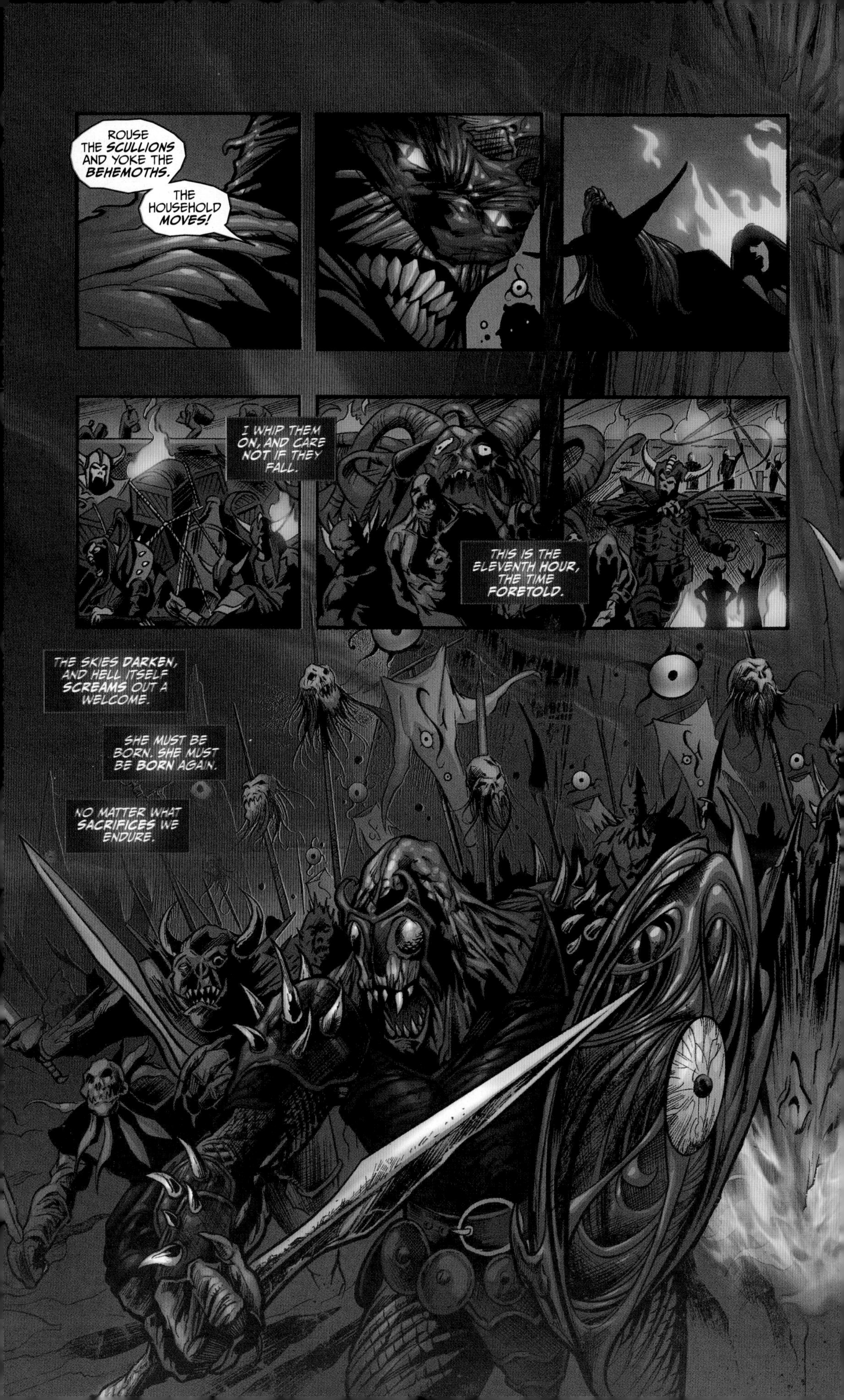
ROUSE THE SCULLIONS AND YOKE THE BEHEMOTHS.
THE HOUSEHOLD MOVES!
I WHIP THEM ON, AND CARE NOT IF THEY FALL.
THIS IS THE ELEVENTH HOUR, THE TIME FORETOLD.
THE SKIES DARKEN, AND HELL ITSELF SCREAMS OUT A WELCOME.
SHE MUST BE BORN. SHE MUST BE BORN AGAIN.
NO MATTER WHAT SACRIFICES WE ENDURE.

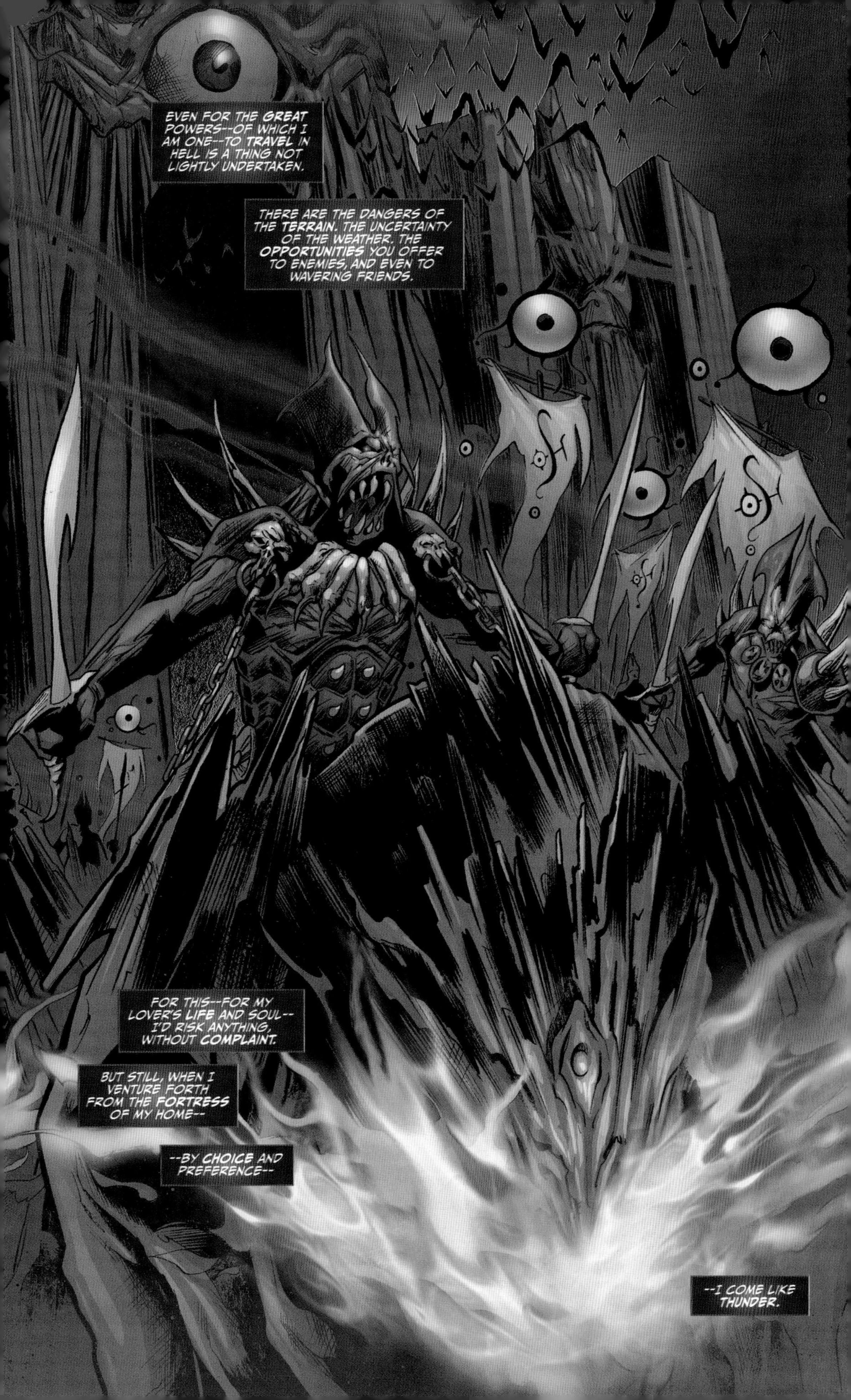
EVEN FOR THE GREAT POWERS--OF WHICH I AM ONE--TO TRAVEL IN HELL IS A THING NOT LIGHTLY UNDERTAKEN.
THERE ARE THE DANGERS OF THE TERRAIN. THE UNCERTAINTY OF THE WEATHER. THE OPPORTUNITIES YOU OFFER TO ENEMIES, AND EVEN TO WAVERING FRIENDS.
FOR THIS--FOR MY LOVER'S LIFE AND SOUL--I'D RISK ANYTHING, WITHOUT COMPLAINT.
BUT STILL, WHEN I VENTURE FORTH FROM THE FORTRESS OF MY HOME--
--BY CHOICE AND PREFERENCE--
--I COME LIKE THUNDER.

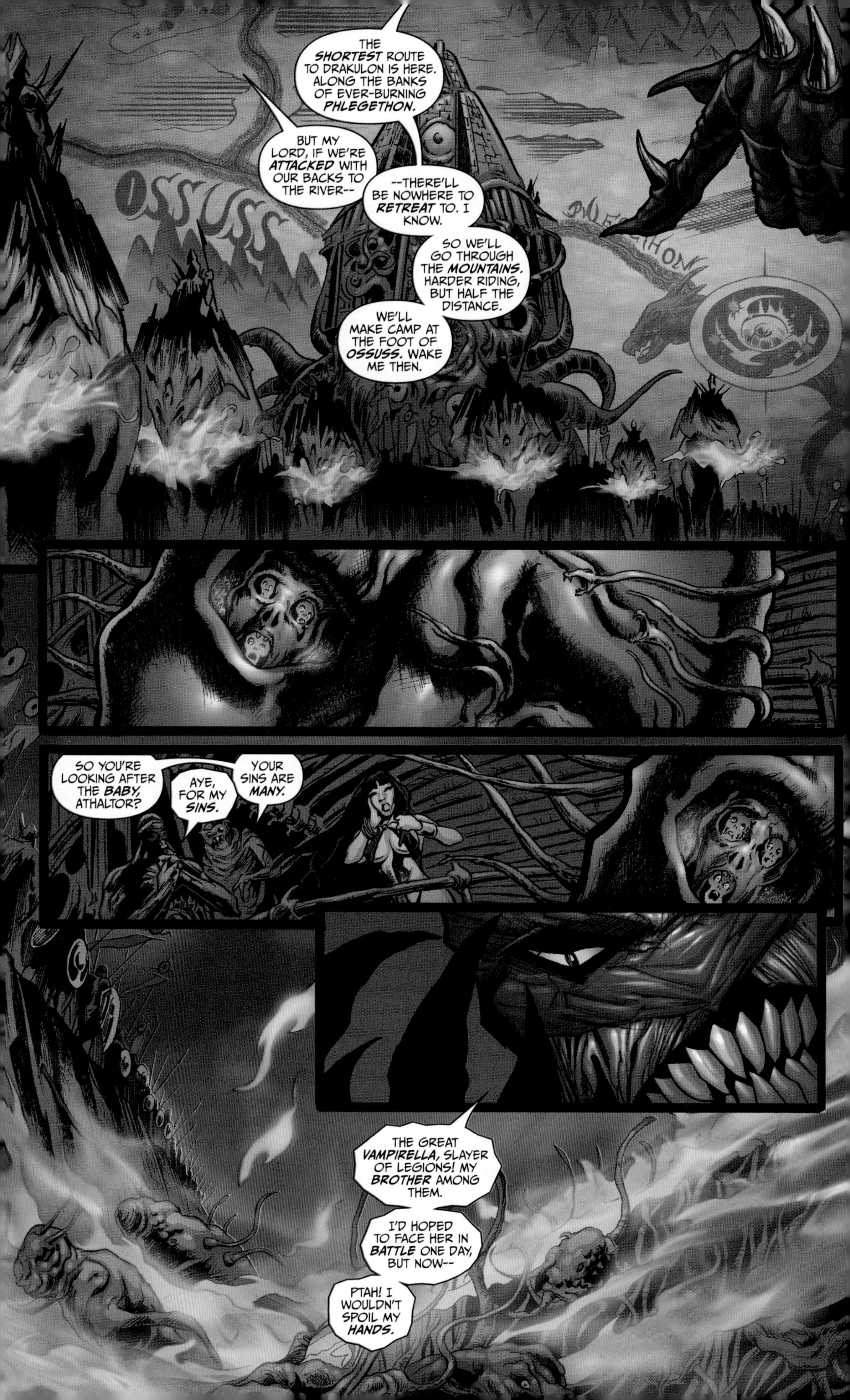
OSSUSS
PHLEGETHON
THE SHORTEST ROUTE TO DRAKULON IS HERE. ALONG THE BANKS OF EVER-BURNING PHLEGETHON.
BUT MY LORD, IF WE'RE ATTACKED WITH OUR BACKS TO THE RIVER--
--THERE'LL BE NOWHERE TO RETREAT TO. I KNOW.
SO WE'LL GO THROUGH THE MOUNTAINS. HARDER RIDING, BUT HALF THE DISTANCE.
WE'LL MAKE CAMP AT THE FOOT OF OSSUSS. WAKE ME THEN.
SO YOU'RE LOOKING AFTER THE BABY, ATHALTOR?
AYE, FOR MY SINS.
YOUR SINS ARE MANY.
THE GREAT VAMPIRELLA, SLAYER OF LEGIONS! MY BROTHER AMONG THEM.
I'D HOPED TO FACE HER IN BATTLE ONE DAY, BUT NOW--
PTAH! I WOULDN'T SPOIL MY HANDS.

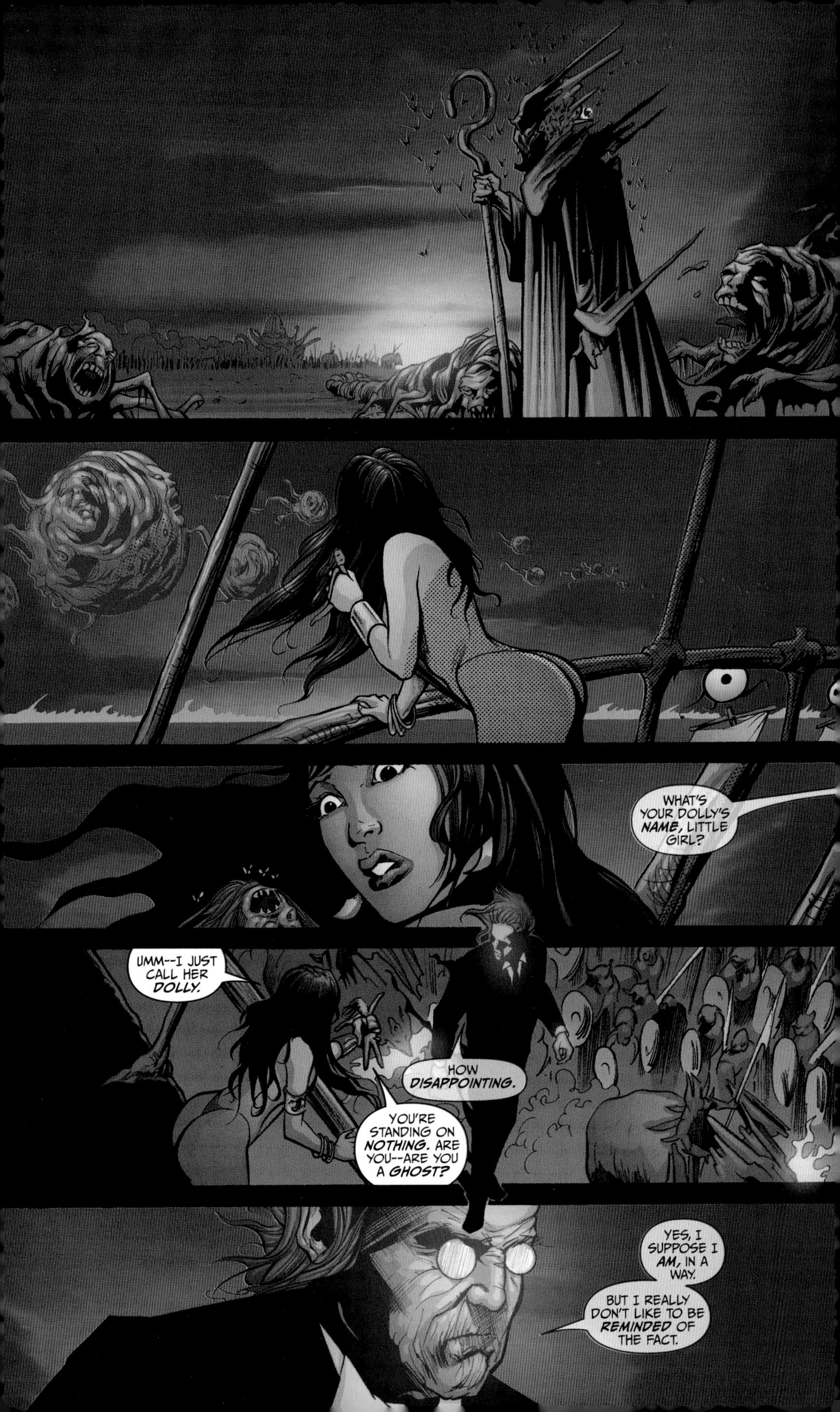

WHAT'S YOUR DOLLY'S NAME, LITTLE GIRL?
UMM--I JUST CALL HER DOLLY.
HOW DISAPPOINTING.
YOU'RE STANDING ON NOTHING. ARE YOU--ARE YOU A GHOST?
YES, I SUPPOSE I AM, IN A WAY.
BUT I REALLY DON'T LIKE TO BE REMINDED OF THE FACT.

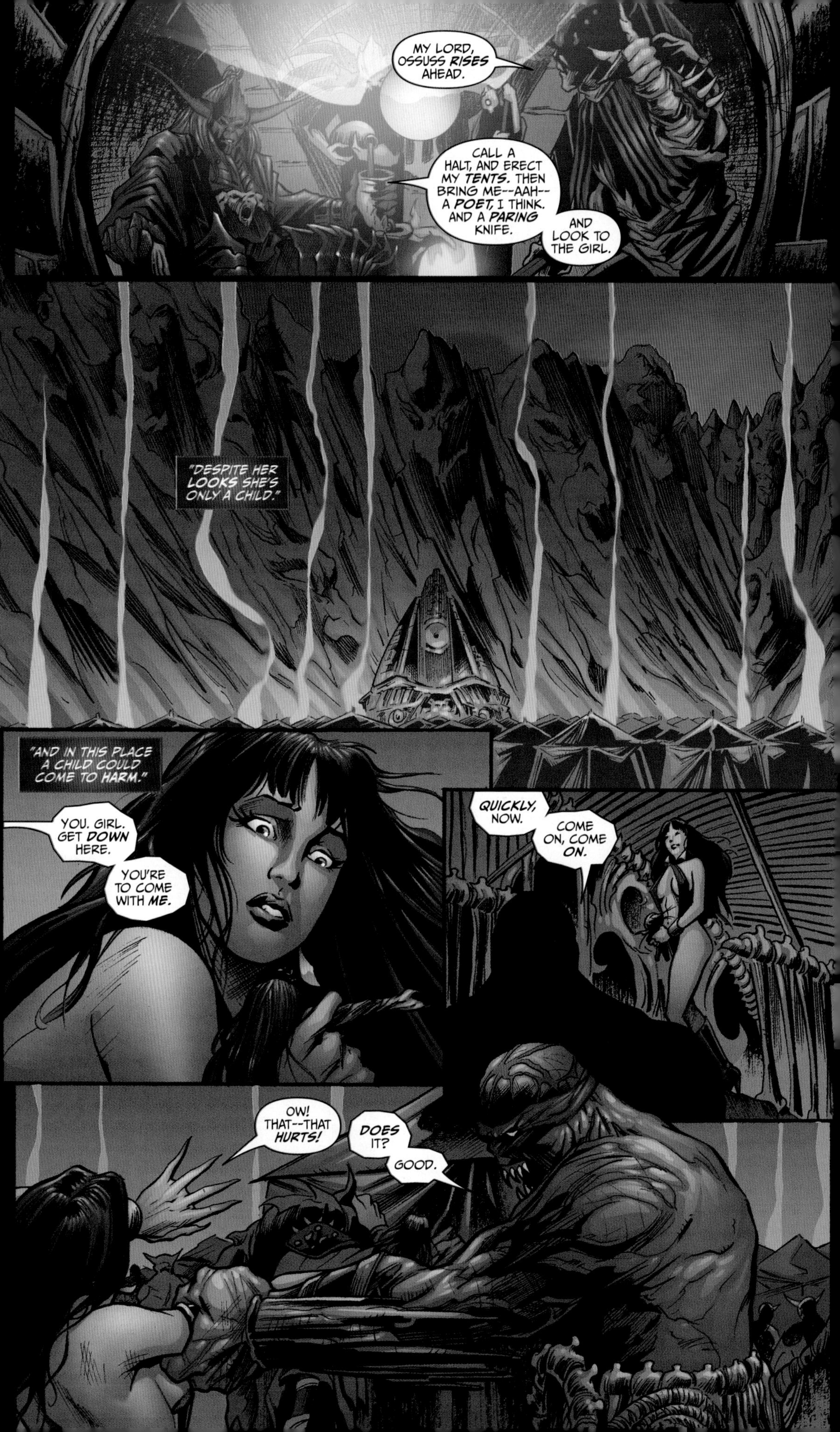
MY LORD, OSSUSS RISES AHEAD.
CALL A HALT, AND ERECT MY TENTS. THEN BRING ME--AAH-- A POET, I THINK. AND A PARING KNIFE.
AND LOOK TO THE GIRL.
"DESPITE HER LOOKS SHE'S ONLY A CHILD."
"AND IN THIS PLACE A CHILD COULD COME TO HARM."
YOU. GIRL. GET DOWN HERE.
YOU'RE TO COME WITH ME.
QUICKLY, NOW.
COME ON, COME ON.
OW! THAT--THAT HURTS!
DOES IT?
GOOD.

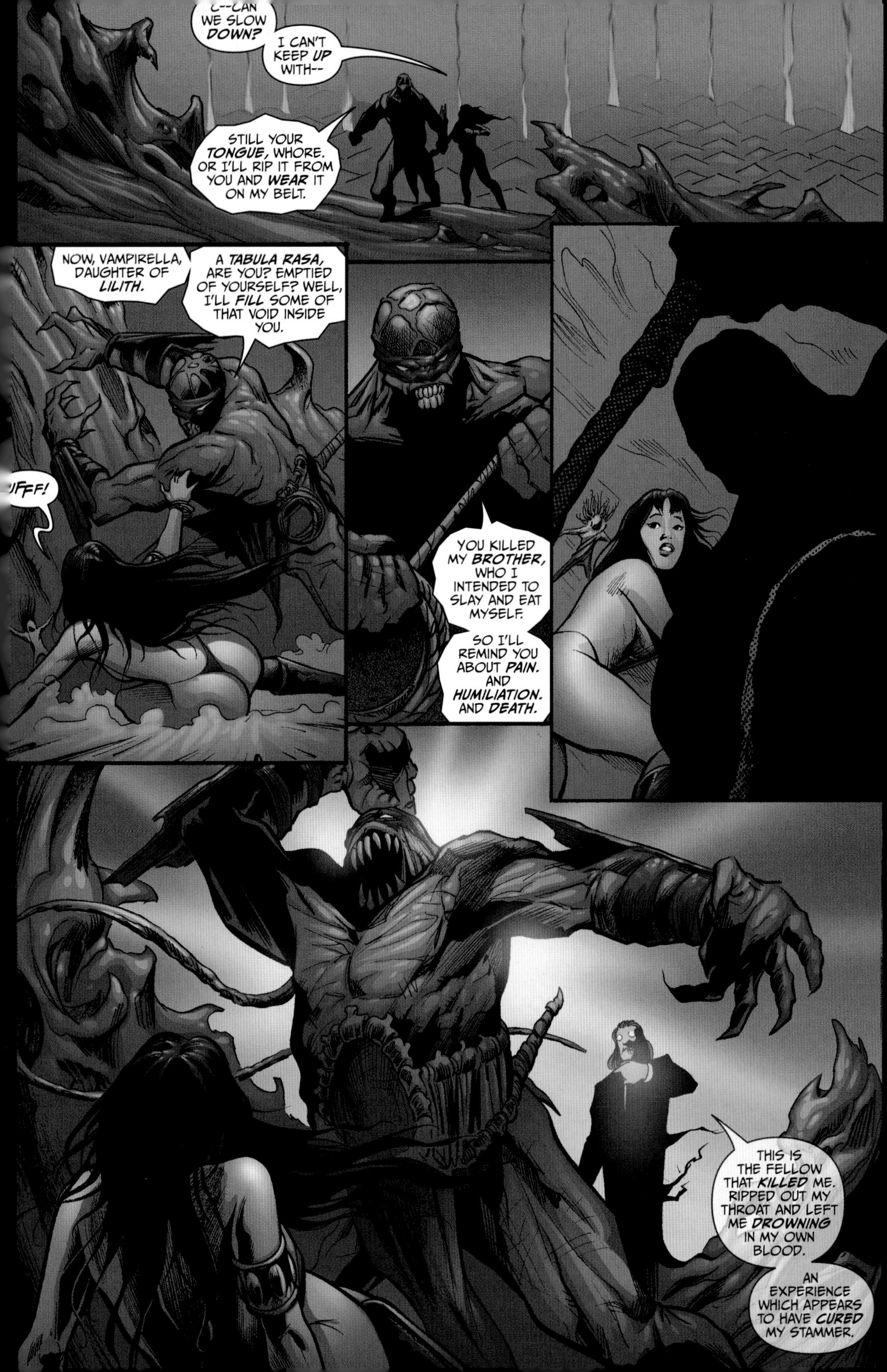

C--CAN WE SLOW DOWN?
I CAN'T KEEP UP WITH--
STILL YOUR TONGUE, WHORE. OR I'LL RIP IT FROM YOU AND WEAR IT ON MY BELT.
NOW, VAMPIRELLA, DAUGHTER OF LILITH.
A TABULA RASA, ARE YOU? EMPTIED OF YOURSELF? WELL, I'LL FILL SOME OF THAT VOID INSIDE YOU.
UFFF!
YOU KILLED MY BROTHER, WHO I INTENDED TO SLAY AND EAT MYSELF.
SO I'LL REMIND YOU ABOUT PAIN. AND HUMILIATION. AND DEATH.
THIS IS THE FELLOW THAT KILLED ME. RIPPED OUT MY THROAT AND LEFT ME DROWNING IN MY OWN BLOOD.
AN EXPERIENCE WHICH APPEARS TO HAVE CURED MY STAMMER.

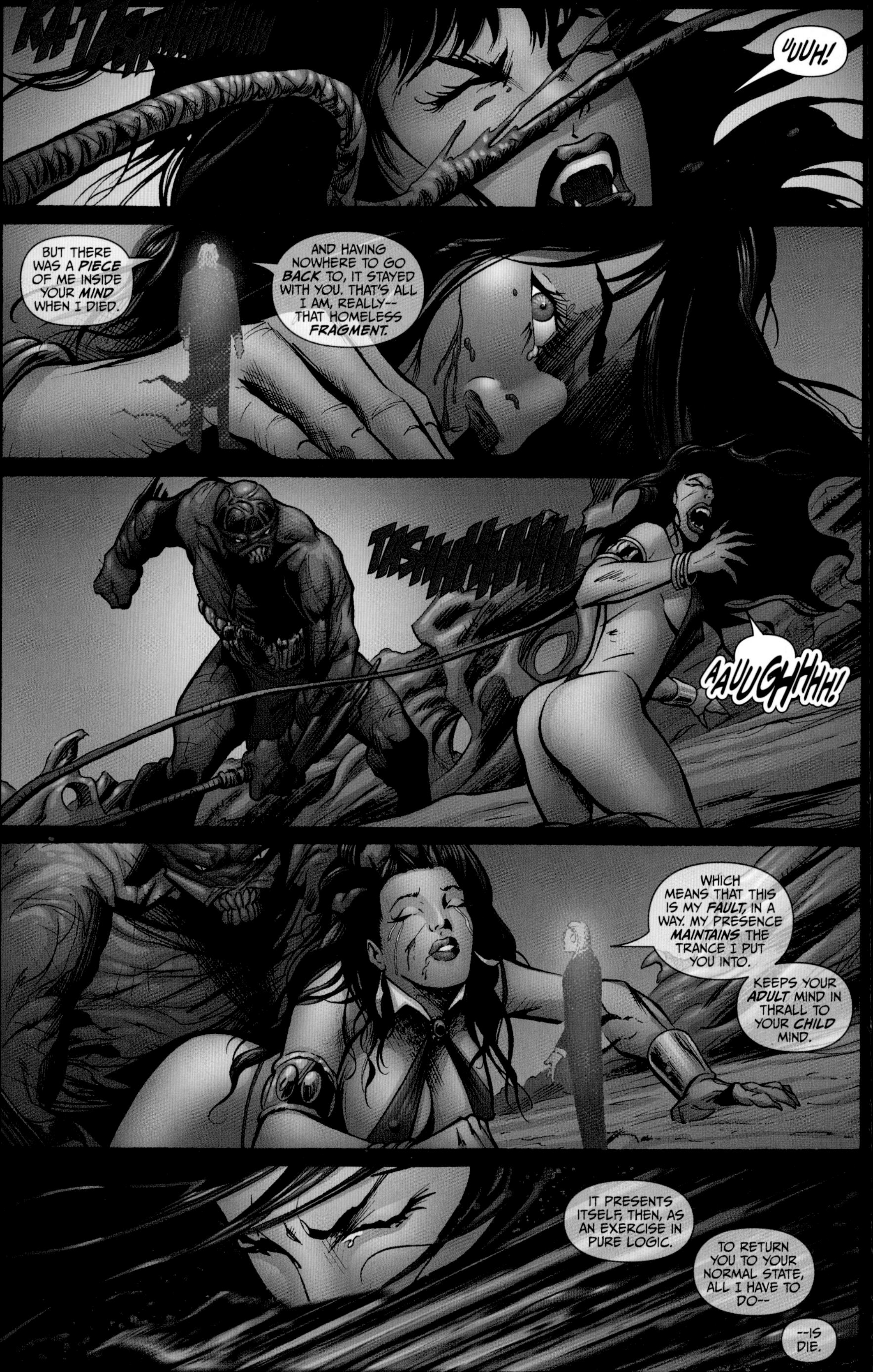
KA-TSSHHHHHHH
UUUH!
BUT THERE WAS A PIECE OF ME INSIDE YOUR MIND WHEN I DIED.
AND HAVING NOWHERE TO GO BACK TO, IT STAYED WITH YOU. THAT'S ALL I AM, REALLY-- THAT HOMELESS FRAGMENT.
TSHHHHHHHH
AAUUGHHHH!
WHICH MEANS THAT THIS IS MY FAULT, IN A WAY. MY PRESENCE MAINTAINS THE TRANCE I PUT YOU INTO.
KEEPS YOUR ADULT MIND IN THRALL TO YOUR CHILD MIND.
IT PRESENTS ITSELF, THEN, AS AN EXERCISE IN PURE LOGIC.
TO RETURN YOU TO YOUR NORMAL STATE, ALL I HAVE TO DO--
--IS DIE.

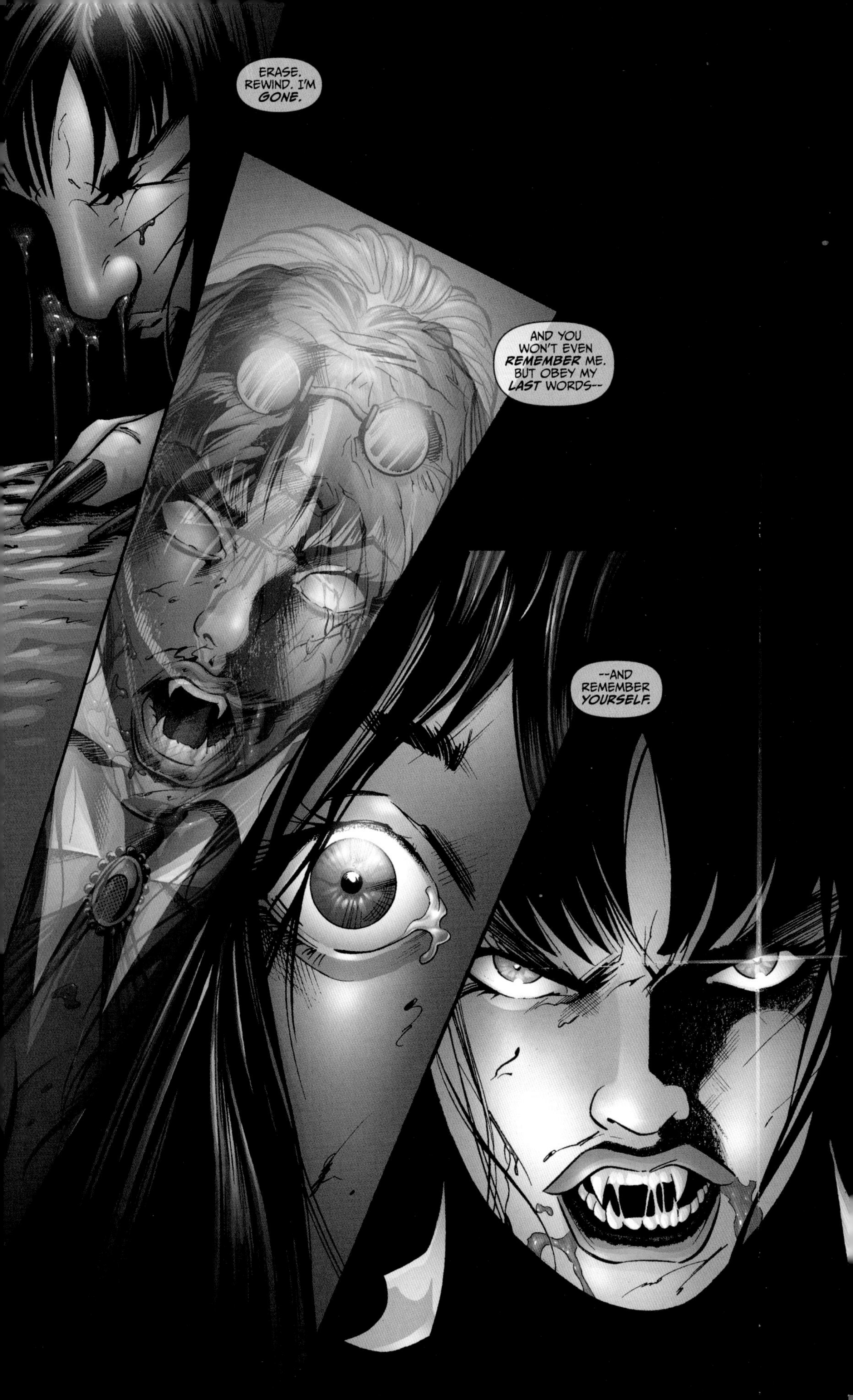

ERASE. REWIND. I'M GONE.
AND YOU WON'T EVEN REMEMBER ME. BUT OBEY MY LAST WORDS--
--AND REMEMBER YOURSELF.

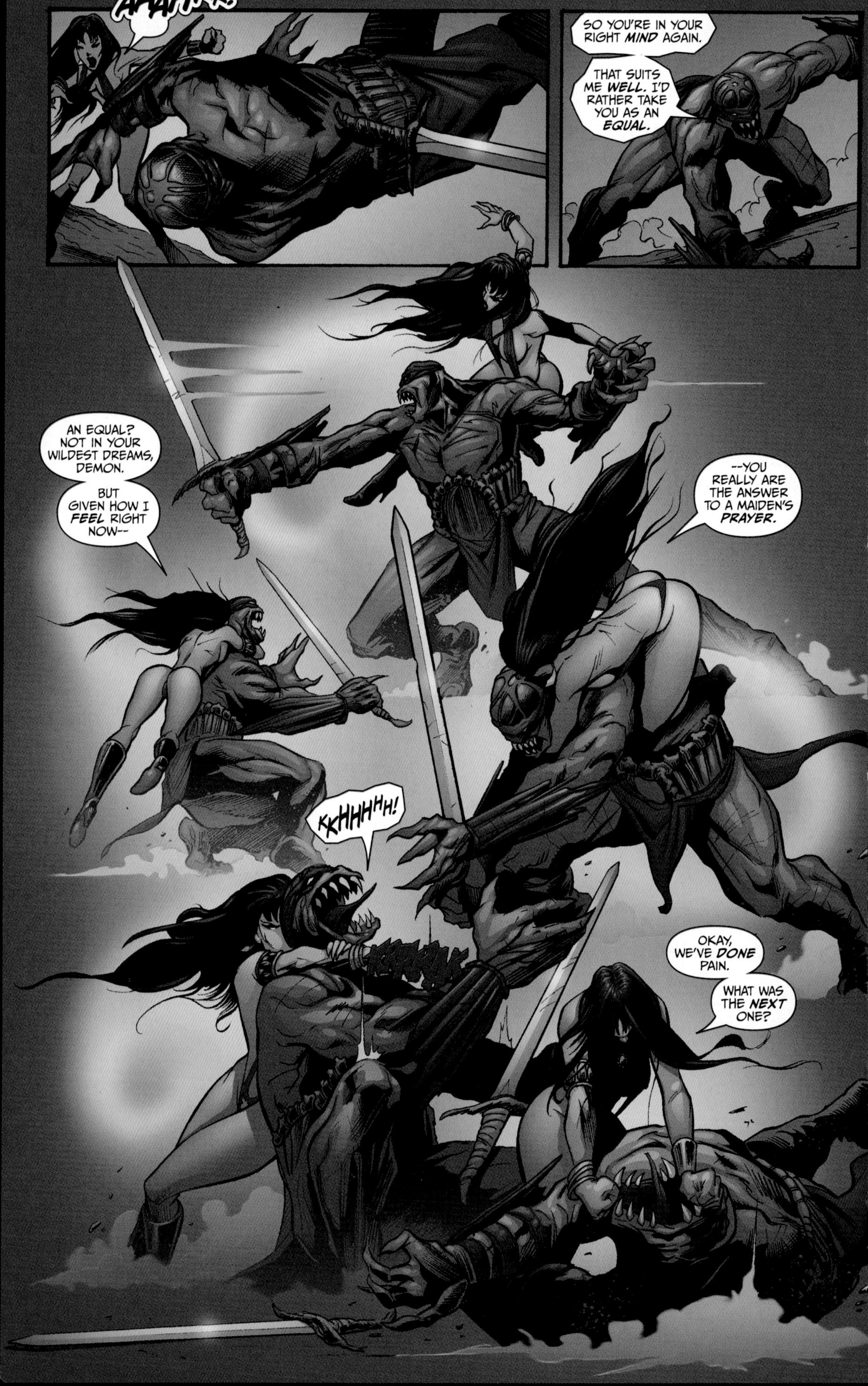

AAAHRR!
SO YOU'RE IN YOUR RIGHT MIND AGAIN.
THAT SUITS ME WELL. I'D RATHER TAKE YOU AS AN EQUAL.
AN EQUAL? NOT IN YOUR WILDEST DREAMS, DEMON.
BUT GIVEN HOW I FEEL RIGHT NOW--
--YOU REALLY ARE THE ANSWER TO A MAIDEN'S PRAYER.
KKHHHHH!
OKAY, WE'VE DONE PAIN.
WHAT WAS THE NEXT ONE?

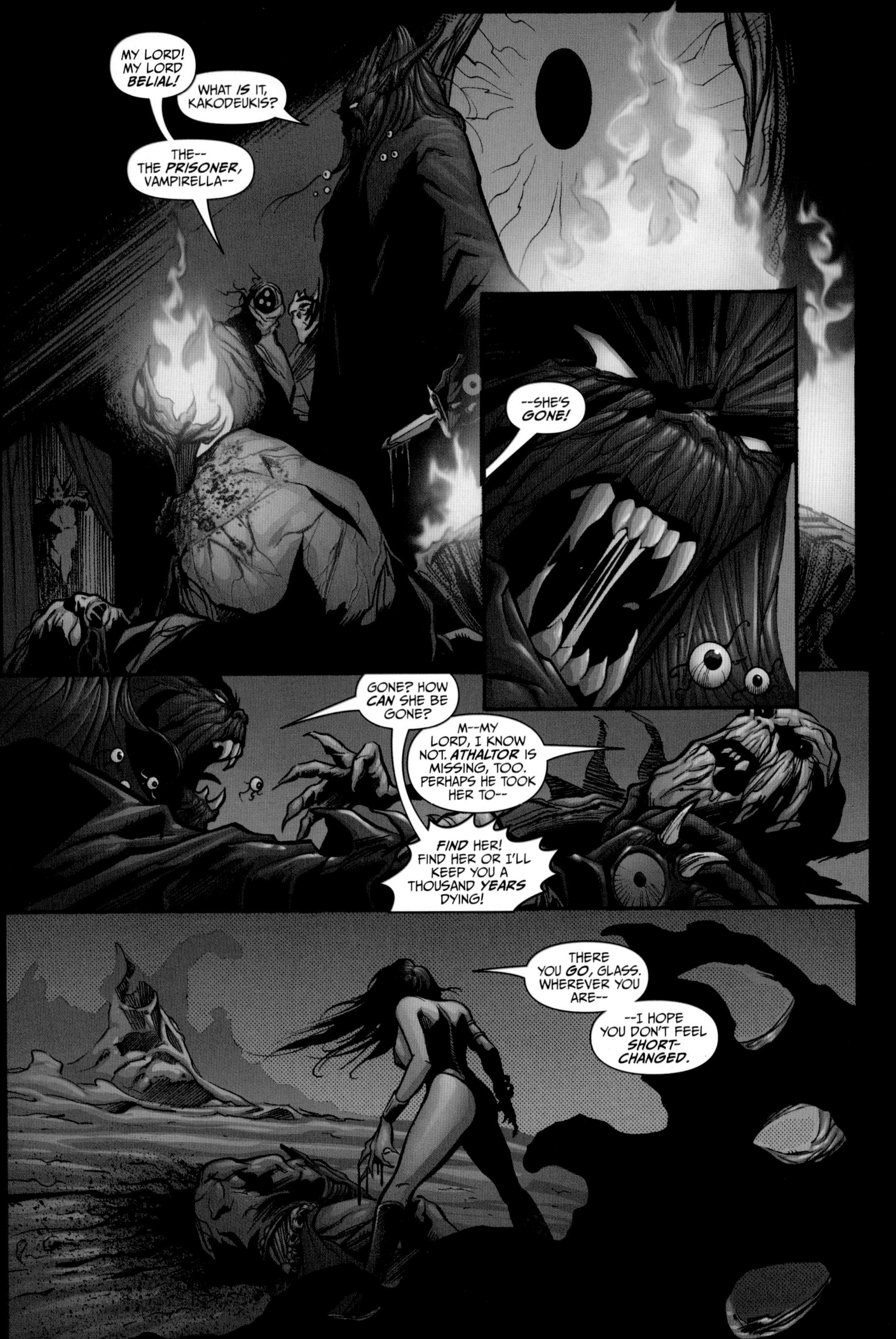
MY LORD! MY LORD *BELIAL!*
WHAT *IS* IT, KAKODEUKIS?
THE-- THE *PRISONER,* VAMPIRELLA--
--SHE'S *GONE!*
GONE? HOW *CAN* SHE BE GONE?
M--MY LORD, I KNOW NOT. *ATHALTOR* IS MISSING, TOO. PERHAPS HE TOOK HER TO--
FIND HER! FIND HER OR I'LL KEEP YOU A THOUSAND *YEARS* DYING!
THERE YOU *GO,* GLASS. WHEREVER YOU ARE--
--I HOPE YOU DON'T FEEL *SHORT-CHANGED.*

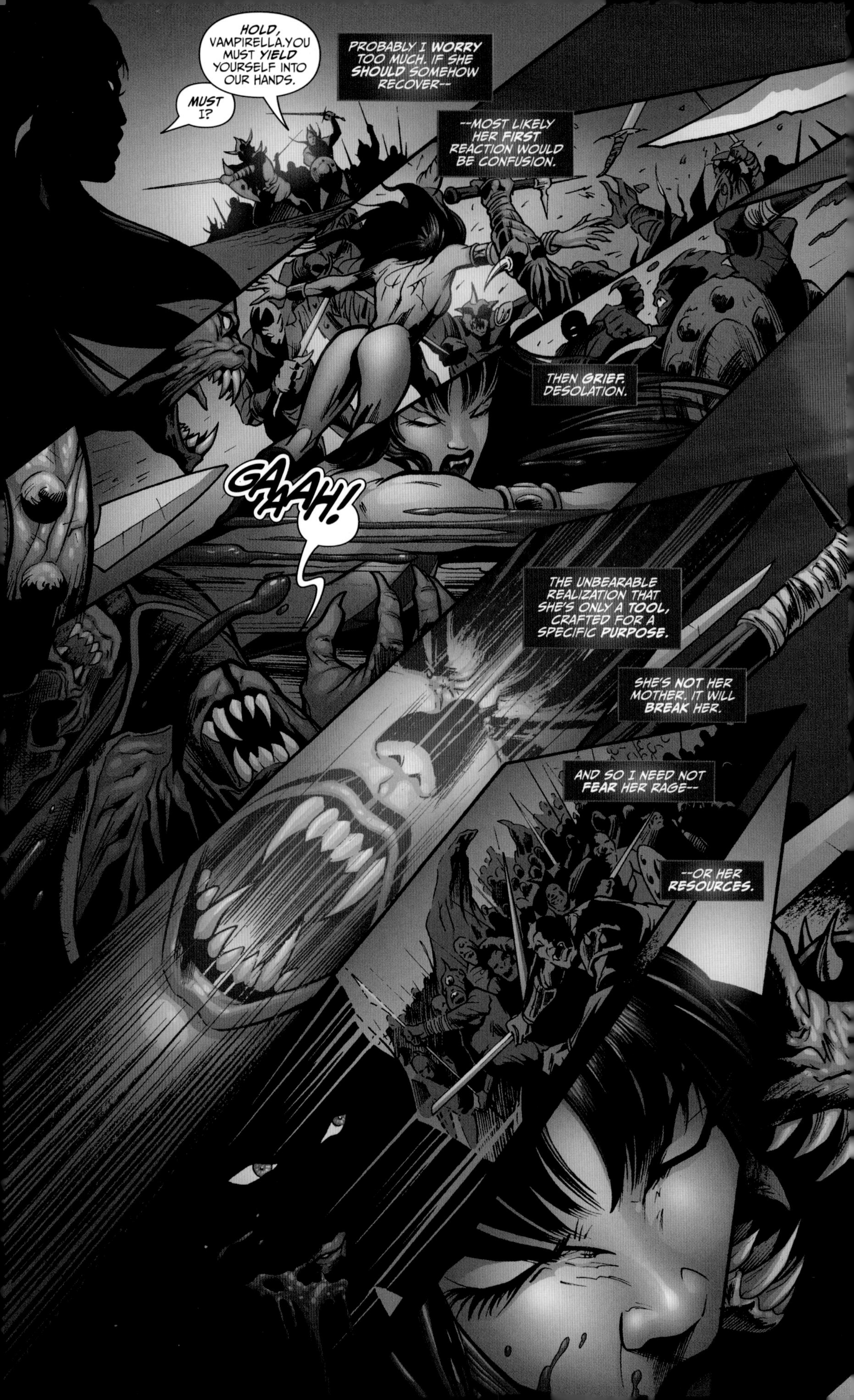
HOLD, VAMPIRELLA. YOU MUST YIELD YOURSELF INTO OUR HANDS.
MUST I?
PROBABLY I WORRY TOO MUCH. IF SHE SHOULD SOMEHOW RECOVER--
--MOST LIKELY HER FIRST REACTION WOULD BE CONFUSION.
THEN GRIEF. DESOLATION.
GAAAH!
THE UNBEARABLE REALIZATION THAT SHE'S ONLY A TOOL, CRAFTED FOR A SPECIFIC PURPOSE.
SHE'S NOT HER MOTHER. IT WILL BREAK HER.
AND SO I NEED NOT FEAR HER RAGE--
--OR HER RESOURCES.

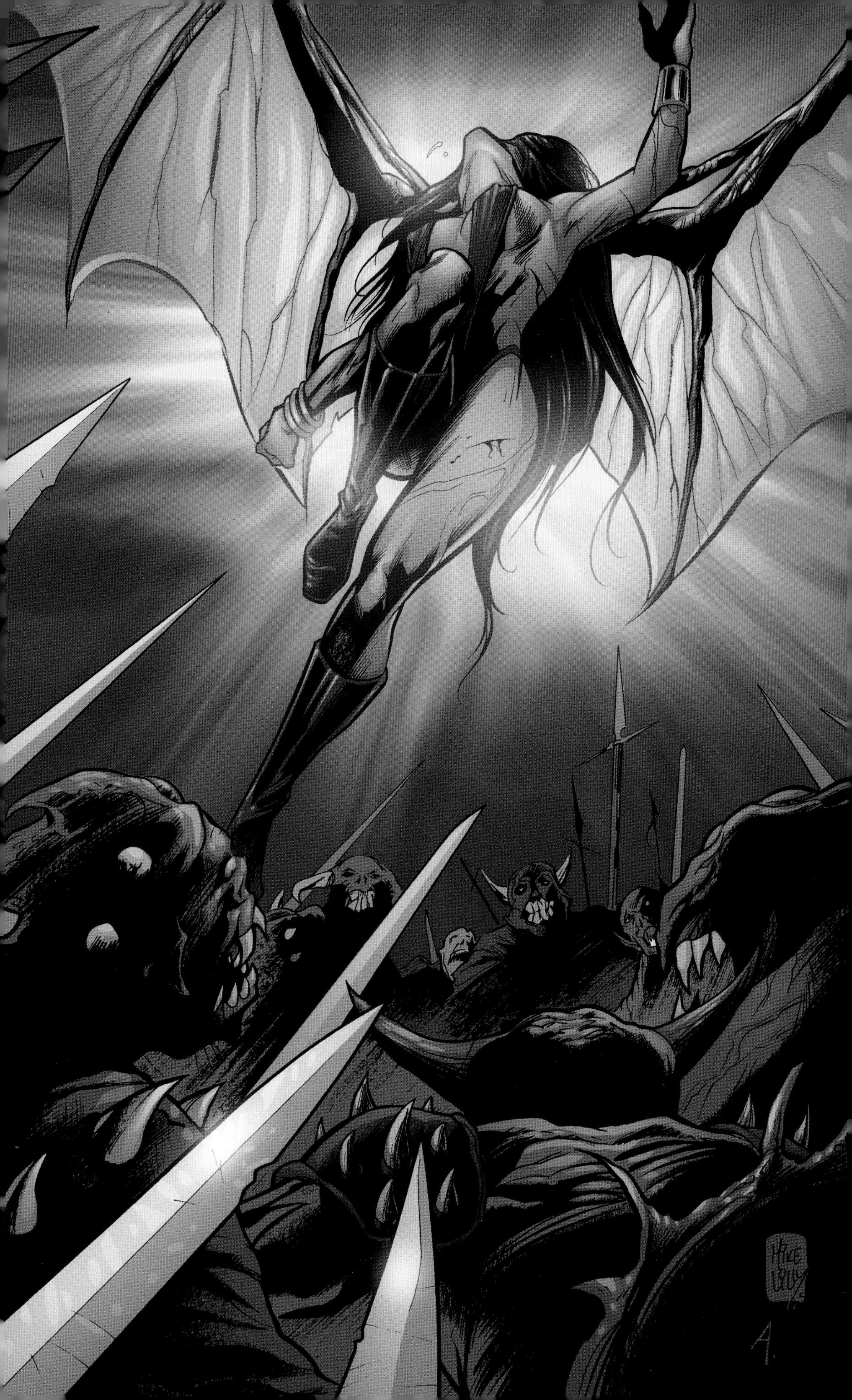

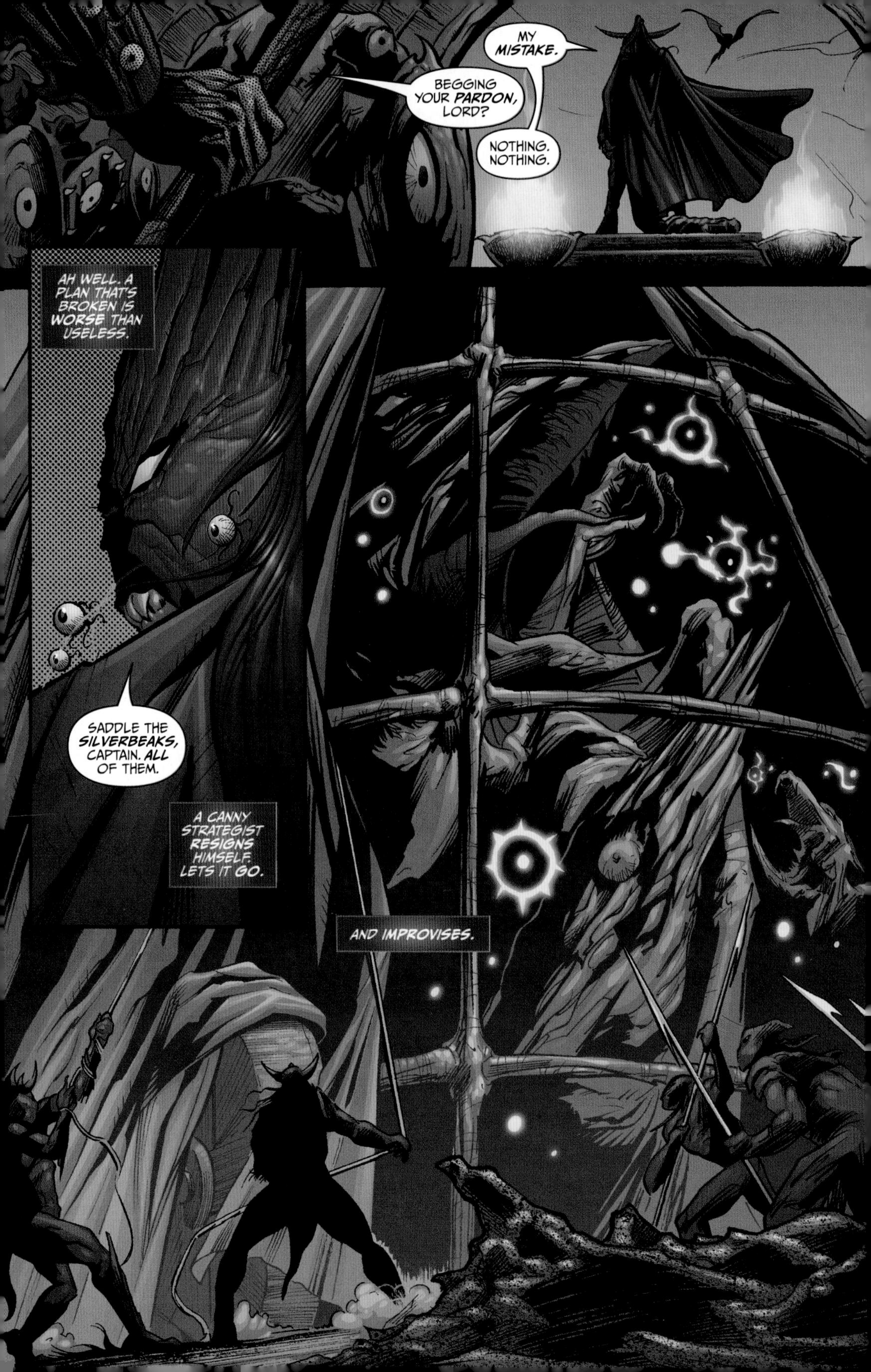

MY MISTAKE.
BEGGING YOUR PARDON, LORD?
NOTHING. NOTHING.
AH WELL. A PLAN THAT'S BROKEN IS WORSE THAN USELESS.
SADDLE THE SILVERBEAKS, CAPTAIN. ALL OF THEM.
A CANNY STRATEGIST RESIGNS HIMSELF. LETS IT GO.
AND IMPROVISES.

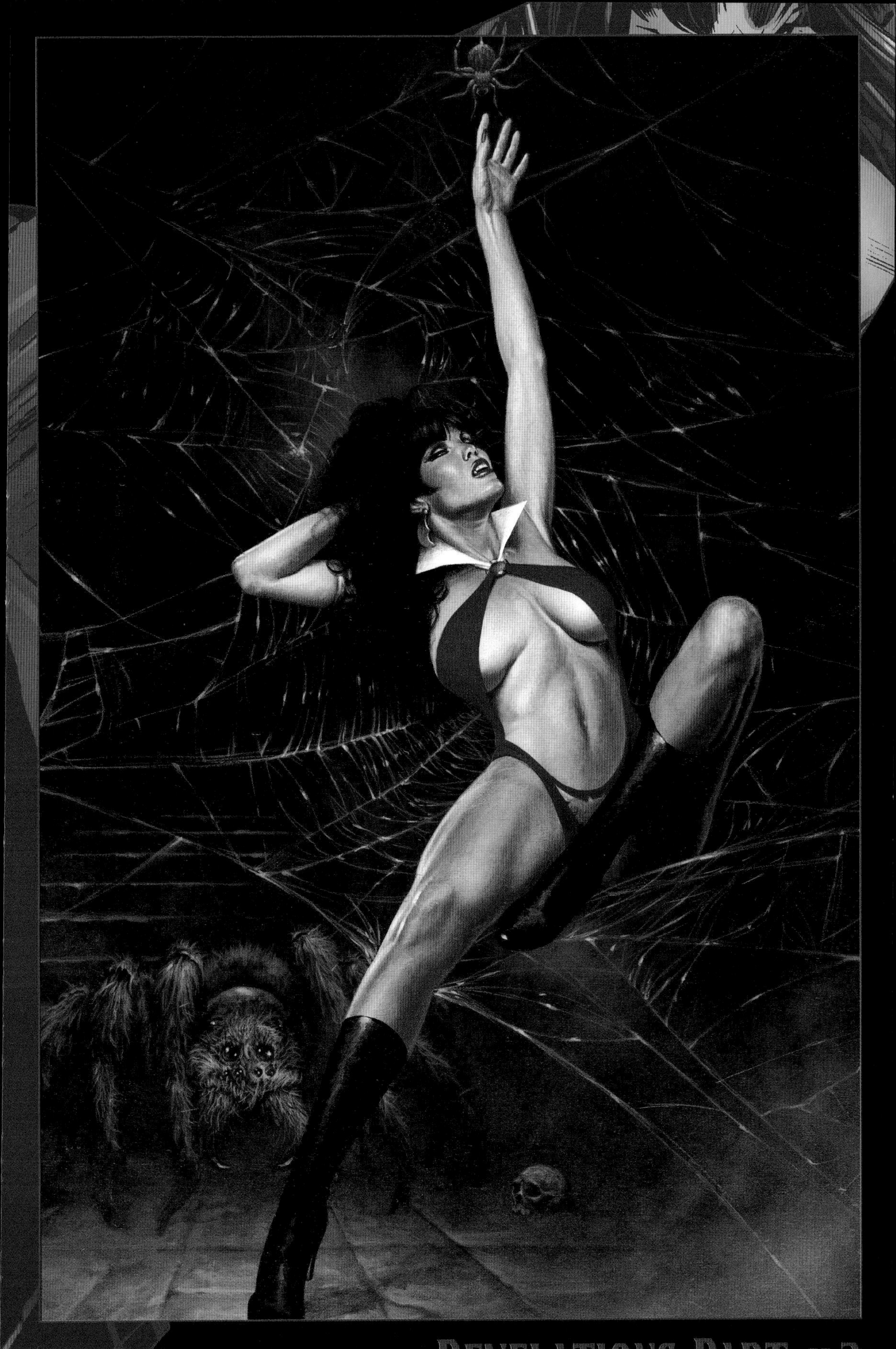

REVELATIONS PART #3

Vampirella: Revelations #3 cover by Joe Jusko

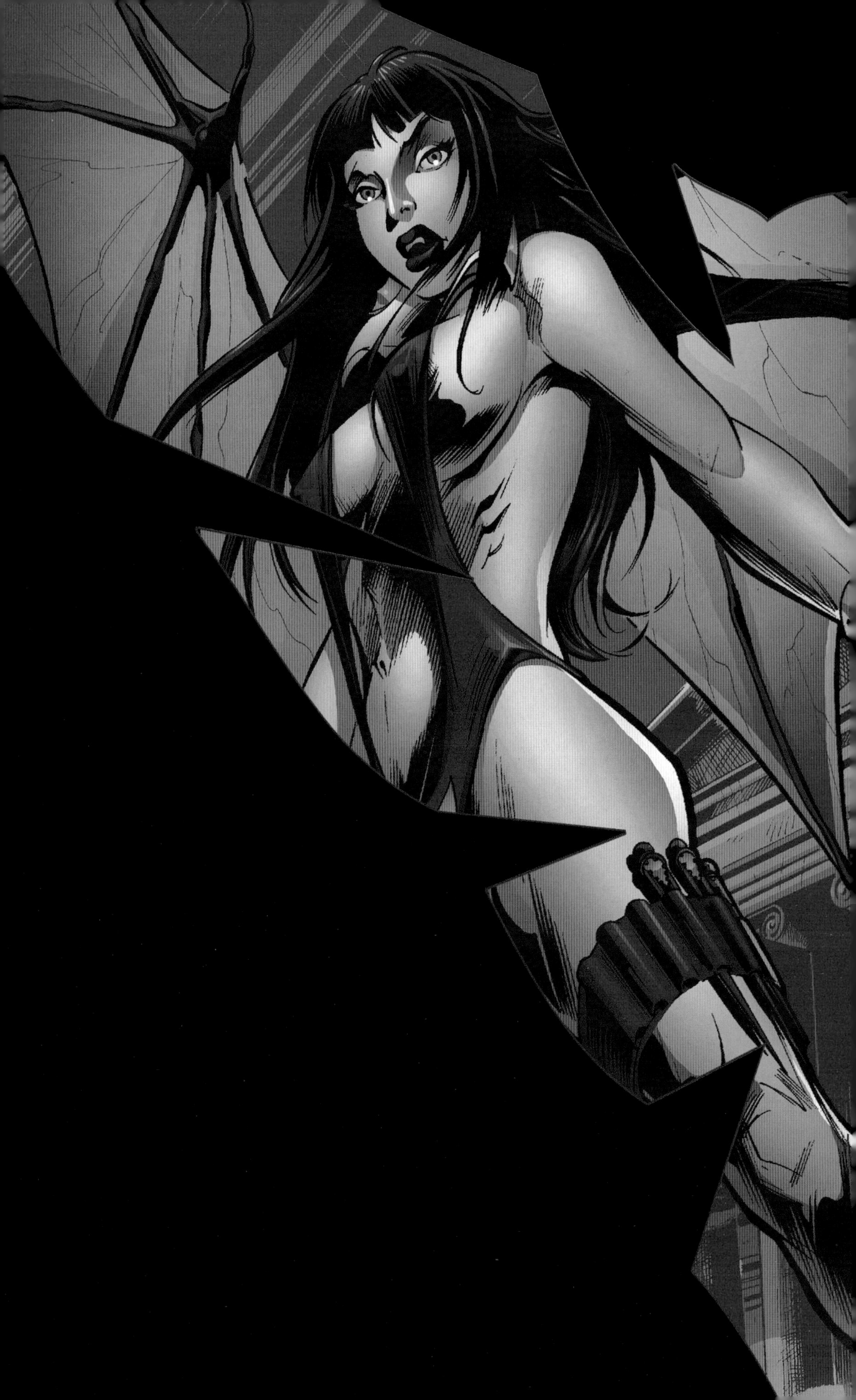

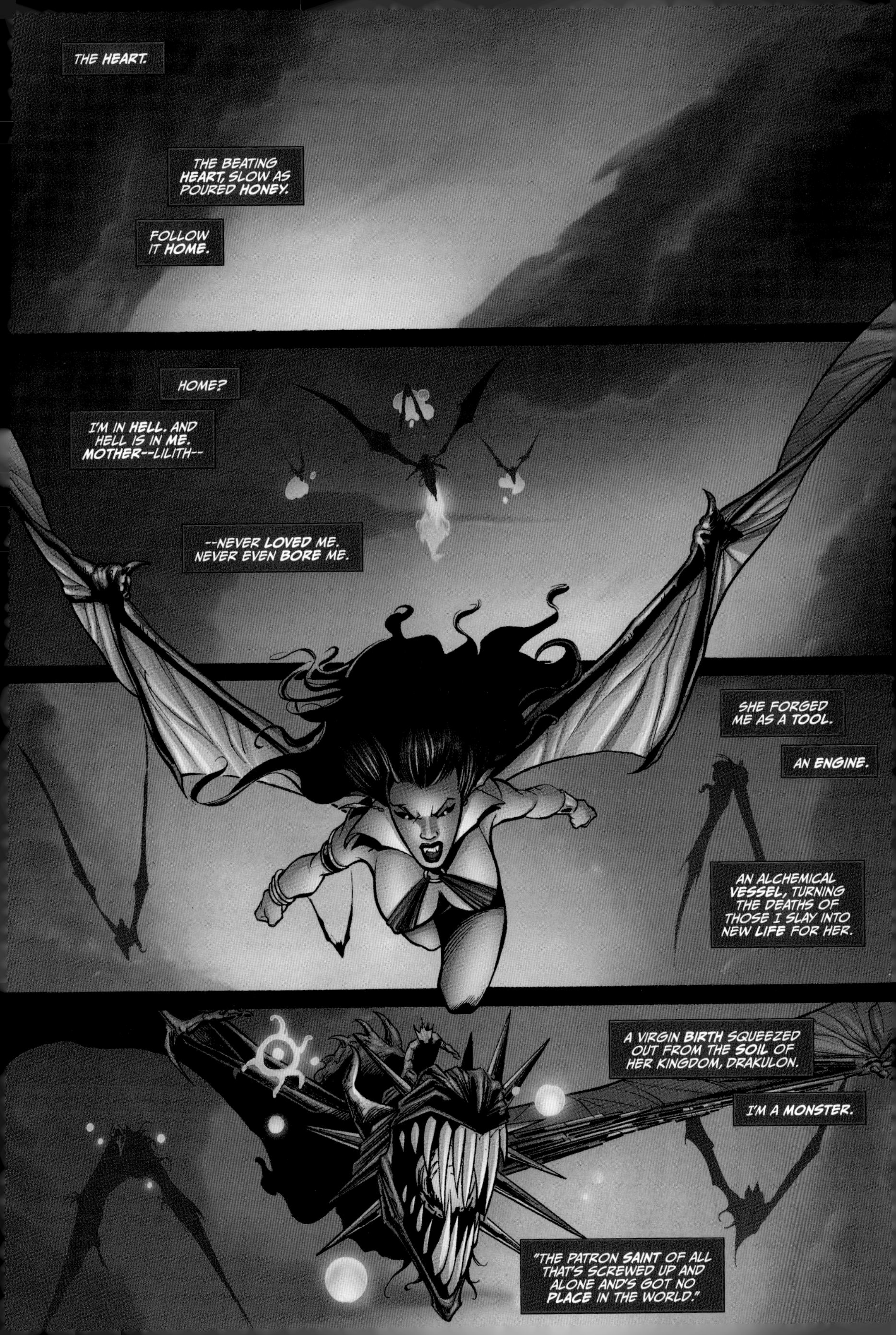
THE HEART.
THE BEATING HEART, SLOW AS POURED HONEY.
FOLLOW IT HOME.
HOME?
I'M IN HELL. AND HELL IS IN ME. MOTHER--LILITH--
--NEVER LOVED ME. NEVER EVEN BORE ME.
SHE FORGED ME AS A TOOL.
AN ENGINE.
AN ALCHEMICAL VESSEL, TURNING THE DEATHS OF THOSE I SLAY INTO NEW LIFE FOR HER.
A VIRGIN BIRTH SQUEEZED OUT FROM THE SOIL OF HER KINGDOM, DRAKULON.
I'M A MONSTER.
"THE PATRON SAINT OF ALL THAT'S SCREWED UP AND ALONE AND'S GOT NO PLACE IN THE WORLD."

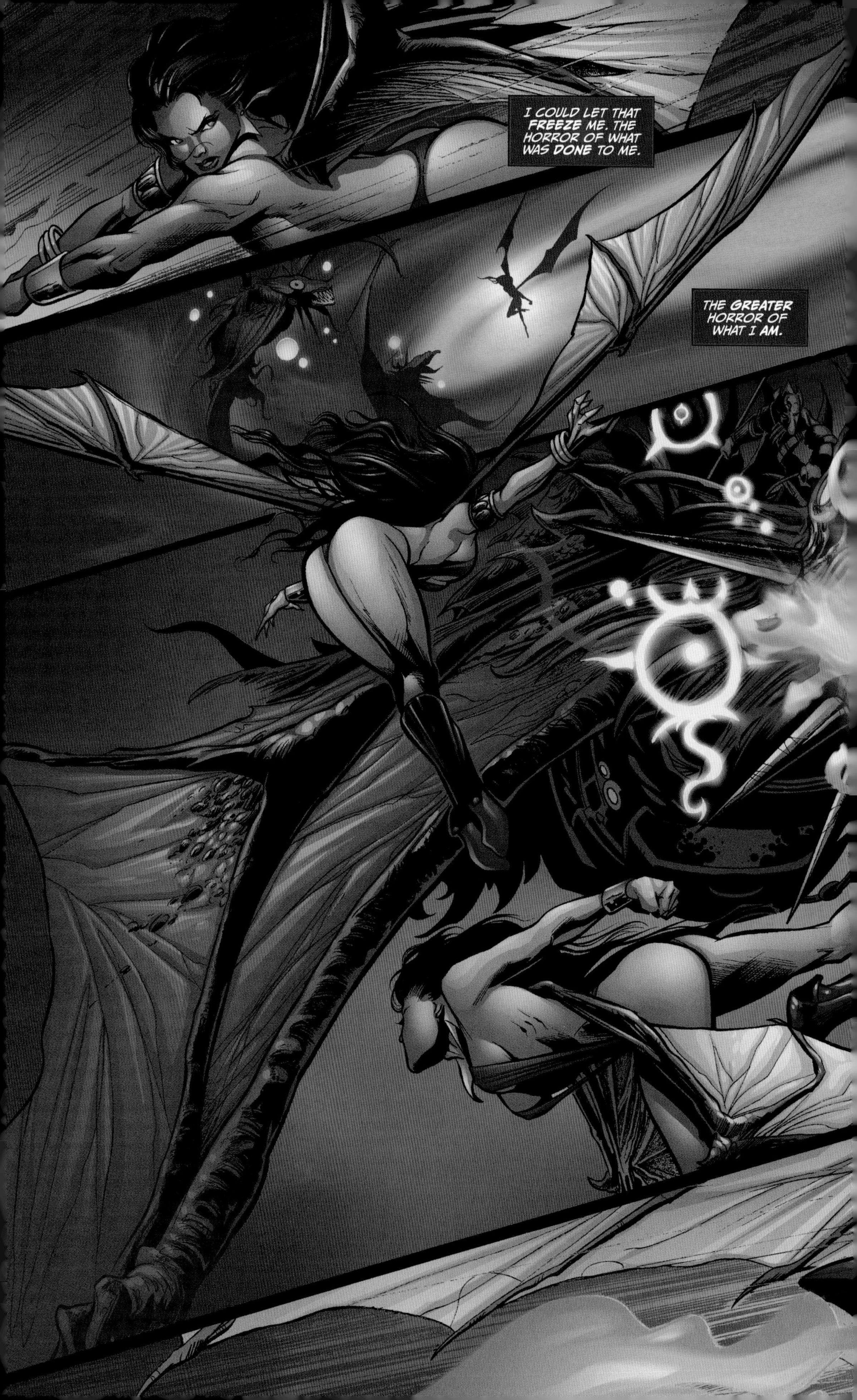
I COULD LET THAT FREEZE ME. THE HORROR OF WHAT WAS DONE TO ME.
THE GREATER HORROR OF WHAT I AM.

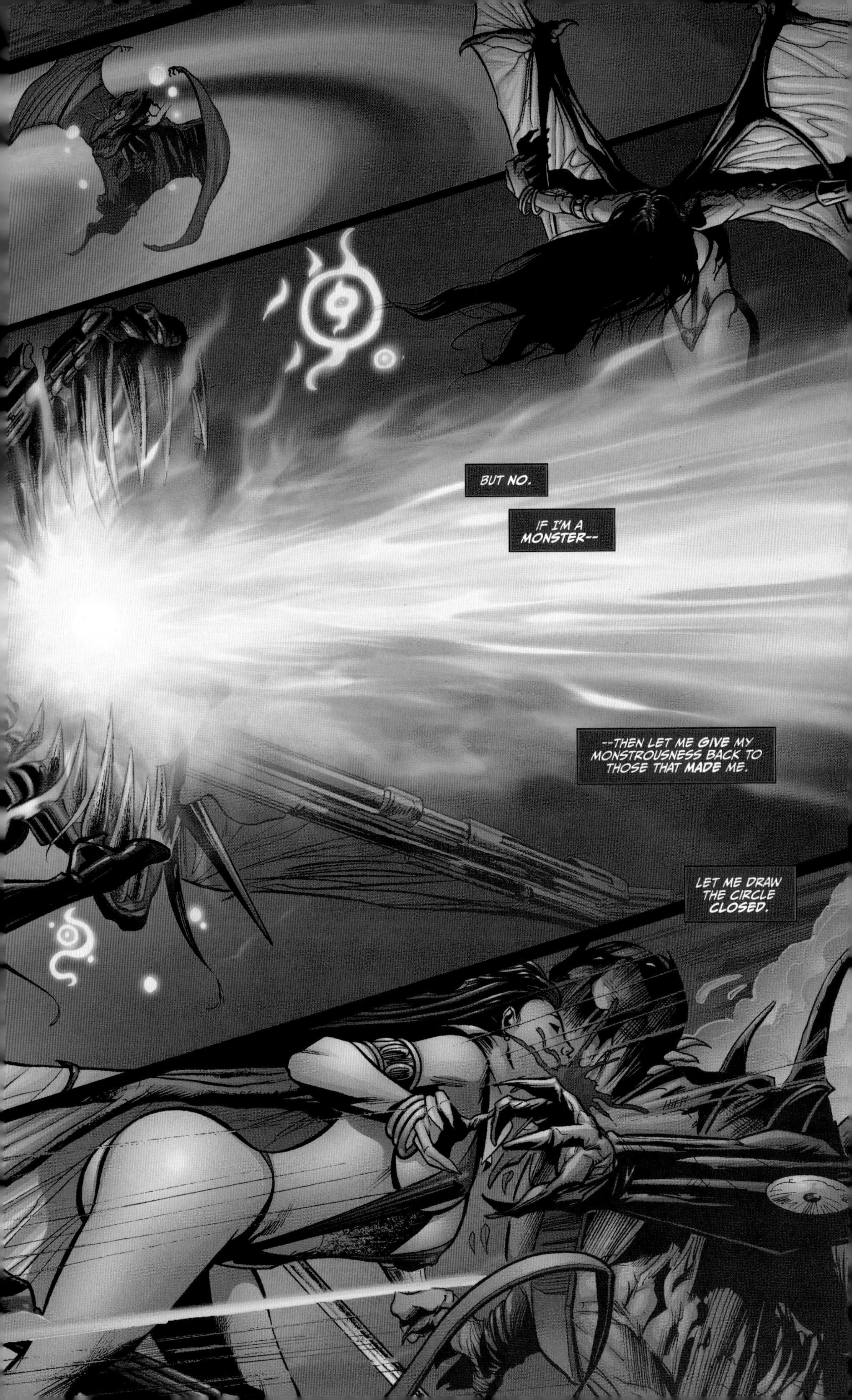
BUT NO.
IF I'M A MONSTER--
--THEN LET ME GIVE MY MONSTROUSNESS BACK TO THOSE THAT MADE ME.
LET ME DRAW THE CIRCLE CLOSED.

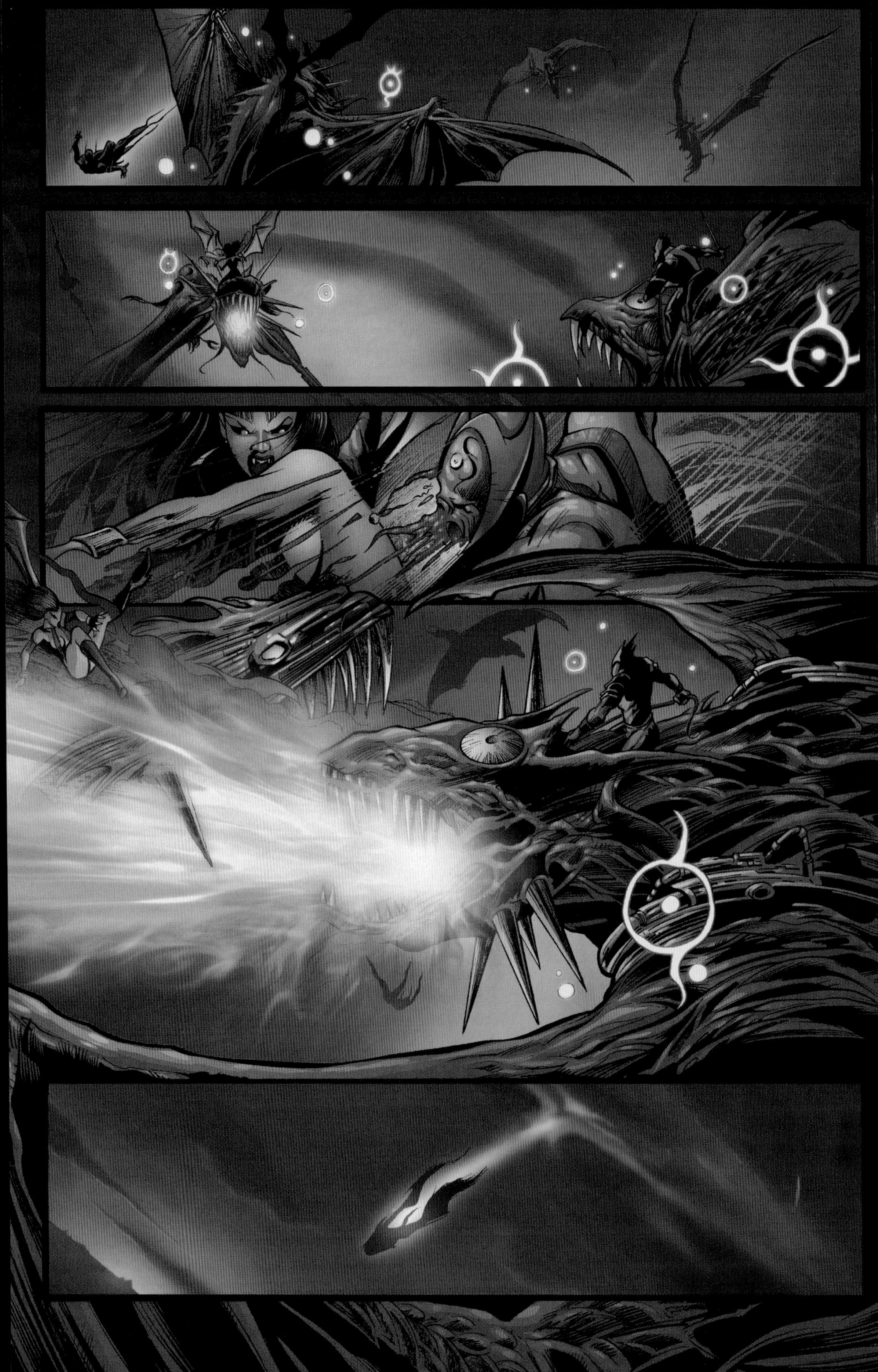

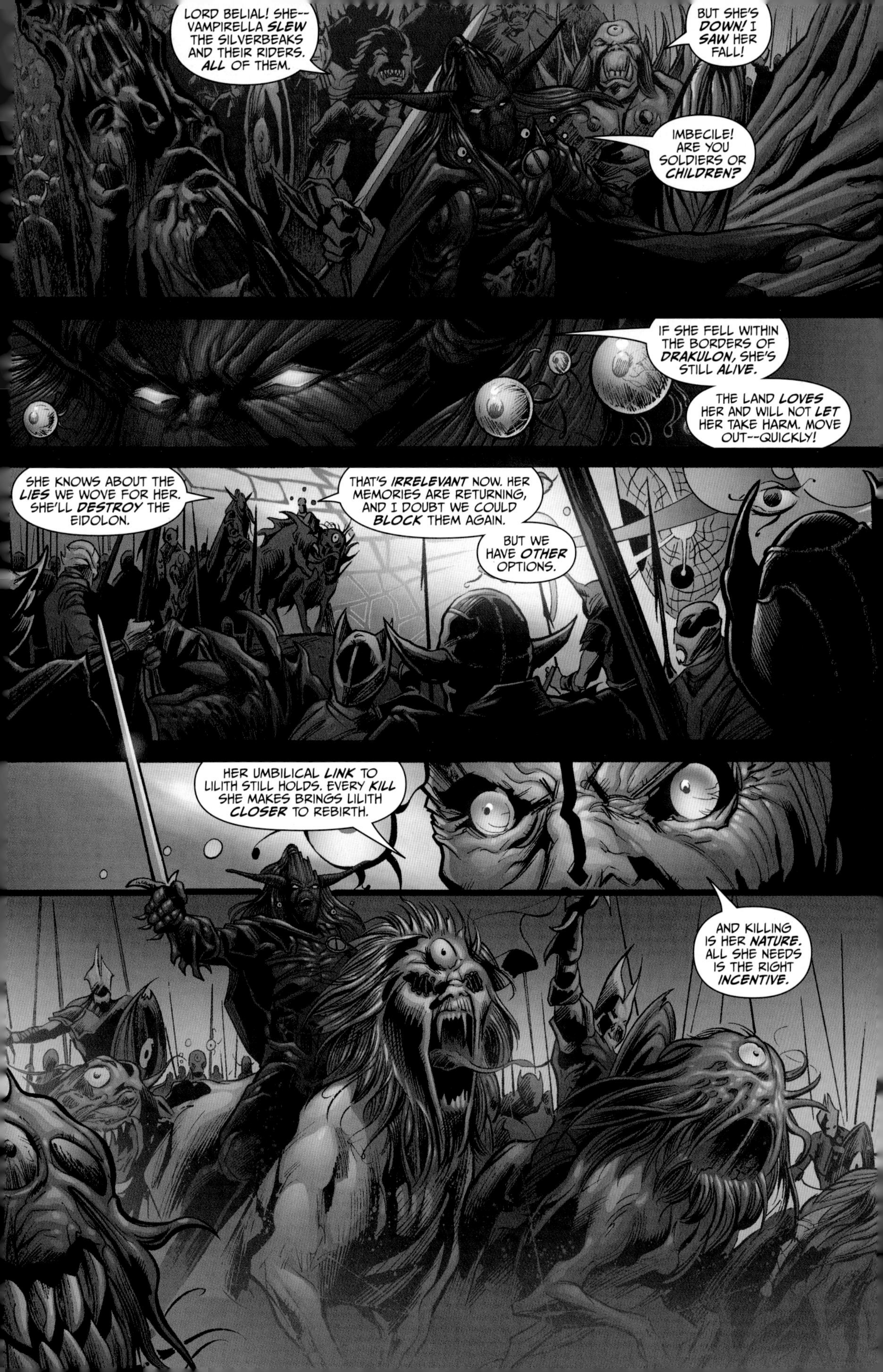
LORD BELIAL! SHE-- VAMPIRELLA SLEW THE SILVERBEAKS AND THEIR RIDERS. ALL OF THEM.
BUT SHE'S DOWN! I SAW HER FALL!
IMBECILE! ARE YOU SOLDIERS OR CHILDREN?
IF SHE FELL WITHIN THE BORDERS OF DRAKULON, SHE'S STILL ALIVE.
THE LAND LOVES HER AND WILL NOT LET HER TAKE HARM. MOVE OUT--QUICKLY!
SHE KNOWS ABOUT THE LIES WE WOVE FOR HER. SHE'LL DESTROY THE EIDOLON.
THAT'S IRRELEVANT NOW. HER MEMORIES ARE RETURNING, AND I DOUBT WE COULD BLOCK THEM AGAIN.
BUT WE HAVE OTHER OPTIONS.
HER UMBILICAL LINK TO LILITH STILL HOLDS. EVERY KILL SHE MAKES BRINGS LILITH CLOSER TO REBIRTH.
AND KILLING IS HER NATURE. ALL SHE NEEDS IS THE RIGHT INCENTIVE.

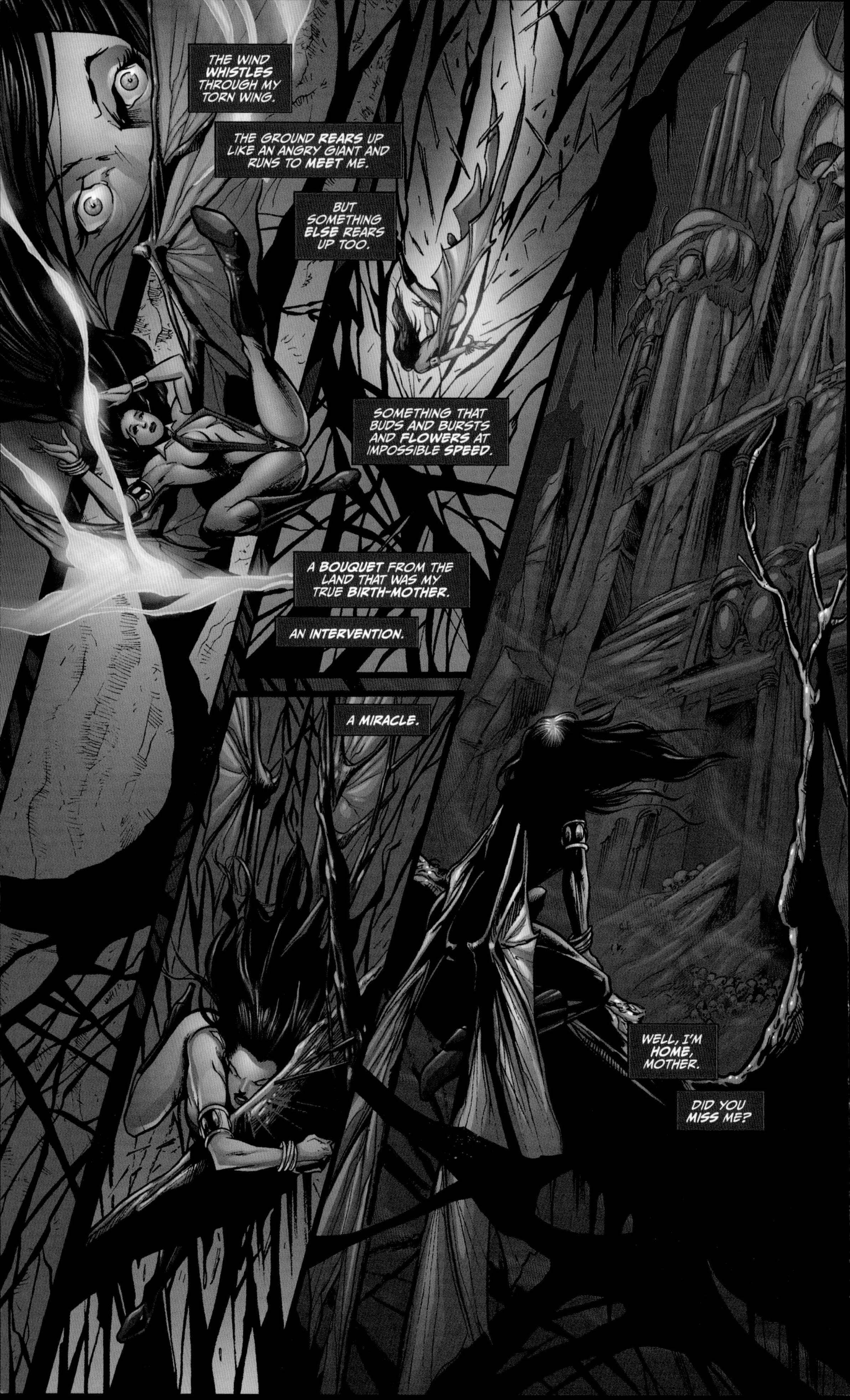
THE WIND WHISTLES THROUGH MY TORN WING.
THE GROUND REARS UP LIKE AN ANGRY GIANT AND RUNS TO MEET ME.
BUT SOMETHING ELSE REARS UP TOO.
SOMETHING THAT BUDS AND BURSTS AND FLOWERS AT IMPOSSIBLE SPEED.
A BOUQUET FROM THE LAND THAT WAS MY TRUE BIRTH-MOTHER.
AN INTERVENTION.
A MIRACLE.
WELL, I'M HOME, MOTHER.
DID YOU MISS ME?

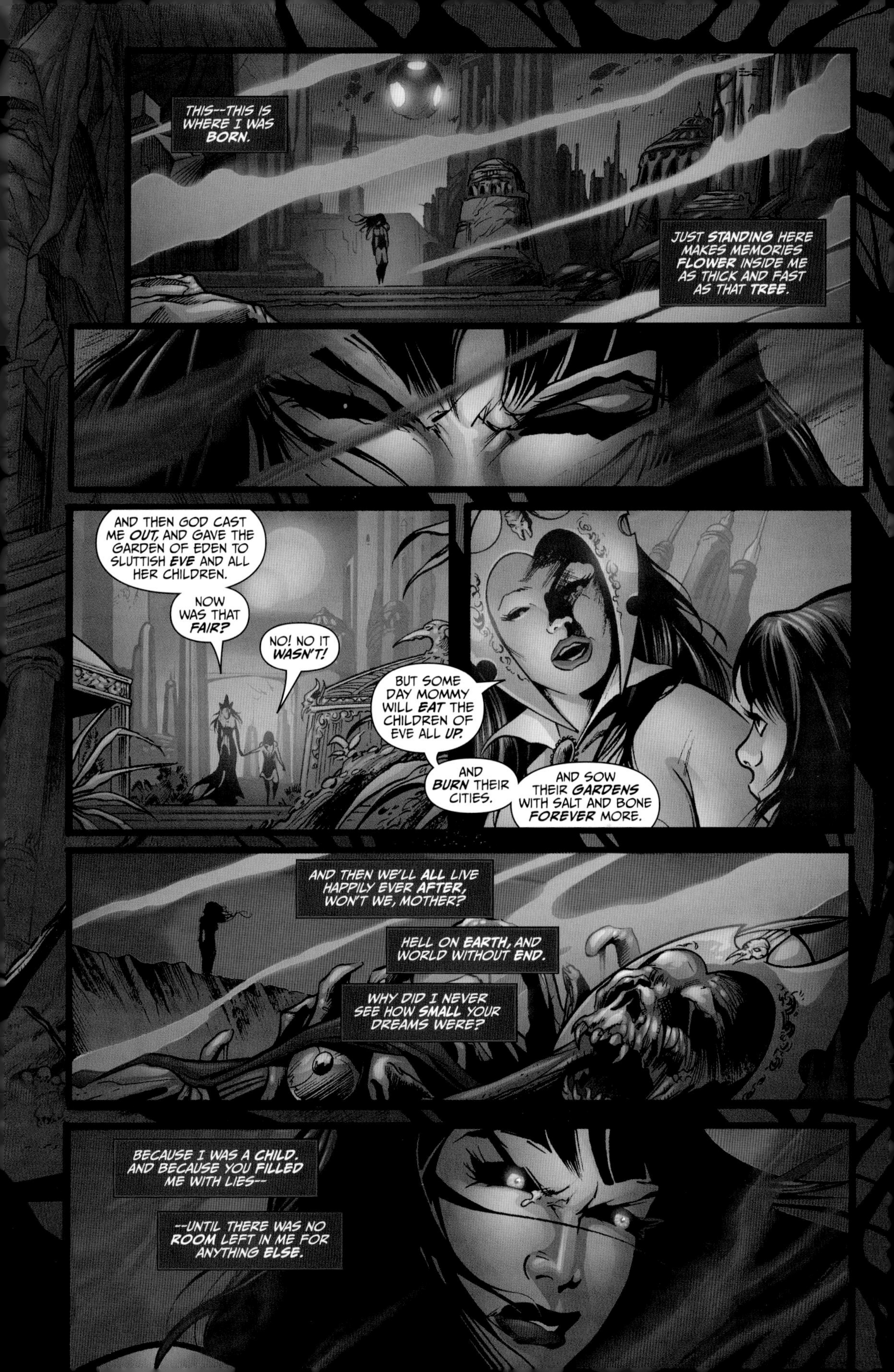
THIS--THIS IS WHERE I WAS BORN.
JUST STANDING HERE MAKES MEMORIES FLOWER INSIDE ME AS THICK AND FAST AS THAT TREE.
AND THEN GOD CAST ME OUT, AND GAVE THE GARDEN OF EDEN TO SLUTTISH EVE AND ALL HER CHILDREN.
NOW WAS THAT FAIR?
NO! NO IT WASN'T!
BUT SOME DAY MOMMY WILL EAT THE CHILDREN OF EVE ALL UP.
AND BURN THEIR CITIES.
AND SOW THEIR GARDENS WITH SALT AND BONE FOREVER MORE.
AND THEN WE'LL ALL LIVE HAPPILY EVER AFTER, WON'T WE, MOTHER?
HELL ON EARTH, AND WORLD WITHOUT END.
WHY DID I NEVER SEE HOW SMALL YOUR DREAMS WERE?
BECAUSE I WAS A CHILD. AND BECAUSE YOU FILLED ME WITH LIES--
--UNTIL THERE WAS NO ROOM LEFT IN ME FOR ANYTHING ELSE.

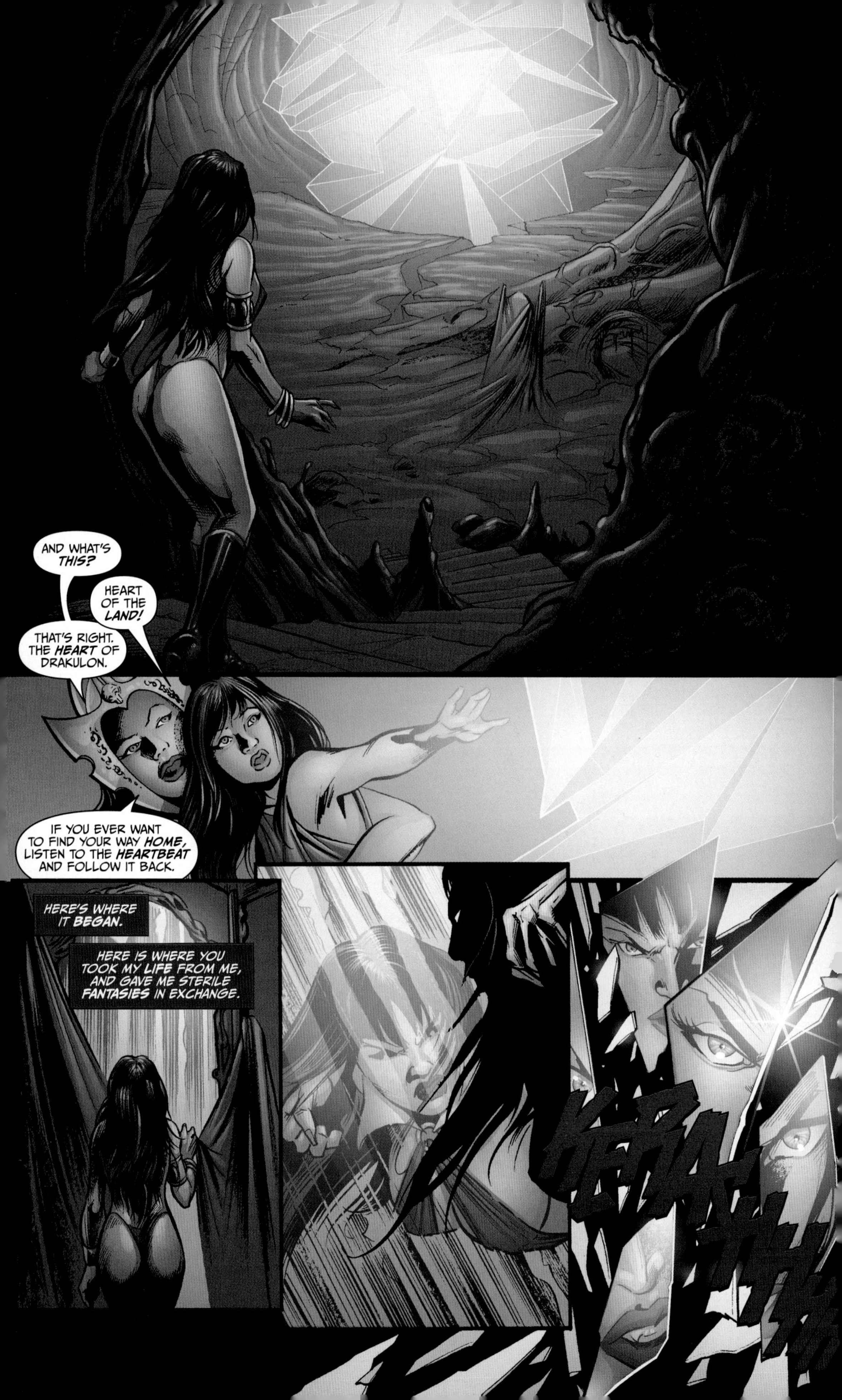
AND WHAT'S THIS?
HEART OF THE LAND!
THAT'S RIGHT. THE HEART OF DRAKULON.
IF YOU EVER WANT TO FIND YOUR WAY HOME, LISTEN TO THE HEARTBEAT AND FOLLOW IT BACK.
HERE'S WHERE IT BEGAN.
HERE IS WHERE YOU TOOK MY LIFE FROM ME, AND GAVE ME STERILE FANTASIES IN EXCHANGE.

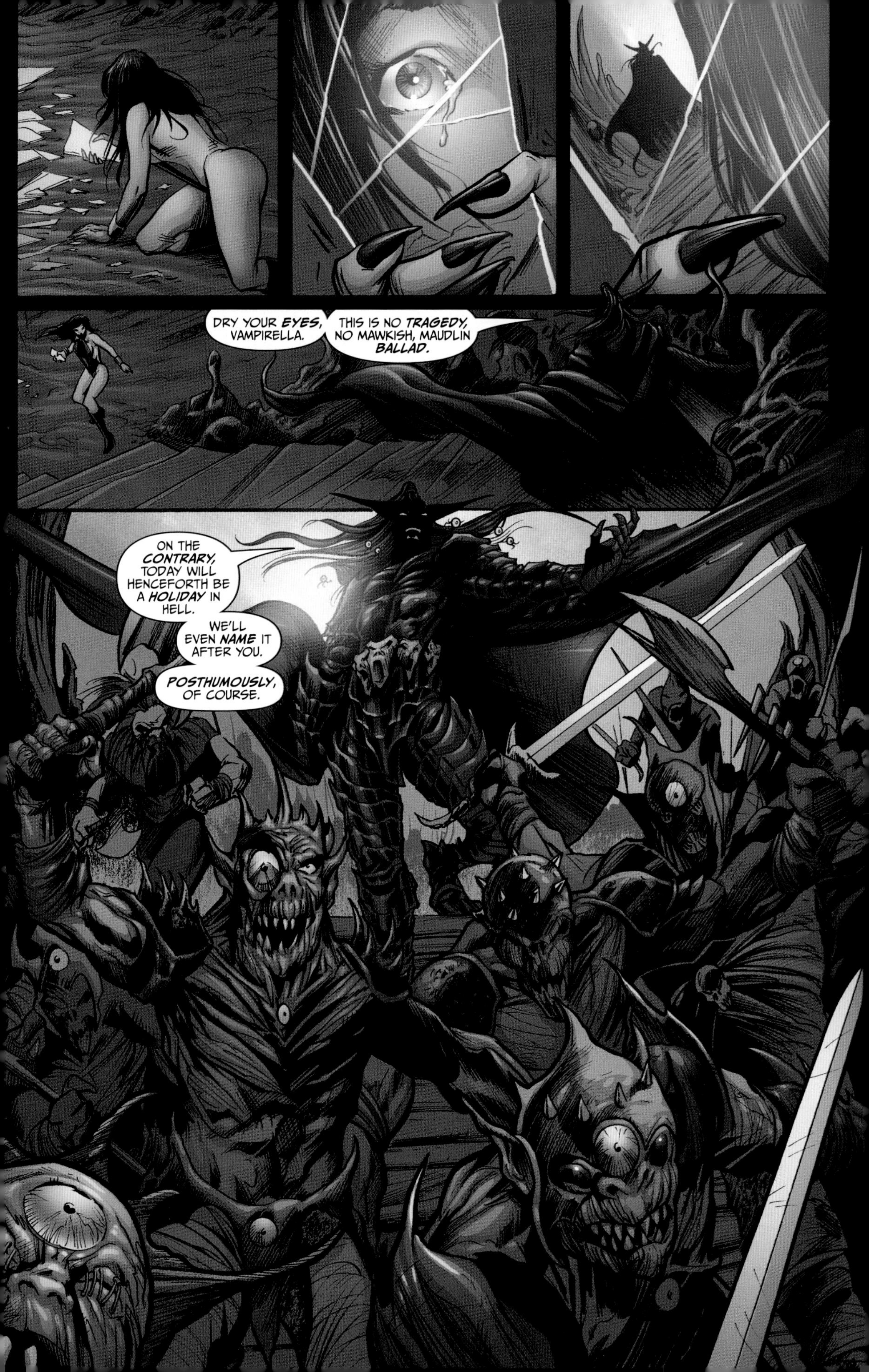
DRY YOUR *EYES*, VAMPIRELLA.
THIS IS NO *TRAGEDY*, NO MAWKISH, MAUDLIN *BALLAD*.
ON THE *CONTRARY*, TODAY WILL HENCEFORTH BE A *HOLIDAY* IN HELL.
WE'LL EVEN *NAME* IT AFTER YOU.
POSTHUMOUSLY, OF COURSE.

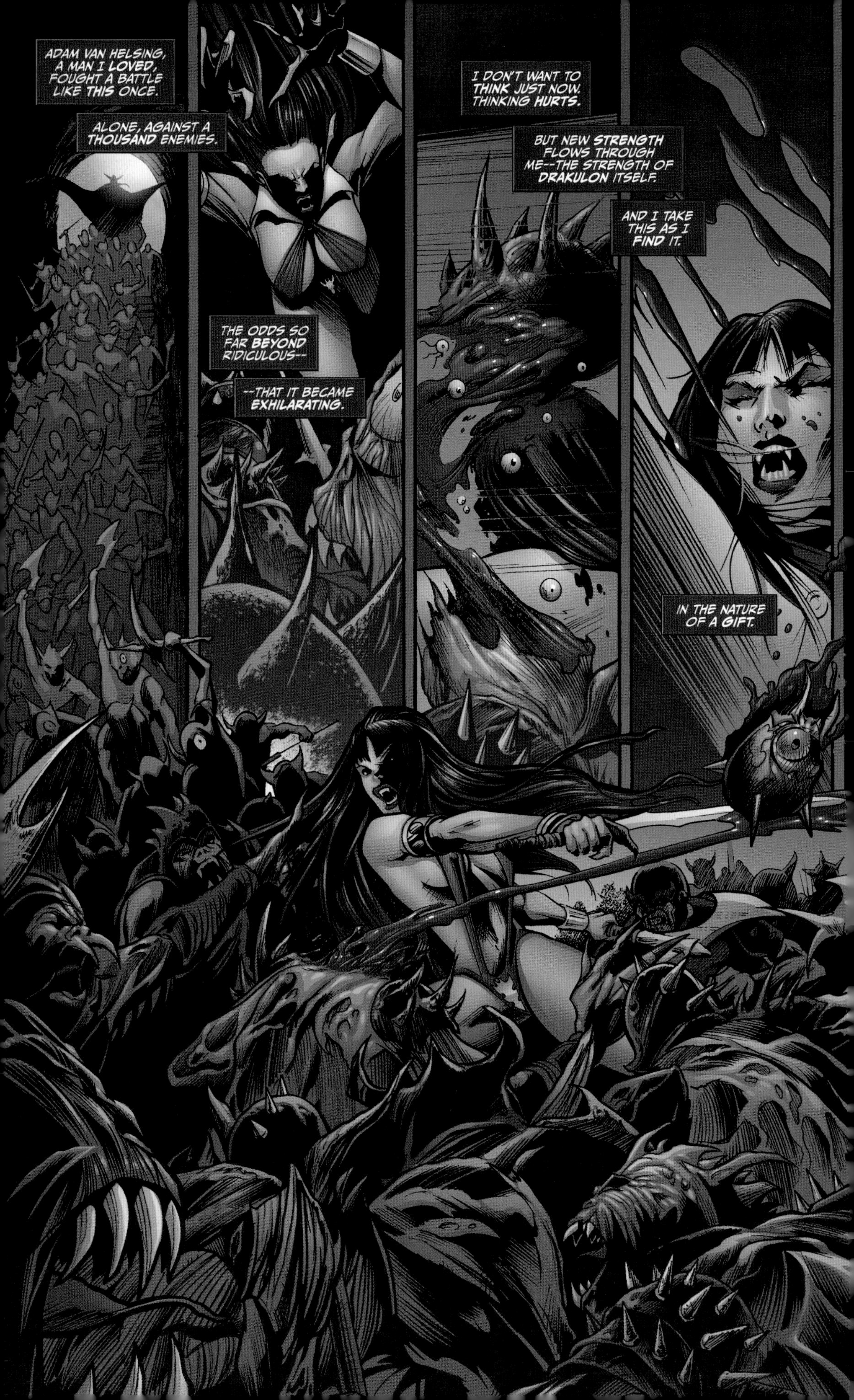
ADAM VAN HELSING, A MAN I LOVED, FOUGHT A BATTLE LIKE THIS ONCE.
ALONE, AGAINST A THOUSAND ENEMIES.
THE ODDS SO FAR BEYOND RIDICULOUS--
--THAT IT BECAME EXHILARATING.
I DON'T WANT TO THINK JUST NOW. THINKING HURTS.
BUT NEW STRENGTH FLOWS THROUGH ME--THE STRENGTH OF DRAKULON ITSELF.
AND I TAKE THIS AS I FIND IT.
IN THE NATURE OF A GIFT.

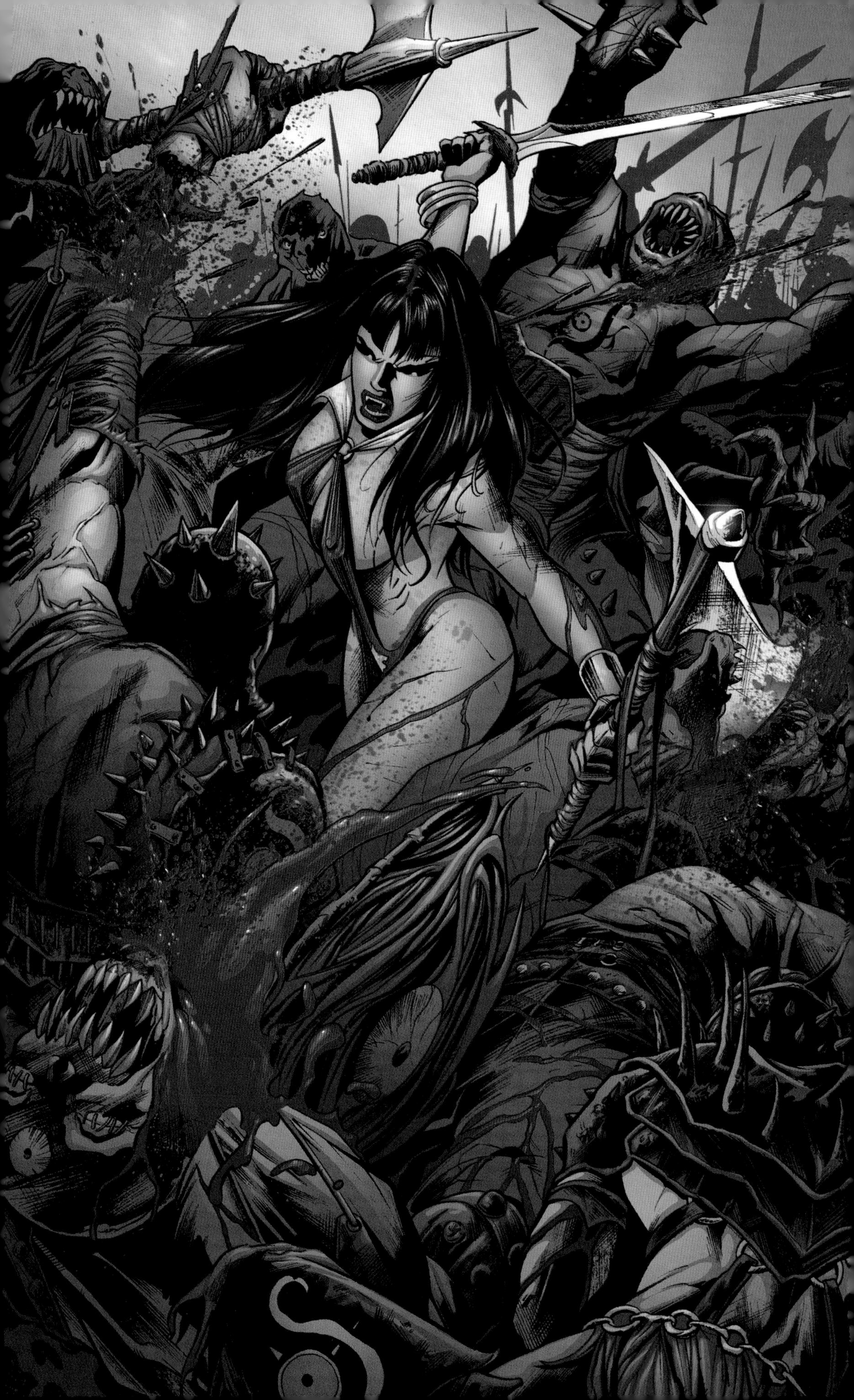

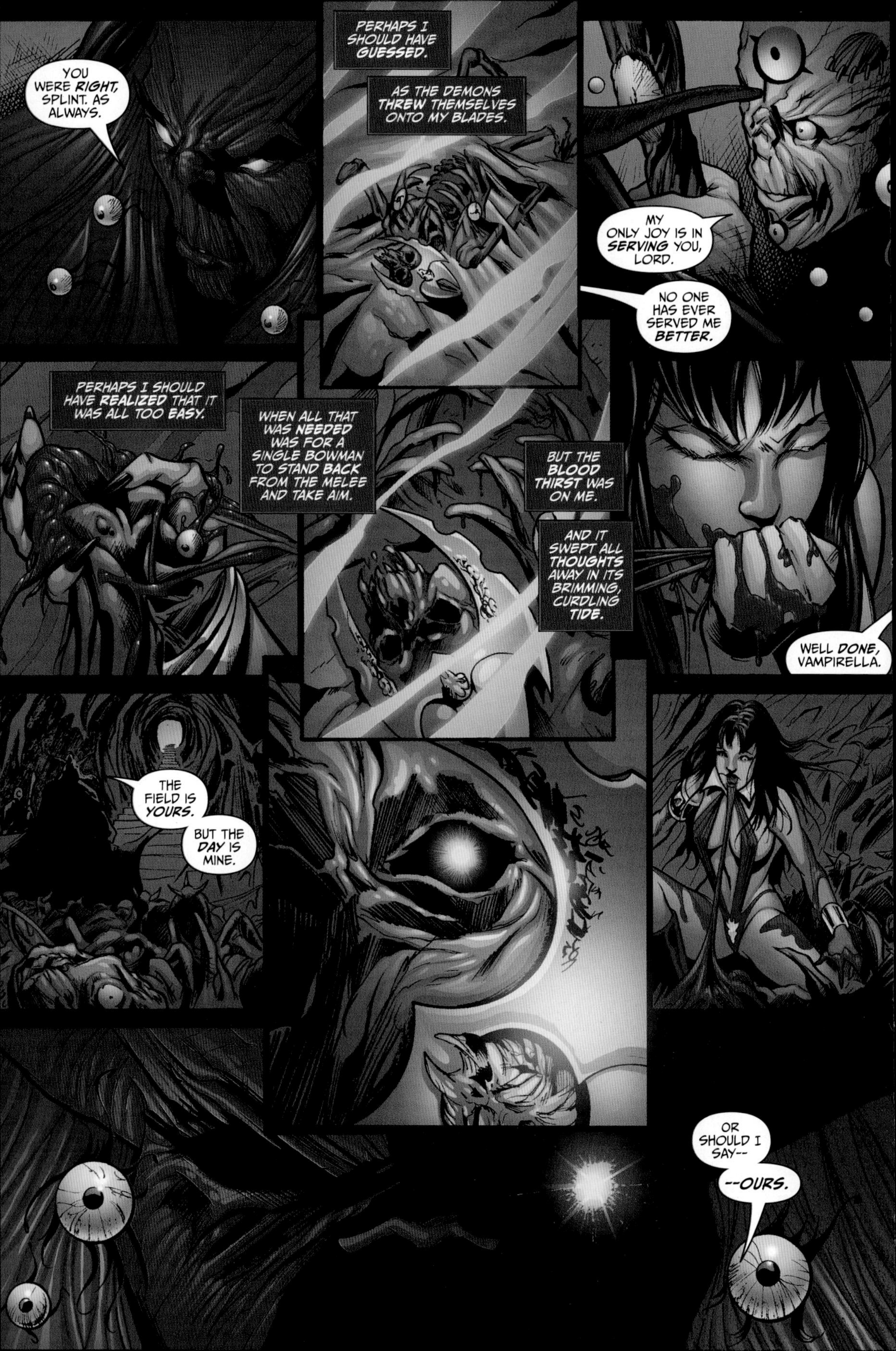
YOU WERE RIGHT, SPLINT. AS ALWAYS.
PERHAPS I SHOULD HAVE GUESSED.
AS THE DEMONS THREW THEMSELVES ONTO MY BLADES.
MY ONLY JOY IS IN SERVING YOU, LORD.
NO ONE HAS EVER SERVED ME BETTER.
PERHAPS I SHOULD HAVE REALIZED THAT IT WAS ALL TOO EASY.
WHEN ALL THAT WAS NEEDED WAS FOR A SINGLE BOWMAN TO STAND BACK FROM THE MELEE AND TAKE AIM.
BUT THE BLOOD THIRST WAS ON ME.
AND IT SWEPT ALL THOUGHTS AWAY IN ITS BRIMMING, CURDLING TIDE.
WELL DONE, VAMPIRELLA.
THE FIELD IS YOURS.
BUT THE DAY IS MINE.
OR SHOULD I SAY--
--OURS.

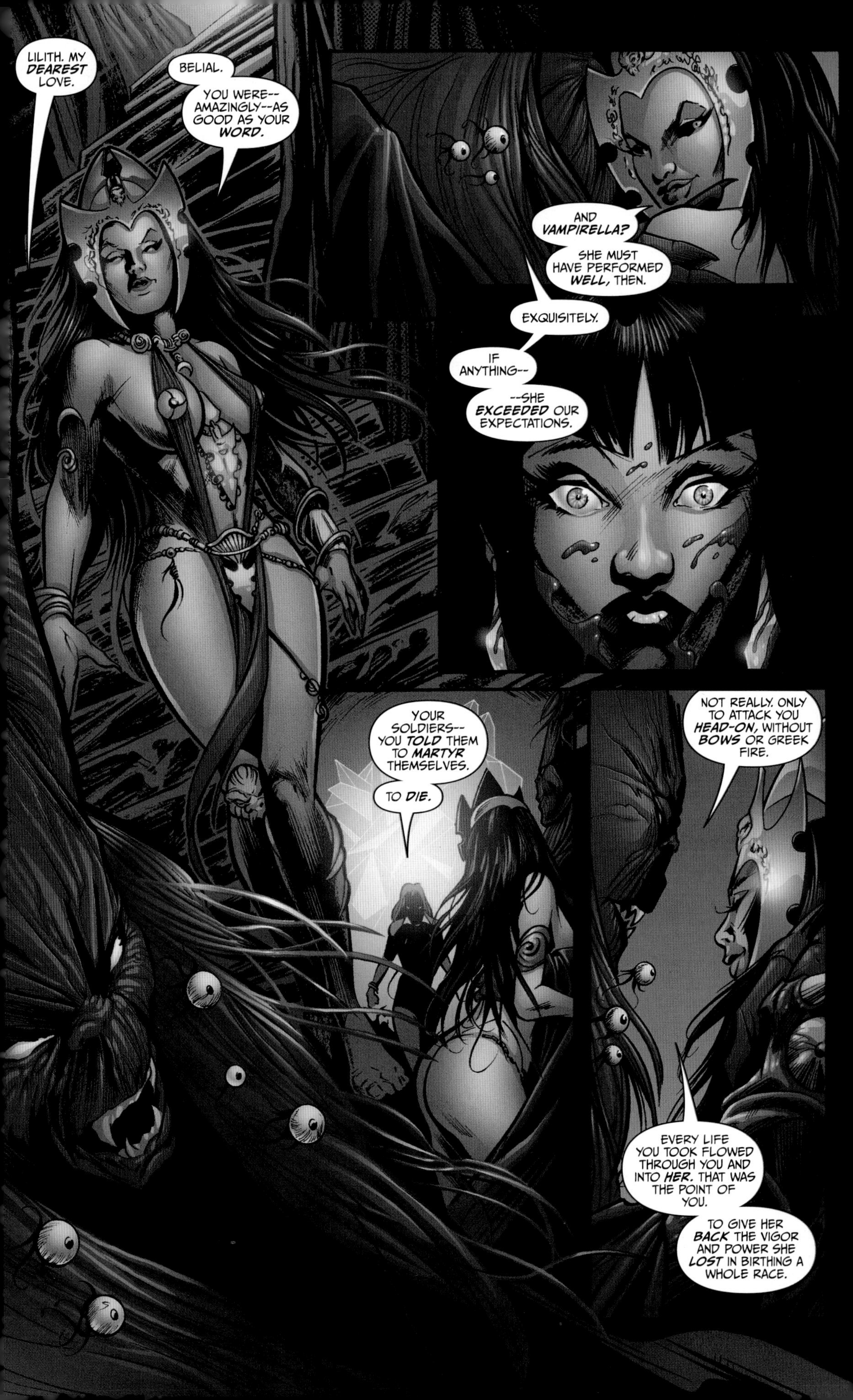
LILITH. MY DEAREST LOVE.
BELIAL.
YOU WERE-- AMAZINGLY--AS GOOD AS YOUR WORD.
AND VAMPIRELLA?
SHE MUST HAVE PERFORMED WELL, THEN.
EXQUISITELY.
IF ANYTHING--
--SHE EXCEEDED OUR EXPECTATIONS.
YOUR SOLDIERS-- YOU TOLD THEM TO MARTYR THEMSELVES.
TO DIE.
NOT REALLY. ONLY TO ATTACK YOU HEAD-ON, WITHOUT BOWS OR GREEK FIRE.
EVERY LIFE YOU TOOK FLOWED THROUGH YOU AND INTO HER. THAT WAS THE POINT OF YOU.
TO GIVE HER BACK THE VIGOR AND POWER SHE LOST IN BIRTHING A WHOLE RACE.

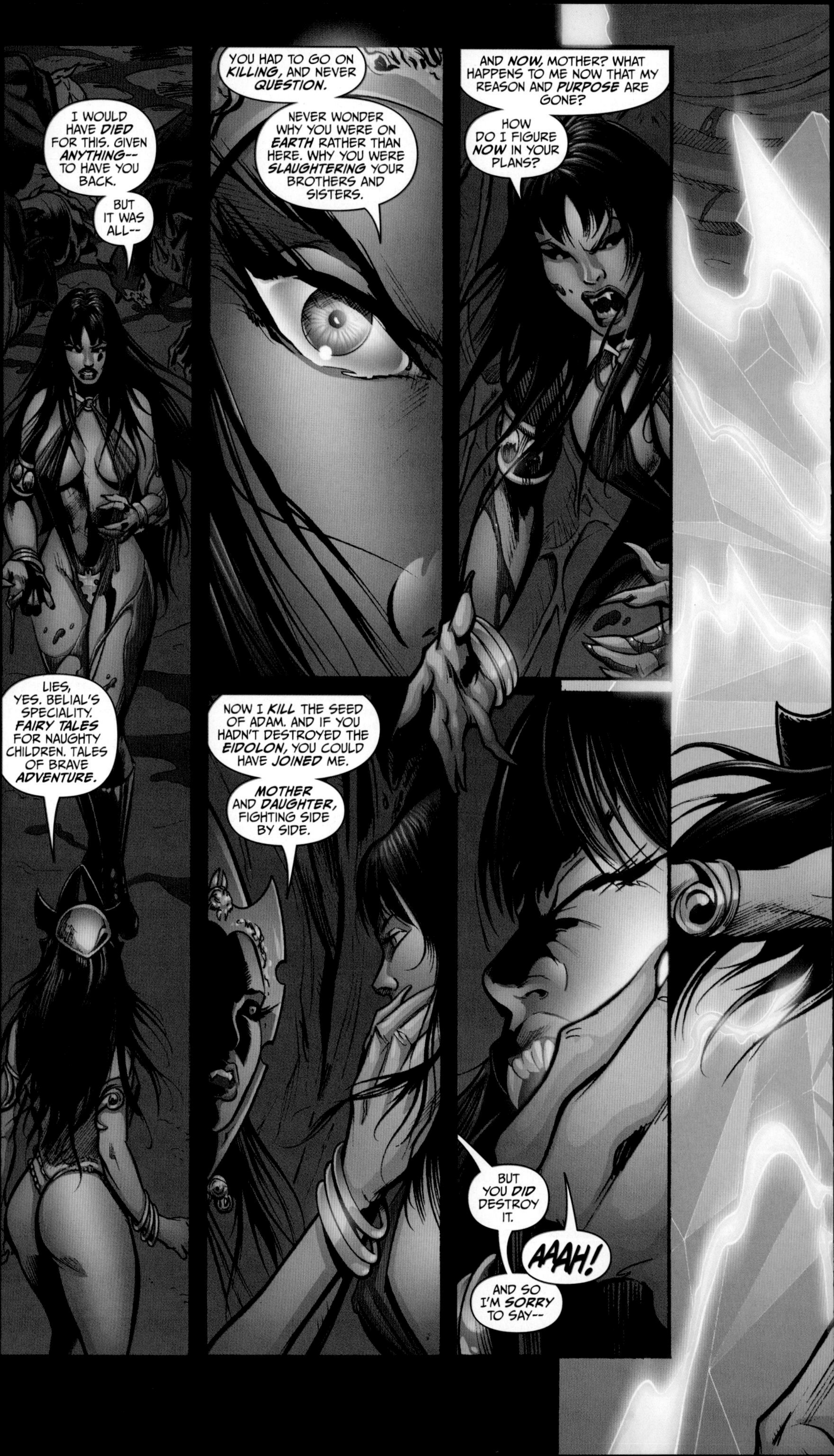
I WOULD HAVE DIED FOR THIS. GIVEN ANYTHING-- TO HAVE YOU BACK.
BUT IT WAS ALL--
YOU HAD TO GO ON KILLING, AND NEVER QUESTION.
NEVER WONDER WHY YOU WERE ON EARTH RATHER THAN HERE. WHY YOU WERE SLAUGHTERING YOUR BROTHERS AND SISTERS.
AND NOW, MOTHER? WHAT HAPPENS TO ME NOW THAT MY REASON AND PURPOSE ARE GONE?
HOW DO I FIGURE NOW IN YOUR PLANS?
LIES, YES. BELIAL'S SPECIALITY. FAIRY TALES FOR NAUGHTY CHILDREN. TALES OF BRAVE ADVENTURE.
NOW I KILL THE SEED OF ADAM. AND IF YOU HADN'T DESTROYED THE EIDOLON, YOU COULD HAVE JOINED ME.
MOTHER AND DAUGHTER, FIGHTING SIDE BY SIDE.
BUT YOU DID DESTROY IT.
AAAH!
AND SO I'M SORRY TO SAY--

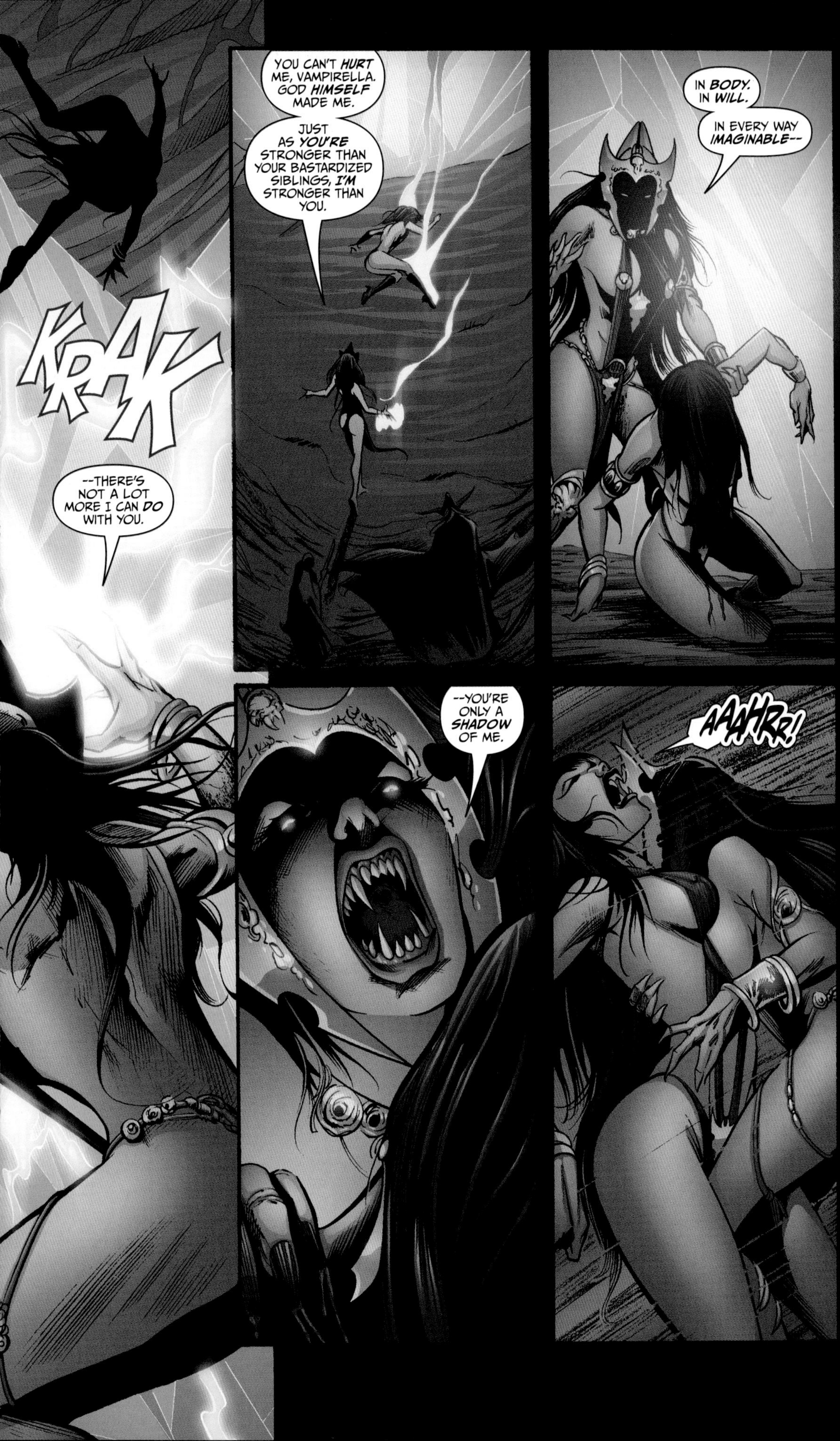

KRAK
--THERE'S NOT A LOT MORE I CAN DO WITH YOU.
YOU CAN'T HURT ME, VAMPIRELLA. GOD HIMSELF MADE ME.
JUST AS YOU'RE STRONGER THAN YOUR BASTARDIZED SIBLINGS, I'M STRONGER THAN YOU.
IN BODY. IN WILL.
IN EVERY WAY IMAGINABLE--
--YOU'RE ONLY A SHADOW OF ME.
AAAHRR!

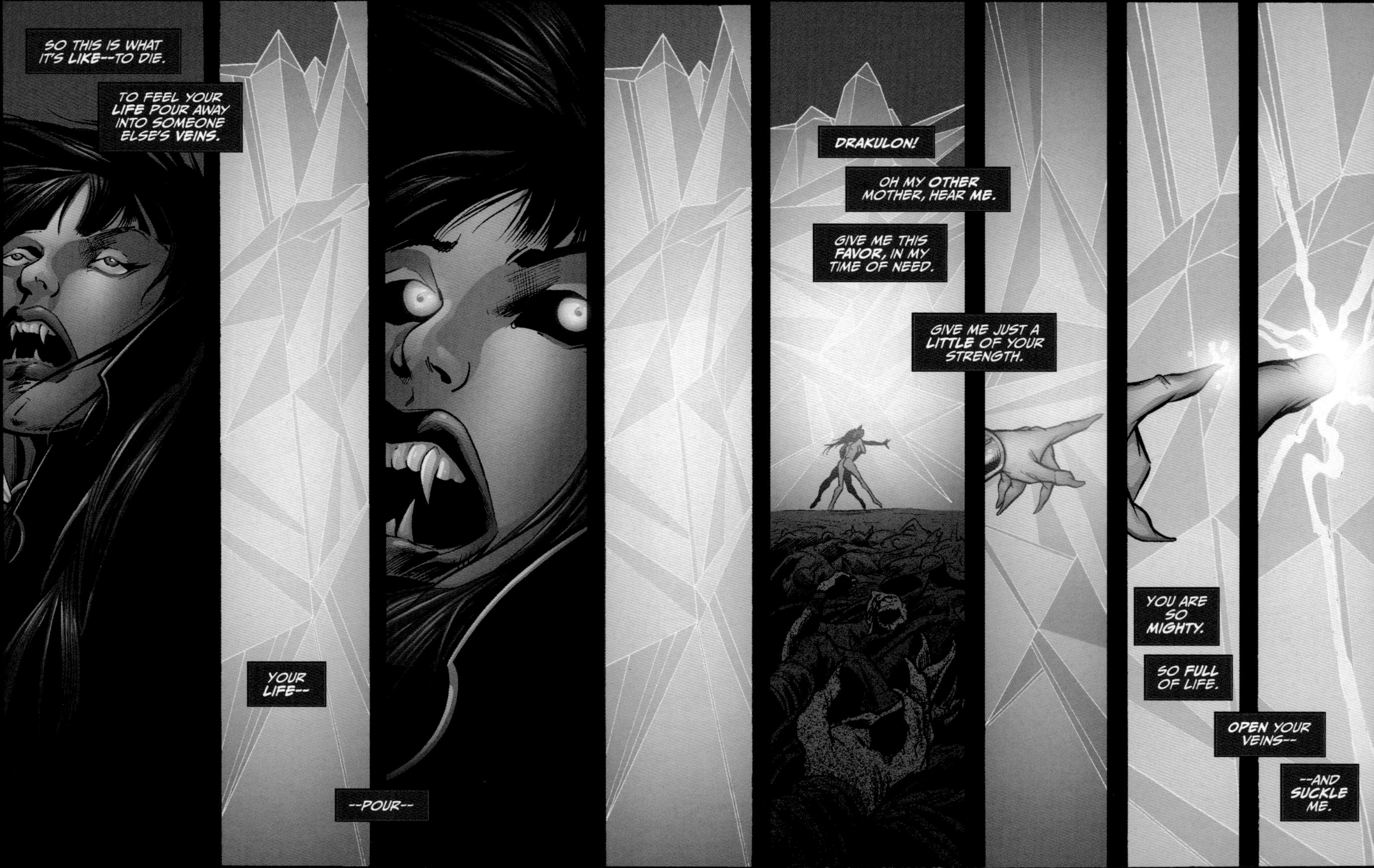
SO THIS IS WHAT IT'S **LIKE**--TO DIE.
TO FEEL YOUR **LIFE** POUR AWAY INTO SOMEONE ELSE'S **VEINS**.
YOUR **LIFE**--
--POUR--
DRAKULON!
OH MY **OTHER** MOTHER, HEAR **ME**.
GIVE ME THIS **FAVOR**, IN MY TIME OF NEED.
GIVE ME JUST A **LITTLE** OF YOUR STRENGTH.
YOU ARE SO **MIGHTY**.
SO **FULL** OF LIFE.
OPEN YOUR VEINS--
--AND **SUCKLE** ME.

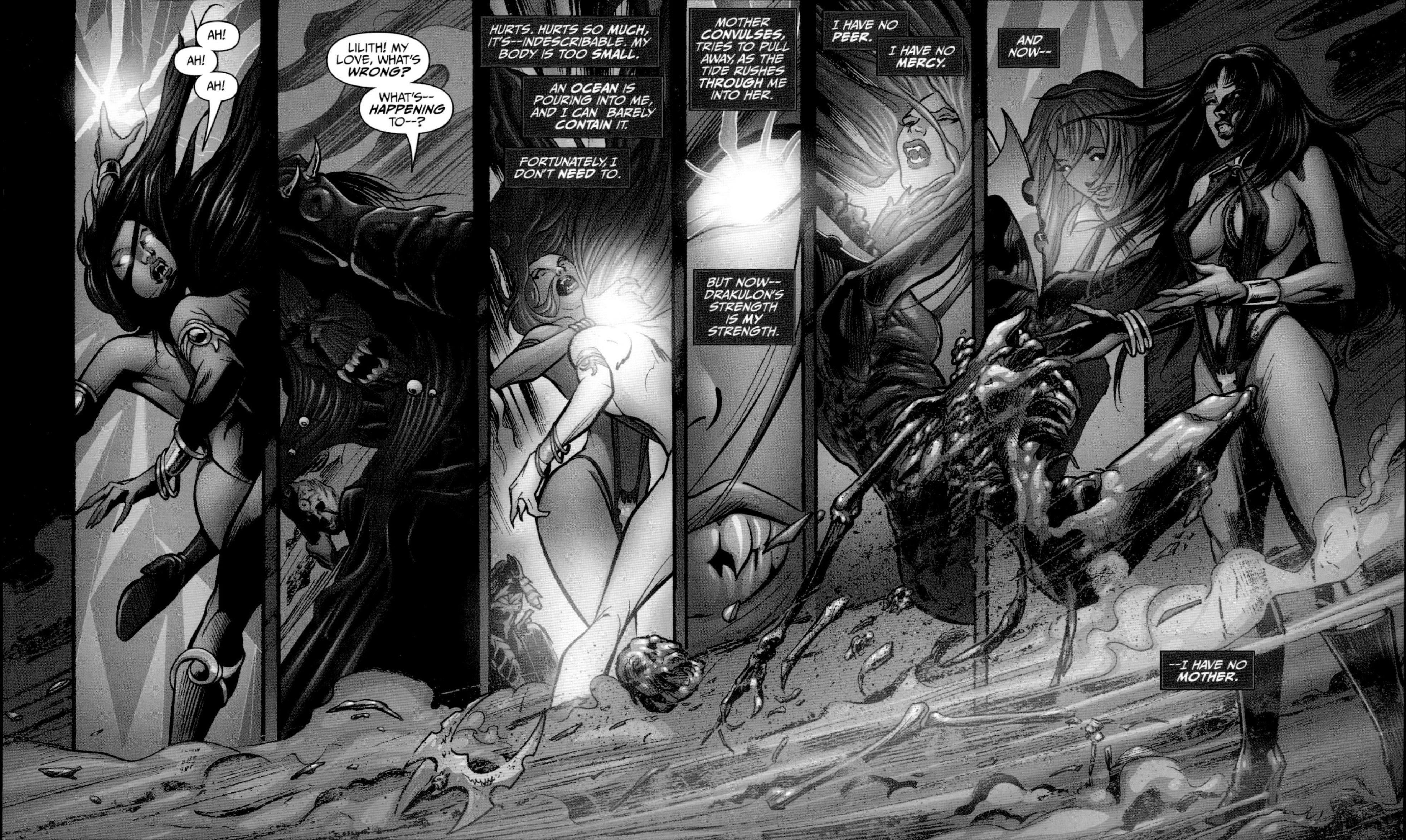
AH!
AH!
AH!
LILITH! MY LOVE, WHAT'S WRONG?
WHAT'S--HAPPENING TO--?
HURTS. HURTS SO MUCH, IT'S--INDESCRIBABLE. MY BODY IS TOO SMALL.
AN OCEAN IS POURING INTO ME, AND I CAN BARELY CONTAIN IT.
FORTUNATELY, I DON'T NEED TO.
MOTHER CONVULSES, TRIES TO PULL AWAY, AS THE TIDE RUSHES THROUGH ME INTO HER.
BUT NOW--DRAKULON'S STRENGTH IS MY STRENGTH.
I HAVE NO PEER.
I HAVE NO MERCY.
AND NOW--
--I HAVE NO MOTHER.

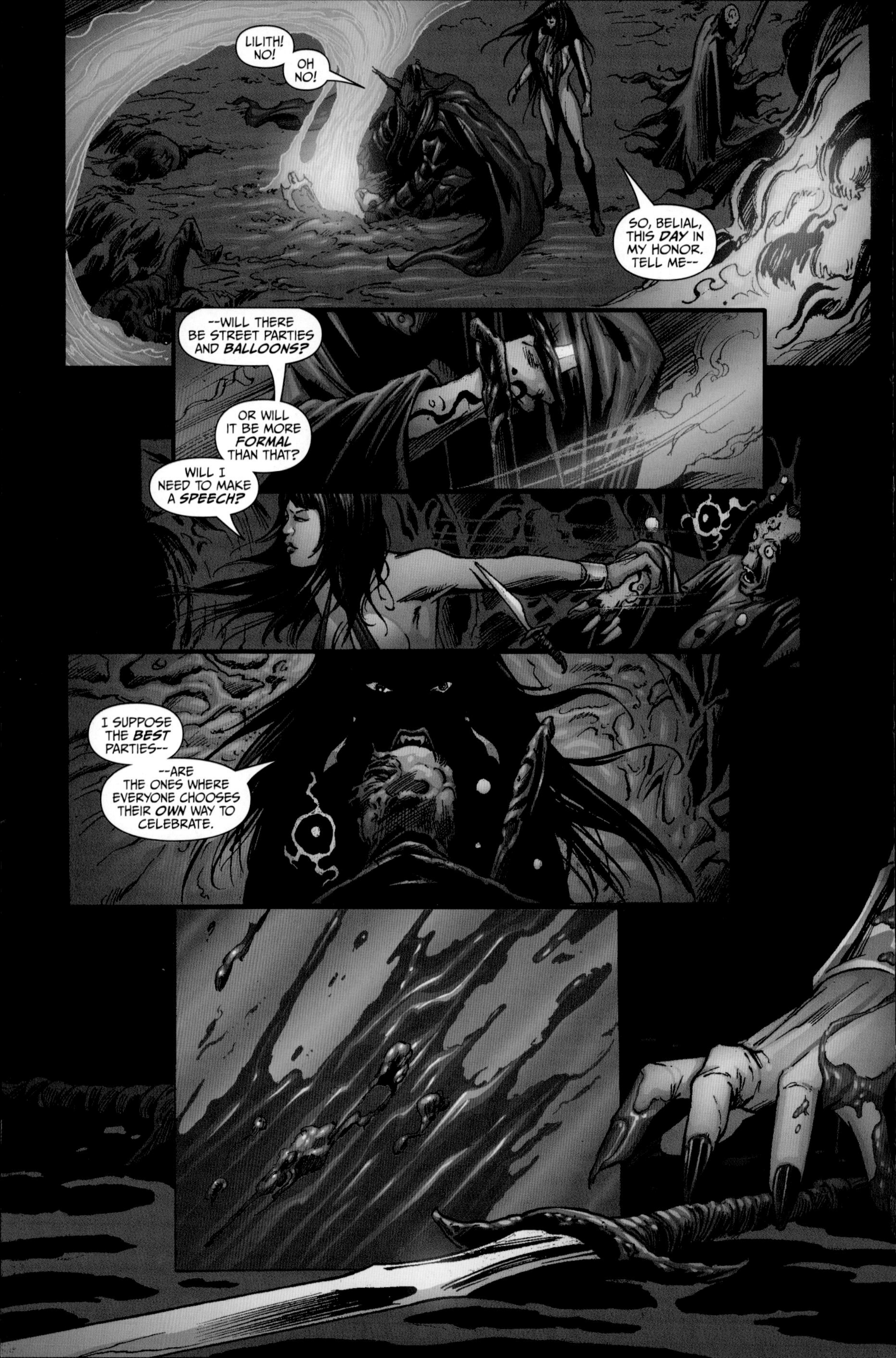
LILITH! NO!
OH NO!
SO, BELIAL, THIS DAY IN MY HONOR. TELL ME--
--WILL THERE BE STREET PARTIES AND BALLOONS?
OR WILL IT BE MORE FORMAL THAN THAT?
WILL I NEED TO MAKE A SPEECH?
I SUPPOSE THE BEST PARTIES--
--ARE THE ONES WHERE EVERYONE CHOOSES THEIR OWN WAY TO CELEBRATE.

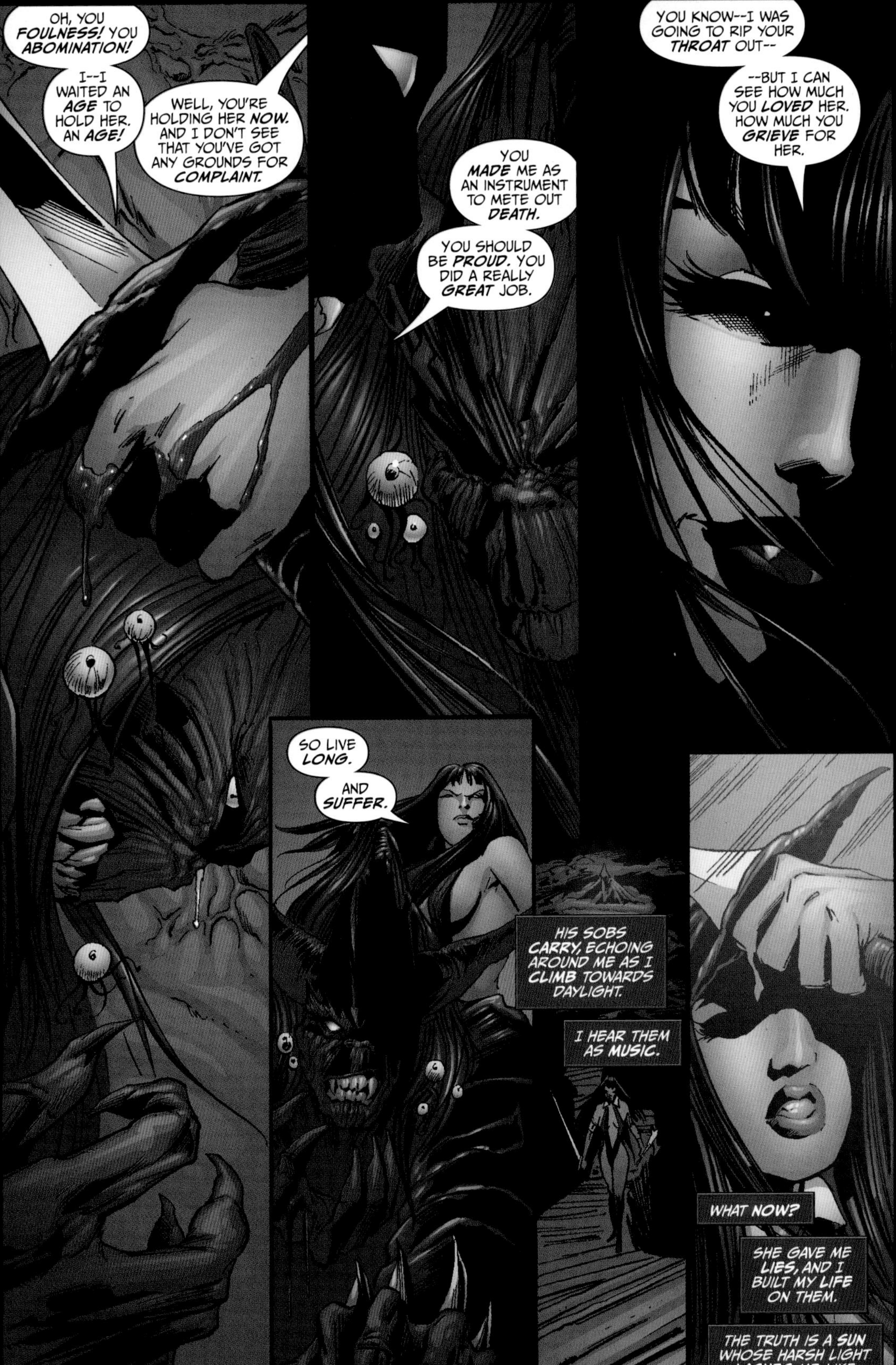
OH, YOU FOULNESS! YOU ABOMINATION!
I--I WAITED AN AGE TO HOLD HER. AN AGE!
WELL, YOU'RE HOLDING HER NOW. AND I DON'T SEE THAT YOU'VE GOT ANY GROUNDS FOR COMPLAINT.
YOU MADE ME AS AN INSTRUMENT TO METE OUT DEATH.
YOU SHOULD BE PROUD. YOU DID A REALLY GREAT JOB.
YOU KNOW--I WAS GOING TO RIP YOUR THROAT OUT--
--BUT I CAN SEE HOW MUCH YOU LOVED HER. HOW MUCH YOU GRIEVE FOR HER.
SO LIVE LONG.
AND SUFFER.
HIS SOBS CARRY, ECHOING AROUND ME AS I CLIMB TOWARDS DAYLIGHT.
I HEAR THEM AS MUSIC.
WHAT NOW?
SHE GAVE ME LIES, AND I BUILT MY LIFE ON THEM.
THE TRUTH IS A SUN WHOSE HARSH LIGHT LASHES ME LIKE KNOTTED ROPES.

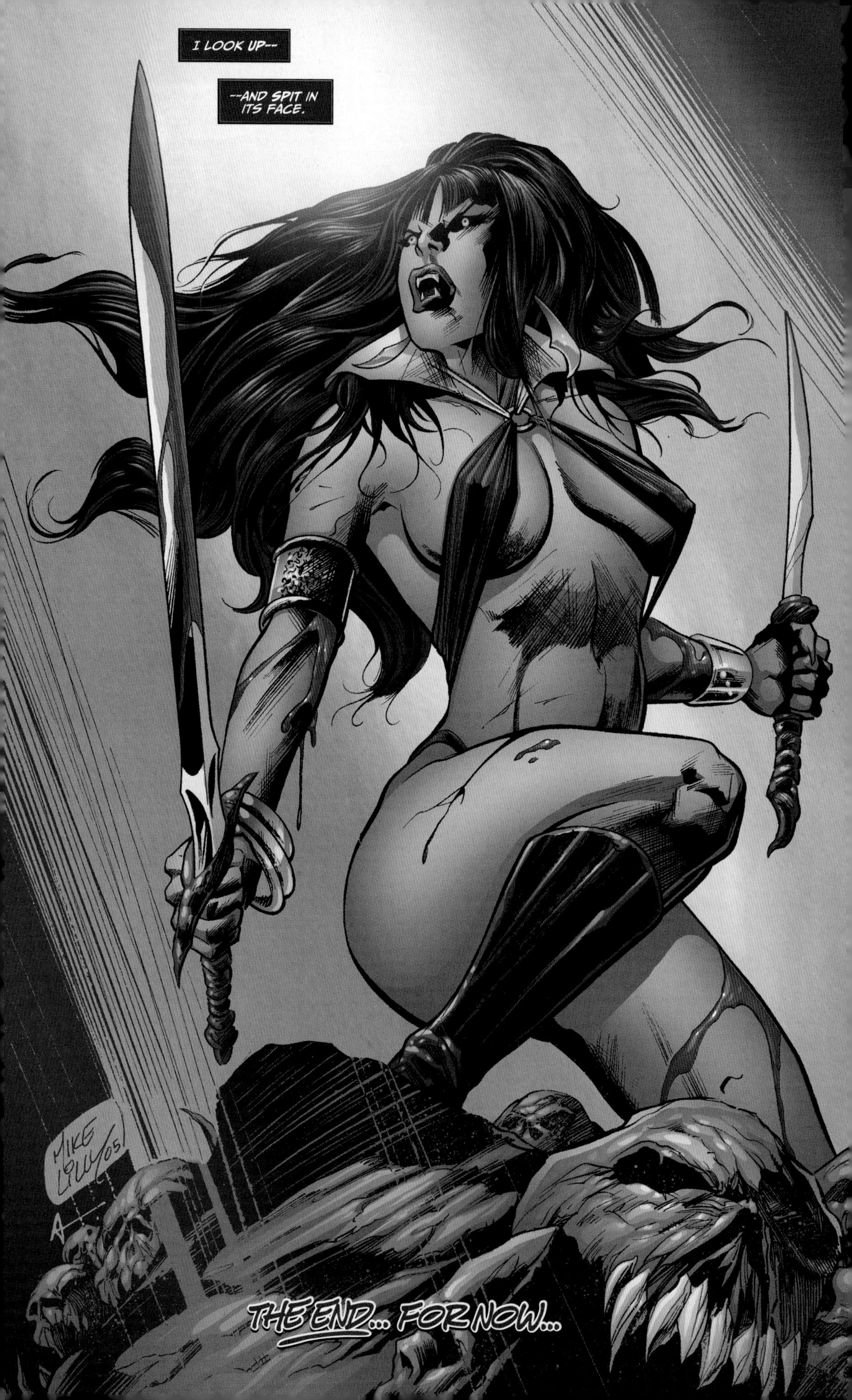
I LOOK UP--
--AND SPIT IN ITS FACE.
THE END... FOR NOW...

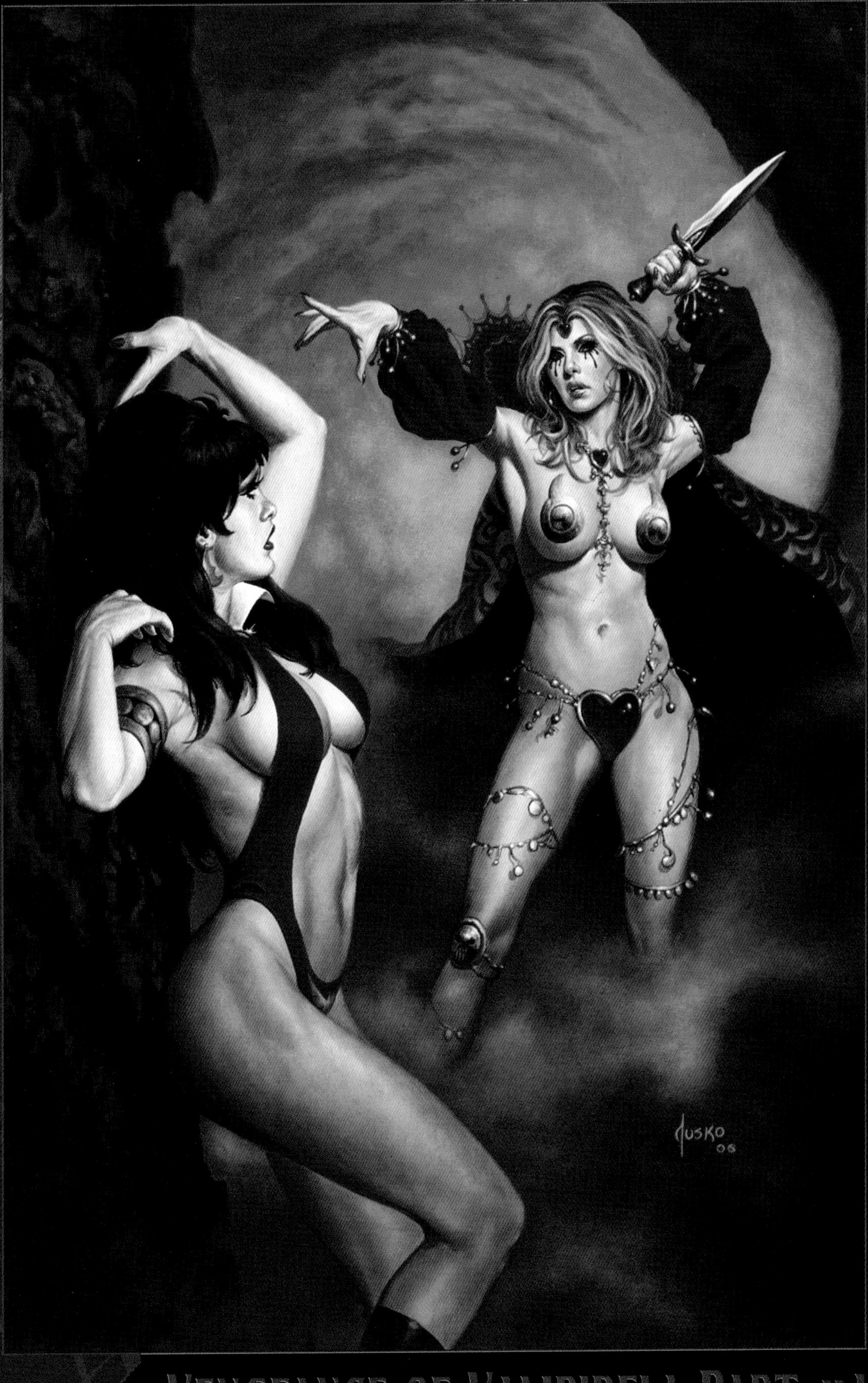
JUSKO 06

VENGEANCE OF VAMPIRELA PART #1

Vampirella Quarterly: Sping 2007 #1 cover by Joe Jusko

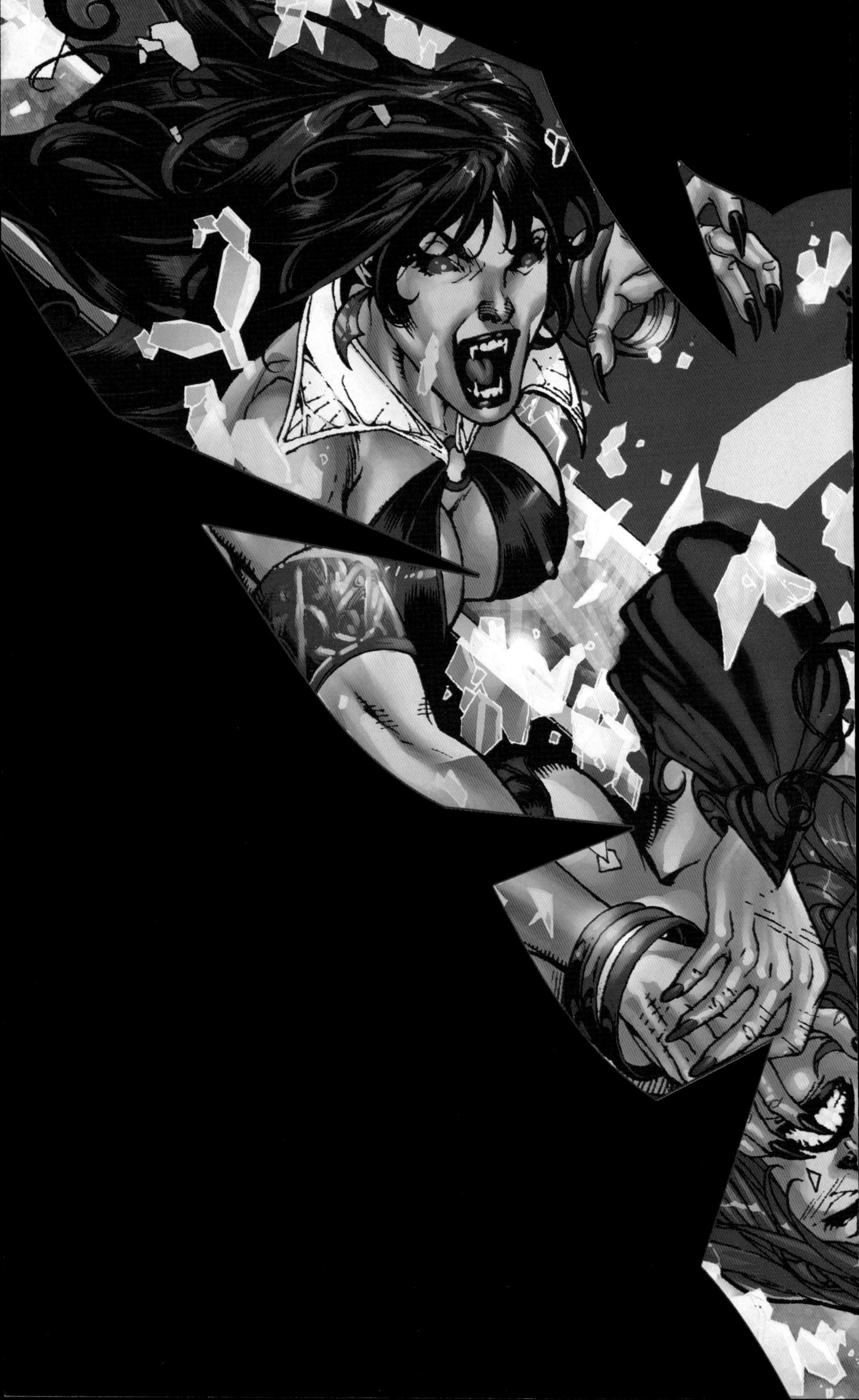

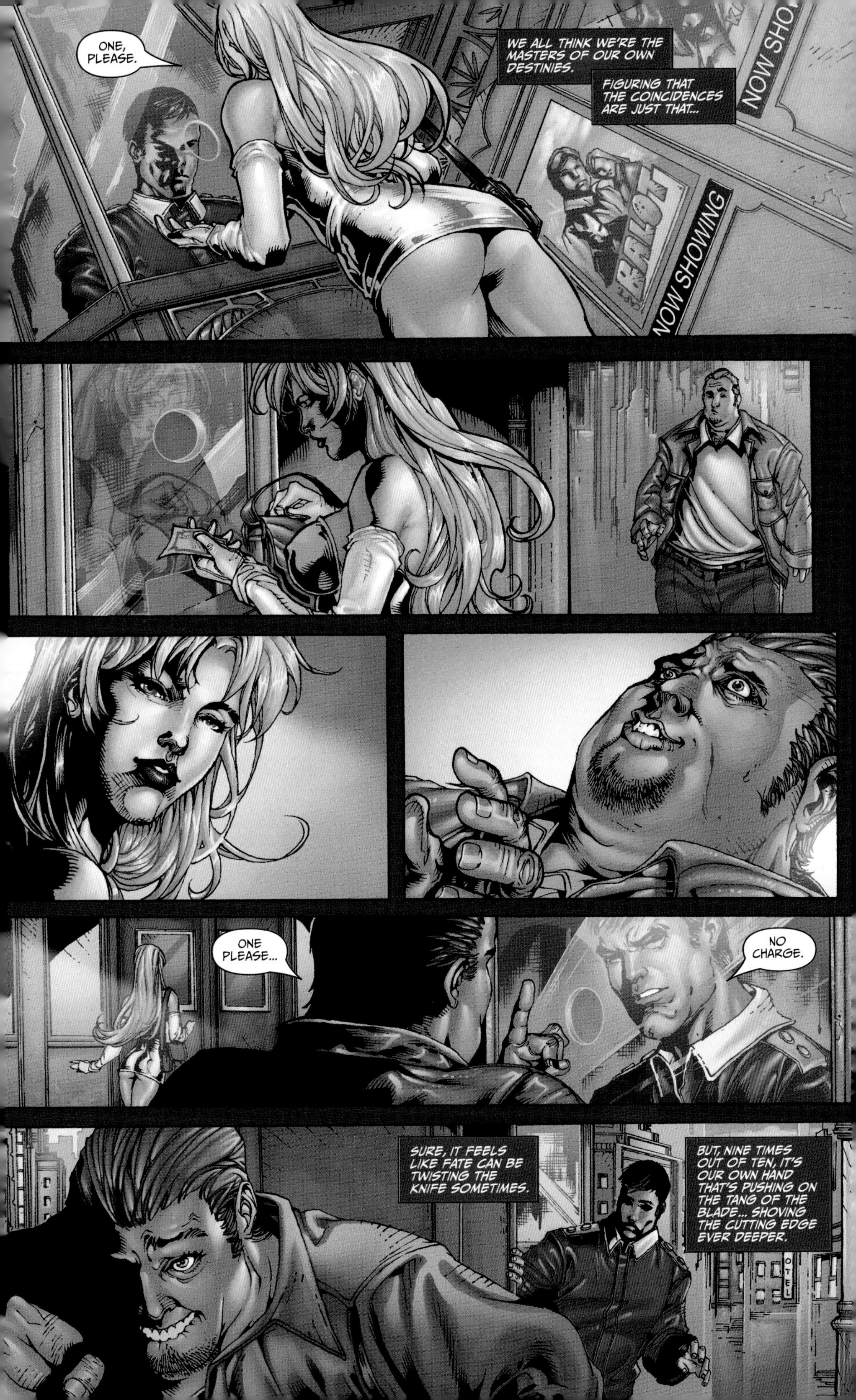
ONE, PLEASE.
WE ALL THINK WE'RE THE MASTERS OF OUR OWN DESTINIES.
FIGURING THAT THE COINCIDENCES ARE JUST THAT...
NOW SHOWING
NOW SHOWING
ONE PLEASE...
NO CHARGE.
SURE, IT FEELS LIKE FATE CAN BE TWISTING THE KNIFE SOMETIMES.
BUT, NINE TIMES OUT OF TEN, IT'S OUR OWN HAND THAT'S PUSHING ON THE TANG OF THE BLADE... SHOVING THE CUTTING EDGE EVER DEEPER.

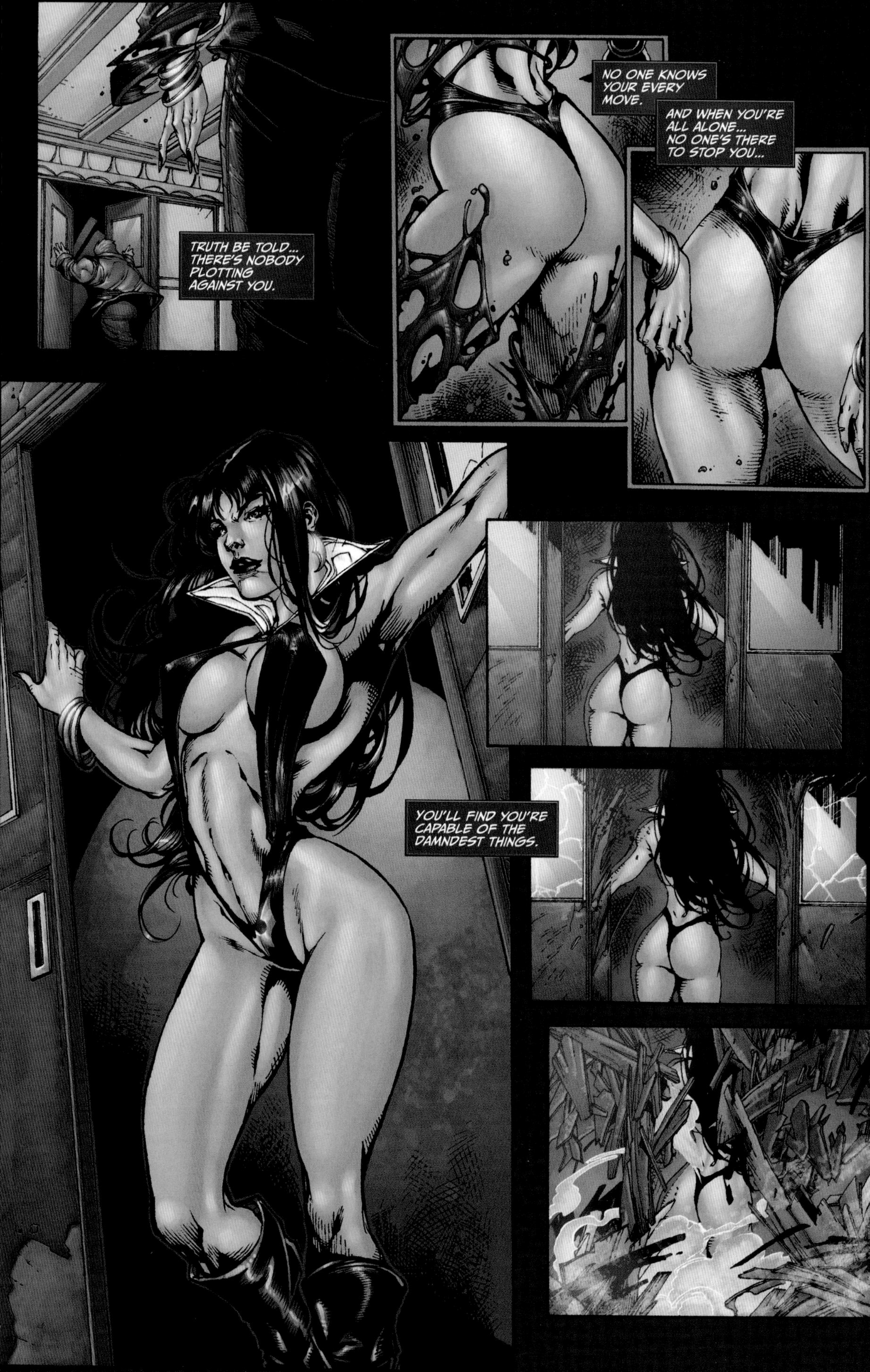
TRUTH BE TOLD... THERE'S NOBODY PLOTTING AGAINST YOU.
NO ONE KNOWS YOUR EVERY MOVE.
AND WHEN YOU'RE ALL ALONE... NO ONE'S THERE TO STOP YOU...
YOU'LL FIND YOU'RE CAPABLE OF THE DAMNDEST THINGS.

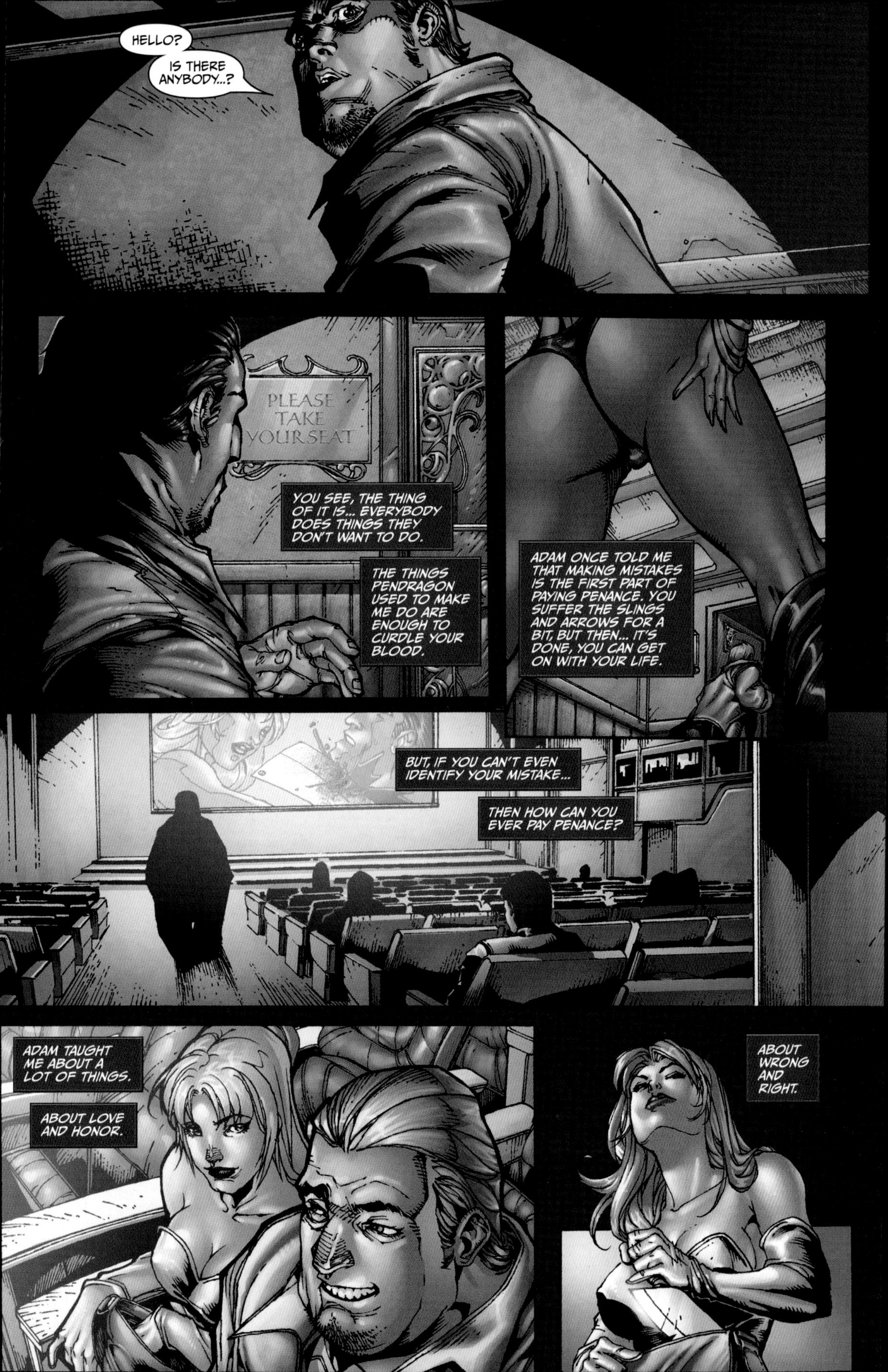
HELLO?
IS THERE ANYBODY...?
PLEASE TAKE YOUR SEAT
YOU SEE, THE THING OF IT IS... EVERYBODY DOES THINGS THEY DON'T WANT TO DO.
THE THINGS PENDRAGON USED TO MAKE ME DO ARE ENOUGH TO CURDLE YOUR BLOOD.
ADAM ONCE TOLD ME THAT MAKING MISTAKES IS THE FIRST PART OF PAYING PENANCE. YOU SUFFER THE SLINGS AND ARROWS FOR A BIT, BUT THEN... IT'S DONE, YOU CAN GET ON WITH YOUR LIFE.
BUT, IF YOU CAN'T EVEN IDENTIFY YOUR MISTAKE...
THEN HOW CAN YOU EVER PAY PENANCE?
ADAM TAUGHT ME ABOUT A LOT OF THINGS.
ABOUT LOVE AND HONOR.
ABOUT WRONG AND RIGHT.

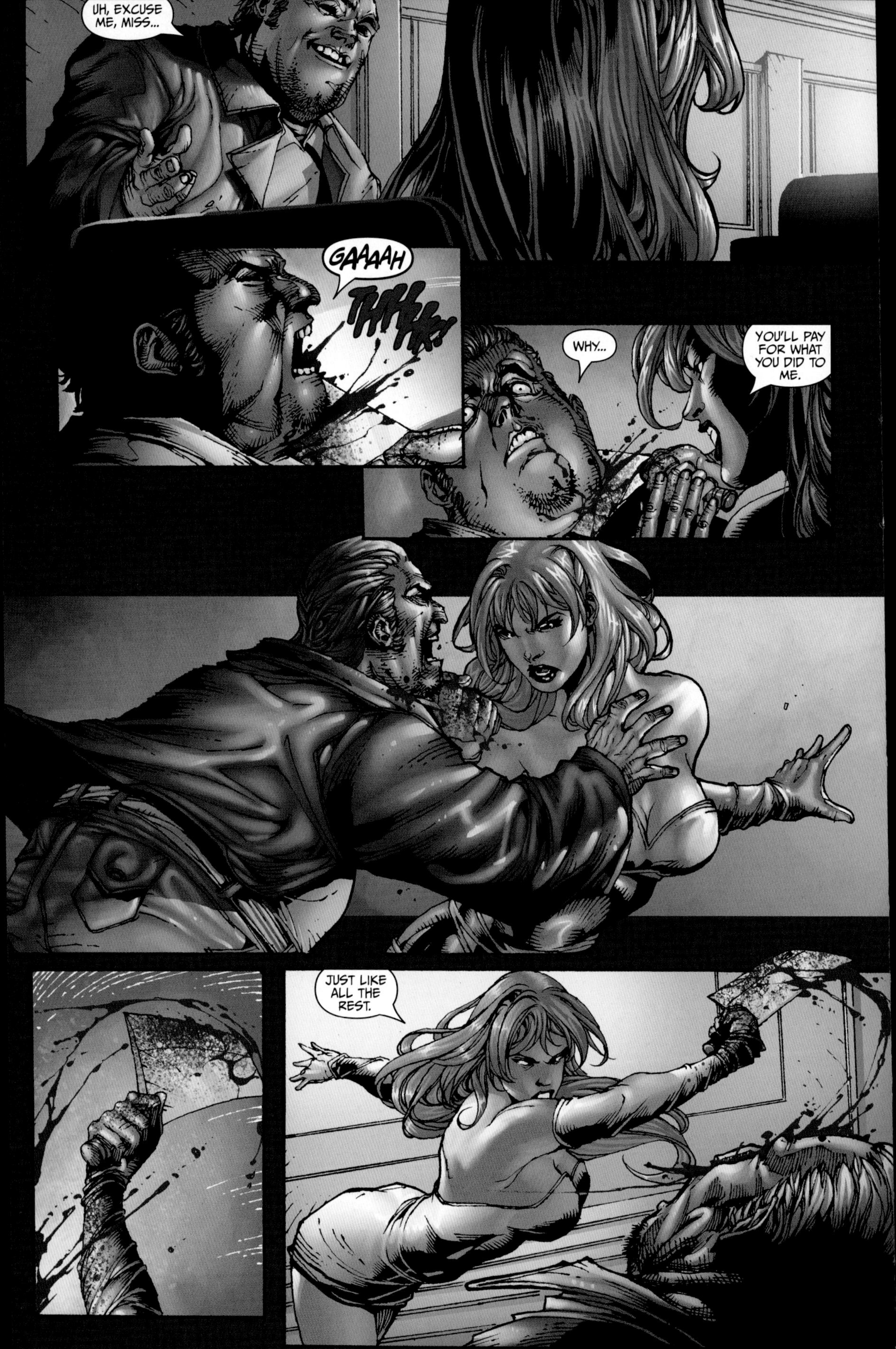

UH, EXCUSE ME, MISS...
GAAAAH
THHHK!
WHY...
YOU'LL PAY FOR WHAT YOU DID TO ME.
JUST LIKE ALL THE REST.

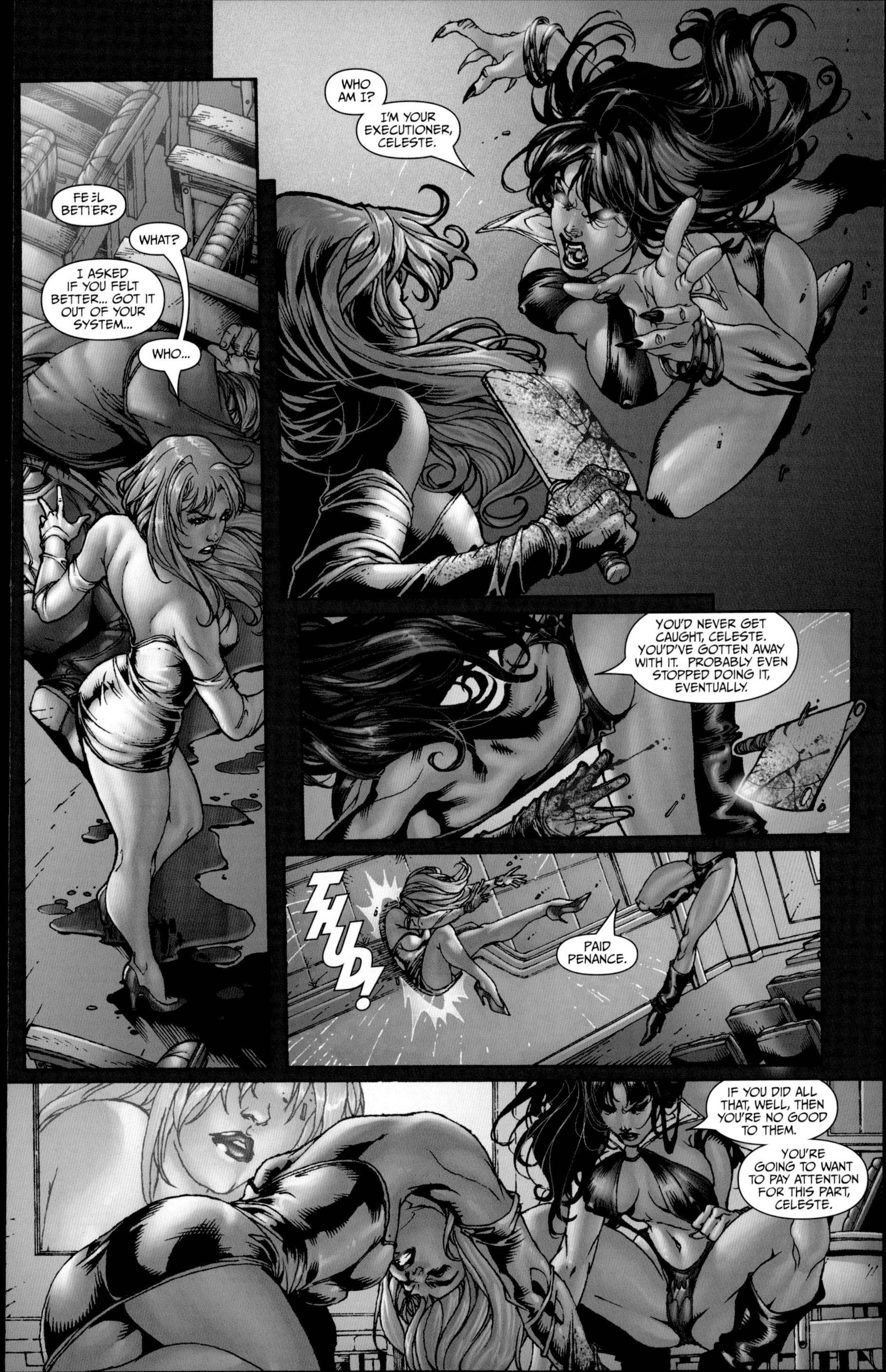
FEEL BETTER?
WHAT?
I ASKED IF YOU FELT BETTER... GOT IT OUT OF YOUR SYSTEM...
WHO...
WHO AM I?
I'M YOUR EXECUTIONER, CELESTE.
YOU'D NEVER GET CAUGHT, CELESTE. YOU'D'VE GOTTEN AWAY WITH IT. PROBABLY EVEN STOPPED DOING IT, EVENTUALLY.
THUD!
PAID PENANCE.
IF YOU DID ALL THAT, WELL, THEN YOU'RE NO GOOD TO THEM.
YOU'RE GOING TO WANT TO PAY ATTENTION FOR THIS PART, CELESTE.

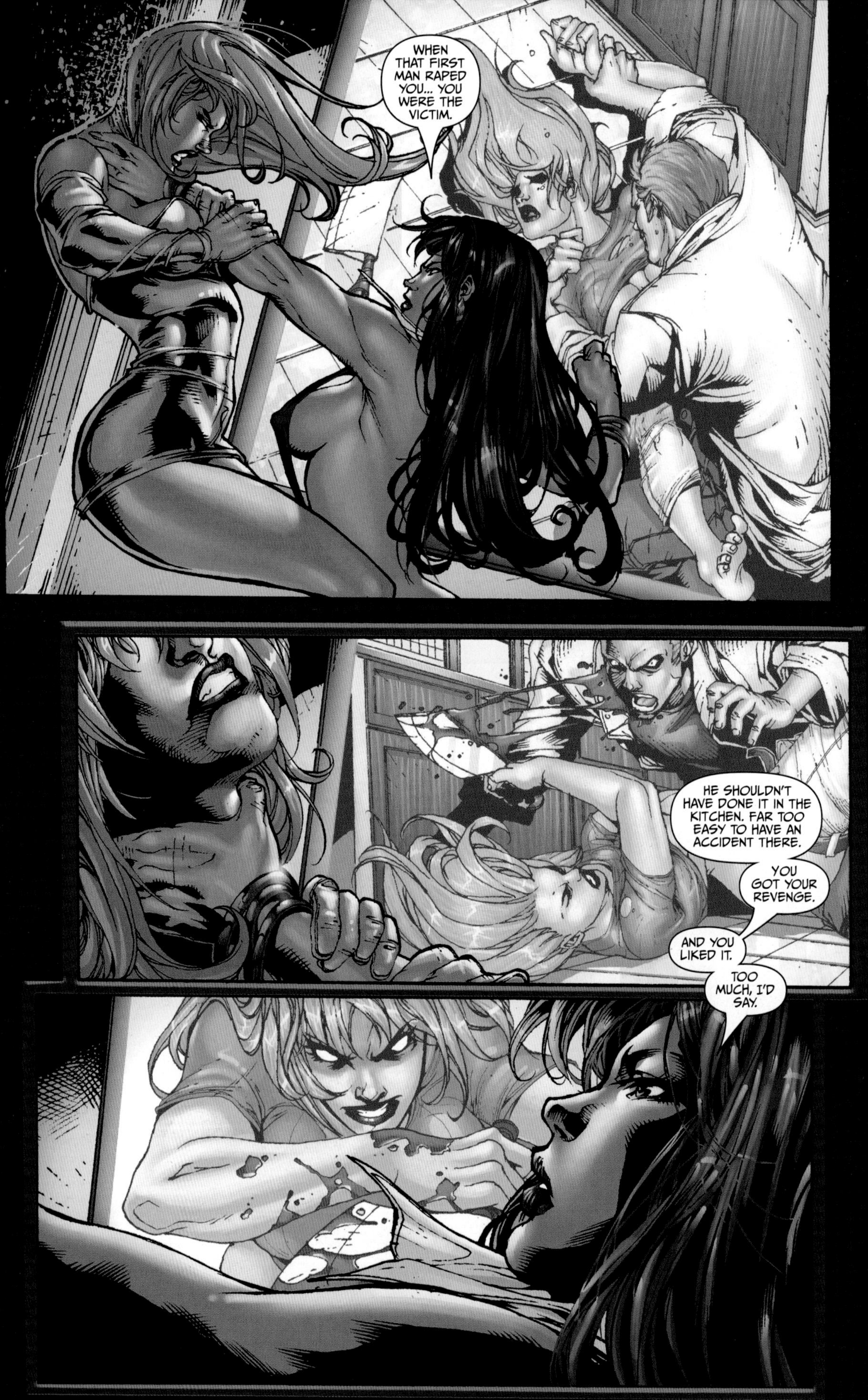
WHEN THAT FIRST MAN RAPED YOU... YOU WERE THE VICTIM.
HE SHOULDN'T HAVE DONE IT IN THE KITCHEN. FAR TOO EASY TO HAVE AN ACCIDENT THERE.
YOU GOT YOUR REVENGE.
AND YOU LIKED IT.
TOO MUCH, I'D SAY.

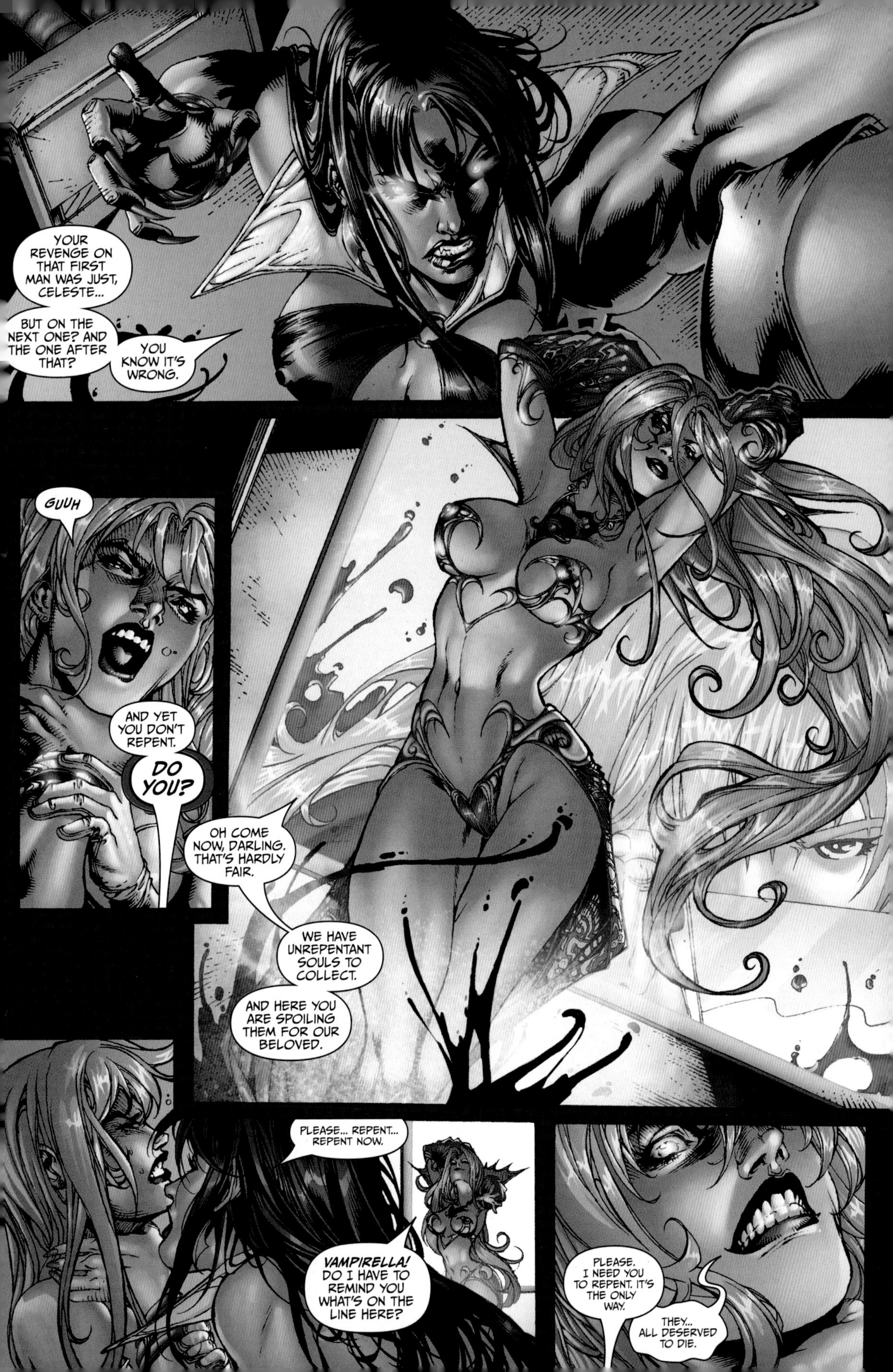
YOUR REVENGE ON THAT FIRST MAN WAS JUST, CELESTE...
BUT ON THE NEXT ONE? AND THE ONE AFTER THAT?
YOU KNOW IT'S WRONG.
GUUH
AND YET YOU DON'T REPENT.
DO YOU?
OH COME NOW, DARLING. THAT'S HARDLY FAIR.
WE HAVE UNREPENTANT SOULS TO COLLECT.
AND HERE YOU ARE SPOILING THEM FOR OUR BELOVED.
PLEASE... REPENT... REPENT NOW.
VAMPIRELLA! DO I HAVE TO REMIND YOU WHAT'S ON THE LINE HERE?
PLEASE. I NEED YOU TO REPENT. IT'S THE ONLY WAY.
THEY... ALL DESERVED TO DIE.

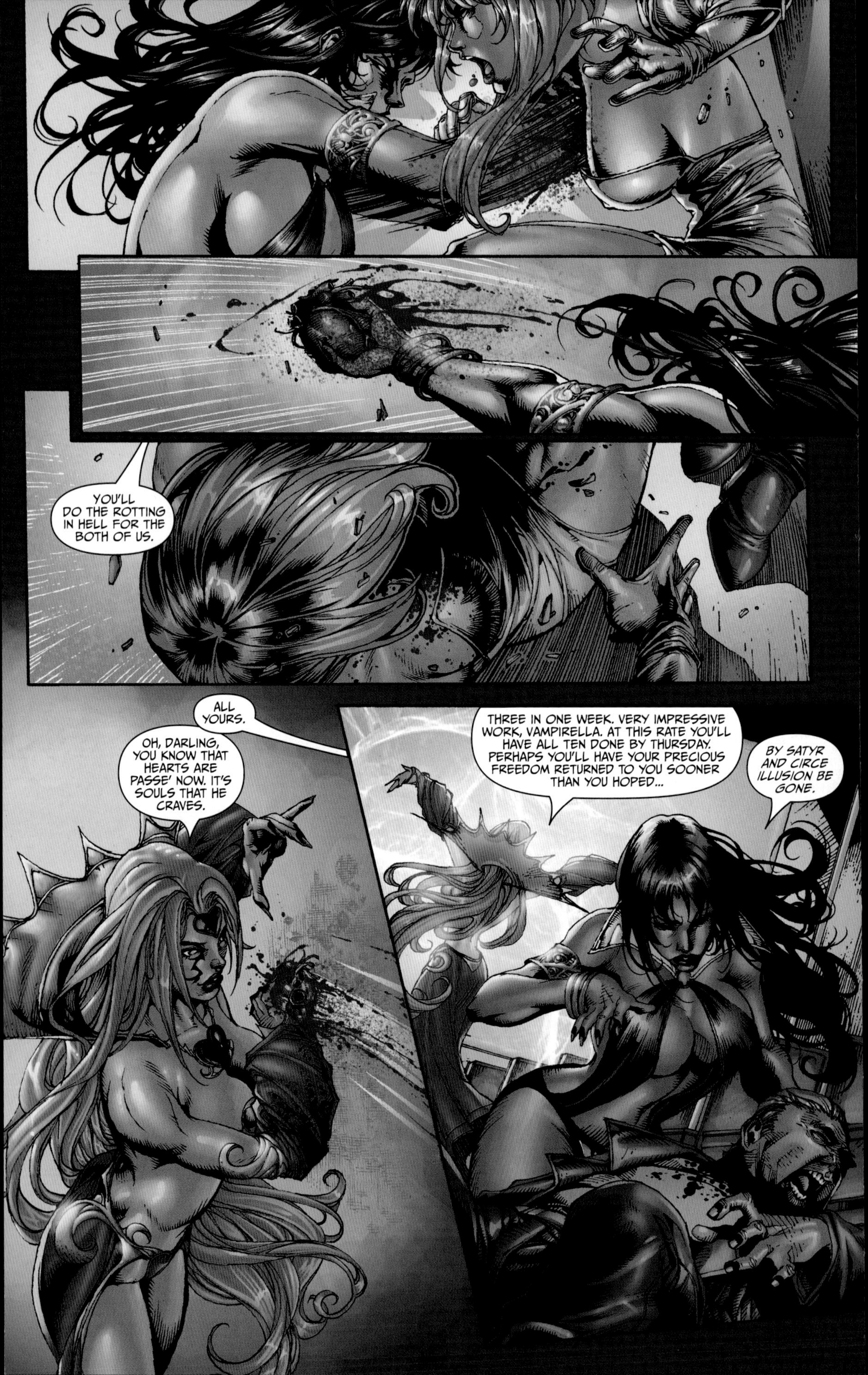
YOU'LL DO THE ROTTING IN HELL FOR THE BOTH OF US.
ALL YOURS.
OH, DARLING, YOU KNOW THAT HEARTS ARE PASSE' NOW. IT'S SOULS THAT HE CRAVES.
THREE IN ONE WEEK. VERY IMPRESSIVE WORK, VAMPIRELLA. AT THIS RATE YOU'LL HAVE ALL TEN DONE BY THURSDAY. PERHAPS YOU'LL HAVE YOUR PRECIOUS FREEDOM RETURNED TO YOU SOONER THAN YOU HOPED...
BY SATYR AND CIRCE ILLUSION BE GONE.

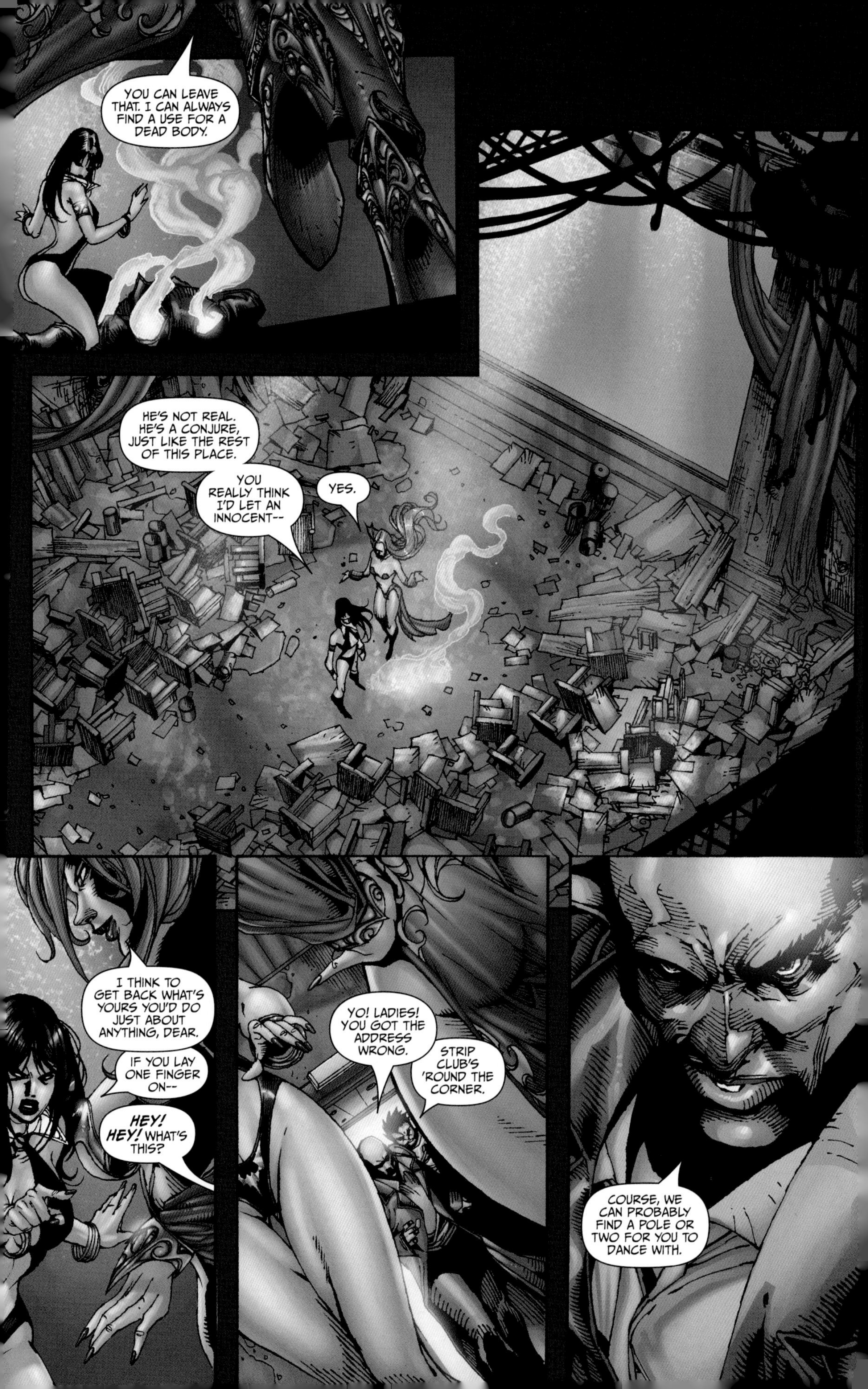
YOU CAN LEAVE THAT. I CAN ALWAYS FIND A USE FOR A DEAD BODY.
HE'S NOT REAL. HE'S A CONJURE, JUST LIKE THE REST OF THIS PLACE.
YOU REALLY THINK I'D LET AN INNOCENT--
YES.
I THINK TO GET BACK WHAT'S YOURS YOU'D DO JUST ABOUT ANYTHING, DEAR.
IF YOU LAY ONE FINGER ON--
HEY! HEY! WHAT'S THIS?
YO! LADIES! YOU GOT THE ADDRESS WRONG.
STRIP CLUB'S 'ROUND THE CORNER.
COURSE, WE CAN PROBABLY FIND A POLE OR TWO FOR YOU TO DANCE WITH.

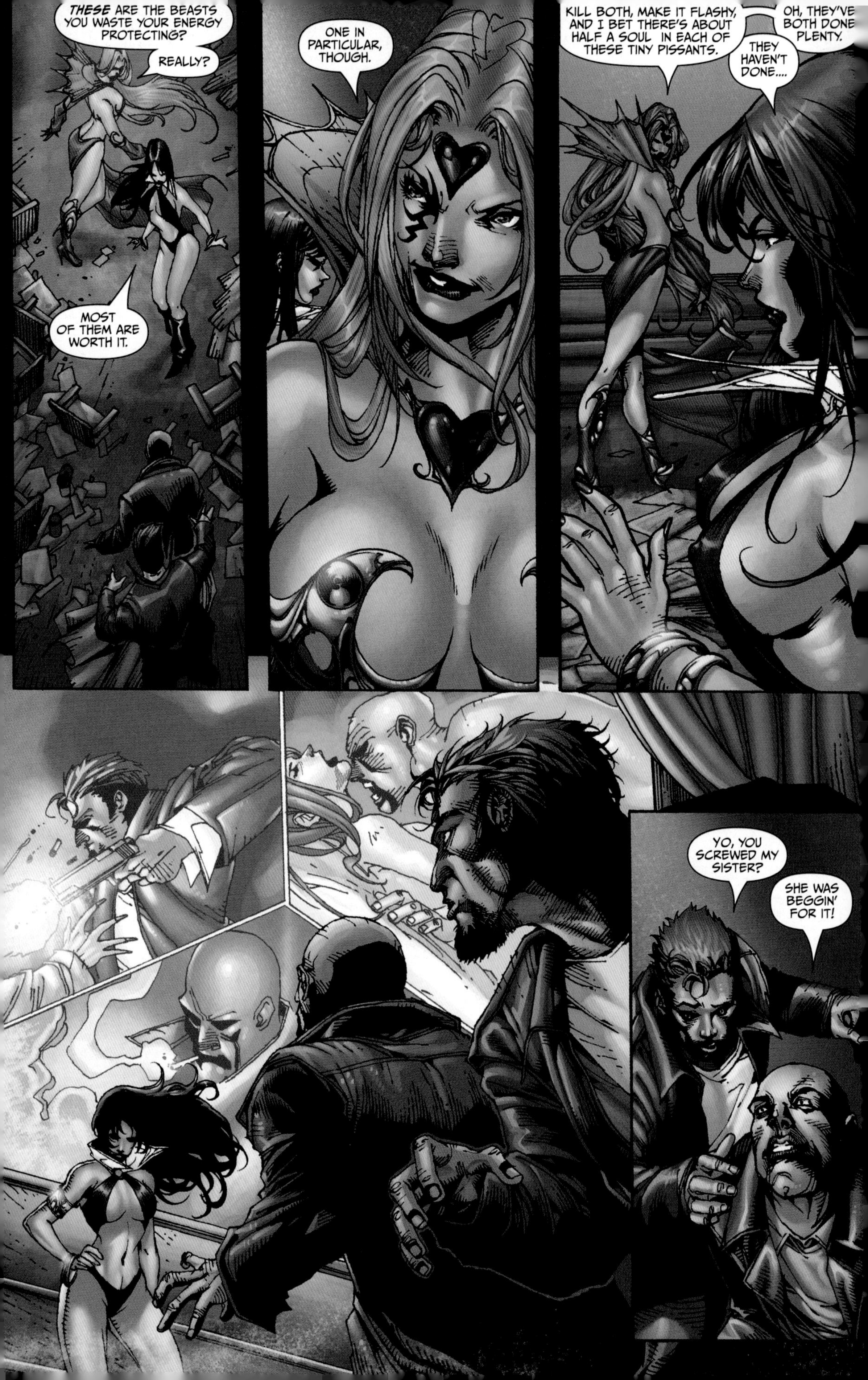
THESE ARE THE BEASTS YOU WASTE YOUR ENERGY PROTECTING?
REALLY?
MOST OF THEM ARE WORTH IT.
ONE IN PARTICULAR, THOUGH.
KILL BOTH, MAKE IT FLASHY, AND I BET THERE'S ABOUT HALF A SOUL IN EACH OF THESE TINY PISSANTS.
THEY HAVEN'T DONE....
OH, THEY'VE BOTH DONE PLENTY.
YO, YOU SCREWED MY SISTER?
SHE WAS BEGGIN' FOR IT!

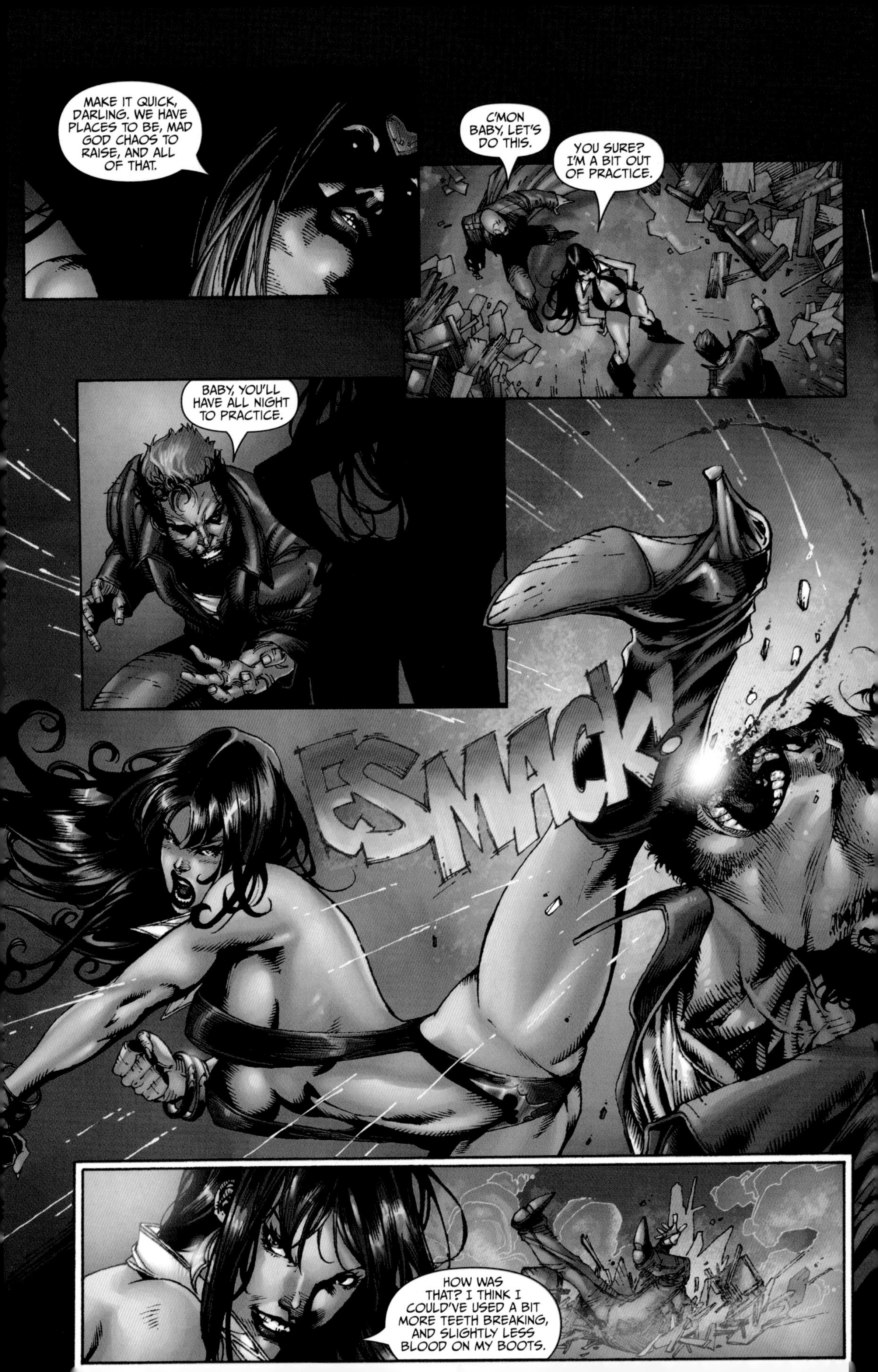
MAKE IT QUICK, DARLING. WE HAVE PLACES TO BE, MAD GOD CHAOS TO RAISE, AND ALL OF THAT.
C'MON BABY, LET'S DO THIS.
YOU SURE? I'M A BIT OUT OF PRACTICE.
BABY, YOU'LL HAVE ALL NIGHT TO PRACTICE.
SMACK
HOW WAS THAT? I THINK I COULD'VE USED A BIT MORE TEETH BREAKING, AND SLIGHTLY LESS BLOOD ON MY BOOTS.

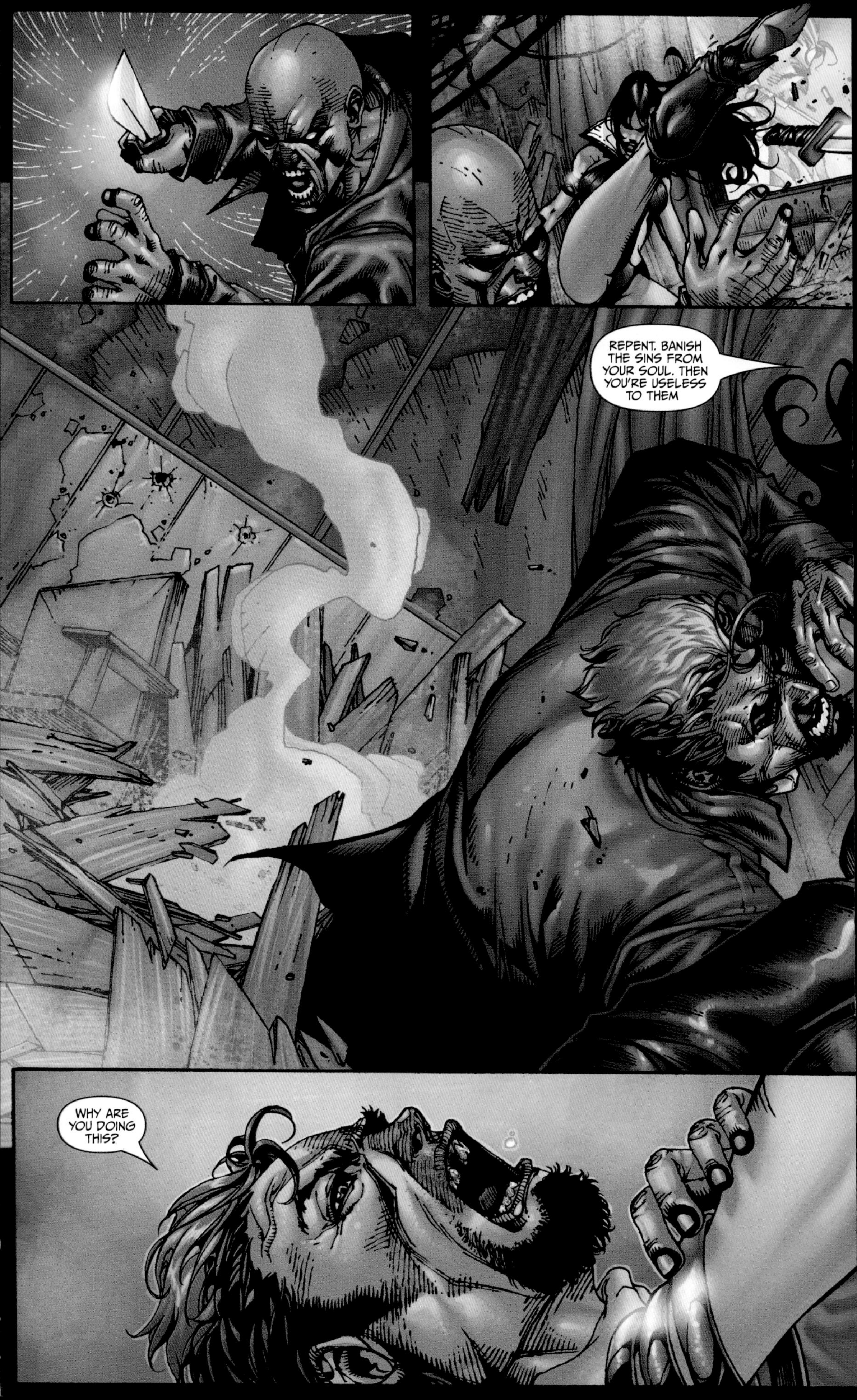
REPENT. BANISH THE SINS FROM YOUR SOUL. THEN YOU'RE USELESS TO THEM
WHY ARE YOU DOING THIS?

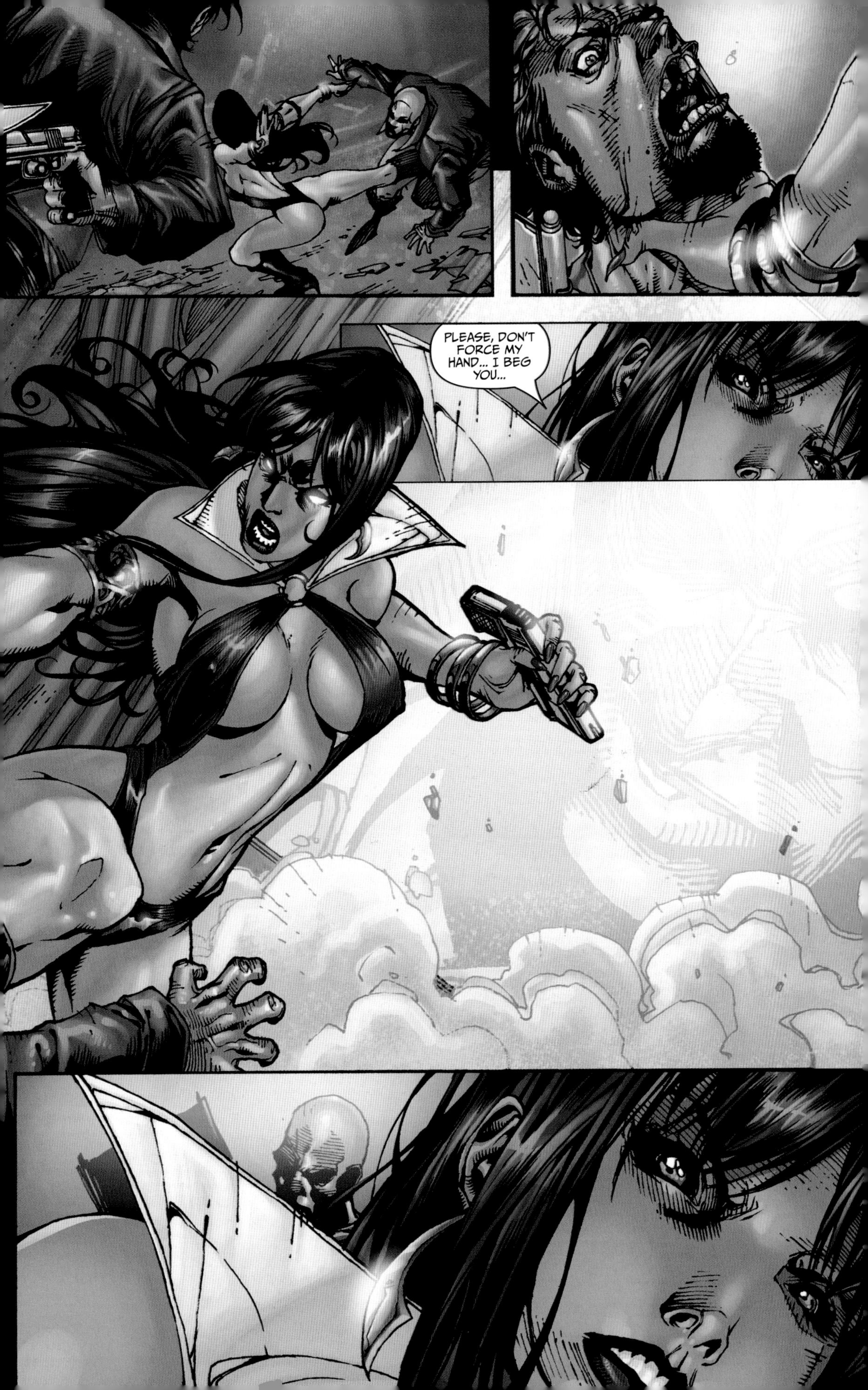
PLEASE, DON'T FORCE MY HAND... I BEG YOU...

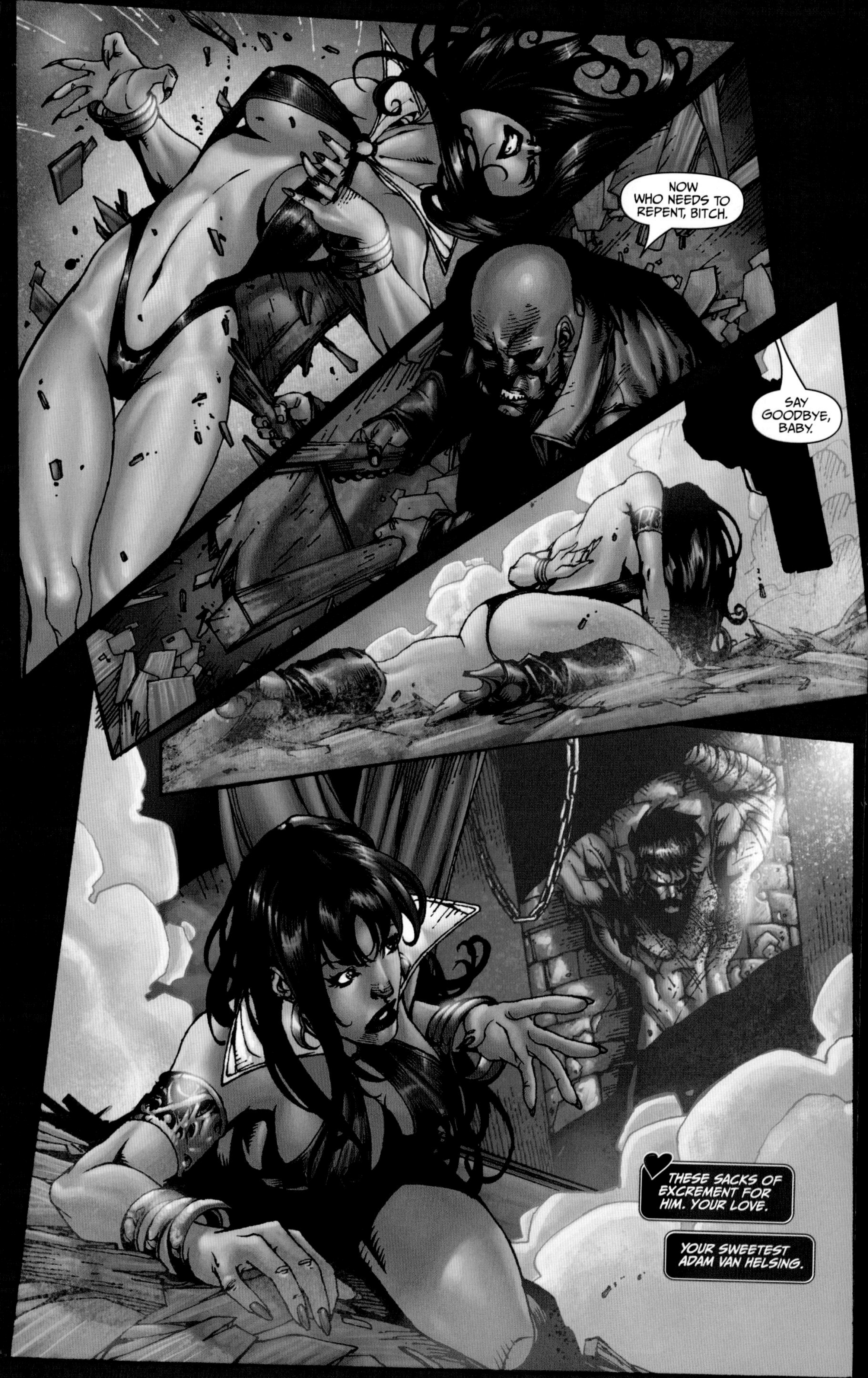
NOW WHO NEEDS TO REPENT, BITCH.
SAY GOODBYE, BABY.
THESE SACKS OF EXCREMENT FOR HIM. YOUR LOVE.
YOUR SWEETEST ADAM VAN HELSING.

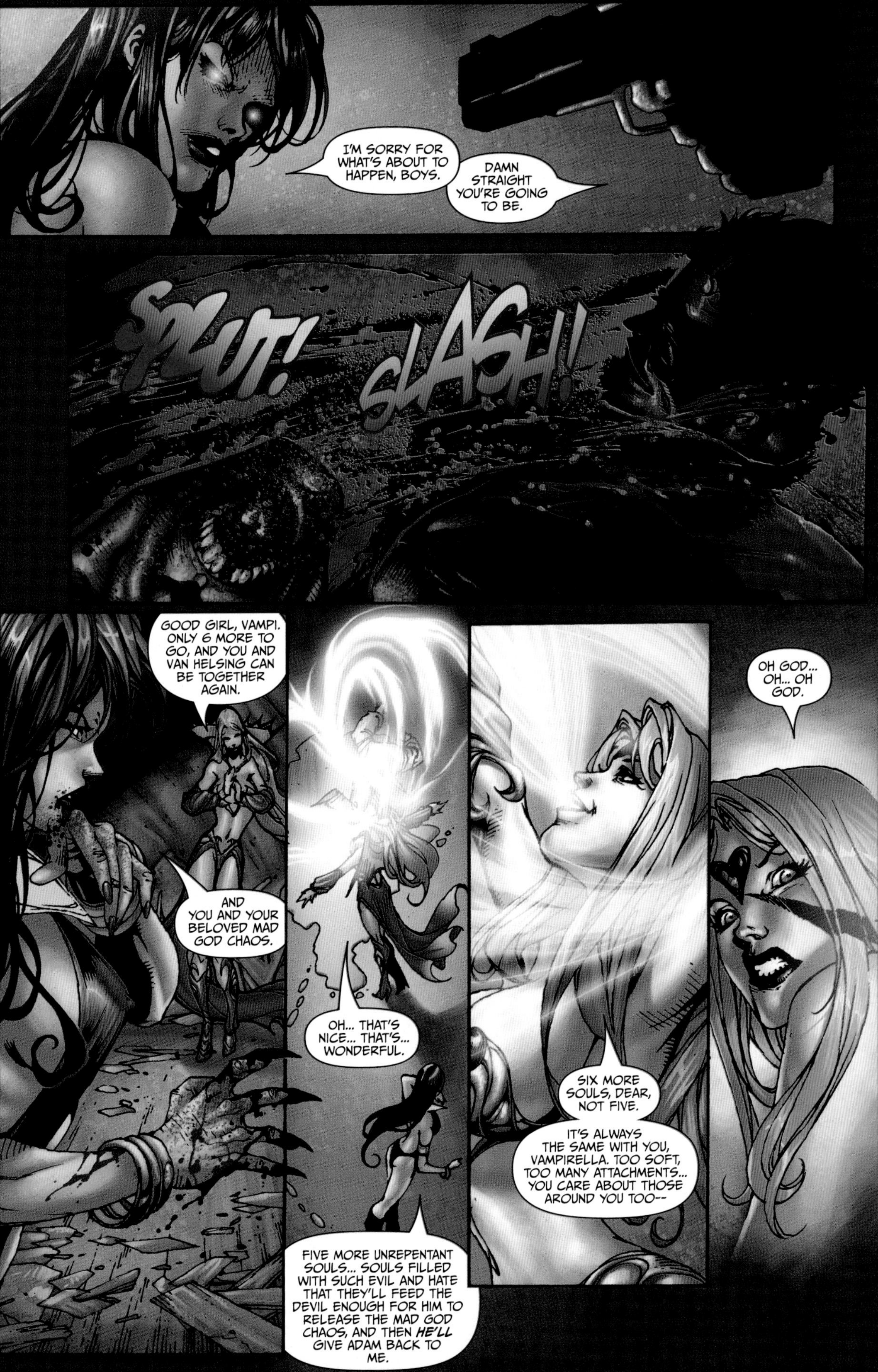
I'M SORRY FOR WHAT'S ABOUT TO HAPPEN, BOYS.
DAMN STRAIGHT YOU'RE GOING TO BE.
SPLUT!
SLASH!
GOOD GIRL, VAMPI. ONLY 6 MORE TO GO, AND YOU AND VAN HELSING CAN BE TOGETHER AGAIN.
AND YOU AND YOUR BELOVED MAD GOD CHAOS.
OH... THAT'S NICE... THAT'S... WONDERFUL.
FIVE MORE UNREPENTANT SOULS... SOULS FILLED WITH SUCH EVIL AND HATE THAT THEY'LL FEED THE DEVIL ENOUGH FOR HIM TO RELEASE THE MAD GOD CHAOS, AND THEN HE'LL GIVE ADAM BACK TO ME.
SIX MORE SOULS, DEAR, NOT FIVE.
IT'S ALWAYS THE SAME WITH YOU, VAMPIRELLA. TOO SOFT, TOO MANY ATTACHMENTS... YOU CARE ABOUT THOSE AROUND YOU TOO--
OH GOD... OH... OH GOD.

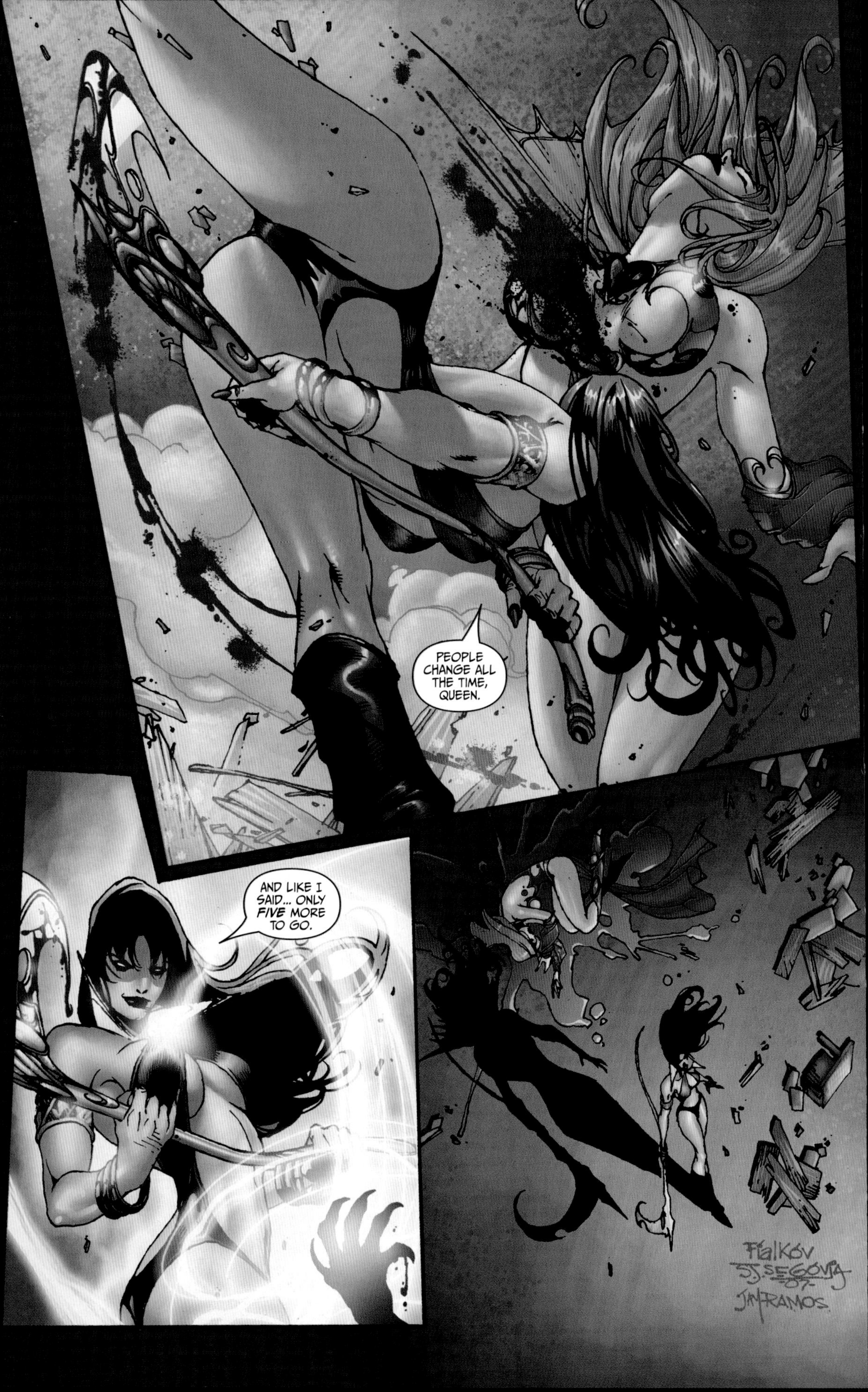
PEOPLE CHANGE ALL THE TIME, QUEEN.
AND LIKE I SAID... ONLY *FIVE* MORE TO GO.
FIALKOV
S.J. SEGOVIA '07
JAY RAMOS

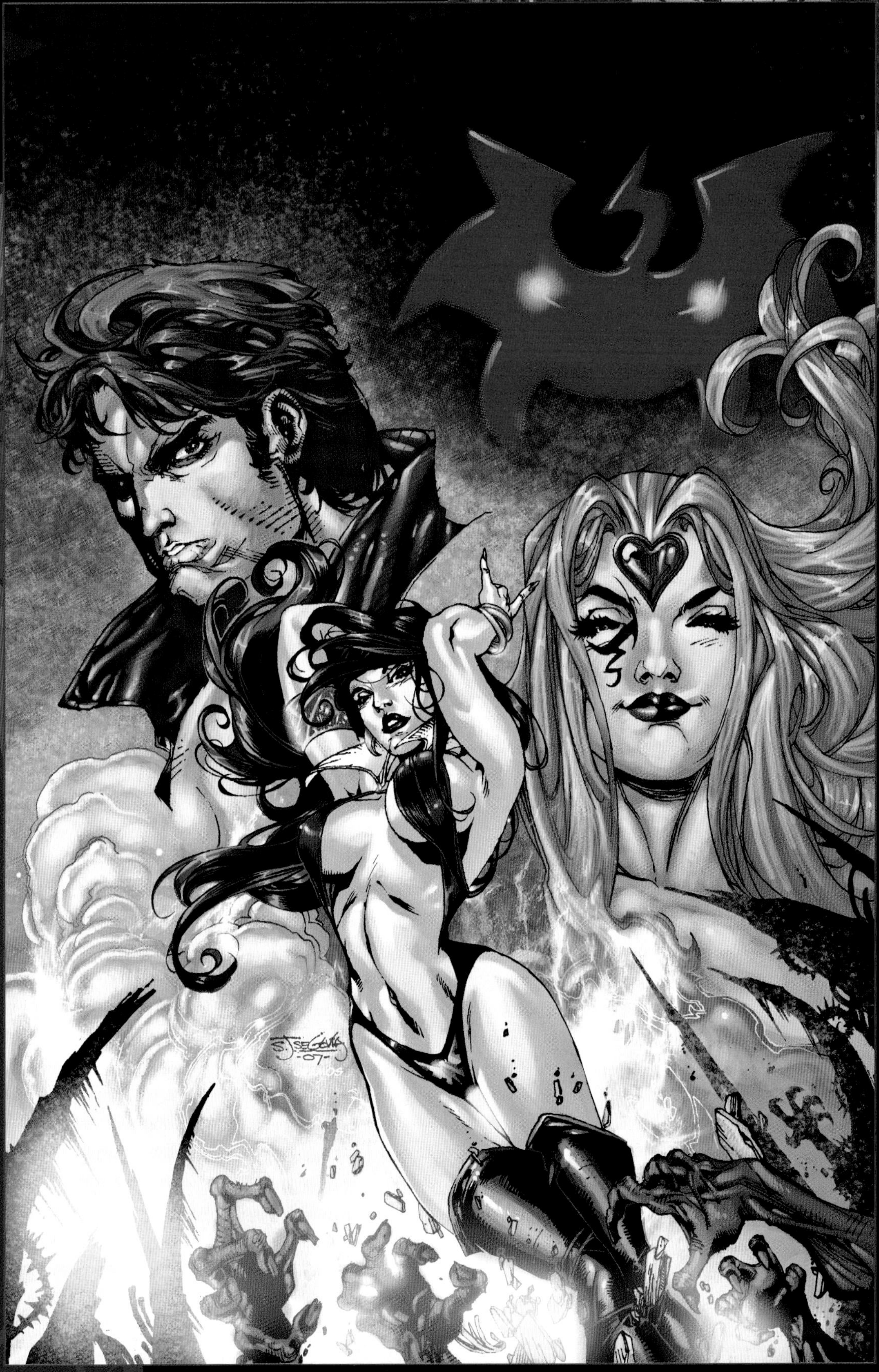

VENGEANCE OF VAMPIRELA PART #2

Vampirella Quarterly: Summer 2007 #1 cover by Stephen Segovia

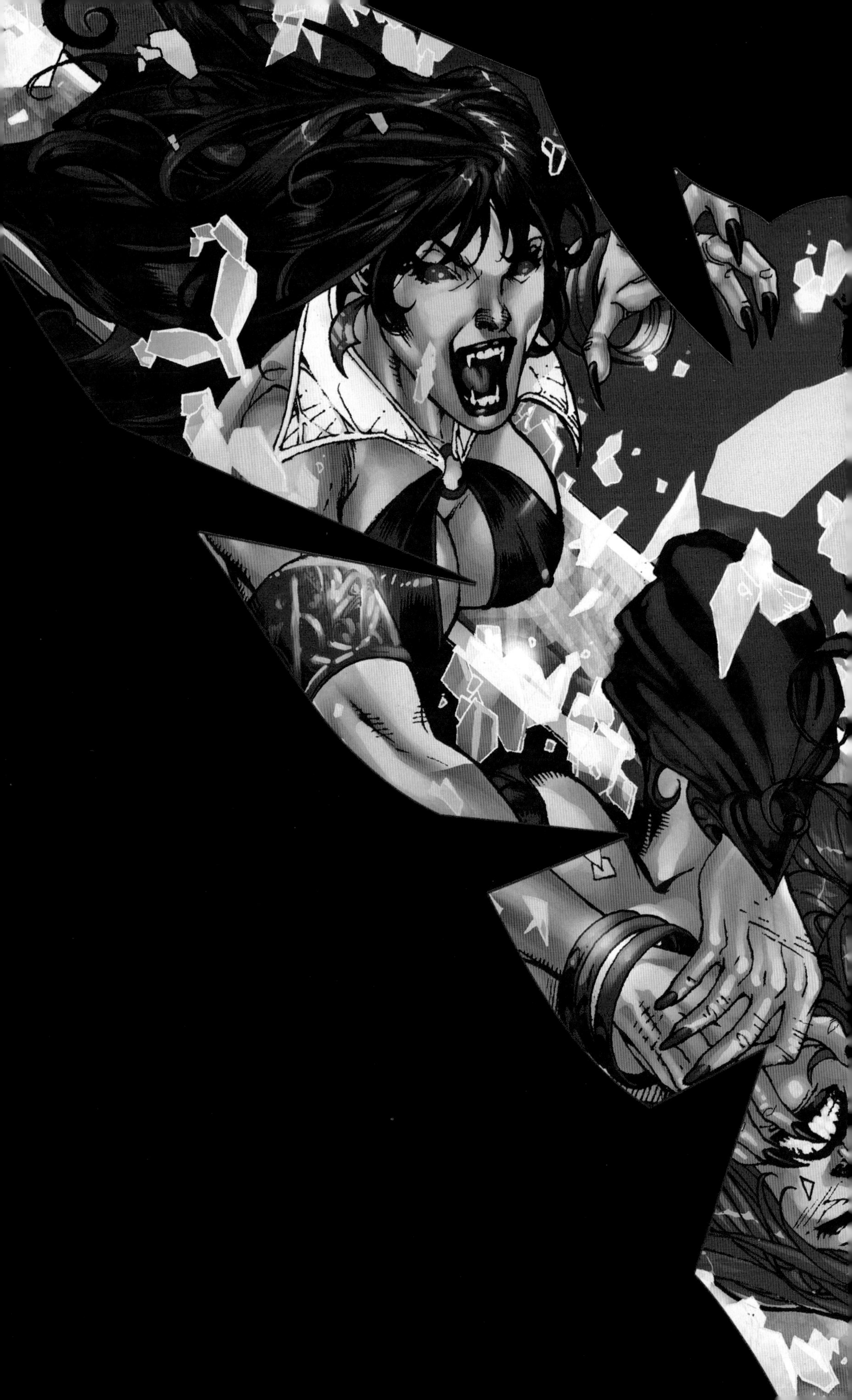

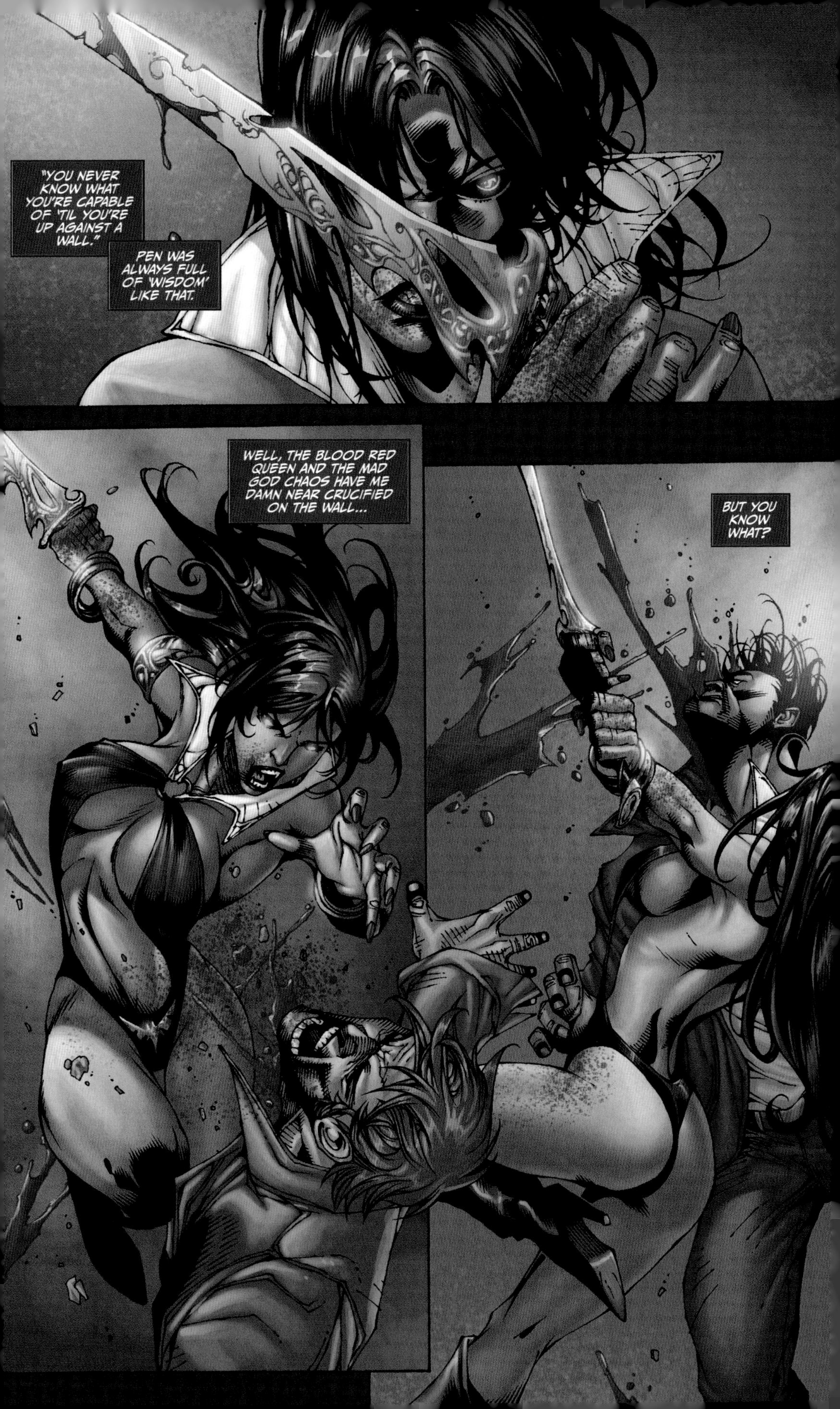
"YOU NEVER KNOW WHAT YOU'RE CAPABLE OF 'TIL YOU'RE UP AGAINST A WALL."
PEN WAS ALWAYS FULL OF 'WISDOM' LIKE THAT.
WELL, THE BLOOD RED QUEEN AND THE MAD GOD CHAOS HAVE ME DAMN NEAR CRUCIFIED ON THE WALL...
BUT YOU KNOW WHAT?

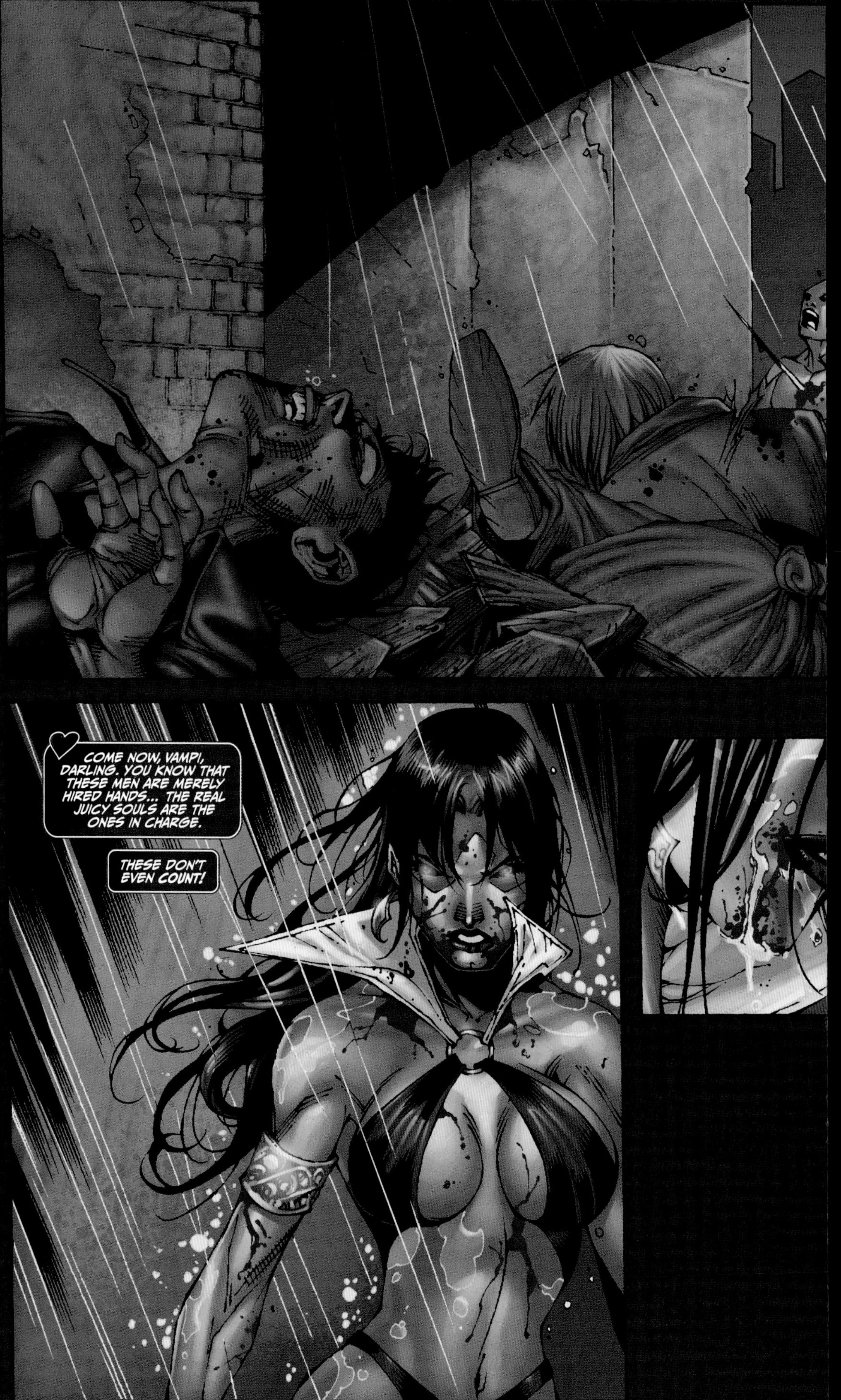
COME NOW, VAMPI, DARLING. YOU KNOW THAT THESE MEN ARE MERELY HIRED HANDS... THE REAL JUICY SOULS ARE THE ONES IN CHARGE.
THESE DON'T EVEN COUNT!

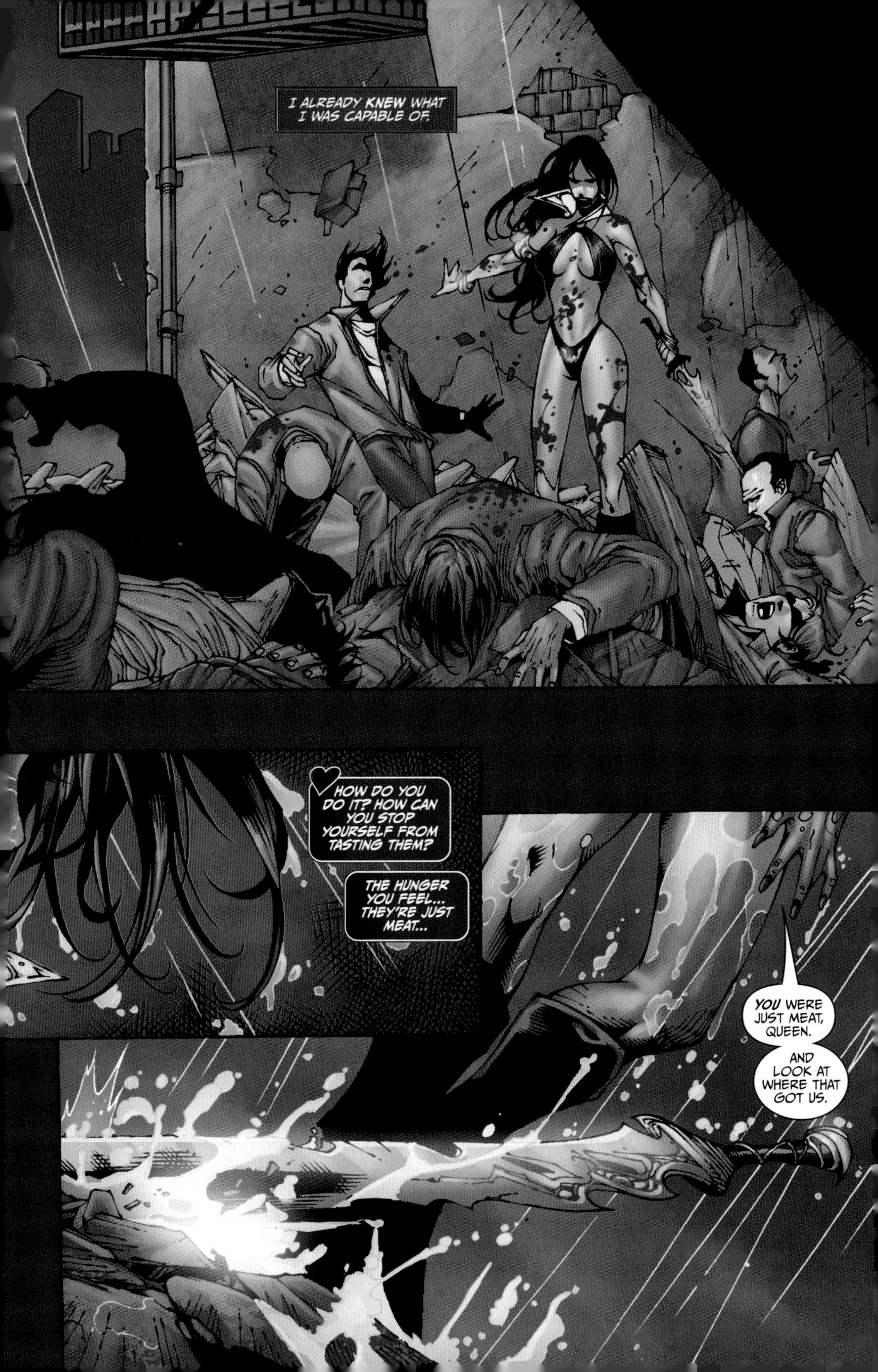
I ALREADY KNEW WHAT I WAS CAPABLE OF.
HOW DO YOU DO IT? HOW CAN YOU STOP YOURSELF FROM TASTING THEM?
THE HUNGER YOU FEEL... THEY'RE JUST MEAT...
YOU WERE JUST MEAT, QUEEN.
AND LOOK AT WHERE THAT GOT US.

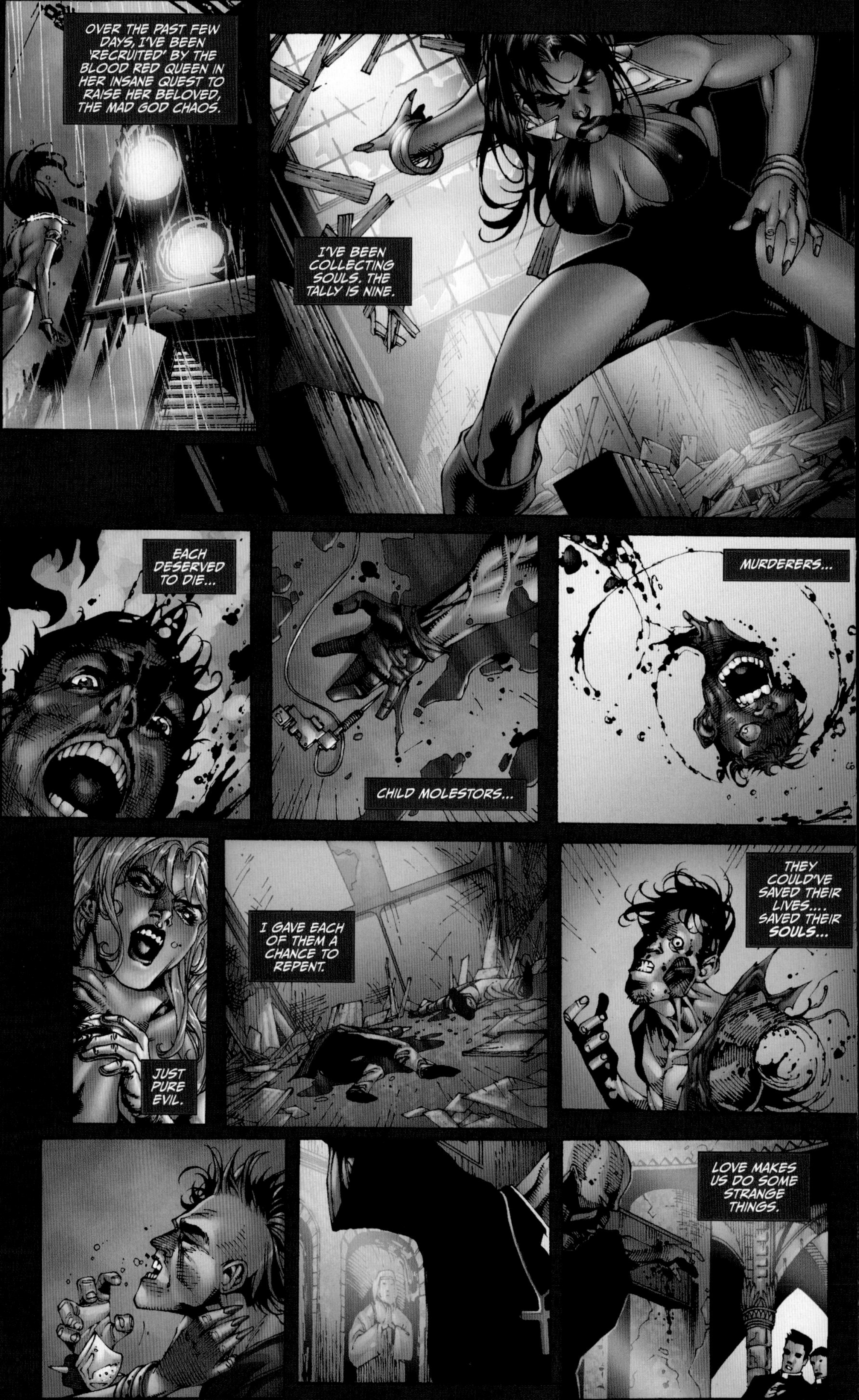
OVER THE PAST FEW DAYS, I'VE BEEN 'RECRUITED' BY THE BLOOD RED QUEEN IN HER INSANE QUEST TO RAISE HER BELOVED, THE MAD GOD CHAOS.
I'VE BEEN COLLECTING SOULS. THE TALLY IS NINE.
EACH DESERVED TO DIE...
CHILD MOLESTORS...
MURDERERS...
JUST PURE EVIL.
I GAVE EACH OF THEM A CHANCE TO REPENT.
THEY COULD'VE SAVED THEIR LIVES.... SAVED THEIR SOULS...
LOVE MAKES US DO SOME STRANGE THINGS.

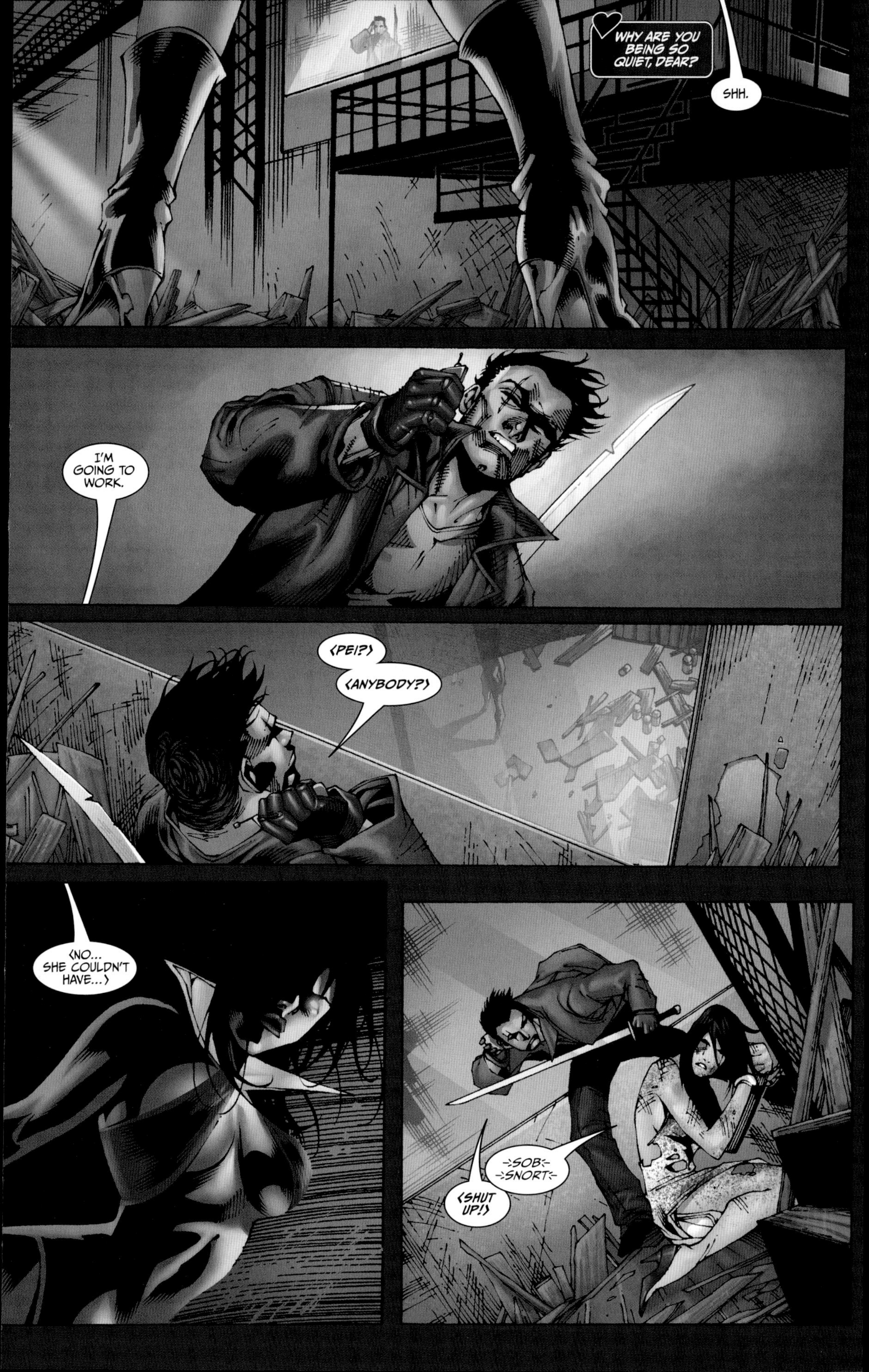

WHY ARE YOU BEING SO QUIET, DEAR?
SHH.
I'M GOING TO WORK.
‹PEI!?›
‹ANYBODY?›
‹NO... SHE COULDN'T HAVE...›
-SOB-
-SNORT-
‹SHUT UP!›

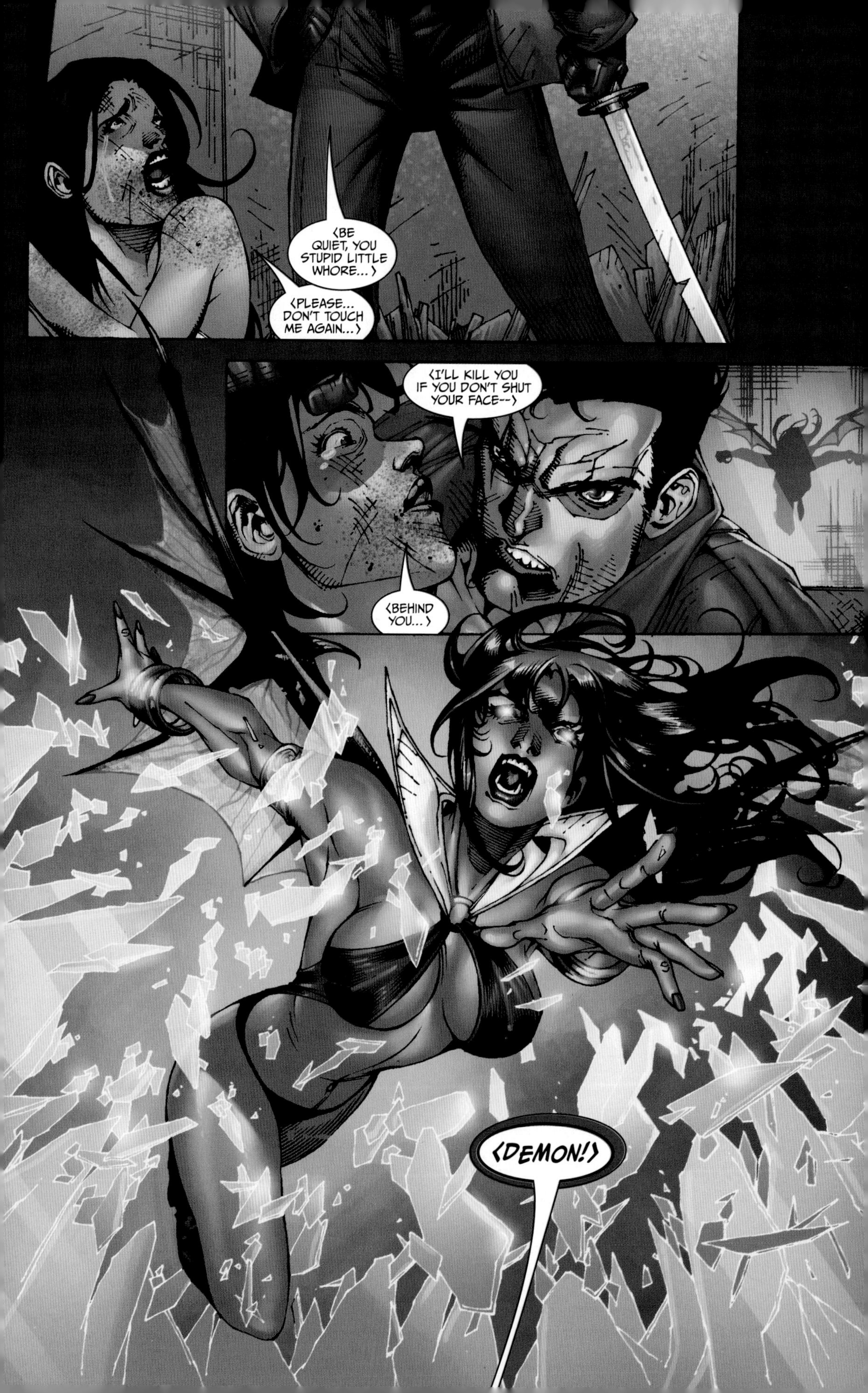
‹BE QUIET, YOU STUPID LITTLE WHORE...›
‹PLEASE... DON'T TOUCH ME AGAIN...›
‹I'LL KILL YOU IF YOU DON'T SHUT YOUR FACE--›
‹BEHIND YOU...›
‹DEMON!›

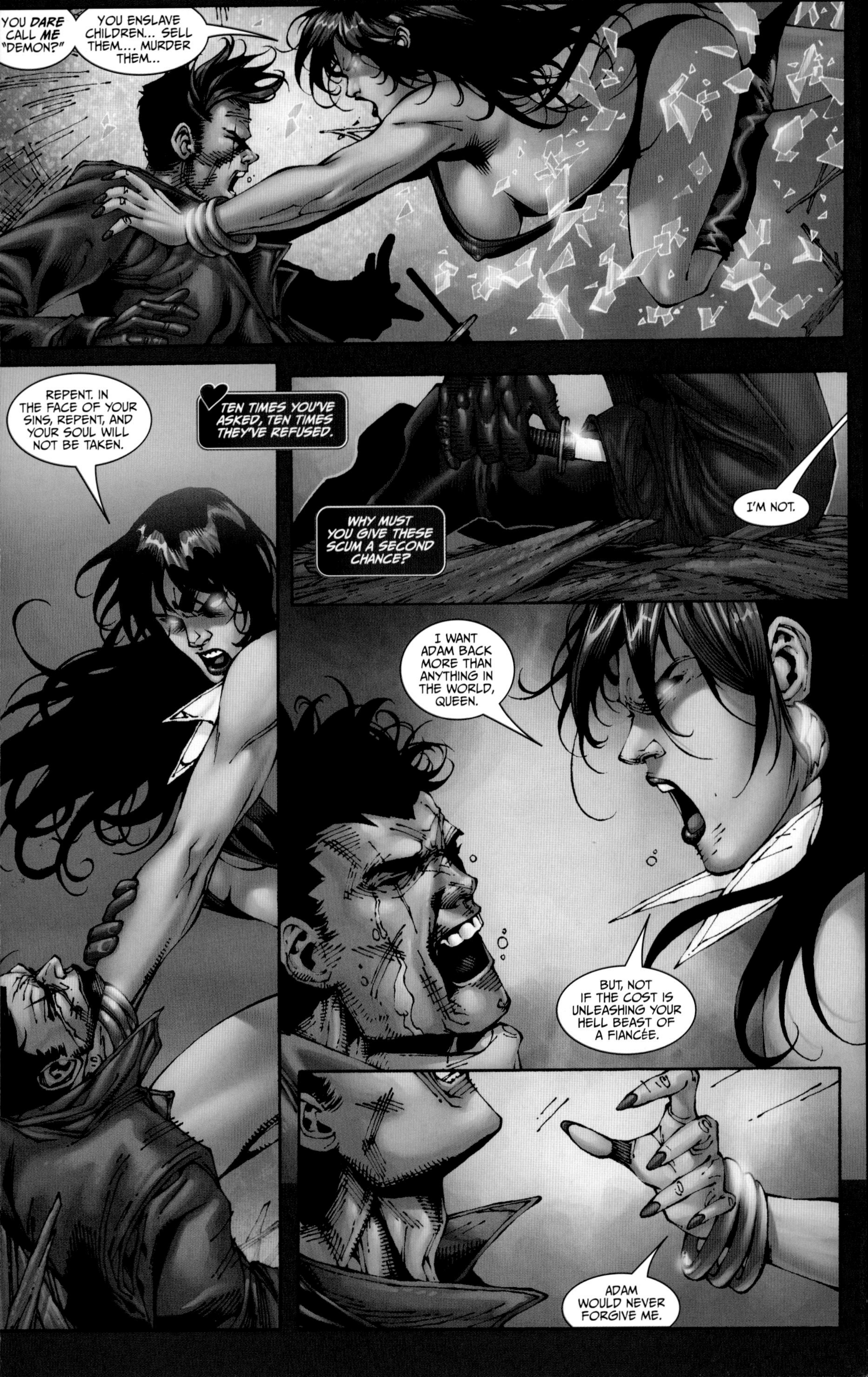
YOU DARE CALL ME "DEMON?"
YOU ENSLAVE CHILDREN... SELL THEM.... MURDER THEM...
REPENT. IN THE FACE OF YOUR SINS, REPENT, AND YOUR SOUL WILL NOT BE TAKEN.
TEN TIMES YOU'VE ASKED, TEN TIMES THEY'VE REFUSED.
WHY MUST YOU GIVE THESE SCUM A SECOND CHANCE?
I'M NOT.
I WANT ADAM BACK MORE THAN ANYTHING IN THE WORLD, QUEEN.
BUT, NOT IF THE COST IS UNLEASHING YOUR HELL BEAST OF A FIANCÉE.
ADAM WOULD NEVER FORGIVE ME.

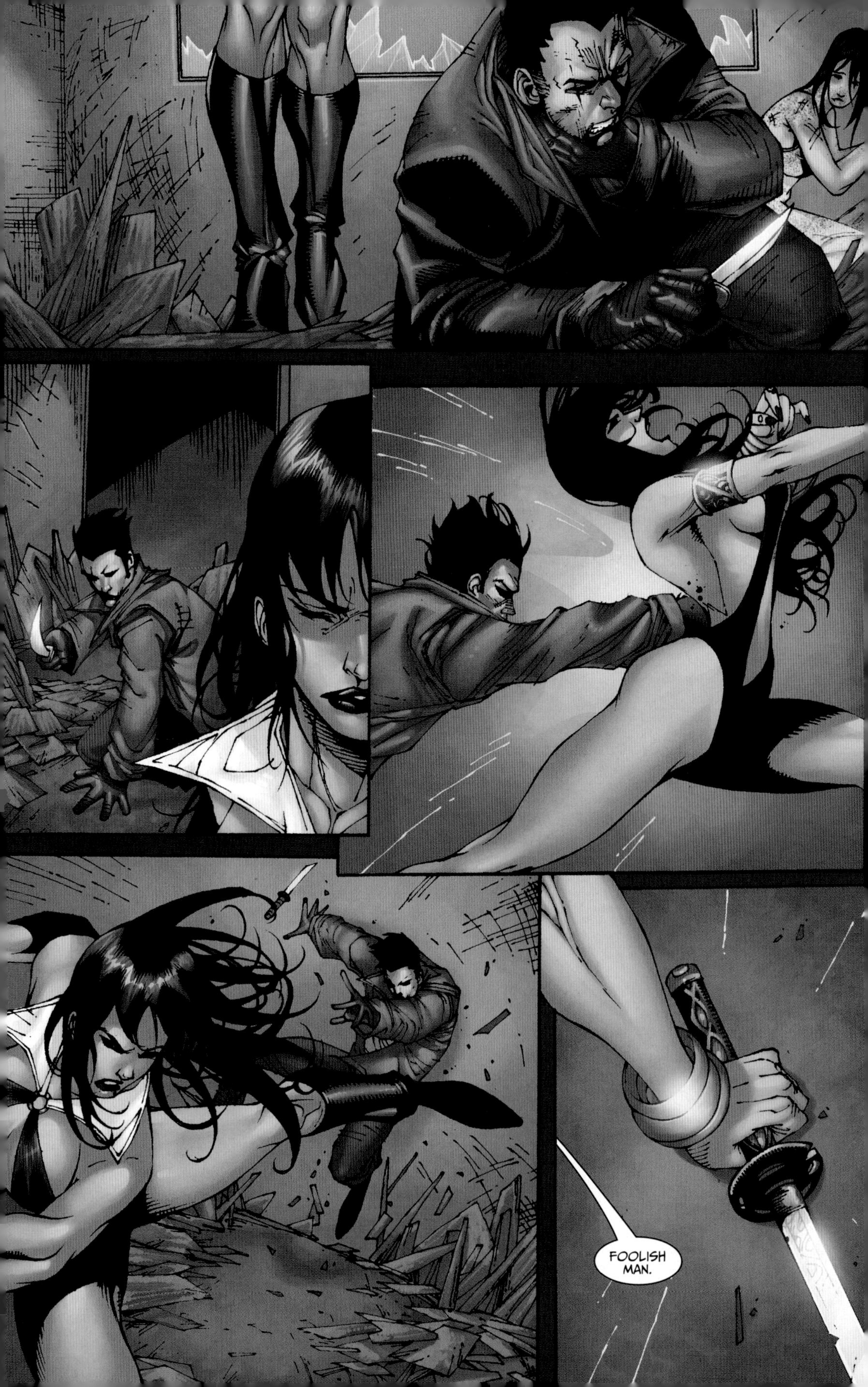
FOOLISH MAN.

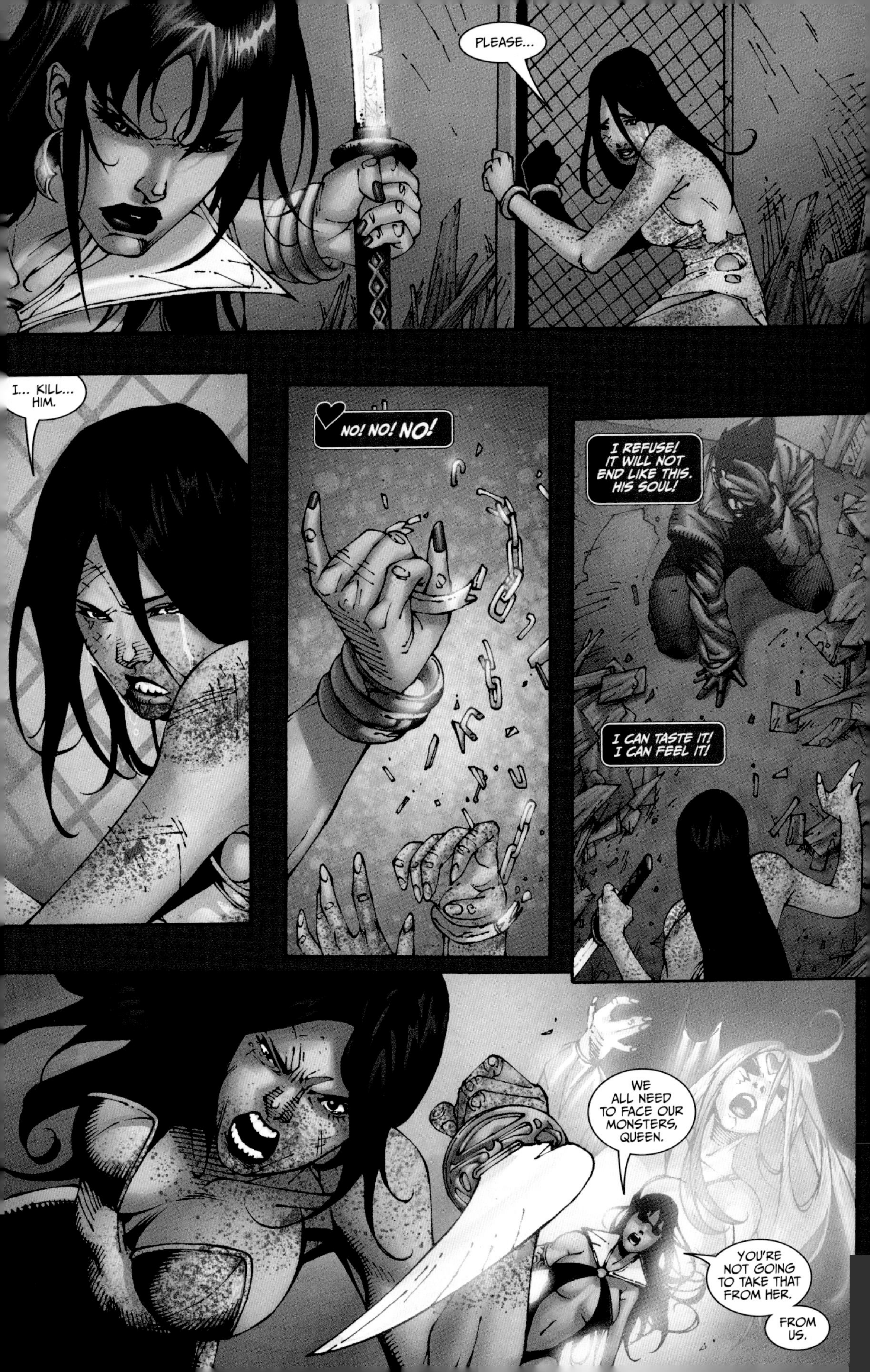
PLEASE...
I... KILL... HIM.
NO! NO! NO!
I REFUSE! IT WILL NOT END LIKE THIS. HIS SOUL!
I CAN TASTE IT! I CAN FEEL IT!
WE ALL NEED TO FACE OUR MONSTERS, QUEEN.
YOU'RE NOT GOING TO TAKE THAT FROM HER.
FROM US.

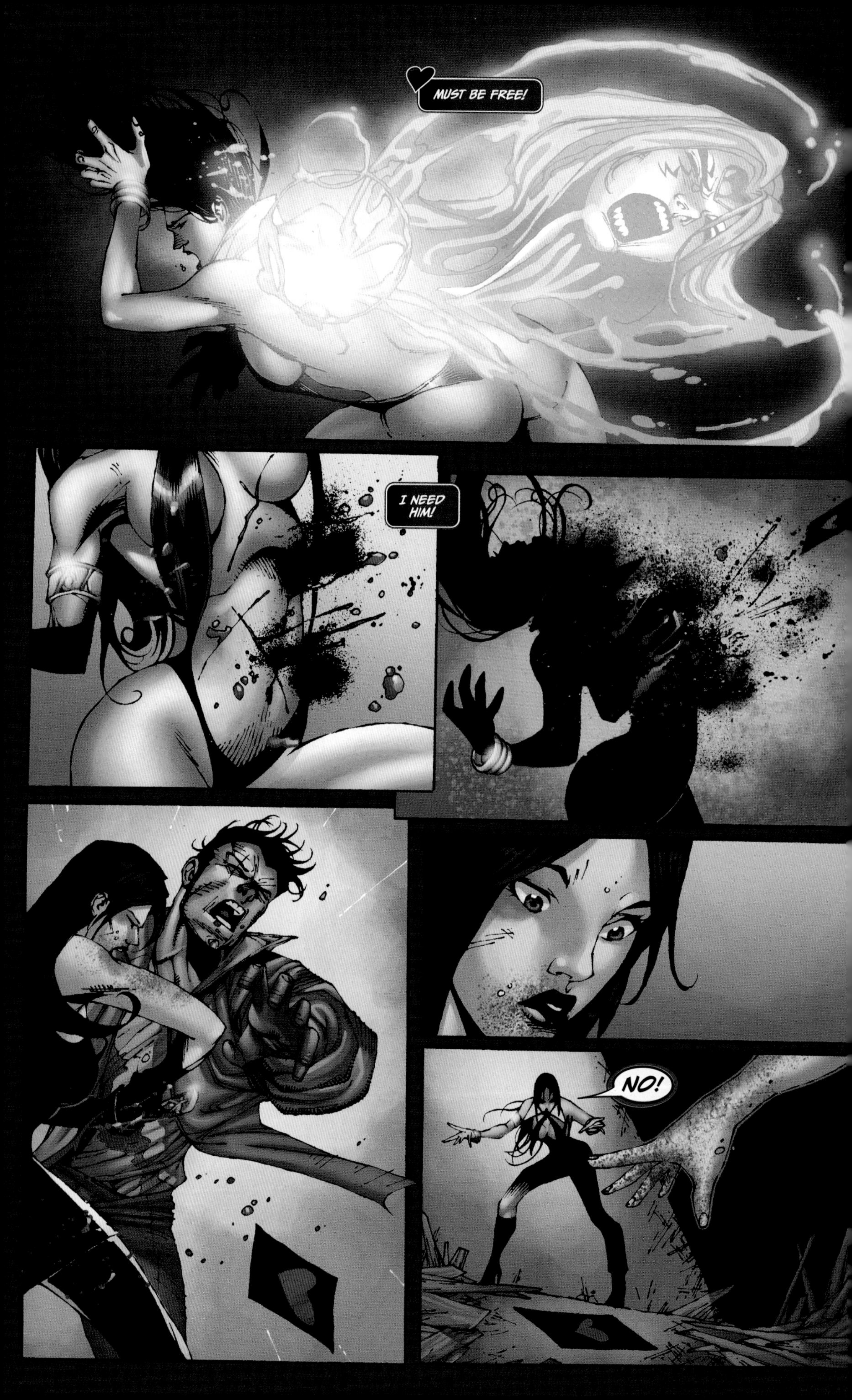
MUST BE FREE!
I NEED HIM!
NO!

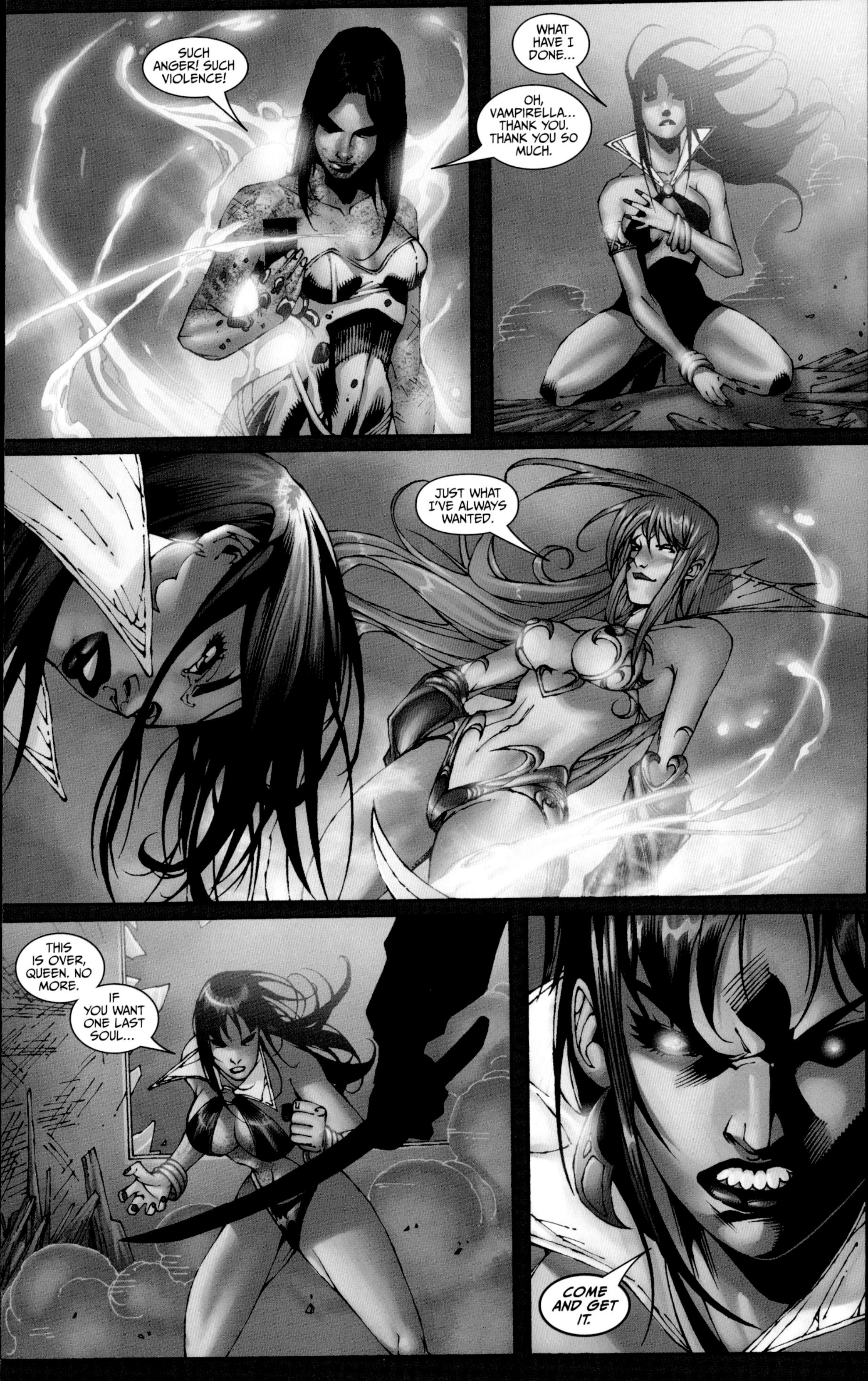
SUCH ANGER! SUCH VIOLENCE!
WHAT HAVE I DONE...
OH, VAMPIRELLA... THANK YOU. THANK YOU SO MUCH.
JUST WHAT I'VE ALWAYS WANTED.
THIS IS OVER, QUEEN. NO MORE.
IF YOU WANT ONE LAST SOUL...
COME AND GET IT.

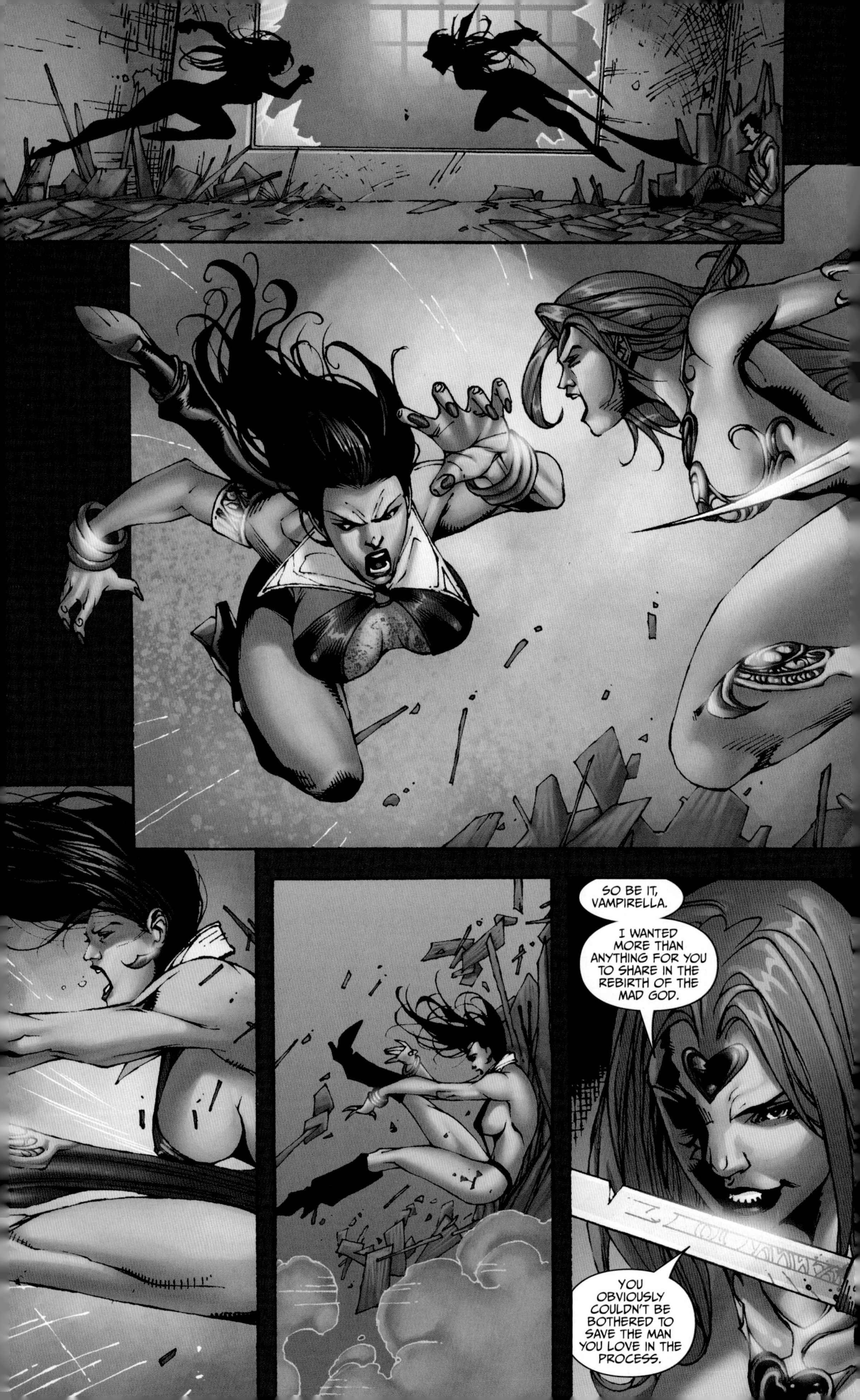
SO BE IT, VAMPIRELLA.
I WANTED MORE THAN ANYTHING FOR YOU TO SHARE IN THE REBIRTH OF THE MAD GOD.
YOU OBVIOUSLY COULDN'T BE BOTHERED TO SAVE THE MAN YOU LOVE IN THE PROCESS.

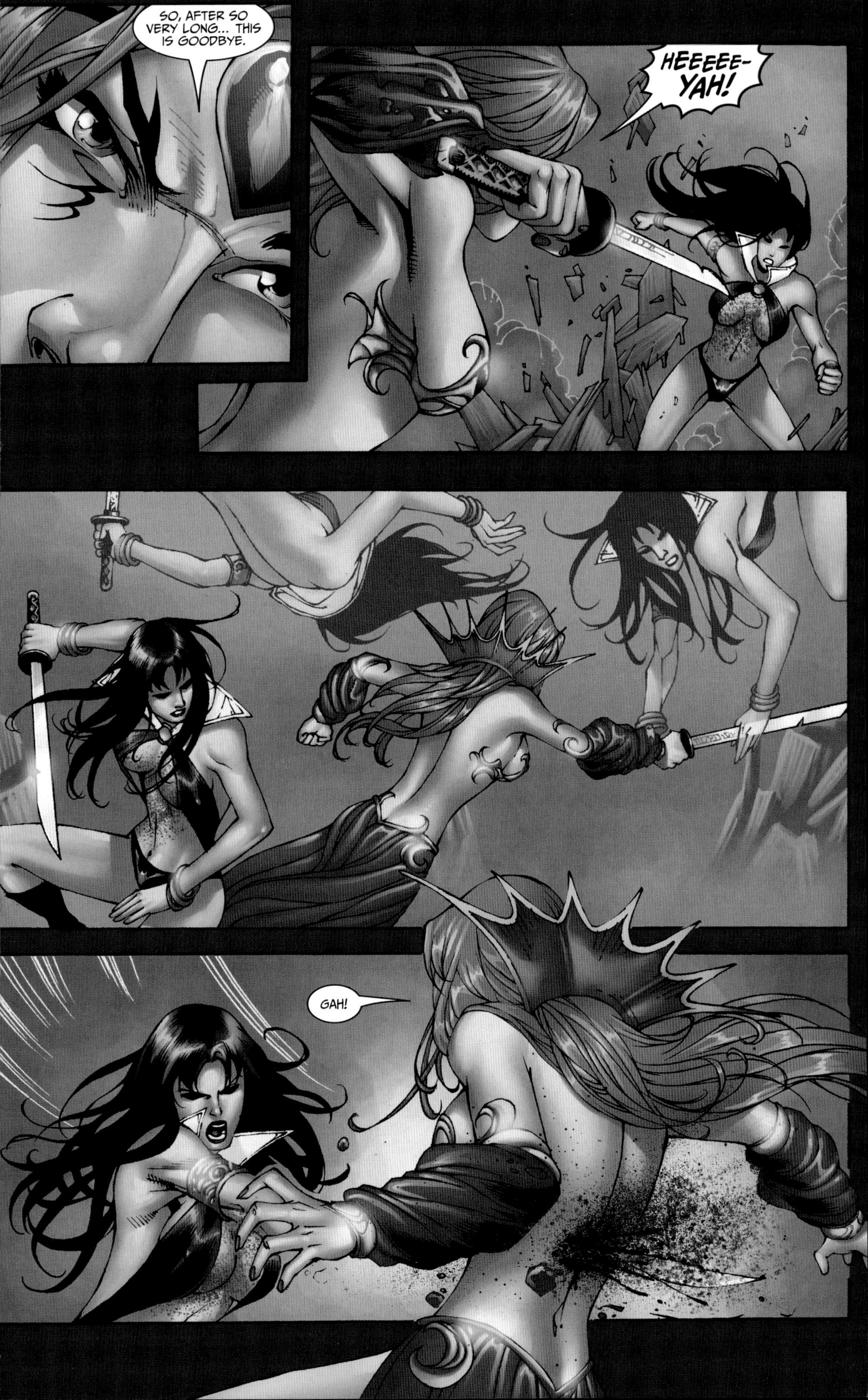
SO, AFTER SO VERY LONG... THIS IS GOODBYE.
HEEEEE-YAH!
GAH!

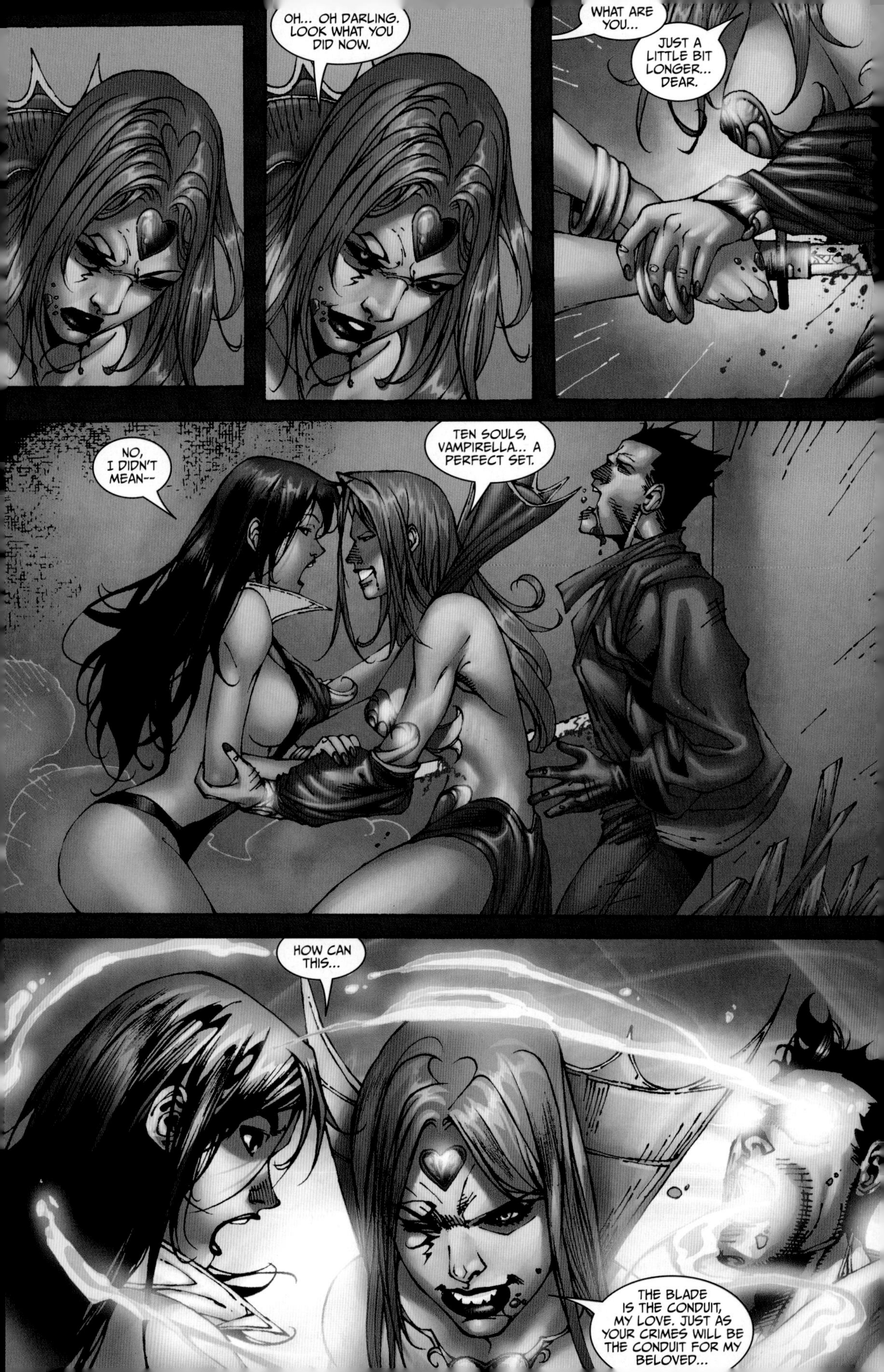
OH... OH DARLING. LOOK WHAT YOU DID NOW.
WHAT ARE YOU...
JUST A LITTLE BIT LONGER... DEAR.
NO, I DIDN'T MEAN--
TEN SOULS, VAMPIRELLA... A PERFECT SET.
HOW CAN THIS...
THE BLADE IS THE CONDUIT, MY LOVE. JUST AS YOUR CRIMES WILL BE THE CONDUIT FOR MY BELOVED...

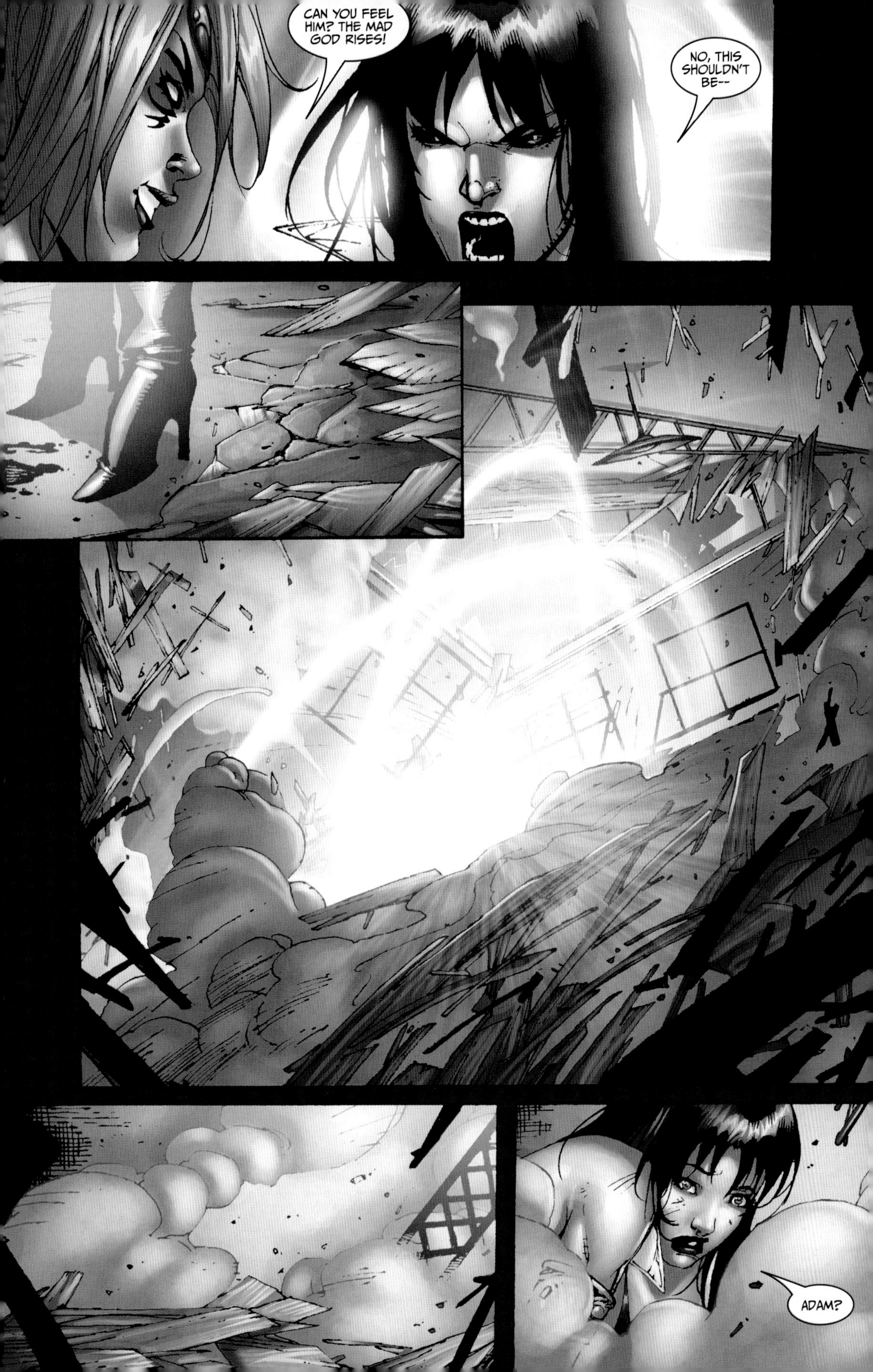
CAN YOU FEEL HIM? THE MAD GOD RISES!
NO, THIS SHOULDN'T BE--
ADAM?

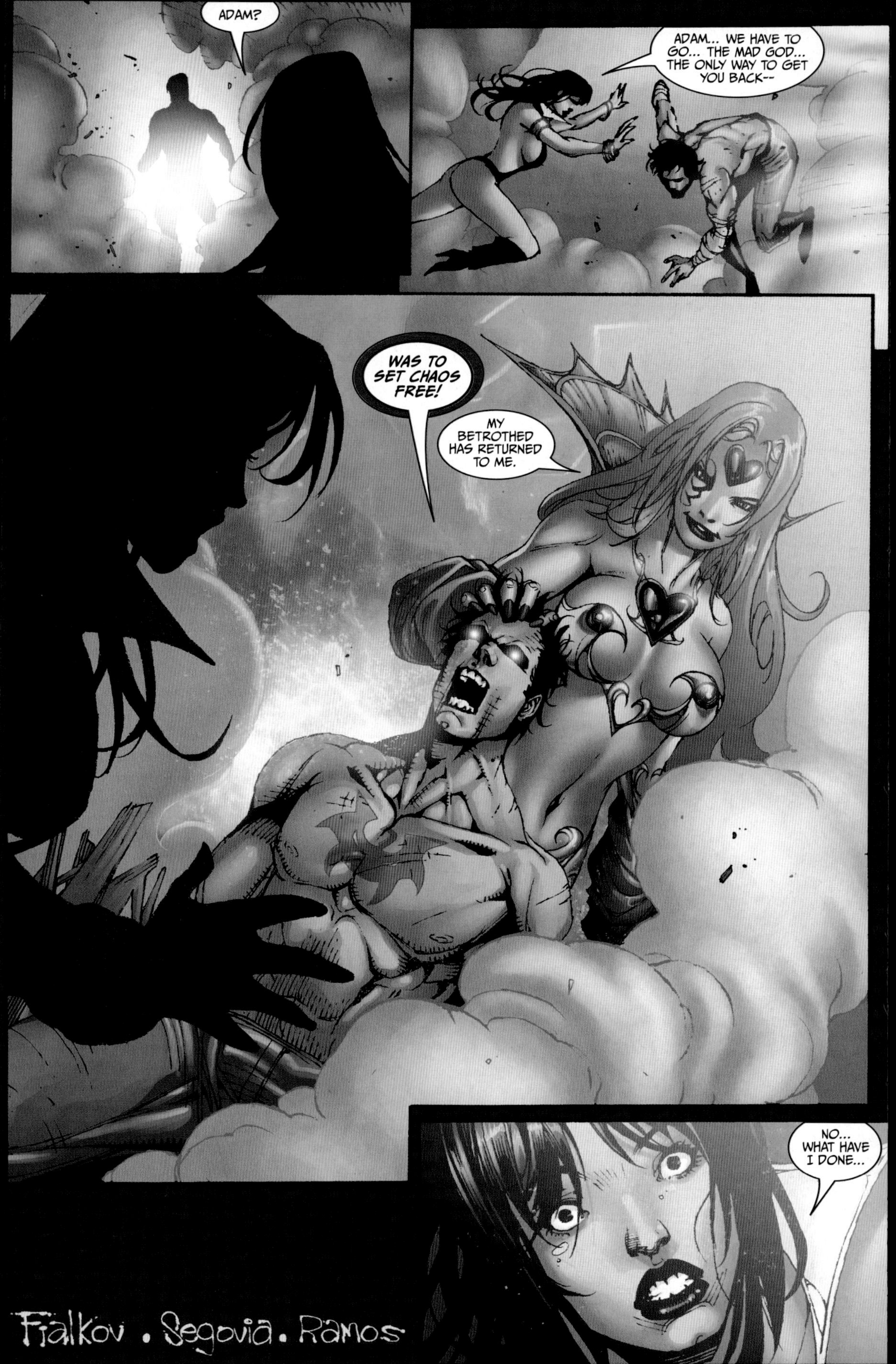
ADAM?
ADAM... WE HAVE TO GO... THE MAD GOD... THE ONLY WAY TO GET YOU BACK--
WAS TO SET CHAOS FREE!
MY BETROTHED HAS RETURNED TO ME.
NO... WHAT HAVE I DONE...
Fialkov . Segovia . Ramos

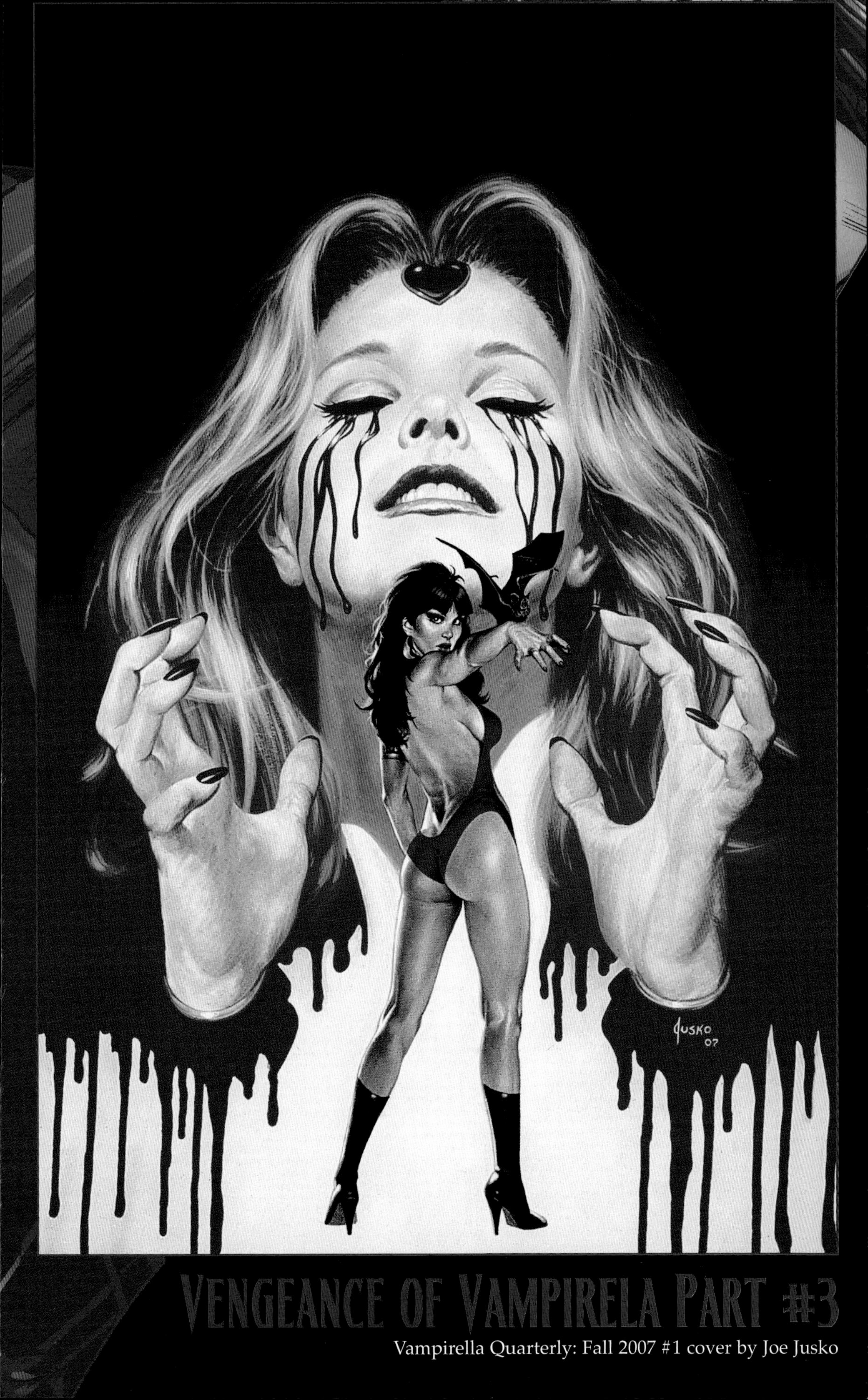
JUSKO
07

VENGEANCE OF VAMPIRELA PART #3

Vampirella Quarterly: Fall 2007 #1 cover by Joe Jusko

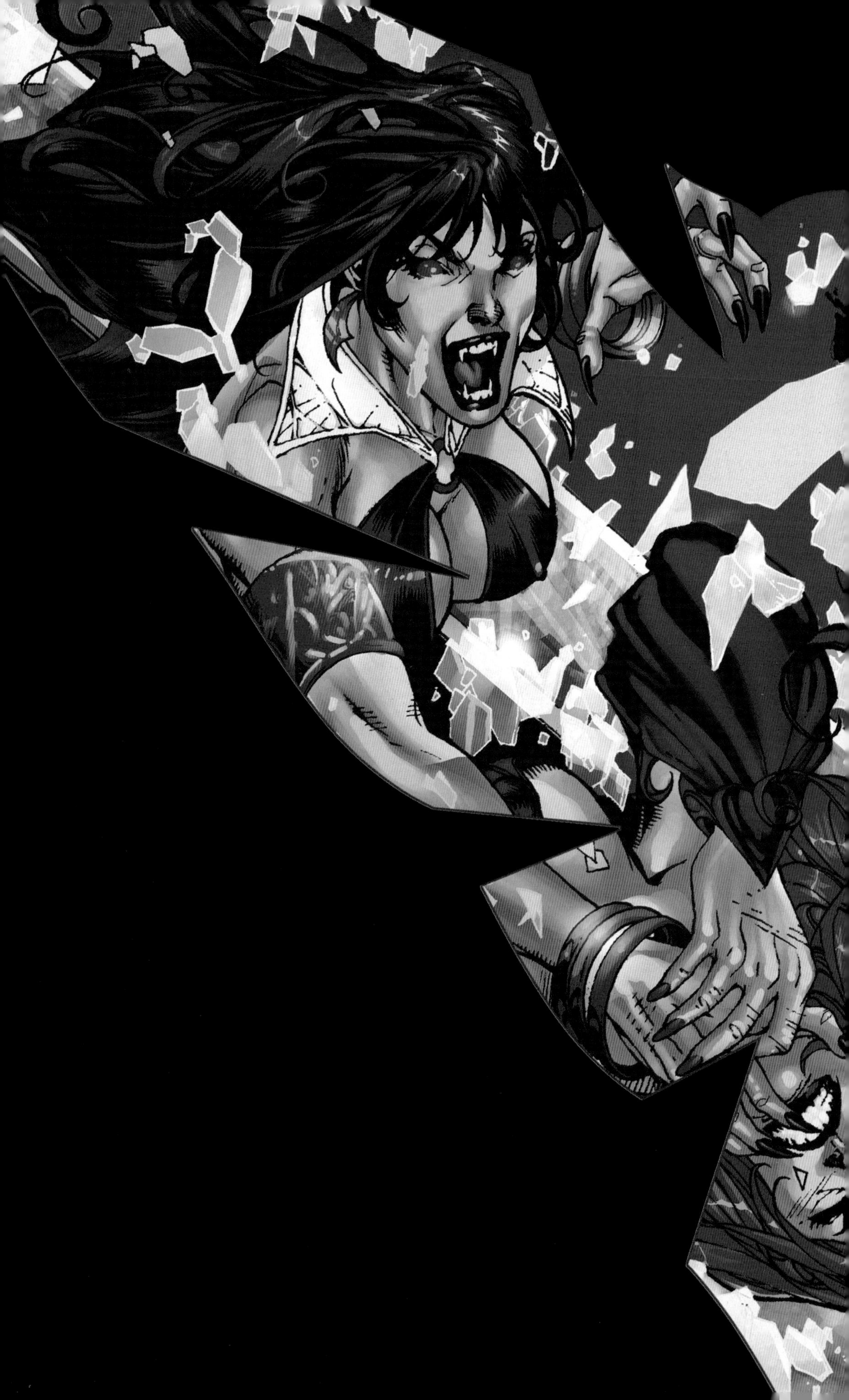

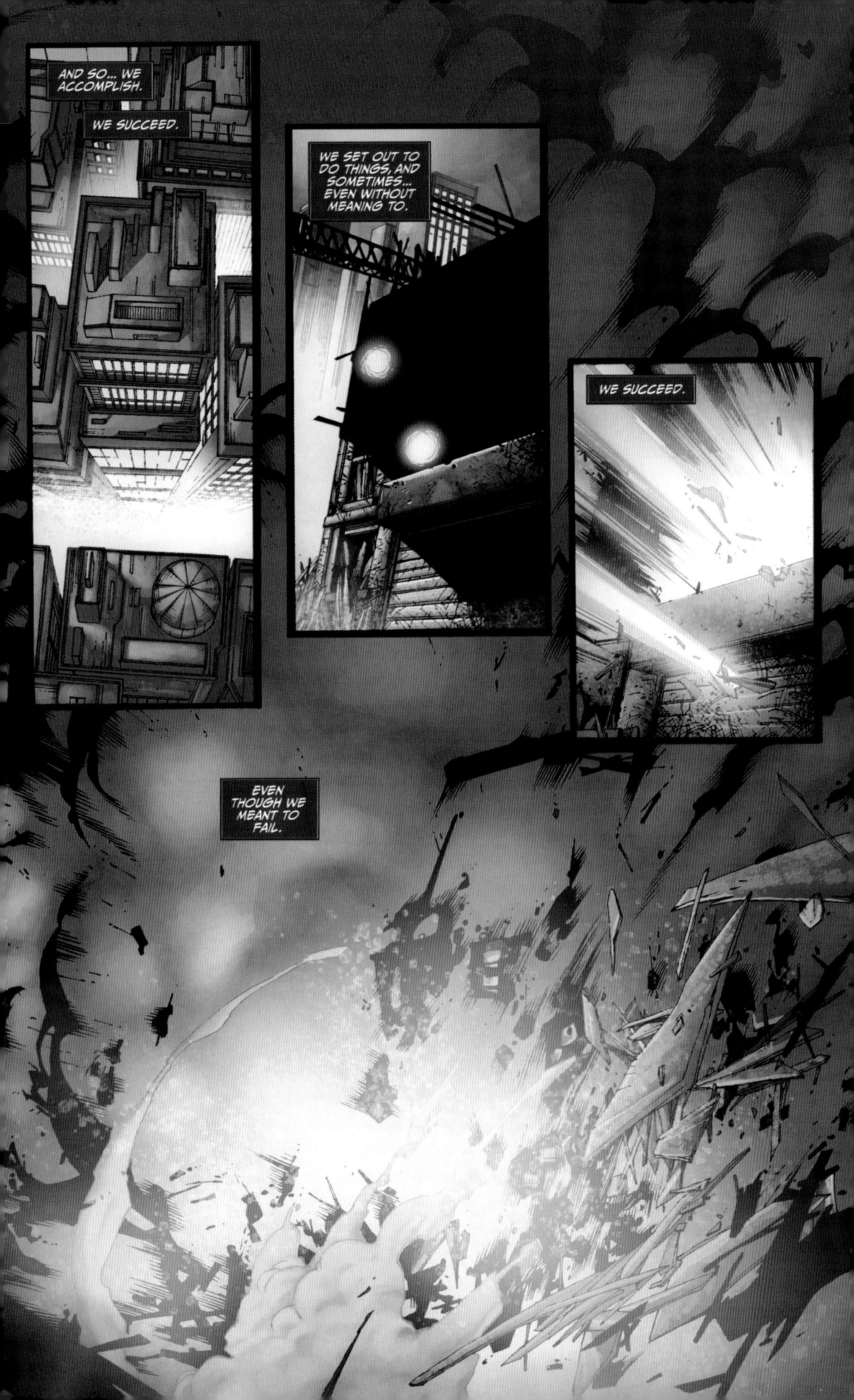
AND SO... WE ACCOMPLISH.
WE SUCCEED.
WE SET OUT TO DO THINGS, AND SOMETIMES... EVEN WITHOUT MEANING TO.
WE SUCCEED.
EVEN THOUGH WE MEANT TO FAIL.

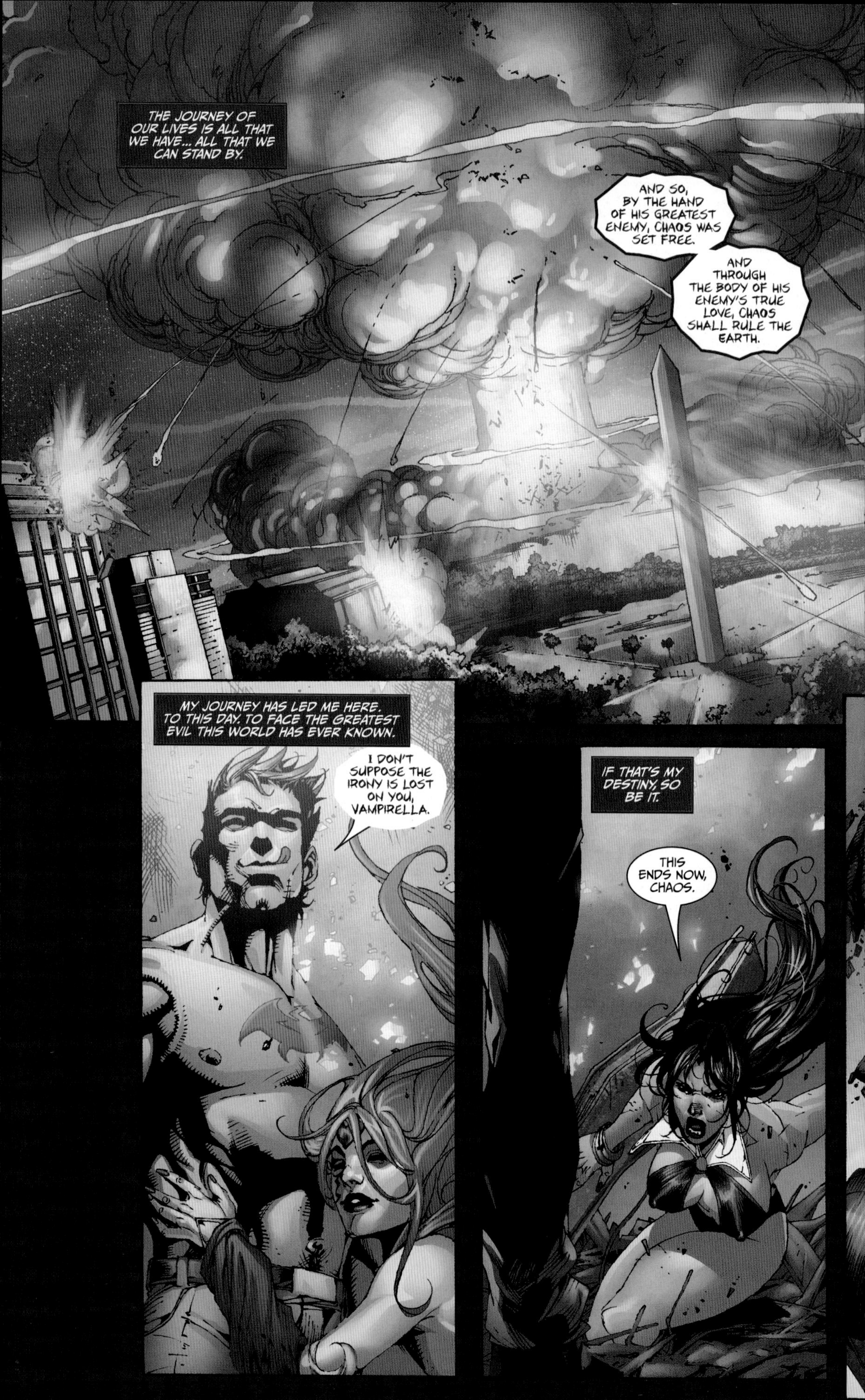
THE JOURNEY OF OUR LIVES IS ALL THAT WE HAVE... ALL THAT WE CAN STAND BY.
AND SO, BY THE HAND OF HIS GREATEST ENEMY, CHAOS WAS SET FREE.
AND THROUGH THE BODY OF HIS ENEMY'S TRUE LOVE, CHAOS SHALL RULE THE EARTH.
MY JOURNEY HAS LED ME HERE. TO THIS DAY. TO FACE THE GREATEST EVIL THIS WORLD HAS EVER KNOWN.
I DON'T SUPPOSE THE IRONY IS LOST ON YOU, VAMPIRELLA.
IF THAT'S MY DESTINY, SO BE IT.
THIS ENDS NOW, CHAOS.

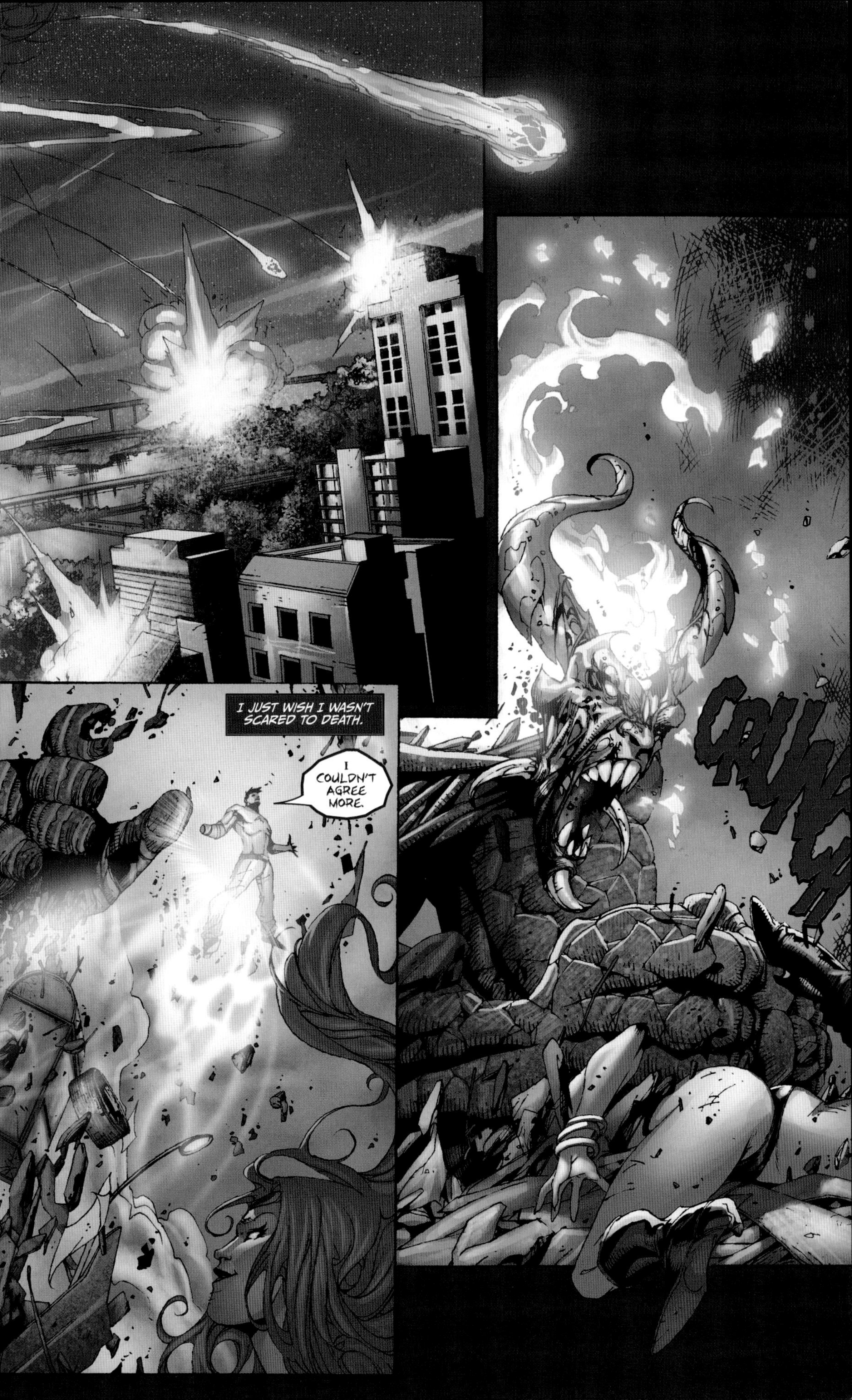
I JUST WISH I WASN'T SCARED TO DEATH.
I COULDN'T AGREE MORE.

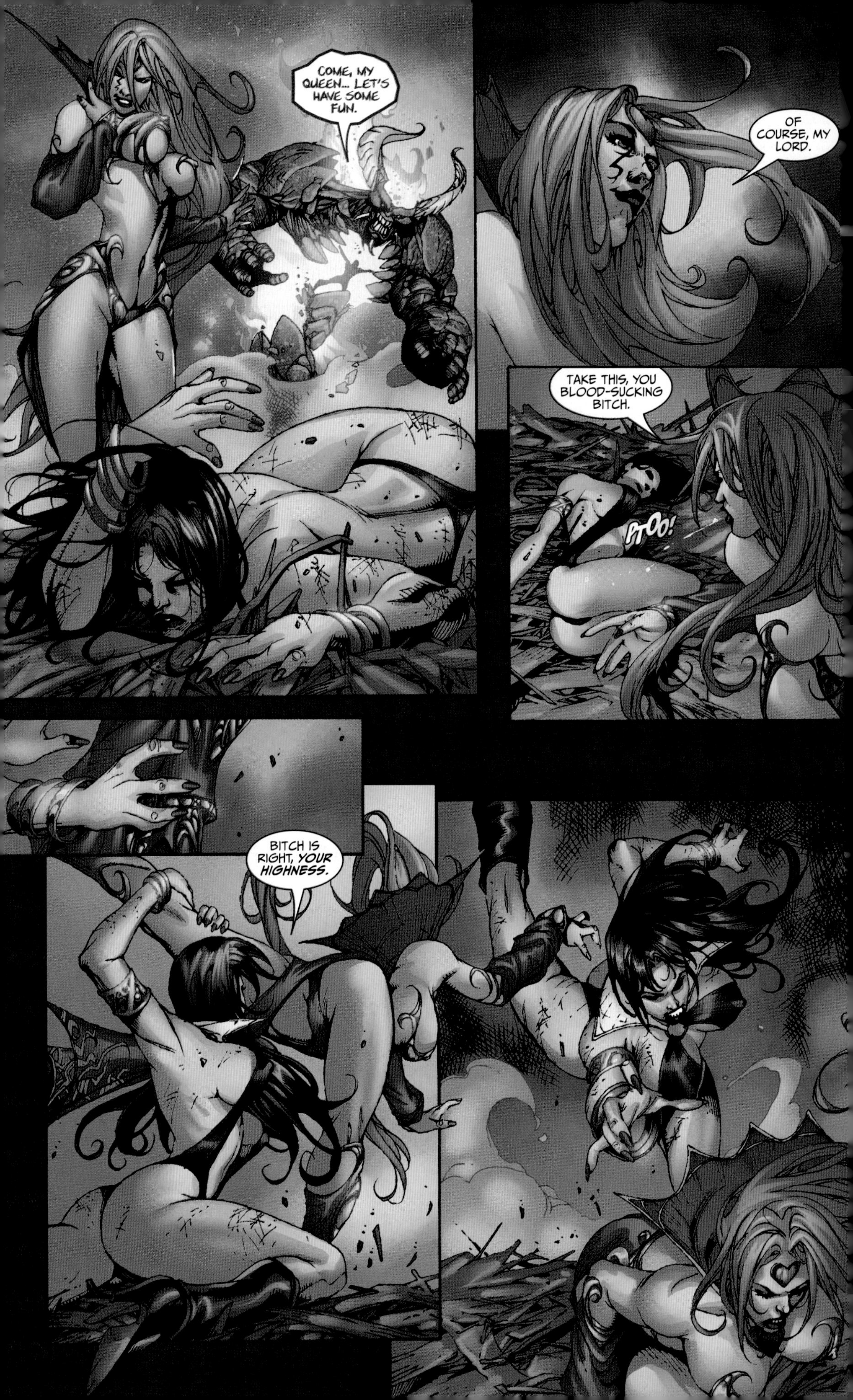
COME, MY QUEEN... LET'S HAVE SOME FUN.
OF COURSE, MY LORD.
TAKE THIS, YOU BLOOD-SUCKING BITCH.
PTOO!
BITCH IS RIGHT, *YOUR HIGHNESS.*

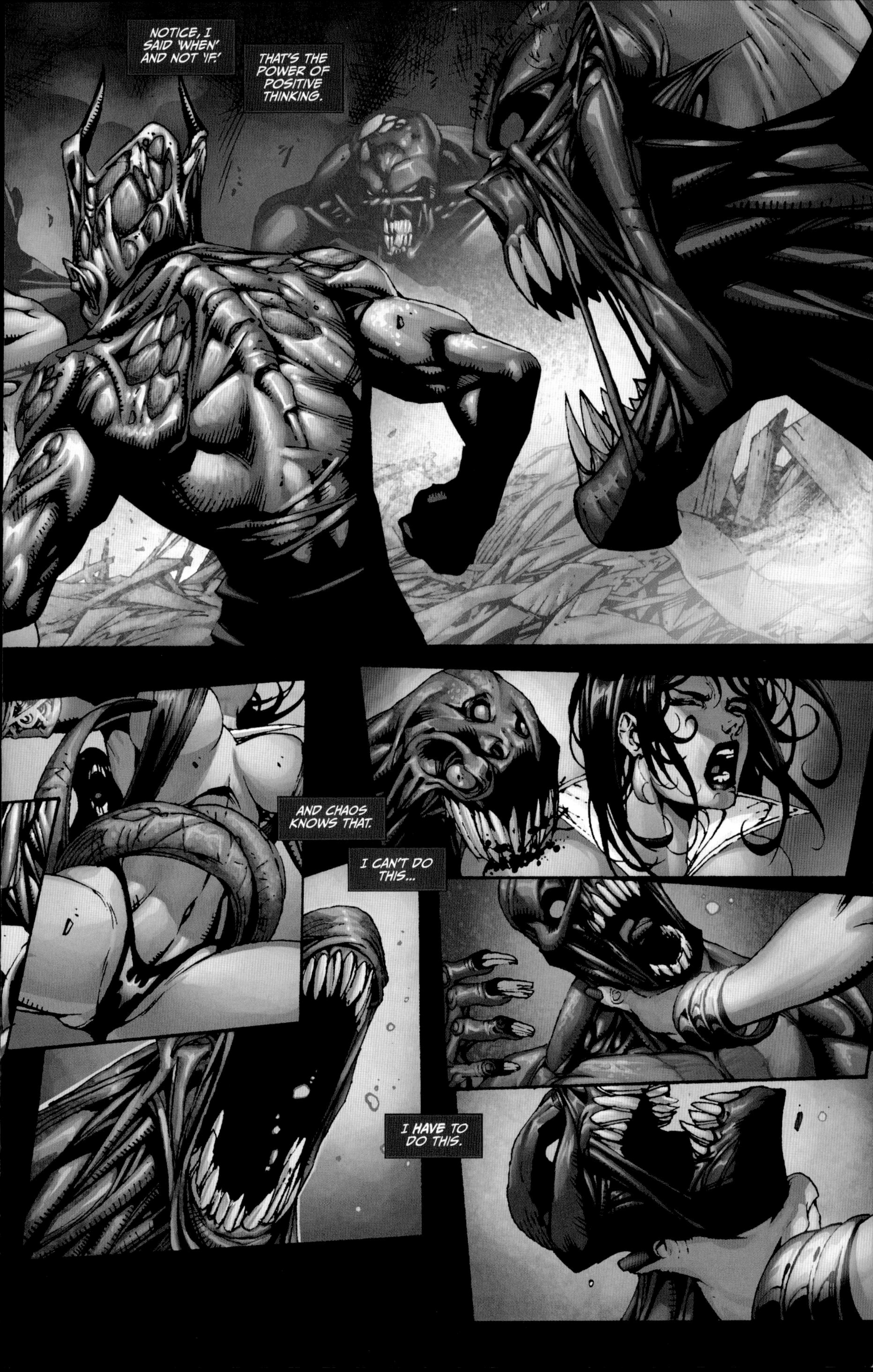
NOTICE, I SAID 'WHEN' AND NOT 'IF.'
THAT'S THE POWER OF POSITIVE THINKING.
AND CHAOS KNOWS THAT.
I CAN'T DO THIS...
I HAVE TO DO THIS.

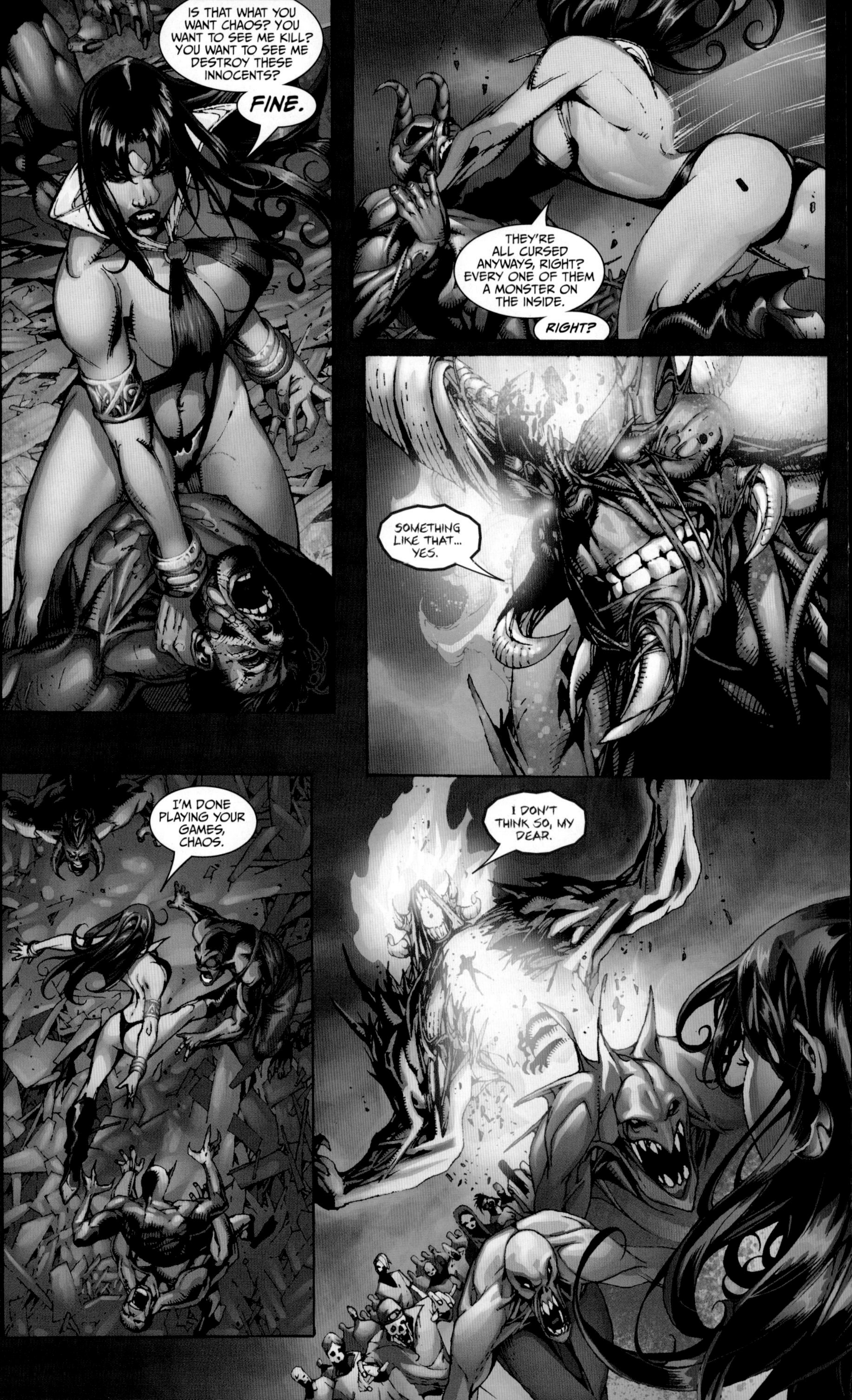
IS THAT WHAT YOU WANT CHAOS? YOU WANT TO SEE ME KILL? YOU WANT TO SEE ME DESTROY THESE INNOCENTS?
FINE.
THEY'RE ALL CURSED ANYWAYS, RIGHT? EVERY ONE OF THEM A MONSTER ON THE INSIDE.
RIGHT?
SOMETHING LIKE THAT... YES.
I'M DONE PLAYING YOUR GAMES, CHAOS.
I DON'T THINK SO, MY DEAR.

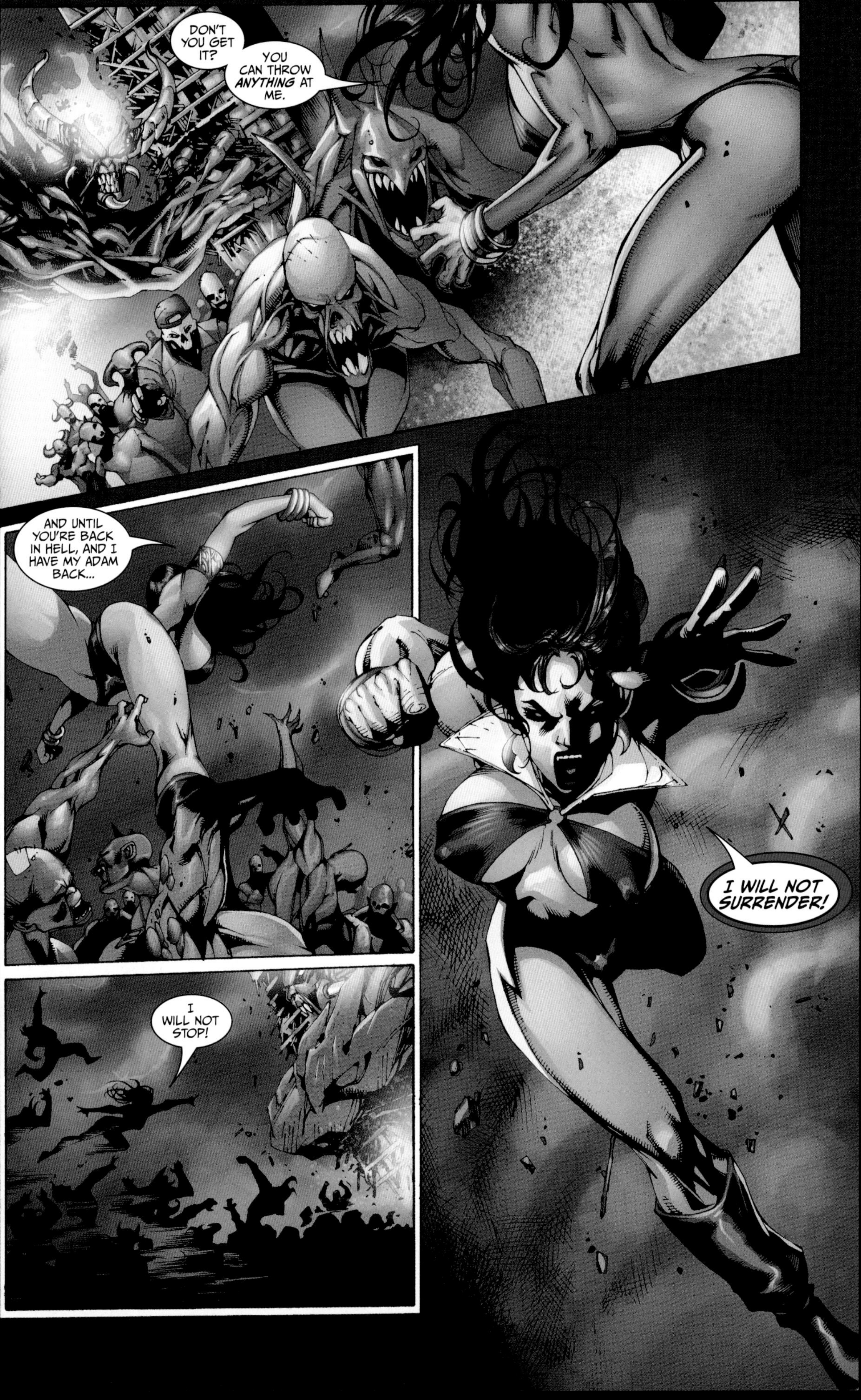
DON'T YOU GET IT?
YOU CAN THROW ANYTHING AT ME.
AND UNTIL YOU'RE BACK IN HELL, AND I HAVE MY ADAM BACK...
I WILL NOT STOP!
I WILL NOT SURRENDER!

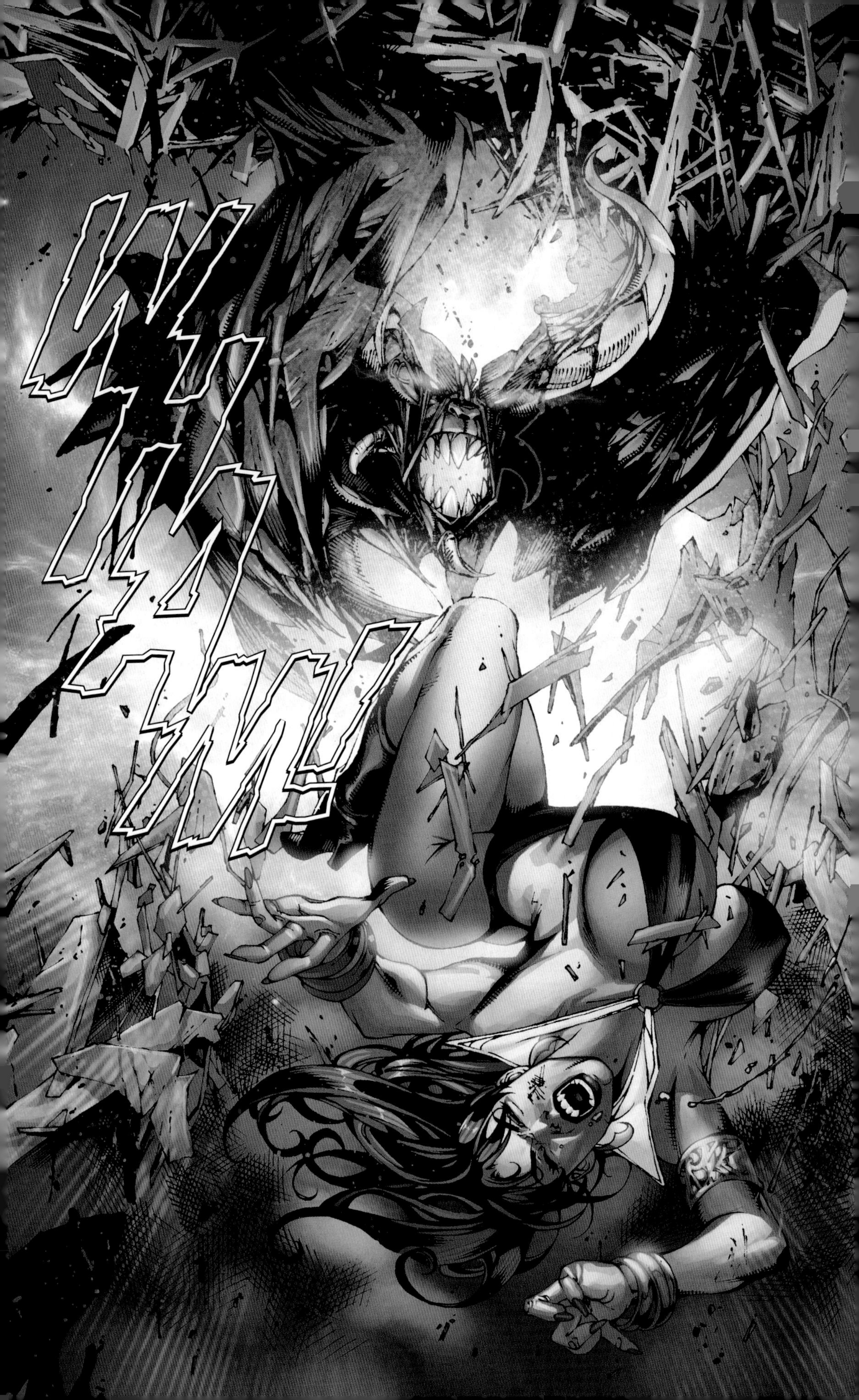

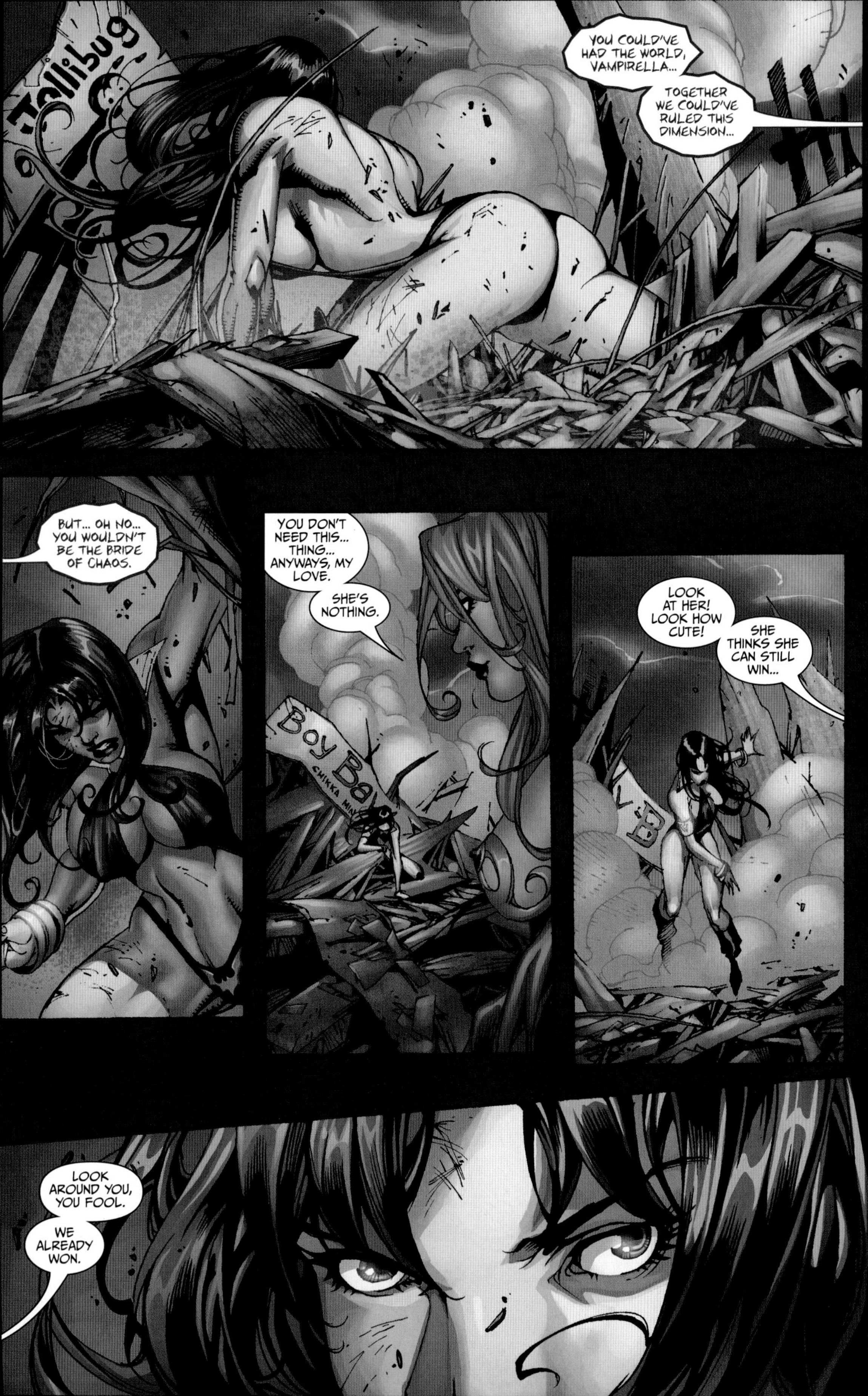
Jollibug
YOU COULD'VE HAD THE WORLD, VAMPIRELLA...
TOGETHER WE COULD'VE RULED THIS DIMENSION...
BUT... OH NO... YOU WOULDN'T BE THE BRIDE OF CHAOS.
YOU DON'T NEED THIS... THING... ANYWAYS, MY LOVE.
SHE'S NOTHING.
Boy Ba
LOOK AT HER! LOOK HOW CUTE!
SHE THINKS SHE CAN STILL WIN...
LOOK AROUND YOU, YOU FOOL.
WE ALREADY WON.

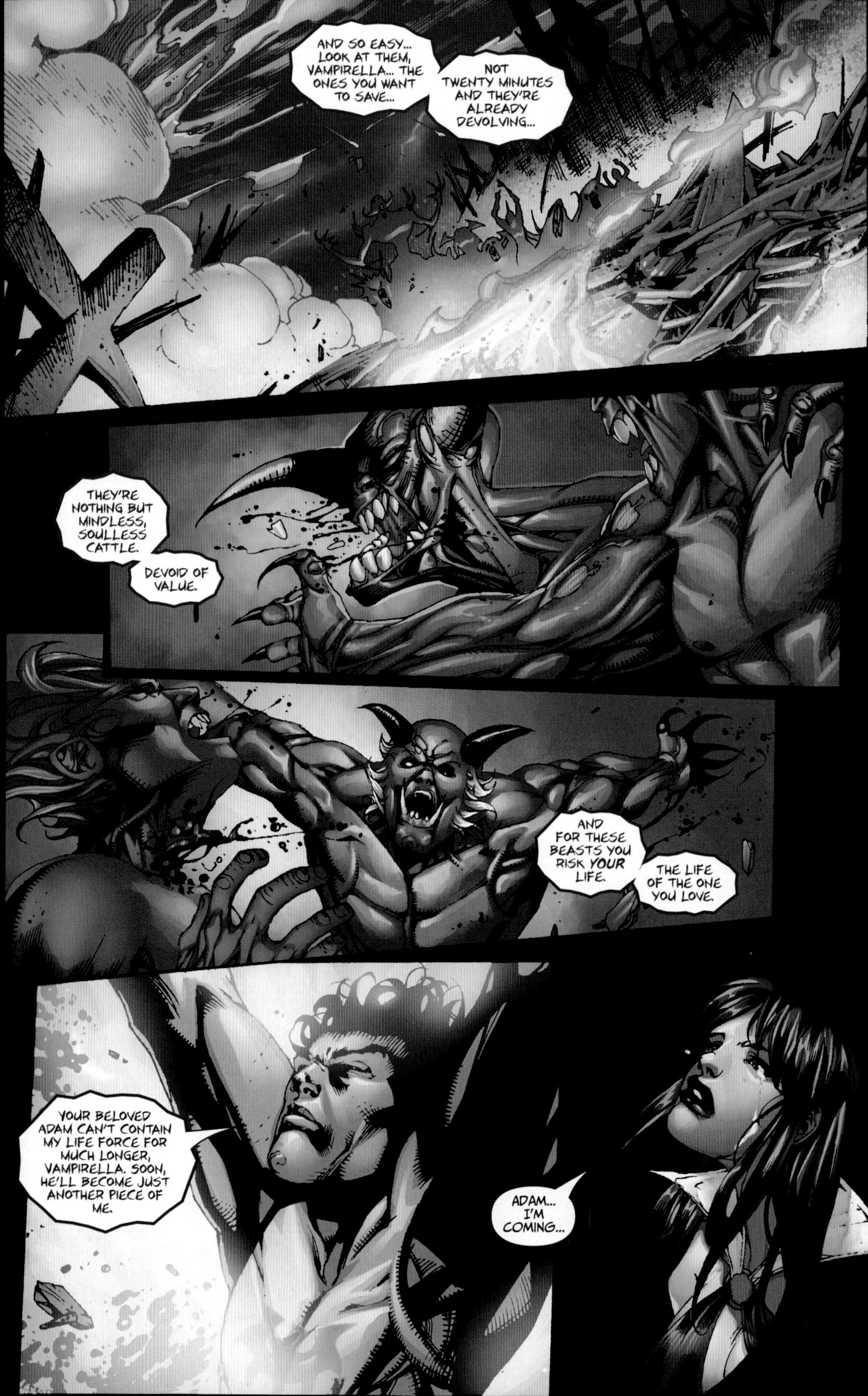
AND SO EASY... LOOK AT THEM, VAMPIRELLA... THE ONES YOU WANT TO SAVE...
NOT TWENTY MINUTES AND THEY'RE ALREADY DEVOLVING...
THEY'RE NOTHING BUT MINDLESS, SOULLESS CATTLE.
DEVOID OF VALUE.
AND FOR THESE BEASTS YOU RISK YOUR LIFE.
THE LIFE OF THE ONE YOU LOVE.
YOUR BELOVED ADAM CAN'T CONTAIN MY LIFE FORCE FOR MUCH LONGER, VAMPIRELLA. SOON, HE'LL BECOME JUST ANOTHER PIECE OF ME.
ADAM... I'M COMING...

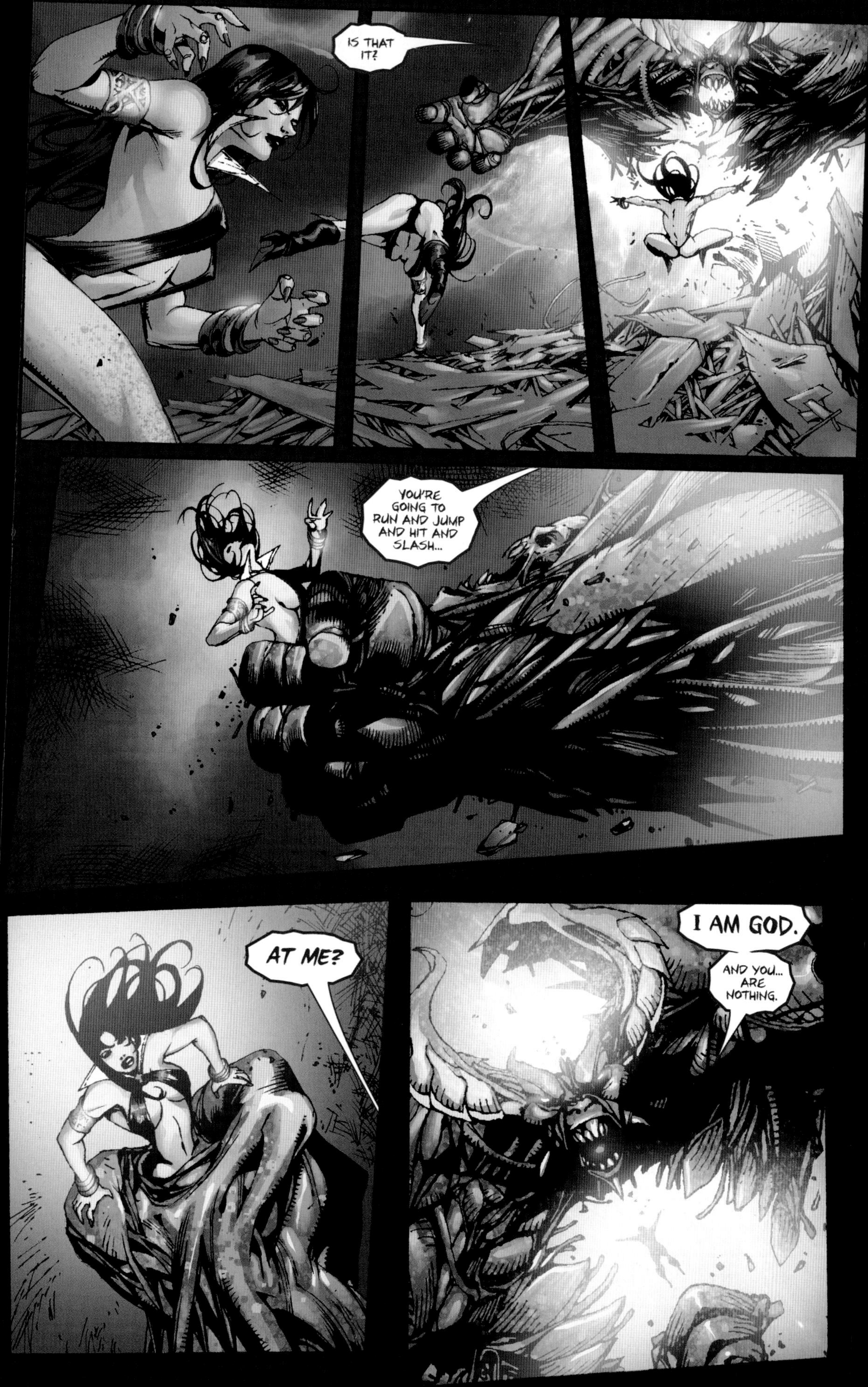
IS THAT IT?
YOU'RE GOING TO RUN AND JUMP AND HIT AND SLASH...
AT ME?
I AM GOD.
AND YOU... ARE NOTHING.

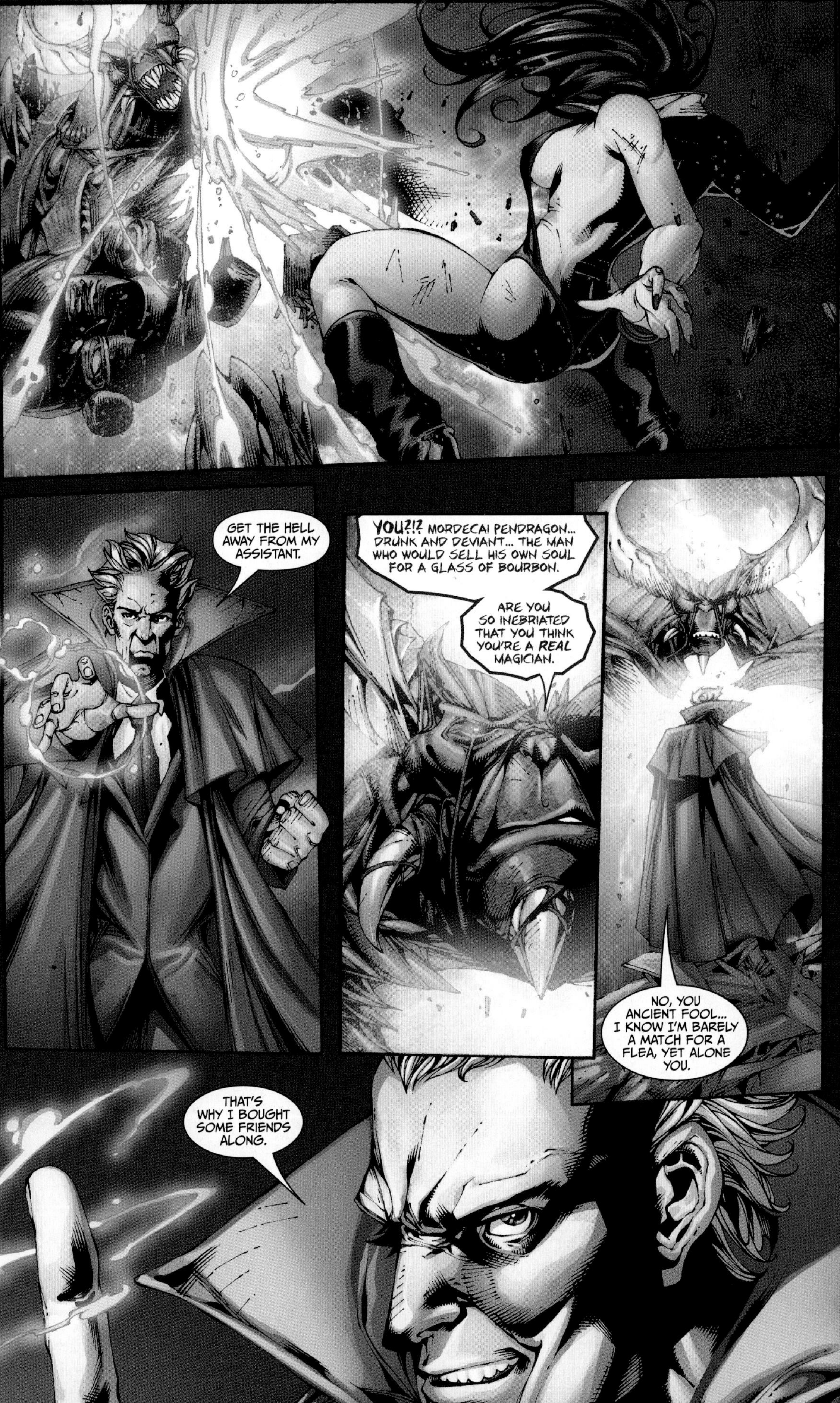
GET THE HELL AWAY FROM MY ASSISTANT.
YOU?!? MORDECAI PENDRAGON... DRUNK AND DEVIANT... THE MAN WHO WOULD SELL HIS OWN SOUL FOR A GLASS OF BOURBON.
ARE YOU SO INEBRIATED THAT YOU THINK YOU'RE A REAL MAGICIAN.
NO, YOU ANCIENT FOOL... I KNOW I'M BARELY A MATCH FOR A FLEA, YET ALONE YOU.
THAT'S WHY I BOUGHT SOME FRIENDS ALONG.

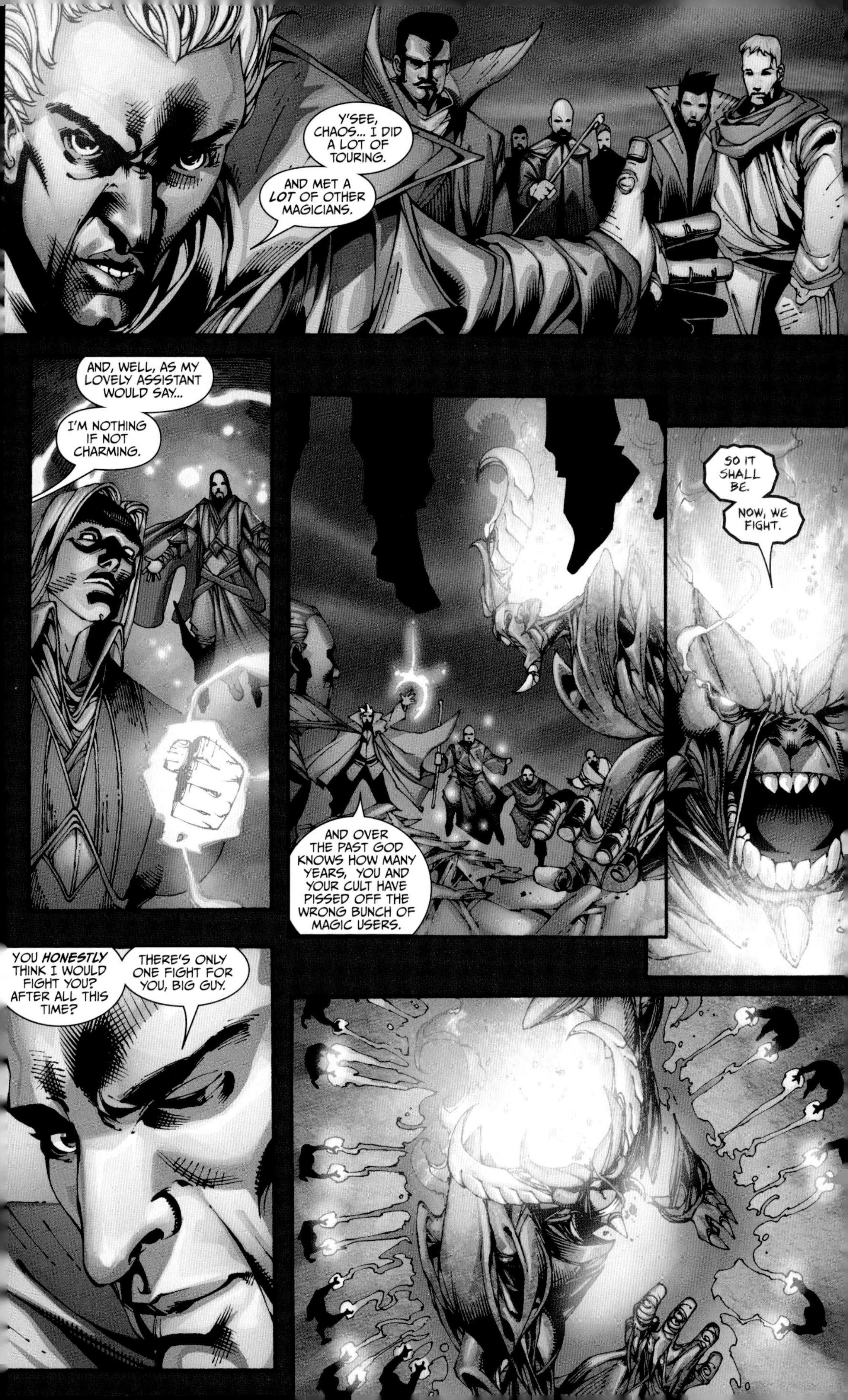
Y'SEE, CHAOS... I DID A LOT OF TOURING.
AND MET A LOT OF OTHER MAGICIANS.
AND, WELL, AS MY LOVELY ASSISTANT WOULD SAY...
I'M NOTHING IF NOT CHARMING.
AND OVER THE PAST GOD KNOWS HOW MANY YEARS, YOU AND YOUR CULT HAVE PISSED OFF THE WRONG BUNCH OF MAGIC USERS.
SO IT SHALL BE.
NOW, WE FIGHT.
YOU HONESTLY THINK I WOULD FIGHT YOU? AFTER ALL THIS TIME?
THERE'S ONLY ONE FIGHT FOR YOU, BIG GUY.

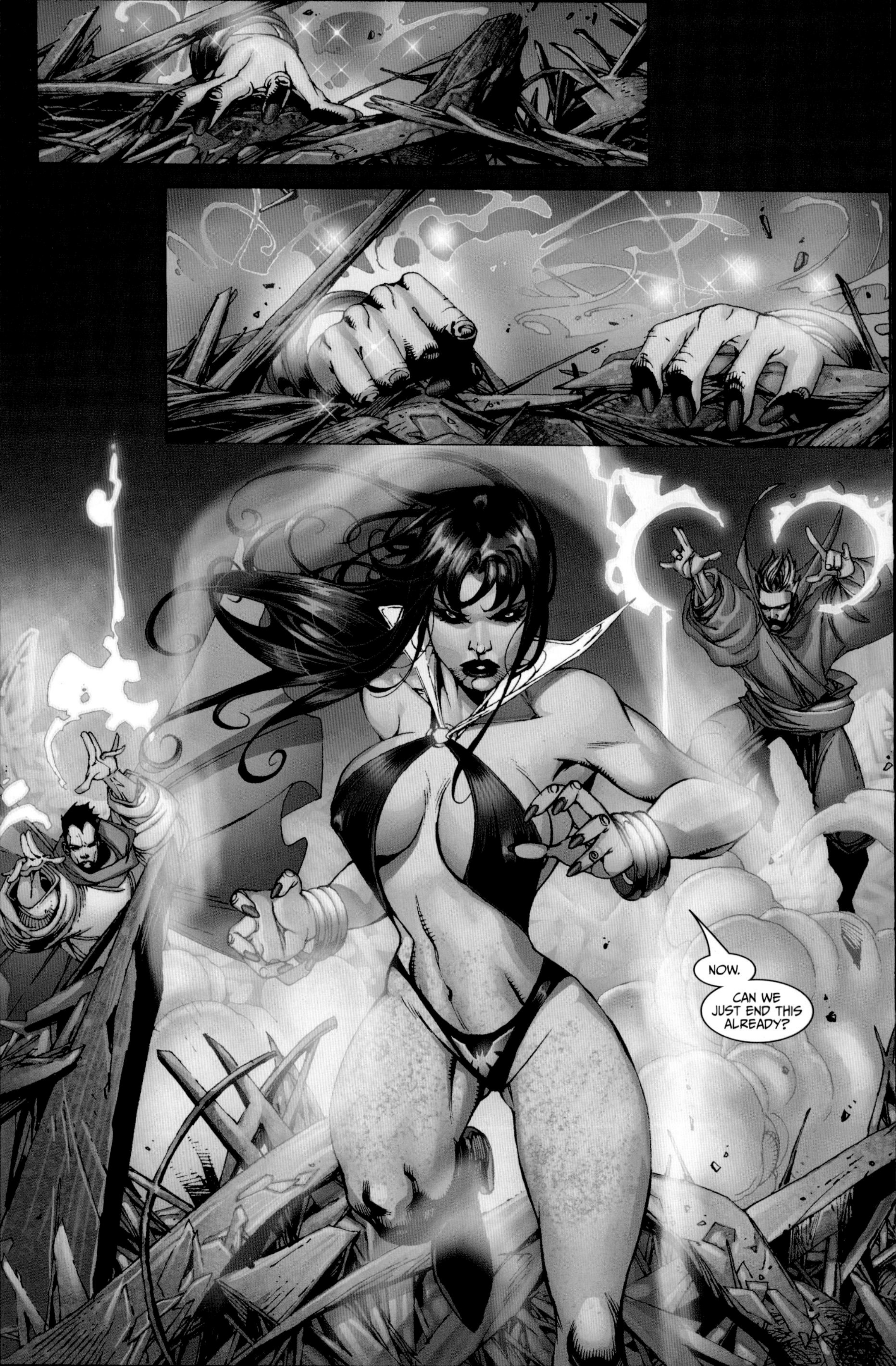
NOW.
CAN WE JUST END THIS ALREADY?

— Fialkov • Segovia • Ramos —

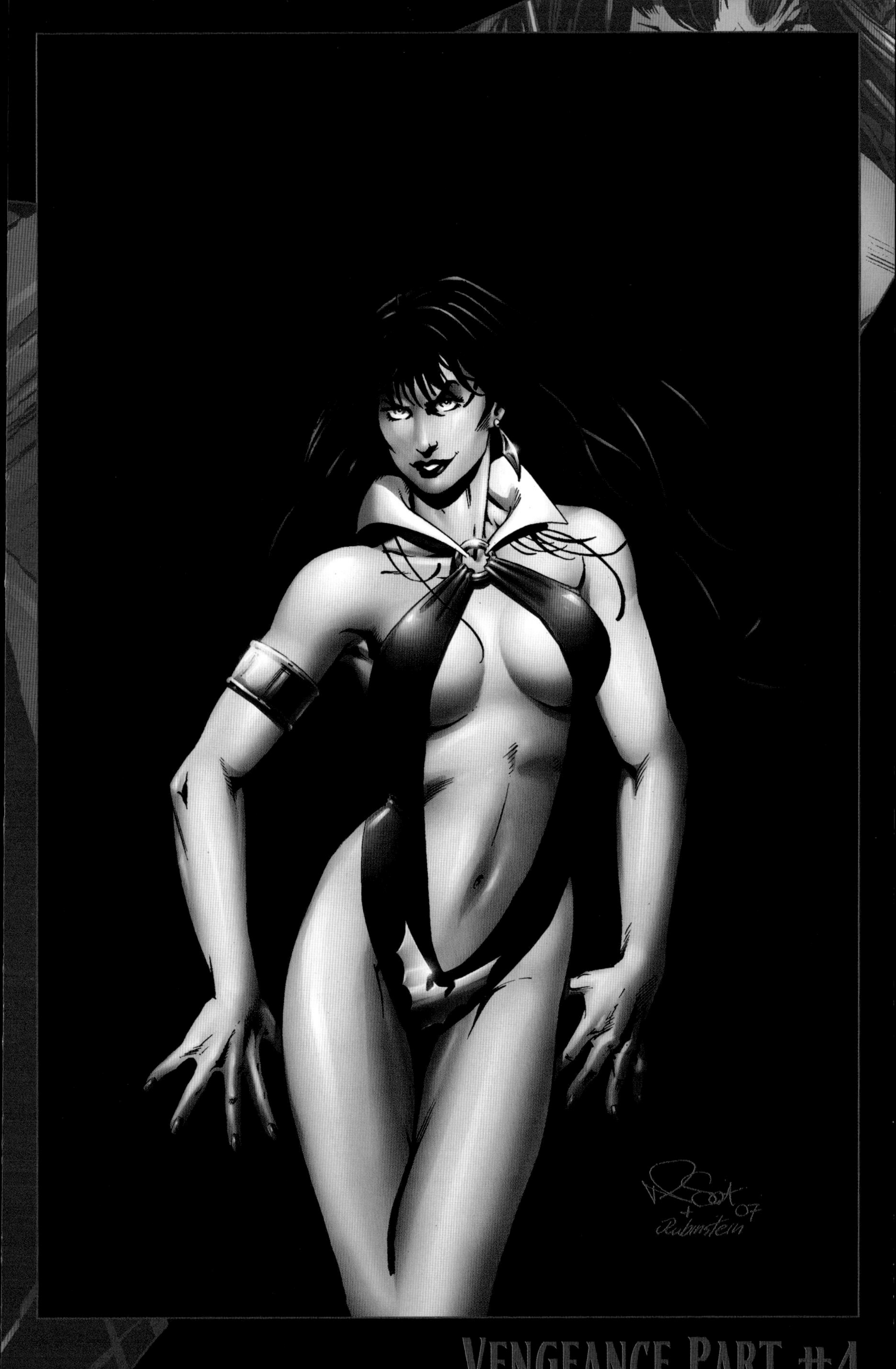

VENGEANCE PART #4

Vampirella Quarterly: Fall 2007 #1 cover by Nicola Scott

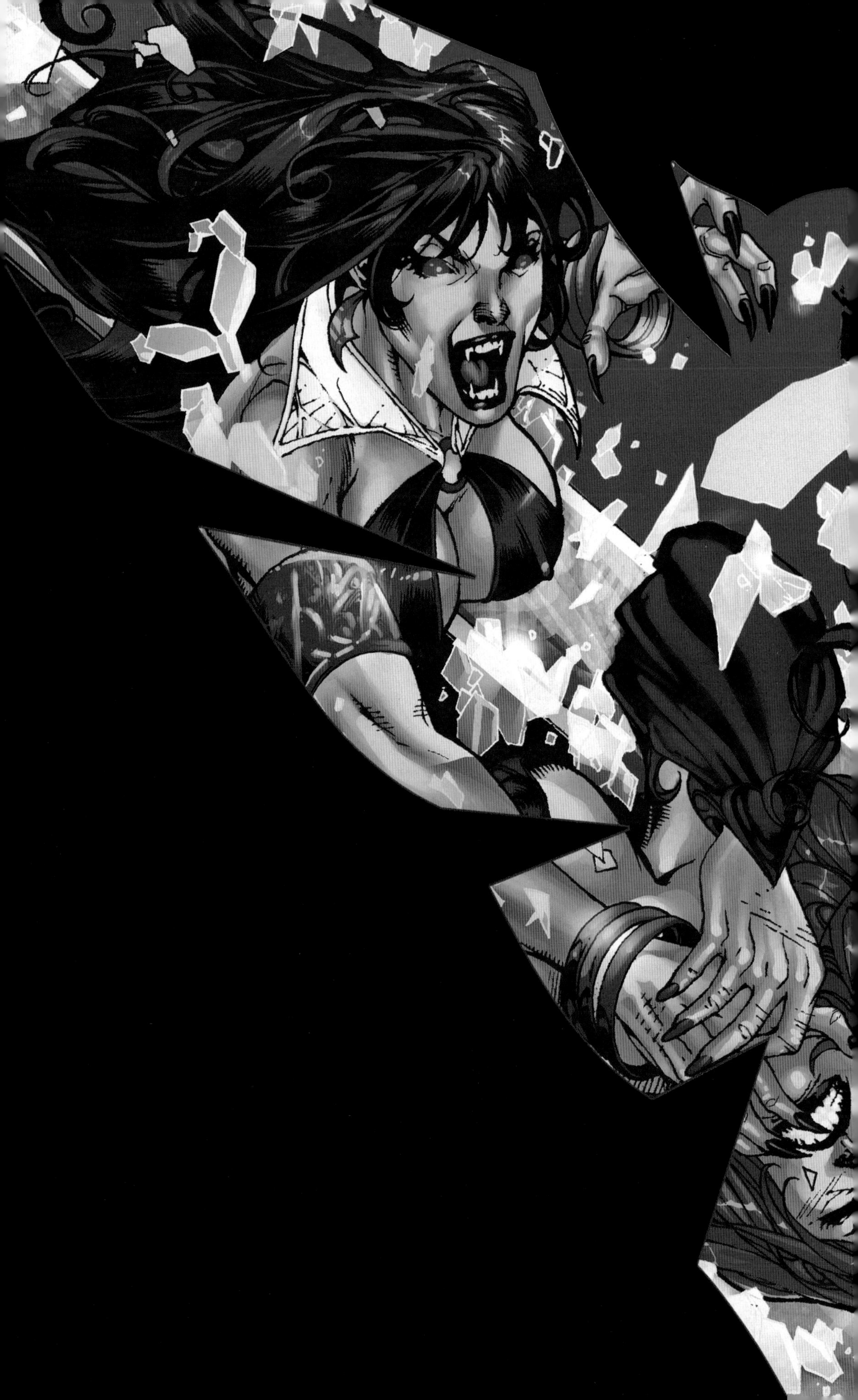

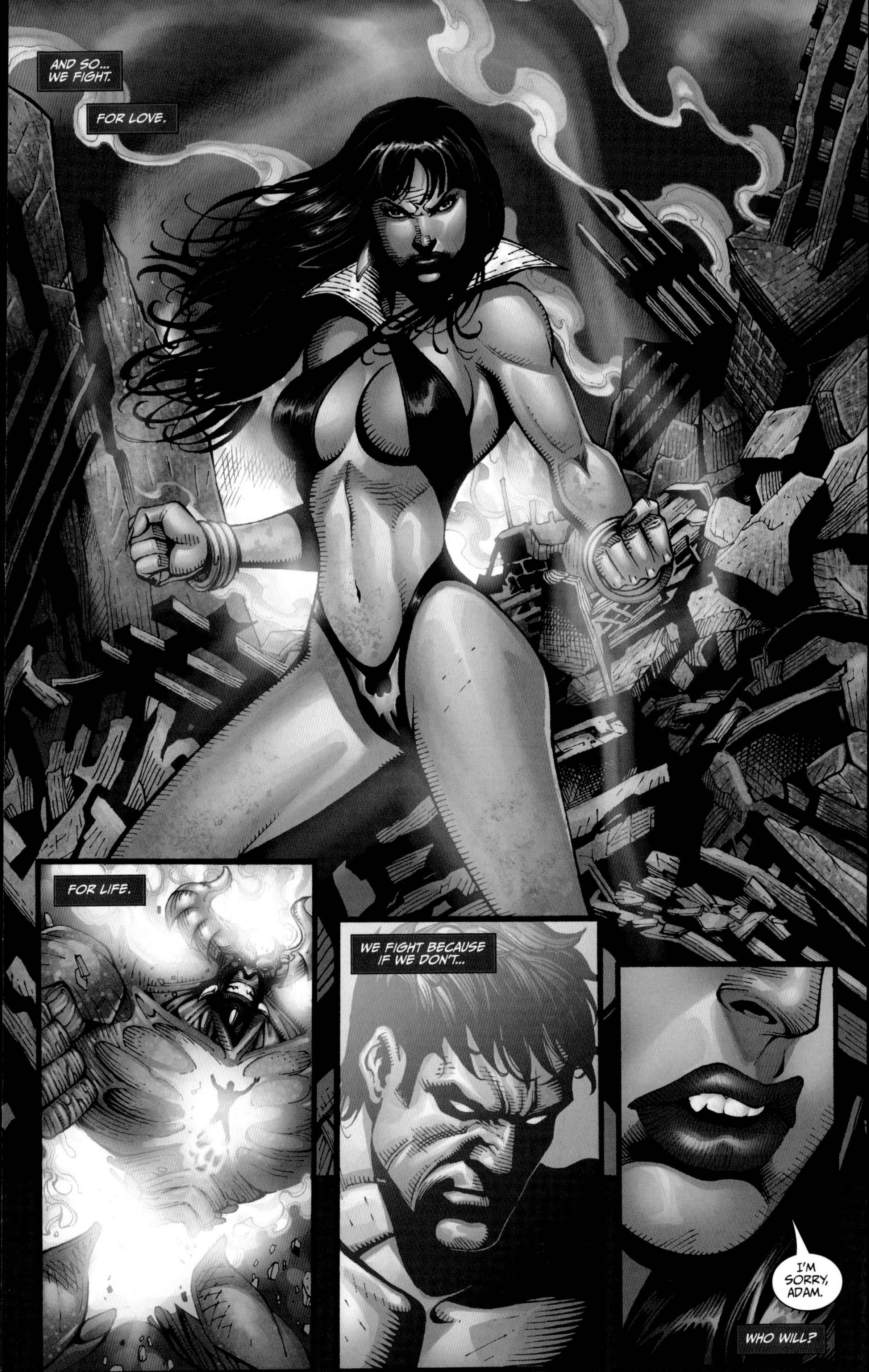
AND SO... WE FIGHT.
FOR LOVE.
FOR LIFE.
WE FIGHT BECAUSE IF WE DON'T...
I'M SORRY, ADAM.
WHO WILL?

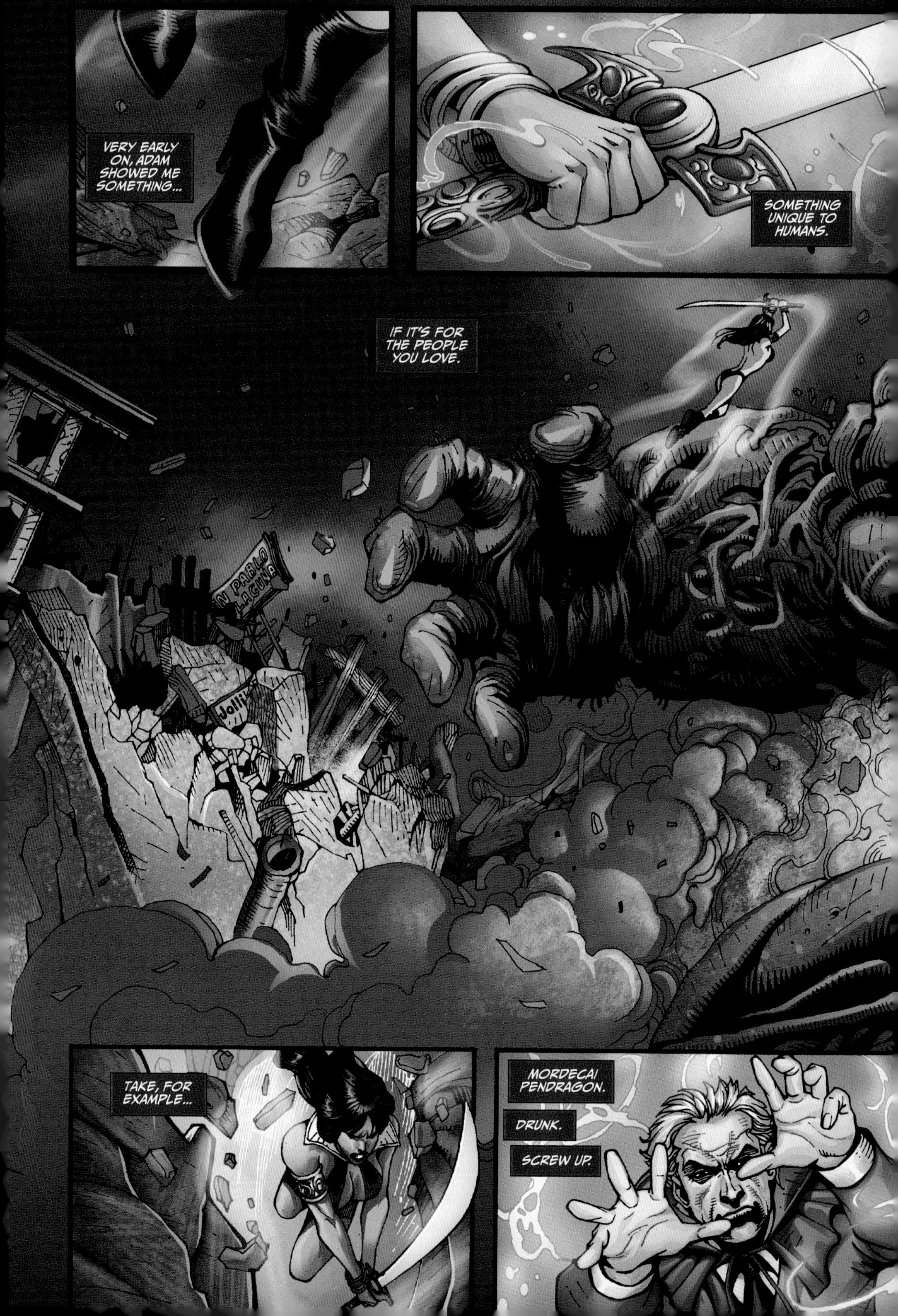

VERY EARLY ON, ADAM SHOWED ME SOMETHING...
SOMETHING UNIQUE TO HUMANS.
IF IT'S FOR THE PEOPLE YOU LOVE.
TAKE, FOR EXAMPLE...
MORDECAI PENDRAGON.
DRUNK.
SCREW UP.

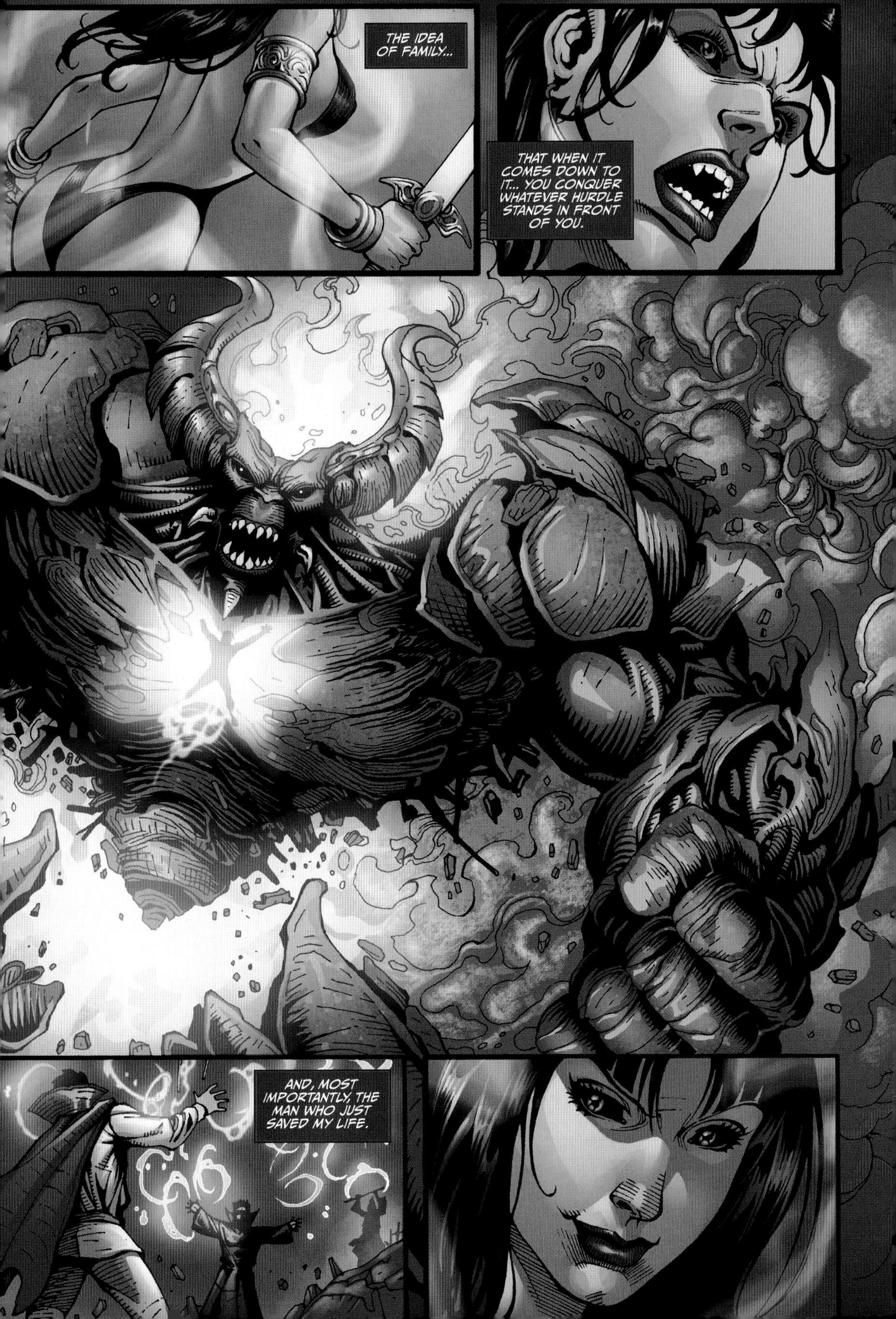
THE IDEA OF FAMILY...
THAT WHEN IT COMES DOWN TO IT... YOU CONQUER WHATEVER HURDLE STANDS IN FRONT OF YOU.
AND, MOST IMPORTANTLY, THE MAN WHO JUST SAVED MY LIFE.

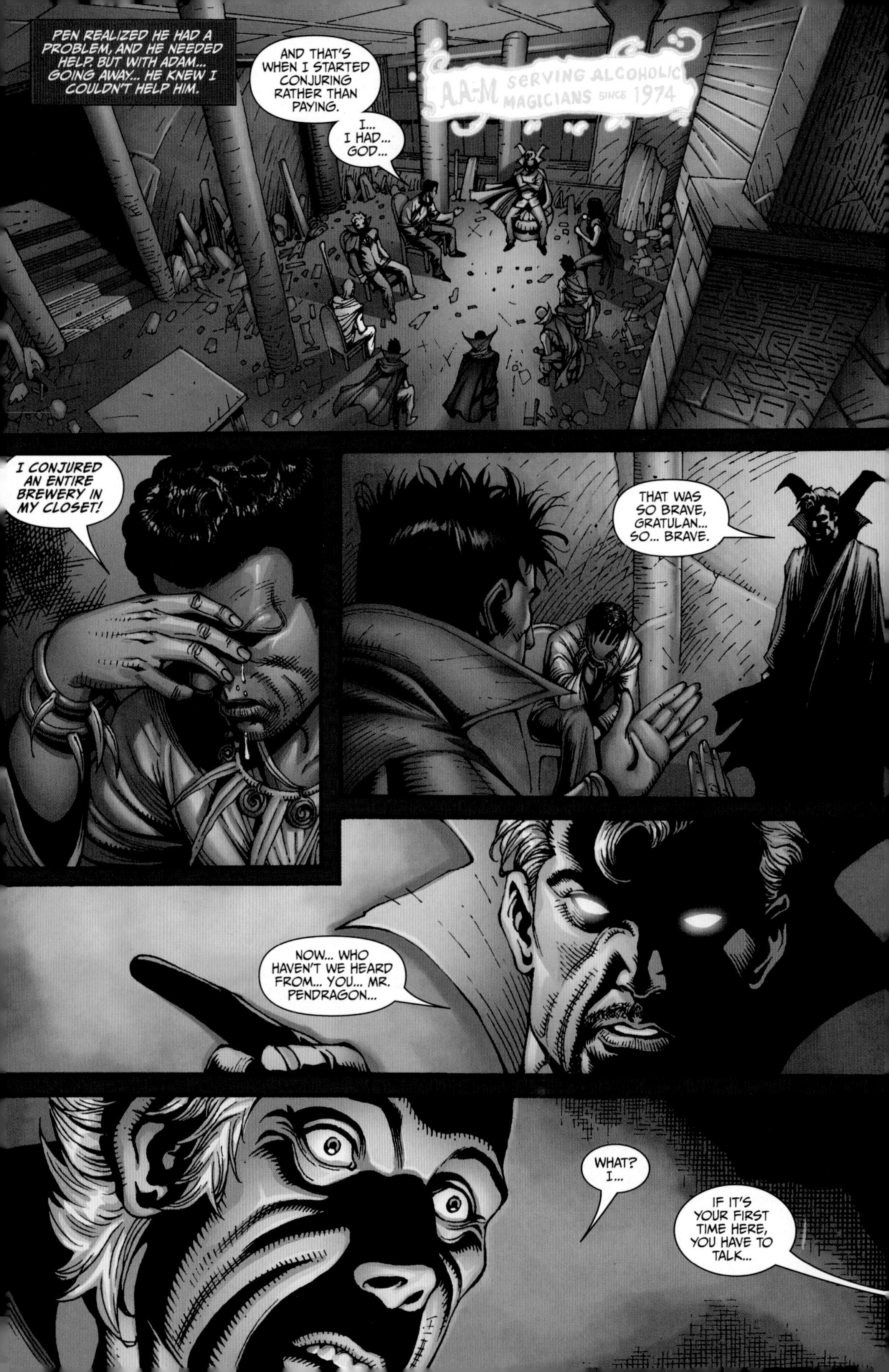
PEN REALIZED HE HAD A PROBLEM, AND HE NEEDED HELP. BUT WITH ADAM... GOING AWAY... HE KNEW I COULDN'T HELP HIM.
AND THAT'S WHEN I STARTED CONJURING RATHER THAN PAYING.
AA-M SERVING ALCOHOLIC MAGICIANS SINCE 1974
I... I HAD... GOD...
I CONJURED AN ENTIRE BREWERY IN MY CLOSET!
THAT WAS SO BRAVE, GRATULAN... SO... BRAVE.
NOW... WHO HAVEN'T WE HEARD FROM... YOU... MR. PENDRAGON...
WHAT? I...
IF IT'S YOUR FIRST TIME HERE, YOU HAVE TO TALK...

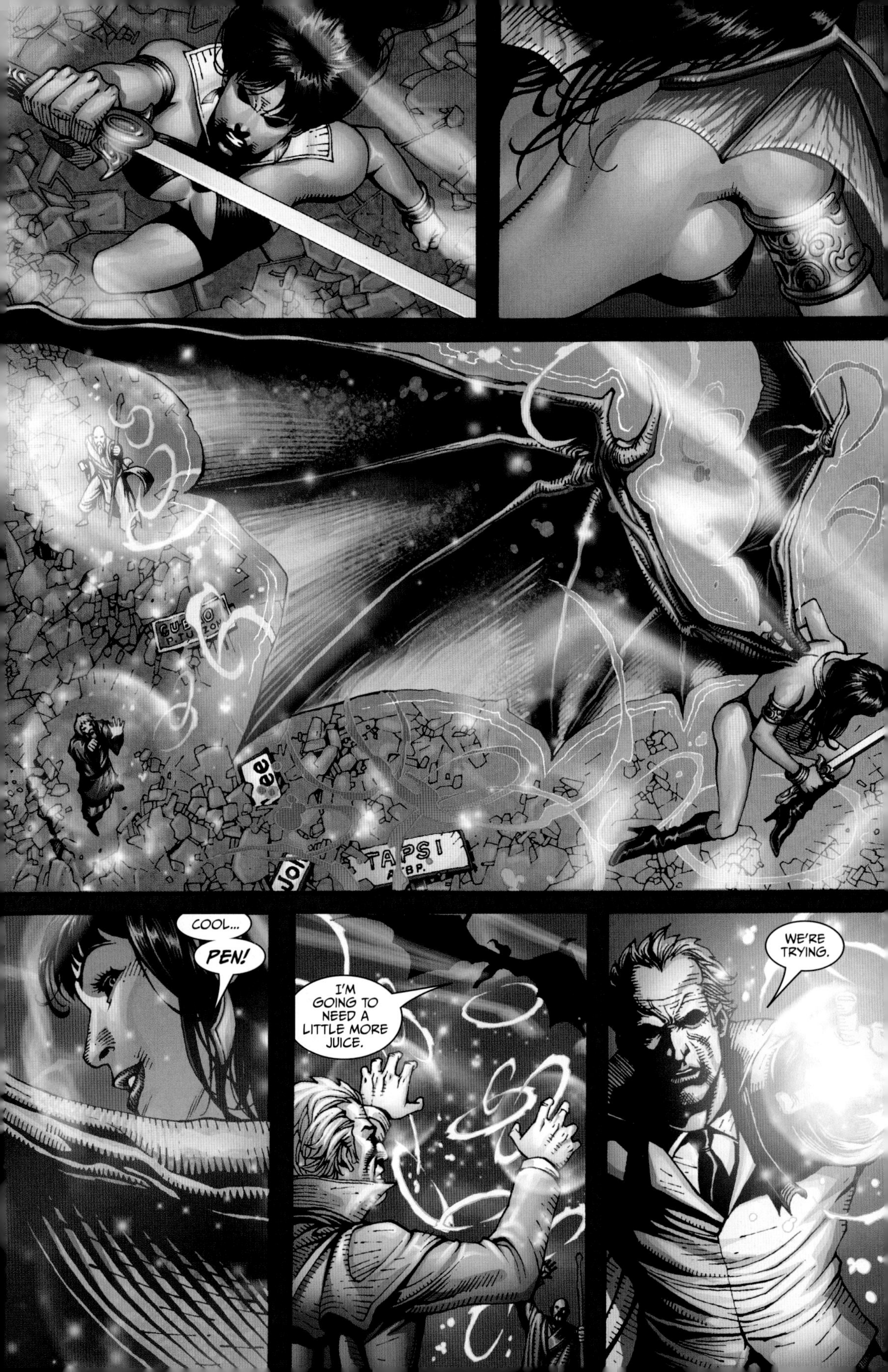
TAPSI
COOL...
PEN!
I'M GOING TO NEED A LITTLE MORE JUICE.
WE'RE TRYING.

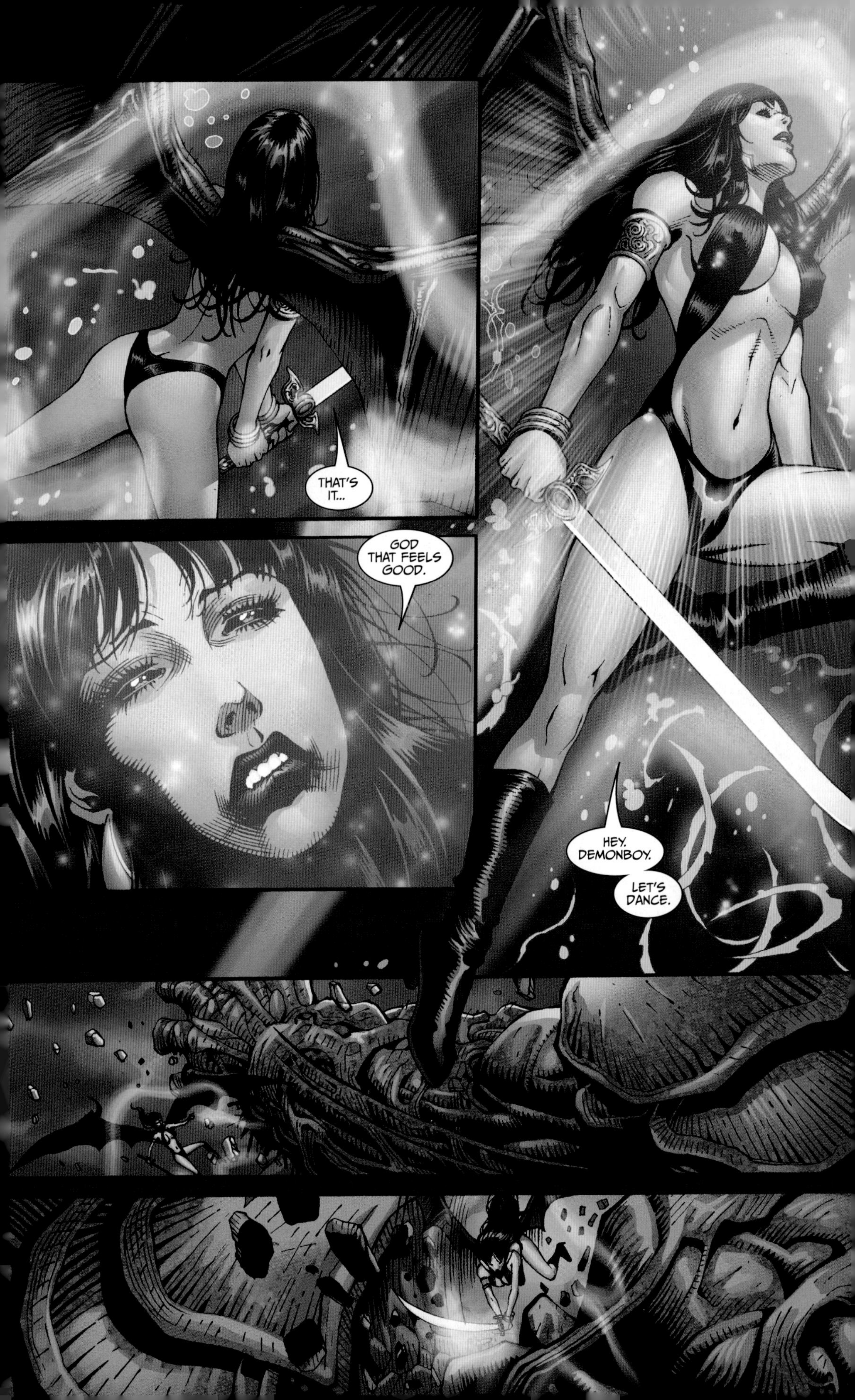
THAT'S IT...
GOD THAT FEELS GOOD.
HEY. DEMONBOY.
LET'S DANCE.

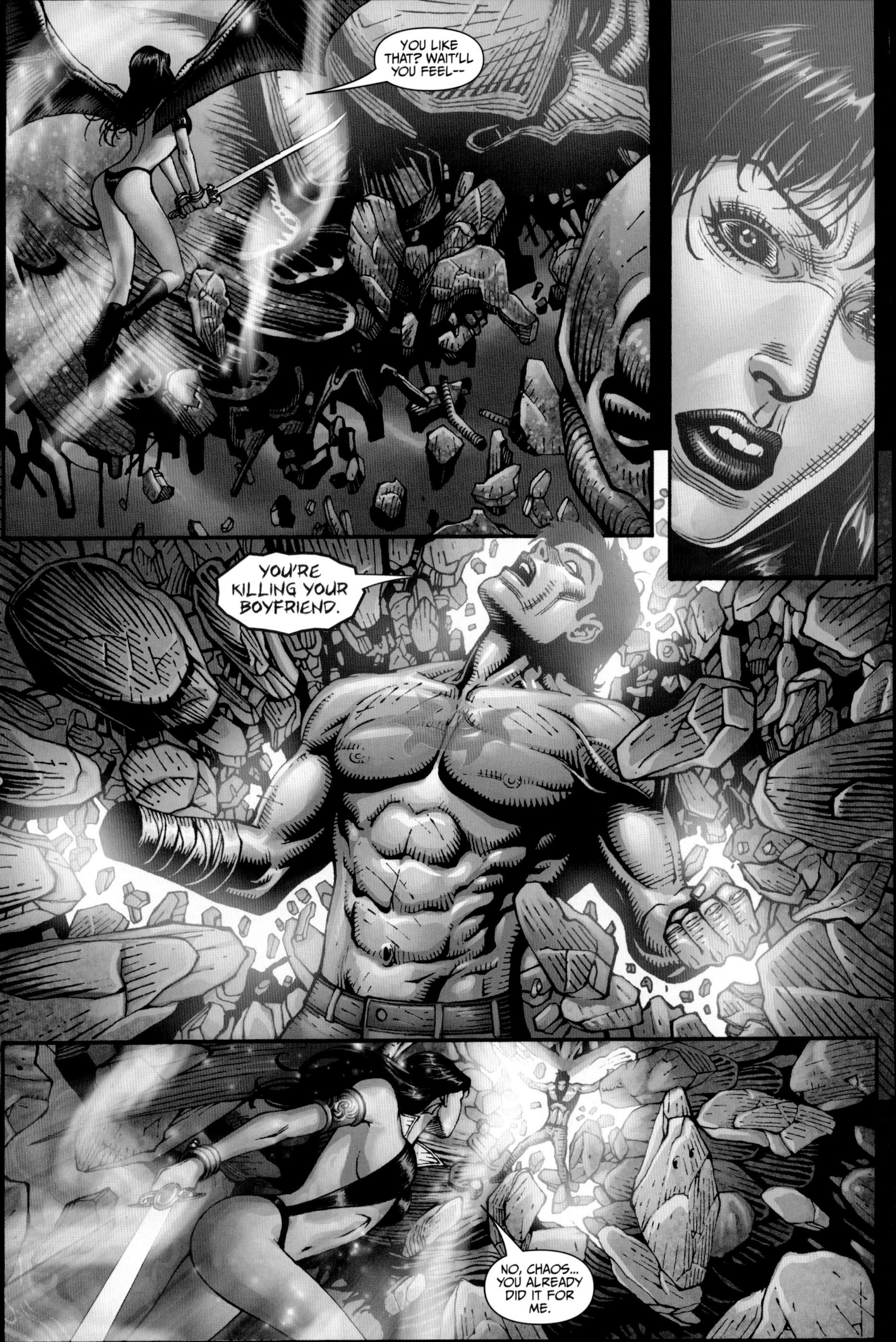
YOU LIKE THAT? WAIT'LL YOU FEEL--
YOU'RE KILLING YOUR BOYFRIEND.
NO, CHAOS... YOU ALREADY DID IT FOR ME.

AND SO...
WE DO
WHAT WE
MUST.

TO PROTECT
THE ONES
WE LOVE...

WE SACRIFICE...
GOD, HOW WE
SACRIFICE.

BUT WE GO
ON BECAUSE
WE LOVE.

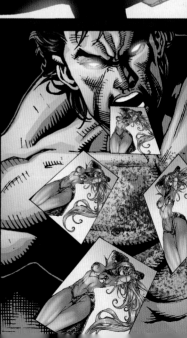

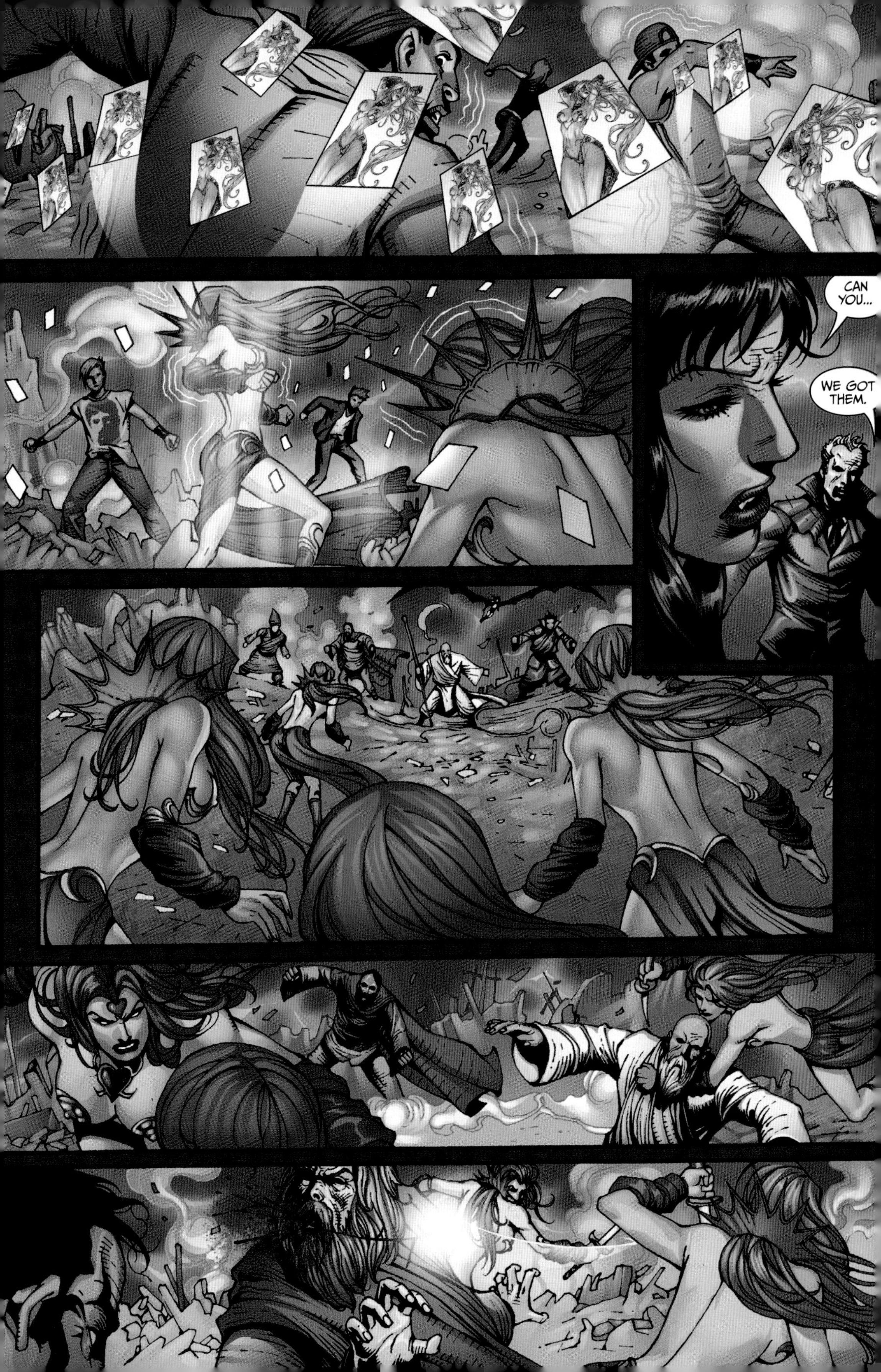
CAN YOU...
WE GOT THEM.

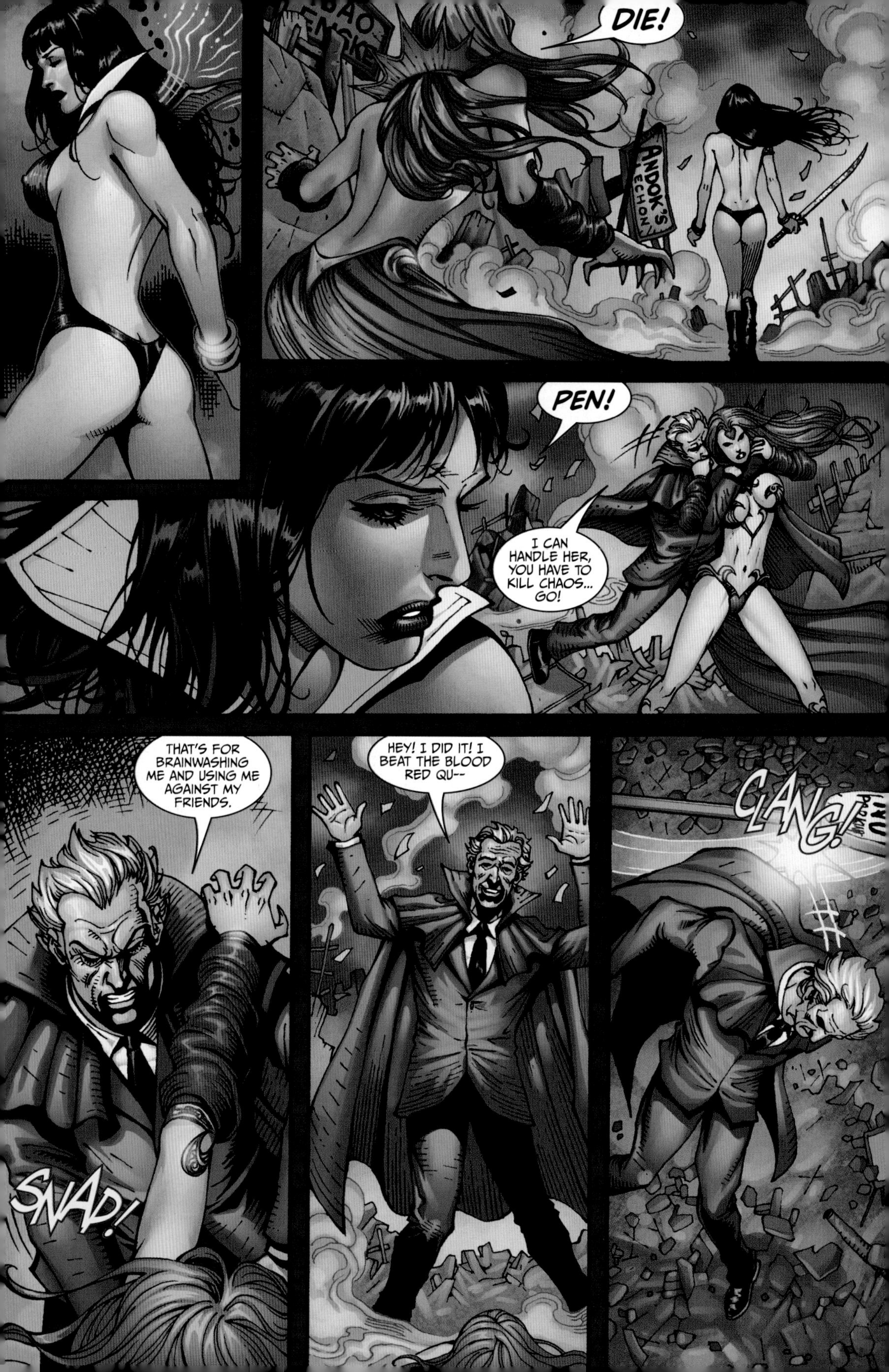
DIE!
ANDOK'S ECHON
PEN!
I CAN HANDLE HER, YOU HAVE TO KILL CHAOS... GO!
THAT'S FOR BRAINWASHING ME AND USING ME AGAINST MY FRIENDS.
SNAP!
HEY! I DID IT! I BEAT THE BLOOD RED QU--
CLANG!

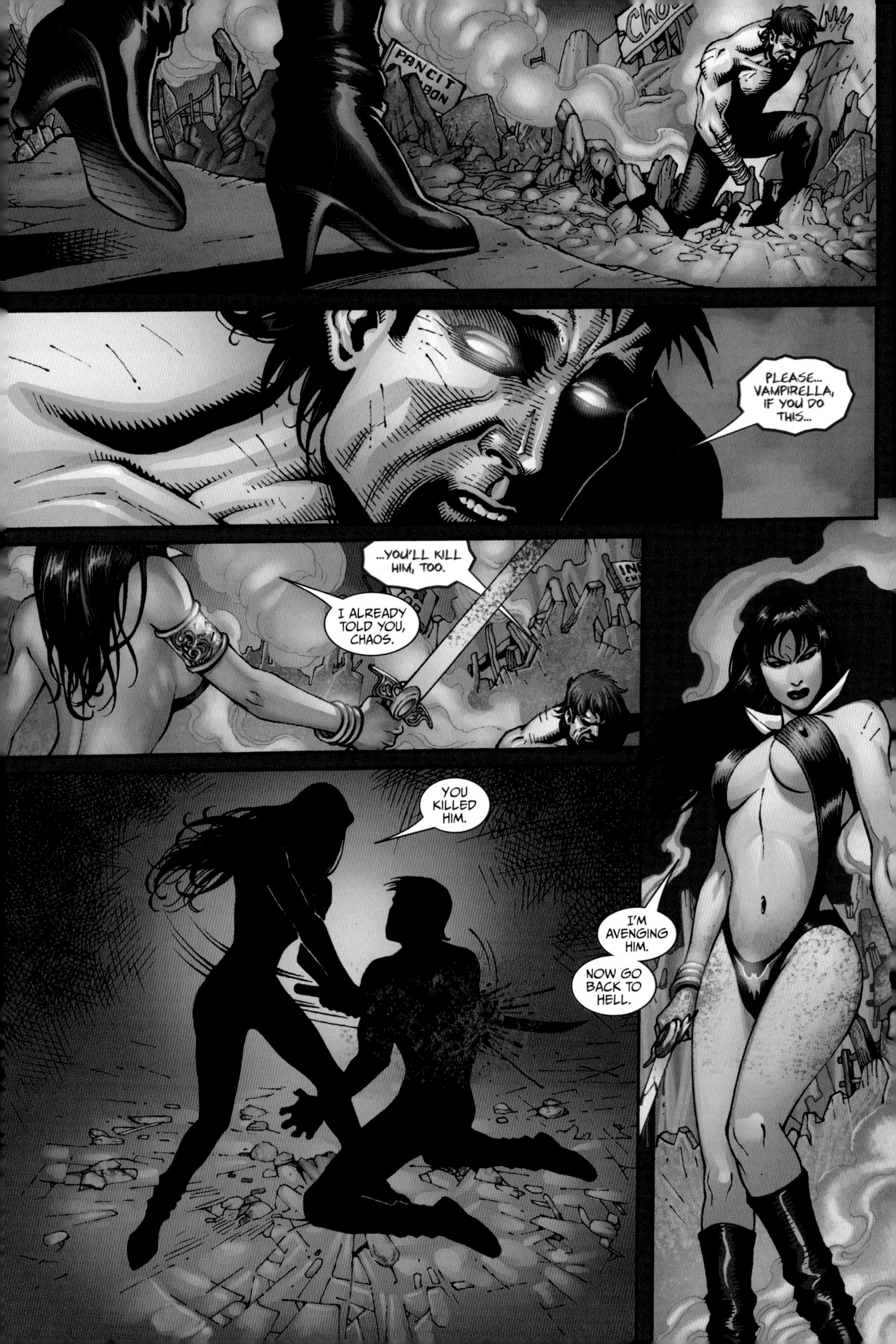
PANCIT
PLEASE... VAMPIRELLA, IF YOU DO THIS...
...YOU'LL KILL HIM, TOO.
I ALREADY TOLD YOU, CHAOS.
YOU KILLED HIM.
I'M AVENGING HIM.
NOW GO BACK TO HELL.

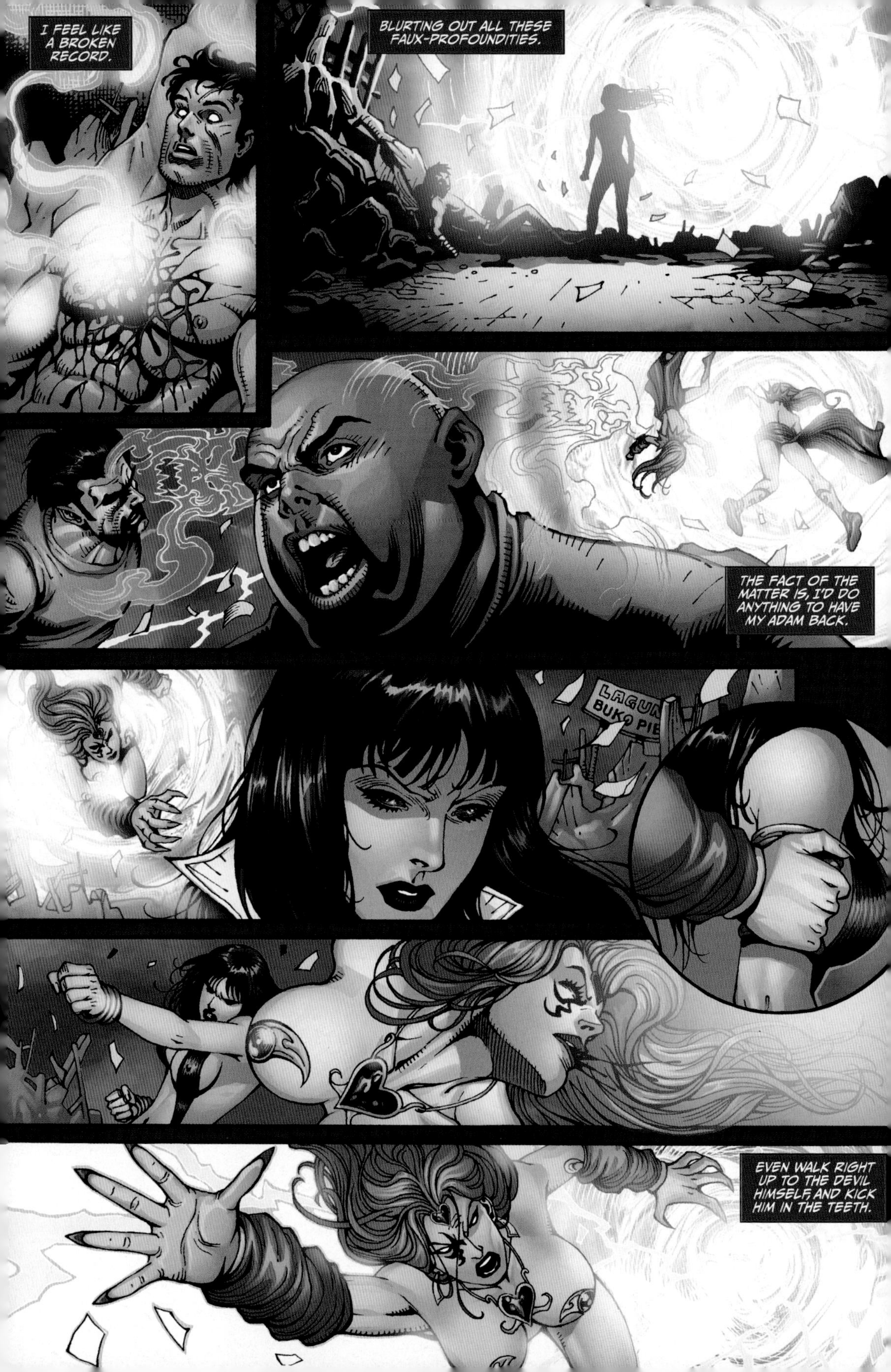
I FEEL LIKE A BROKEN RECORD.
BLURTING OUT ALL THESE FAUX-PROFOUNDITIES.
THE FACT OF THE MATTER IS, I'D DO ANYTHING TO HAVE MY ADAM BACK.
EVEN WALK RIGHT UP TO THE DEVIL HIMSELF, AND KICK HIM IN THE TEETH.

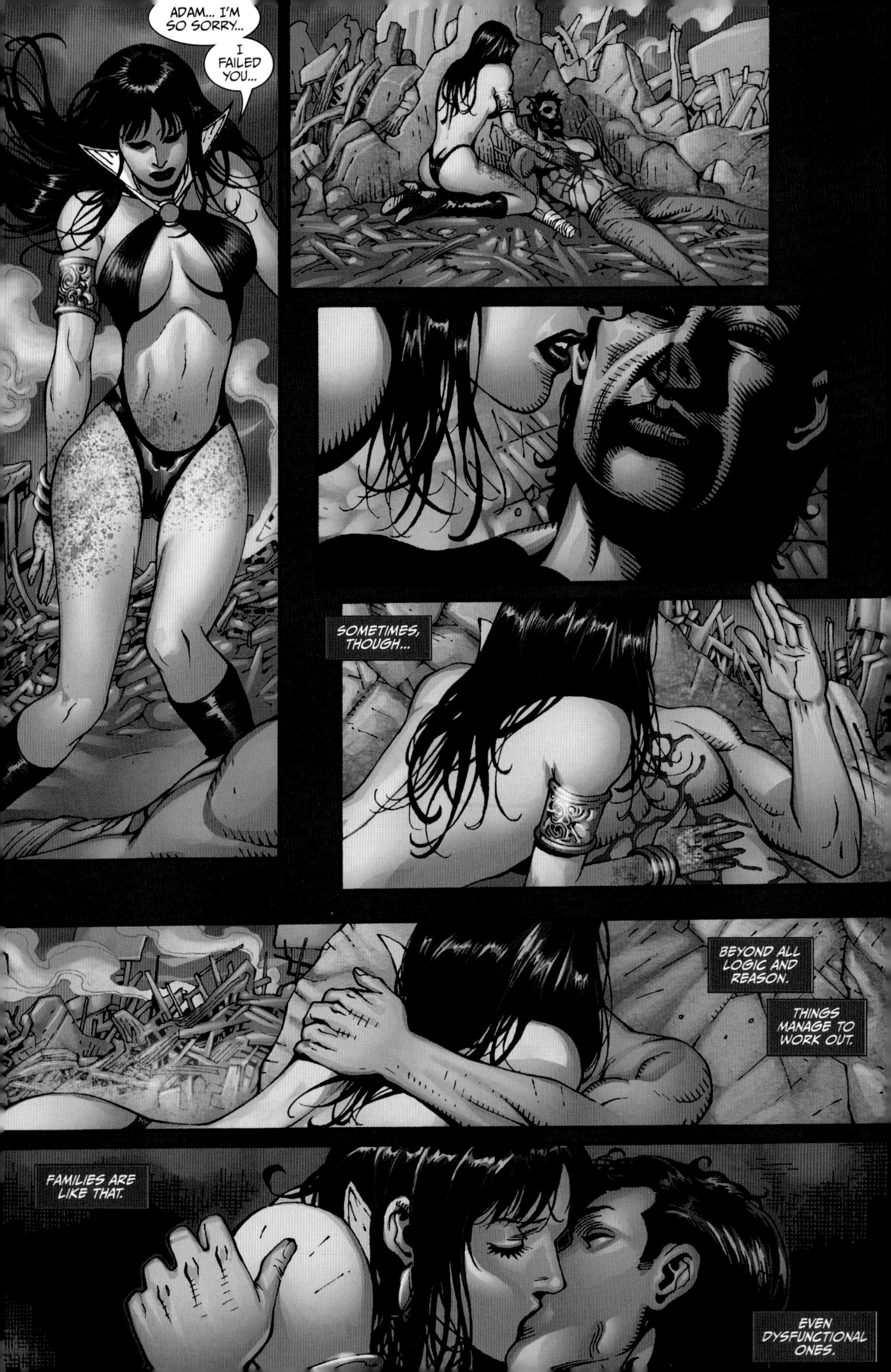
ADAM... I'M SO SORRY...
I FAILED YOU...
SOMETIMES, THOUGH...
BEYOND ALL LOGIC AND REASON.
THINGS MANAGE TO WORK OUT.
FAMILIES ARE LIKE THAT.
EVEN DYSFUNCTIONAL ONES.

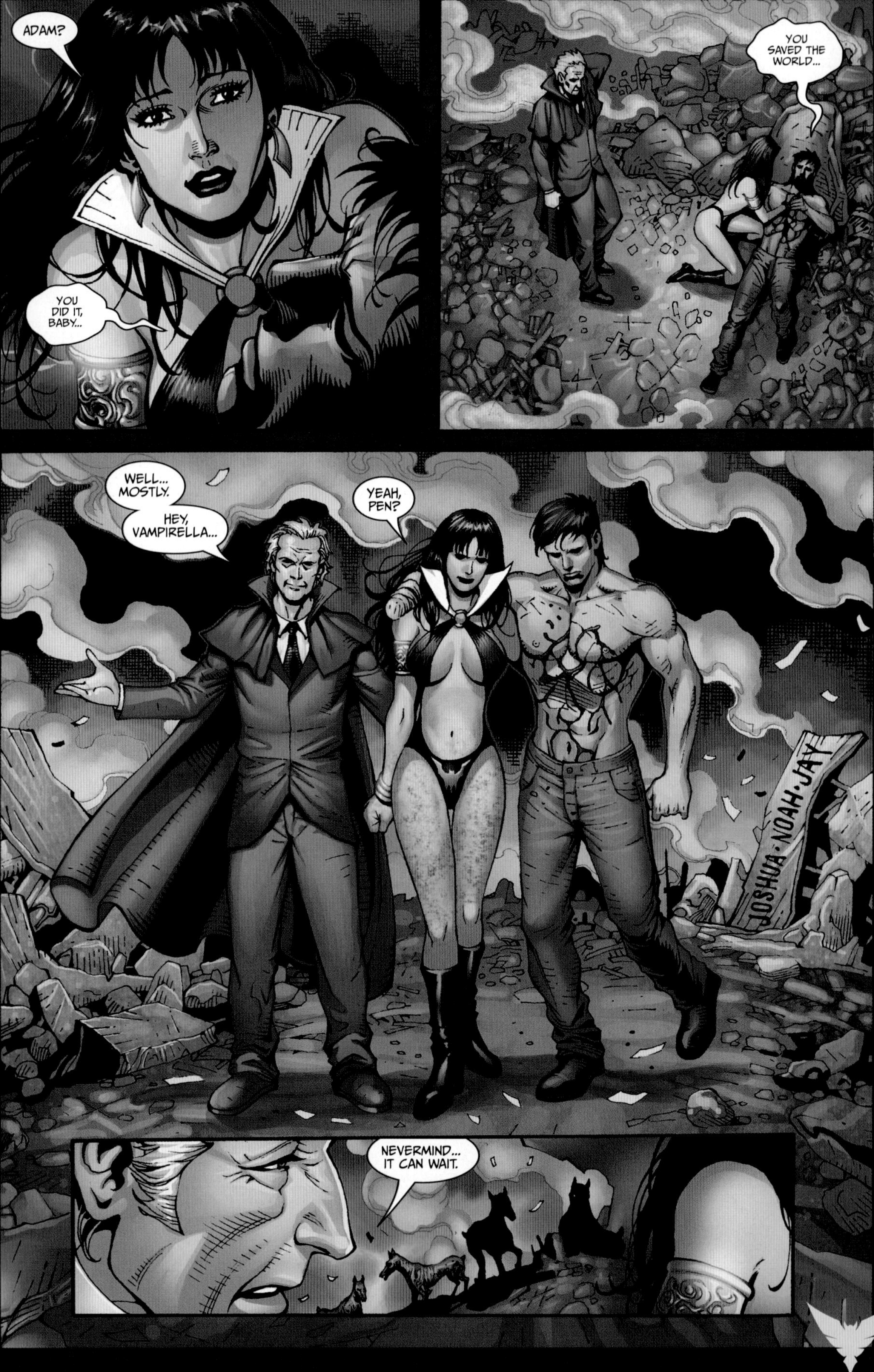
ADAM?
YOU DID IT, BABY...
YOU SAVED THE WORLD...
WELL... MOSTLY.
HEY, VAMPIRELLA...
YEAH, PEN?
JOSHUA • NOAH • JAY
NEVERMIND... IT CAN WAIT.

REVELATIONS
REVEALED!

Get the ultimate look inside the mind of Mike Carey: here's his complete final draft script for Vampirella Revelations #1!

PAGE 1

PANEL 1

Open in flashback/dream sequence—and we'll stay there for the whole of this first page. We're in the Drakulon of Vampi's childhood, and it's still in the "paradise" stage of its life cycle, with lush growth everywhere—a rural idyll in various swards one of the fabled rivers of blood and the deep red flowers which grow along its margins. Vampi's naked foot protrudes into the panel as she walks along the bank of the river: the rest of her is out of shot.

CAPTION: "I went out walking, down by the river. I was picking flowers, I think."

CAPTION: "And the river was arterial. So deep a red, it was almost black."

PANEL 2

Tight on Vampi—head and shoulders shot. She's plucked one of the flowers and she inhales its scent, eyes closed, savouring the sensation with every appearance of intense but tranquil pleasure.

CAPTION: "Oh god, the smell of the roses that bloom along those banks—their roots yards deep in the pulsing flow."

CAPTION: "The smell of a massacre in Heaven. You can't imagine."

PANEL 3

Out wide. Vampi wades out across a field of wild flowers—a young girl on a country stroll. To either side of her, strange animals like bovine mosquitoes graze in a peculiar and unsettling way. They have bodies like cattle, but mouthparts like biting insects which they've buried deep into the ground at their feet so that they can suck the blood of Drakulon through the "flesh" of its soil. Vampi pays them no mind—they're harmless and familiar sights.

CAPTION: "Then I walked home through the fields, where shrillkin dug their needle snouts into the integument to drink deep of the land's fullness."

CAPTION: "For Drakulon loves and feeds all her children alike."

PANEL 4

Close-up on Vampirella's face. She looks up and to the side, startled, wide-eyed.

CAPTION: "But then there was a sound. A roaring out of the sky."

CAPTION: "I didn't know enough to be afraid, but I was startled. I looked up—"

PANEL 5

Out wide, high angle. The spaceship which we've seen before in previous versions of Vampi's origin story rides down out of the sky on the white columns of its own incandescent jets.

CAPTION: "—and I saw the thing that would change my world forever."

PAGE 2

PANEL 1

Into present time. We're in a chic, up-market restaurant somewhere in Washington. Tight on Harry Krishna, who is dressed up to the nines—but in his usual louche, slightly frayed-at-the-edges, don't-really-give-a-damn Sean Penn kind of way. He has a glass of wine half-raised to his mouth, a meal half-eaten on the table in front of him. He looks a little skeptical or wary, as if he's not sure about some of what he's heard.

HARRY: Umm—Vampi, I think you told me this one. The ship was from Earth, right?

HARRY: And you hitched a ride back with these astronaut guys because your world was dying.

PANEL 2

Answering tight shot on Vampirella, who is sitting across the table from Harry. She too is in dazzling formal dress, but she's wearing her costume underneath as we'll see in a moment. She looks tense and unhappy. Mike, Bon actually has a possible design in mind for this dress, as being a full-length evening gown which actually incorporates the costume in a sneaky way, so that the reveal doesn't involve her removing the entire outfit to show the costume underneath—it's just whipping off the full-length add-on.

VAMPIRELLA: Yeah. But in this dream it was still lush and beautiful. Its veins—swollen with life. The charnel scents on the wind—

VAMPIRELLA: I'm sorry, Harry. I can see this is making you uncomfortable.

PANEL 3

Out wide. Harry stands, putting his glass down and looking past Vampi over towards the bar area, where a big, heavy-set, very imposing man in a tuxedo (Scald—he's actually a vampire) has just entered. Vampi turns to glance off in the same direction.

HARRY: Takes a lot to put me off my food, darling. But maybe we could finish this conversation later.

HARRY: I think our man just showed up.

PANEL 4

Looking past Harry towards Vampi as he walks away from the table towards the bar. She's still sitting down, watching him go.

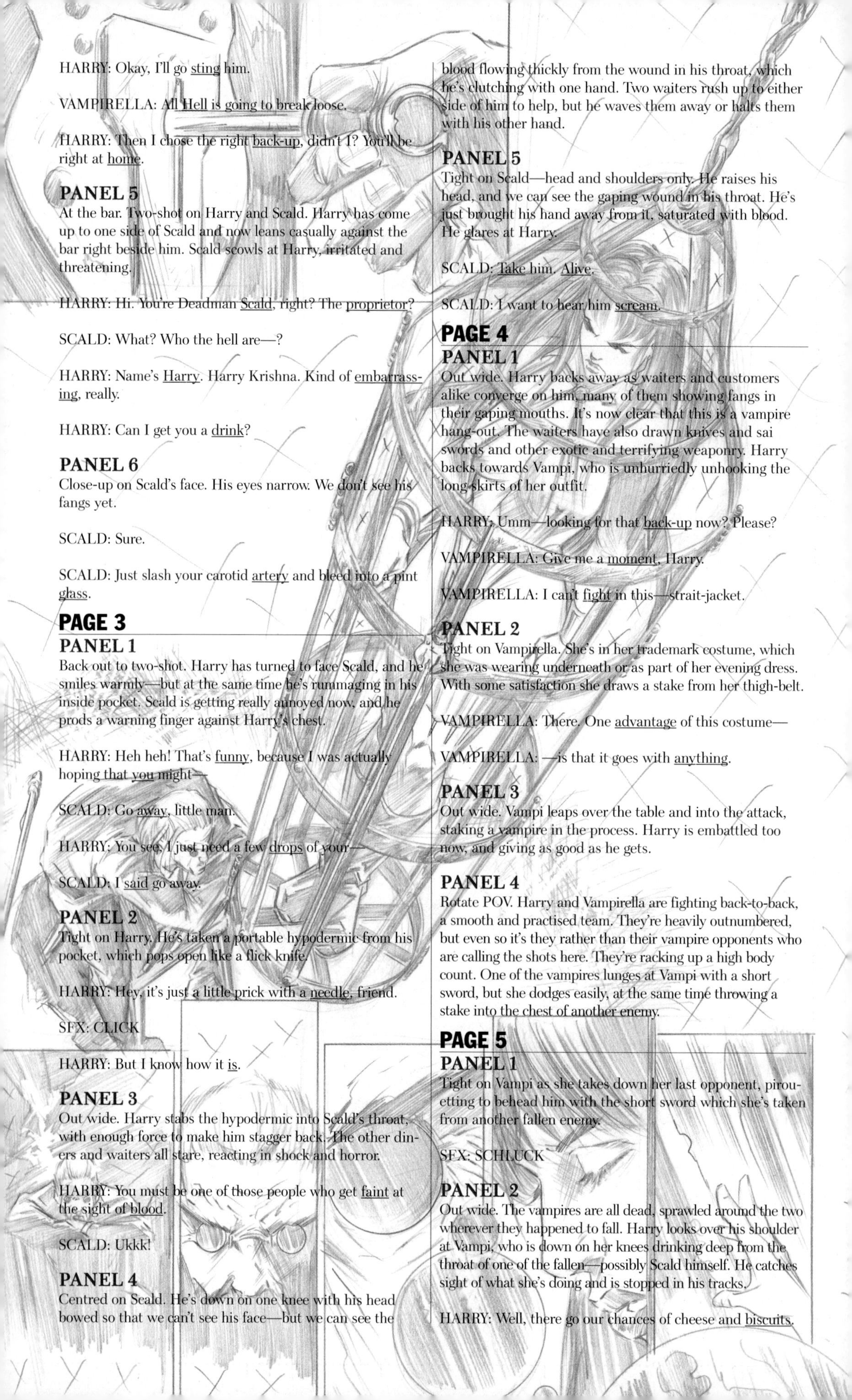

HARRY: Okay, I'll go sting him.

VAMPIRELLA: All Hell is going to break loose.

HARRY: Then I chose the right back-up, didn't I? You'll be right at home.

PANEL 5
At the bar. Two-shot on Harry and Scald. Harry has come up to one side of Scald and now leans casually against the bar right beside him. Scald scowls at Harry, irritated and threatening.

HARRY: Hi. You're Deadman Scald, right? The proprietor?

SCALD: What? Who the hell are—?

HARRY: Name's Harry. Harry Krishna. Kind of embarrassing, really.

HARRY: Can I get you a drink?

PANEL 6
Close-up on Scald's face. His eyes narrow. We don't see his fangs yet.

SCALD: Sure.

SCALD: Just slash your carotid artery and bleed into a pint glass.

PAGE 3

PANEL 1
Back out to two-shot. Harry has turned to face Scald, and he smiles warmly—but at the same time he's rummaging in his inside pocket. Scald is getting really annoyed now, and he prods a warning finger against Harry's chest.

HARRY: Heh heh! That's funny, because I was actually hoping that you might—

SCALD: Go away, little man.

HARRY: You see, I just need a few drops of your—

SCALD: I said go away.

PANEL 2
Tight on Harry. He's taken a portable hypodermic from his pocket, which pops open like a flick knife.

HARRY: Hey, it's just a little prick with a needle, friend.

SFX: CLICK

HARRY: But I know how it is.

PANEL 3
Out wide. Harry stabs the hypodermic into Scald's throat, with enough force to make him stagger back. The other diners and waiters all stare, reacting in shock and horror.

HARRY: You must be one of those people who get faint at the sight of blood.

SCALD: Ukkk!

PANEL 4
Centred on Scald. He's down on one knee with his head bowed so that we can't see his face—but we can see the blood flowing thickly from the wound in his throat, which he's clutching with one hand. Two waiters rush up to either side of him to help, but he waves them away or halts them with his other hand.

PANEL 5
Tight on Scald—head and shoulders only. He raises his head, and we can see the gaping wound in his throat. He's just brought his hand away from it, saturated with blood. He glares at Harry.

SCALD: Take him. Alive.

SCALD: I want to hear him scream.

PAGE 4

PANEL 1
Out wide. Harry backs away as waiters and customers alike converge on him, many of them showing fangs in their gaping mouths. It's now clear that this is a vampire hang-out. The waiters have also drawn knives and sai swords and other exotic and terrifying weaponry. Harry backs towards Vampi, who is unhurriedly unhooking the long skirts of her outfit.

HARRY: Umm—looking for that back-up now? Please?

VAMPIRELLA: Give me a moment, Harry.

VAMPIRELLA: I can't fight in this—strait-jacket.

PANEL 2
Tight on Vampirella. She's in her trademark costume, which she was wearing underneath or as part of her evening dress. With some satisfaction she draws a stake from her thigh-belt.

VAMPIRELLA: There. One advantage of this costume—

VAMPIRELLA: —is that it goes with anything.

PANEL 3
Out wide. Vampi leaps over the table and into the attack, staking a vampire in the process. Harry is embattled too now, and giving as good as he gets.

PANEL 4
Rotate POV. Harry and Vampirella are fighting back-to-back, a smooth and practised team. They're heavily outnumbered, but even so it's they rather than their vampire opponents who are calling the shots here. They're racking up a high body count. One of the vampires lunges at Vampi with a short sword, but she dodges easily, at the same time throwing a stake into the chest of another enemy.

PAGE 5

PANEL 1
Tight on Vampi as she takes down her last opponent, pirouetting to behead him with the short sword which she's taken from another fallen enemy.

SFX: SCHLUCK

PANEL 2
Out wide. The vampires are all dead, sprawled around the two wherever they happened to fall. Harry looks over his shoulder at Vampi, who is down on her knees drinking deep from the throat of one of the fallen—possibly Scald himself. He catches sight of what she's doing and is stopped in his tracks.

HARRY: Well, there go our chances of cheese and biscuits.

HARRY: Maybe we should go back to my place for a—

HARRY: ...

PANEL 3
Tight on Vampi. She looks up from her impromptu meal, unapologetic. Blood courses down her chin.

VAMPIRELLA: What? He was bleeding anyway, and I was hungry.

VAMPIRELLA: The house salad didn't do it for me.

PANEL 4
Out to two-shot. Vampi stands, wiping her mouth with the back of her hand. Harry stares at her with slight unease.

HARRY: I'm sorry. It's just—every once in a while I forget what you are.

VAMPIRELLA: Why, Harry. That's the nicest thing you've ever said to me.

VAMPIRELLA: Back to your place for—?

PANEL 5
Tight on Harry. He looks at the hypodermic, now full of rich, sloshing red.

HARRY: Skip it. I think we're done here.

HARRY: Seventeen samples in three days. Could be a new world record.

PANEL 6
Out wide. Looking towards the two of them from behind as they head for the doors.

VAMPIRELLA: What does the government want with vampire blood samples?

HARRY: They don't tell me, darlin', and I don't ask.

HARRY: Since they closed the Circus down, this is the only way I can justify my expense account.

PAGE 6
PANEL 1
Out on the street. Two-shot on Vampi and Harry, with the restaurant sign visible behind them—CHEZ PAPA MINUIT in flowing cursive script. Vampi is in the lead; Harry looks at her back, thoughtful or concerned.

HARRY: That stuff you were talking about in there—it bothers you?

VAMPIRELLA: What do you think?

VAMPIRELLA: My mind is full of garbage that makes no sense even on its own terms.

PANEL 2
Tight on Vampi. She turns to look back at Harry, her expression bleak.

VAMPIRELLA: Spaceships from Earth, out in the far reaches of the universe?

VAMPIRELLA: And I've been to Drakulon. It's in Hell. So why do I remember a childhood on another planet?

PANEL 3
Two-shot. Harry holds up his wrist-watch to talk into it. Vampi stares at him, deadpan.

HARRY: Bring her round, Jinks—we're done. So you only agreed to come out and play because I said I could help you?

VAMPIRELLA: No. I also got to kill vampires.

VAMPIRELLA: Can you help me, Harry, or was that just your usual bullshit?

PANEL 4
Tight on Harry. He rubs his neck, looks tired and ill at ease.

HARRY: There's this ex-circus guy. Peter Glass. He can—whatever you want to call it—possess people.

HARRY: Send out his spirit, as the judges in the Salem witch trials so quaintly put it.

PANEL 5
Out wide. Harry walks towards a small van which is pulling in at the sidewalk. Vampi follows him. In the van is Jinks, the muscular roustabout seen in Vampirella#11. On the side of the van is the logo of the WORLDS END CIRCUS.

HARRY: Nervous type. He kept on having breakdowns and we kept on putting him back together.

HARRY: Then he went blind—don't ask me how—and we put him out to grass.

VAMPIRELLA: And how does this relate to me?

PANEL 6
Tight on Harry. He's hauled open the side door of the van, but he pauses to look back at Vampi before climbing in.

HARRY: You want someone to take a look inside your head, right? Glass will read you like a book. He may scribble in the margins, though.

HARRY: I'll give him a call. Ask him if he'll see you. After that—

PAGE 7
PANEL 1
Cut to a new location. External establishing shot of a big, almost palatial detached house in Washington. Night. A bat flies down towards the house. It has a very large glass conservatory.

CAPTION [COMPLETING HARRY'S DIALOGUE]: "—you're on your own."

CAPTION: "Like always."

PANEL 2
In tighter. The bat flits past a window which is both closed and barred.

PANEL 3
Tight on a small skylight seen from inside the house. It's wedged slightly open, and this leaves a gap just wide enough for the bat to crawl through—which is what it's doing. The skylight is actually part of the conservatory, where a number of these small windows have been left open high up on the side of the structure.

PANEL 4

Out wide to show the interior of the conservatory. It has a number of tropical plants—palm trees and the like—growing here and there, but it's a space for living in rather than a greenhouse as such. The bat flies across the tiled central area, watched intently and silently by scores of birds—parrots, macaws, lovebirds and so on—which are sitting in the trees. Up ahead there's a partition, partially open, and beyond it we can see a man—his back turned to us—playing a grand piano.

PANEL 5

Tight on the man at the piano, seen from in front now. This is Glass, and since it's our first glimpse of him we need him to make a strong impression. He's a slender, almost cadaverous and in late middle age, dry and hard and seemingly humourless. He has snow-white hair and wears opaque black glasses. There's something about him that's forbidding and scary: he's not a man you'd approach voluntarily or trust readily. The bat hovers in the air immediately behind him as he plays. He seems intent on his music, not reacting to the presence of the bat in any way.

PANEL 6

Identical POV to previous panel, but instead of the bat Vampirella in her human form now stands behind Glass. He looks up and off, frowning, as if he's heard something.

PAGE 8
PANEL 1

Tight on Glass. He arches one eyebrow, not afraid or startled but certainly interested.

GLASS: Extraordinary. You're a—nyctalops. Haemovore. Vampire.

GLASS: I've never seen one from this close.

PANEL 2

Out to two-shot. Glass stands, closing the piano lid. Vampi watches him with suspicion and dislike.

VAMPIRELLA: Seen? Harry said you were blind.

GLASS: Oh yes, oh yes. Hysterical dysfunction of the optic nerve. The eyes send, the brain ignores.

GLASS: But I can see you well enough.

PANEL 3

Out wide, high angle. In the foreground, the brightly coloured birds high up in the trees stare down at Vampirella. She looks up, meeting their gaze, as Glass leads the way across the conservatory.

GLASS: The birds, the birds, the birds. I use their eyes. That's what they're for—just little tiny windows for me to peer through.

GLASS: Follow me—Vampirella.

PAGE 9
PANEL 1

Another room—a sort of study, very luxuriously appointed, with bookcases on the walls, a desk, a leather swivel chair. Vampirella follows Glass in through the doorway.

VAMPIRELLA: Did Harry tell you what it is I want?

GLASS: You want me to enter your thoughts—search for locked rooms, loose floorboards, hidden doors.

GLASS: I can do that. Oh yes, oh yes. I can do more.

PANEL 2

Tight on Glass, possibly high angle. He's stopped in front of something very incongruous—a winch on the wall to which a chain and pulley are attached. He winds the winch, and a skeletal iron structure of some kind—we won't see the details until the next panel—lowers itself into view.

GLASS: But before we go any further—

GLASS: —I think you should slip into something a little less comfortable.

PANEL 3

Out wide. Glass has lowered the bizarre object to ground level. It's a human-shaped cage which hinges on a central axis so that a person can be locked inside it. Vampirella stares at it, her eyes narrowing slightly in anger. Glass remains calm and cold.

VAMPIRELLA: An iron maiden.

GLASS: A gibbet. No spikes. No sharp edges. Very humane—until you starve to death.

VAMPIRELLA: Are you mad?

PANEL 4

Tight on Glass. His expression is deadpan.

GLASS: That's a trick question. You're the one who wants your mind, your past, your soul dissected.

GLASS: Could be nasty. Usually is. Could provoke—extreme reactions.

PANEL 5

Out to two-shot. Vampi glares at Glass. He meets the glare levelly with his sightless eyes, smiling without humour.

VAMPIRELLA: You think I might harm you?

GLASS: I'm determined that you won't.

GLASS: So in you go. Turn the lock, start the clock. You see?

PANEL 6

Close-up on Vampi's face—a reaction shot. She's exasperated and not at all happy, but she hesitates with a biting rejoinder on her lips. Her options don't look all that wide or wonderful here.

PAGE 10
PANEL 1

An identical close-up of Vampi's face, but now the bars of the gibbet have been closed across it. Glass's hand enters shot to turn a key in the gibbet at head height. Vampi's expression is grim, smouldering.

PANEL 2

Out wide. Glass winches the gibbet a foot or so off the floor. Vampi glares down at him.

GLASS: Krishna says your memories are unreliable. Loose. Crumbly. No firm footholds.

VAMPIRELLA: I remember things that couldn't have happened.

VAMPIRELLA: And things that contradict each other.

PANEL 3
Tight on Glass. He pulls up a chair (not the swivel chair—a straight-backed chair), immediately underneath the gibbet.

GLASS: Precisely. And since we are nothing but the sum of our past experiences—

GLASS: —the inescapable conclusion is that you don't know who you are.

PANEL 4
Out wide. Glass sits under the gibbet, backwards on the chair with his arms folded on its back. Vampi looks down on him, which is a strain at this angle.

VAMPIRELLA: You've got a flair for melodrama.

GLASS: For truth. Truth truth truth. Truth is the bedrock of the soul.

GLASS: It stands out, under all the illusions and deceptions of memory, like the outline of a dead stump under moss.

PANEL 5
Close-up on Glass's face. He starts to concentrate, his eyes narrowing.

GLASS: Close your eyes.

GLASS: And think about the earliest moment that you can remember.

PANEL 6
Close-up on Vampi's face—eyes closed, thinking hard.

PANEL 7
Into flashback—a tiny scrap of information, a tiny detail from a larger scene. We're looking at the frame of a mirror (the Eidolon, the magical mirror which we'll meet later on), and we're seeing it from a low angle, as through the eyes of a child. The child's hand—the young Vampirella's hand—comes on from off-panel to touch the bottom of the mirror tentatively.

PAGE 11
PANELS 1, 2, 3
Three narrow panels, side by side on the top tier. The central panel is the mirror again—a repeat of this frozen moment from Vampi's memory. It's flanked on the left by Vampi's face—eyes closed, with an expression of intense concentration—and on the right by Glass's face: he looks sour and unimpressed. The balloons run along the whole of the top tier—so Glass has a lot to say, but it's spread out across three panels.

GLASS: Hmm. That's the best you can do?

GLASS: Very well. It has resonances. It sings. But its voice is too soft to hear.

GLASS: You see—we start outside ourselves.

GLASS: The light that illuminates us—reveals us—explains us—comes from outside.

PANEL 4
Out wide. Vampirella dangles in her cage over Glass's head. She looks down at him, still mistrusting. He rests his chin on his folded arms and stares unseeing into space.

VAMPIRELLA: What does that mean?

GLASS: Context. It means context.

GLASS: It means your memories are encrypted. We need a key.

PANEL 5
Close-up on Glass's face. He glances up at Vampi, suddenly animated and excited.

GLASS: So we dangle this moment into the dead sea of past time. And other moments rise to the bait.

GLASS: Moments not from your life, but from—

GLASS: Aah! Yes yes yes!

PANEL 6
Back to the same frozen instant of Vampi's hand touching the mirror—the third time we've seen it now. But this time is different: this time the image seems to accelerate and blur towards the right of the panel, bleeding off the edge of the page in horizontal speed lines. We're entering a visionary time, a premonition of the past.

GLASS [TAILLESS BALLOON]: It begins.

GLASS [TAILLESS BALLOON]: Hold on tight.

PAGE 12
PANEL 1
Mike, we need the same "speed blur" effect, but reversed this time, so that it comes on from the left of the panel and then disappears or fades as the image "stabilises"—giving us a solid, undistorted image on the right. We've been on a journey and now we've arrived. The image that we're seeing now is another tight close-up—this time of Lilith's face, seen horizontally because she's reclining on a couch. She looks pale and unhappy, even in pain, as she twists and grimaces.

LILITH: I cannot rise to greet you, beloved. I can barely speak.

LILITH: Look in my eyes. Tell me what you see.

PANEL 2
Out wide for an establishing shot. We're in Drakulon, in Lilith's palace: specifically, we're in her luxuriously appointed boudoir. Lilith lies on her bed or on a couch, with a canopy of draperies over her, apparently too weak to rise. Belial stands over her, having just entered. He stares down at her, serious and concerned. Mike, Lilith has been seen before many times, so there's loads of visual reference. Belial is new, and you can basically go to town. He's a demon, obviously, so although he's based on the human template we can give him horns or fangs or antlers or whatever the hell we like. Ideally, what I'd like is for him to be both bestial and fairly sexy/charismatic in appearance: the sort of demon you could imagine making a fool of yourself over, if you were a woman given to that sort of rough trade (as Lilith is). Did you ever read Alan Moore's *Halo Jones*? There's a guy in part three who has two enormous tusks jutting out of his mouth, but Halo still falls for him and it's convincing that she does. That's the effect we want here...

BELIAL: A shadow, Lilith. Death's shadow.

LILITH: You're honest for once, Belial. How very ill-timed.

BELIAL: But you do not need to die.

PANEL 3

Tight on Belial. He gestures, agitated, angry—his anger motivated by his love and concern for Lilith.

BELIAL: It's the children—the wamphyri. They deplete you. They draw their being from you.

BELIAL: It is their curse, and yours. You must act now, or you'll perish by inches and ounces.

PANEL 4

Out wide. Lilith and Belial are frozen in their postures—he reaching out a hand towards her, her trying to rise. We can now see Vampi and Glass watching from the background. Vampi is amazed to be here, and she looks at her mother with both yearning and concern. Glass is entirely matter-of-fact.

VAMPIRELLA: How am I seeing this? What are you doing to me?

GLASS: We're trawling the past—the memories of others, in which you figure. You know these two?

VAMPIRELLA: Not the demon. The—the woman is my mother, Lilith. But she looks so sick!

PANEL 5

Into two-shot on Glass and Vampirella. Glass glances side-long at Vampirella, interested but not emotionally engaged—as if she's a specimen on a slide. She glares back at him, angry and disconcerted.

GLASS: Your mother is central to your conception of yourself, yes?

VAMPIRELLA: I love her.

GLASS: No, no, not that. She defines you. You kill your vampire siblings in order to win redemption for her.

PANEL 6

Two-shot on Glass and Belial. Glass walks around Belial as though he's walking around a museum exhibit: Belial hasn't moved since the previous panel. Glass watches Belial with a musing, interested expression, and flicks out the fingers of his right hand in a commanding gesture.

GLASS: Perhaps that explains the paradox. This moment is before your birth, but still it marks a crux for you.

GLASS: Let's see what comes of it.

PAGE 13
PANEL 1

Another "speed blur" effect, signalling a shift to another crucial moment of past time. This time, when the image stabilises, we're in tight close-up on a dagger which Lilith is drawing from a sheath at her waist.

LILITH: It's ironic.

LILITH: That the solution should look so very much like the problem—

PANEL 2

Out wide for an establishing shot. We're no longer in Lilith's chambers, or in her palace. We're out in the wilds of Drakulon—still a paradise—with the palace rising in the background. Lilith stands in the foreground with the dagger in her hand, steeling herself for some ordeal or ritual still unspecified.

Belial stands at her shoulder, watching her, being both supportive and watchful. Lilith is about to draw the dagger across the open palm of her hand, and her posture should suggest this.

BELIAL: She may look like them, but she'll be different.

BELIAL: She'll be you. Born from your blood, untainted and undiluted. With none of the weaknesses of her siblings.

LILITH: I know that, my love.

PANEL 3

Tight on Lilith. She slashes her hand deeply, holding it tilted so that the blood will run out onto the soil.

LILITH: She'll have two mothers—me, and Drakulon itself. The living land that Satan gave to me.

LILITH: And no father. No other strain or strand to weaken her bond with me.

PANEL 4

Tight on the drops of blood as they fall onto the soil.

LILITH [OP]: And so that bond will grow, as she grows.

LILITH [OP]: Wax strong, as she discovers her strength.

PANEL 5

Staying tight on the same area of ground. It bulges into a gently rounded mound like a pregnant woman's stomach. *Exactly* like a pregnant woman's stomach.

LILITH [OP]: Branch out, umbilically, through every part of her—

PANEL 6

Same POV. The hand of a newborn baby breaks through the crumbly soil of the mound—groping, reaching, being born.

LILITH [OP]: My second self.

LILITH [OP]: My sword.

LILITH [OP]: My surrogate.

PAGE 14

Splash. Mike, this may seem like a weird moment to elevate by means of a splash page, but it's the new focal point which we're putting at the heart of the Vampirella mythos: the moment of her birth. Think religious icons, although I know that's a dodgy analogy. Lilith and Belial stand facing each other, and Lilith has the newborn Vampirella in her arms. An umbilical cord still connects the neonate Vampi to the soil of Drakulon. Lilith looks down at her tenderly, but also eagerly—not a mother's look, because it's somehow too calculating. Belial stands by, taking the role of father in this holy family although he's not genetically involved or at stake here. He loves Lilith: he'll do whatever it takes to keep her alive.

LILITH: Vampirella.

PAGE 15
PANEL 1

Pull back, to show Vampirella and Glass watching the epiphany we've just seen. Vampi is shocked rigid, Glass coolly thoughtful.

VAMPIRELLA: That's—

GLASS: Yes. You. Newborn.

GLASS: To go on from here—it gets risky.

PANEL 2
Tight on Glass. He ponders, touching a knuckle to his lower lip.

GLASS: Hovering around the edges—just watching—that's all very well. Oh yes.

GLASS: When we go on into your childhood, you won't watch. You'll—become.

GLASS: Regress. Rewind. Relive. As long as it lasts.

PANEL 3
Tight two-shot on Vampi and Glass. She turns to stare at him. He's still enjoying this just as an intriguing game of ideas, a conundrum. She stares at him with desperate, feral intensity.

VAMPIRELLA: So?

GLASS: So. You hate the thought of being vulnerable. That's uppermost in your—

VAMPIRELLA: Just do it.

PANEL 4
Out very wide. We're looking towards the Lilith/Belial/baby Vampi holy family moment, but from a distance as the adult Vampi and Glass walk away from it towards us. What they're walking into is a featureless black expanse.

GLASS: In your own head be it.

GLASS: Follow me.

PANEL 5
Identical POV, with Vampi and Glass still walking towards us—but now, the image of child-Vampi's hand touching the frame of the mirror, the memory that started all this, has appeared in the foreground so that Vampi and Glass are walking towards it. Vampi stares at the image, intent: Glass is cold and detached.

GLASS: Remember this?

VAMPIRELLA: My first memory. Where we started from.

GLASS: Exactly.

PANEL 6
Close-up on Vampirella's face. The speed blur effect kicks in to the right of the panel.

GLASS [OP]: That's where we'll go next.

PAGE 16
PANEL 1
Speed blur from left. High angle shot looking down into the face of an angelic child Vampirella, circa six or seven years old. We're looking down on her as through Lilith's eyes, and Lilith's hand comes into shot to stroke her cheek.

LILITH: My good girl. My only good girl.

VAMPIRELLA: 'Cos all my brothers and sisters are bad.

LILITH: Very bad.

PANEL 2
Out wide for an establishing shot. We're in a room in the

palace—the subterranean room where our climax is going to take place in #3. Lilith scoops Vampi up in her arms, smiling at her playfully—although Vampi herself is as serious and solemn as only a child or an archbishop knows how to be. Lilith walks across an expanse of marble floor, heading towards us.

VAMPIRELLA: The demons hurt mommy, and make her sad.

VAMPIRELLA: I'll hurt them right back.

LILITH: Yes you will, my love.

PANEL 3
Rotate POV to bring the heart of Drakulon into shot. It's like a huge, multi-faceted diamond—the millennium—and it hovers unsupported in the centre of the vast chamber. Lilith holds kiddy-Vampirella up to examine it, and Vampirella holds her hand out to touch it although Lilith is careful to hold her just out of reach.

LILITH: And what's this?

VAMPIRELLA: Heart of the land!

LILITH: That's right. The heart of Drakulon.

LILITH: If you ever want to find your way home, listen to the heartbeat and follow it back.

PANEL 4
Into tight two-shot. Lilith brings her face up close to Vampi's, for all the world like a mother who loves her child, and Vampi stares at her with big, soulful eyes.

VAMPIRELLA: Do I have to go away, mommy?

LILITH: Not yet, my love. But soon. You'll be my brave soldier.

LILITH: You'll fight for mommy while she sleeps, and make her all better.

PANEL 5
Cut away to a doorway on the other side of the room. Belial enters, followed by the aged, crotchety Splinter and by two burly demons who wheel the Eidolon in between them. There's a curtain or hanging over the mirror, so that we can't see anything of it besides the general outline.

BELIAL: Lilith. This is Splinter, who made the Eidolon for you—to my specifications.

SPLINTER: An honor, majesty.

BELIAL: He says it's ready now.

PAGE 17
PANEL 1
Out wide. Lilith now leads Vampi by the hand, across the room towards Belial and the Eidolon. Lilith and Belial exchange a tense, meaningful look, while Splinter fusses with the hangings and makes a last-minute inspection of his pride and joy. The demon servitors stand stolidly by.

LILITH: Perhaps there's another way to do this.

BELIAL: There isn't. You need to be strong again.

BELIAL: To win your revenge on the children of Adam. To devour their world.

PANEL 2
Tight on Belial. He reaches out and grasps the edge of the curtain which covers the Eidolon. His expression is stern and cold.

BELIAL: So the equation's <u>simple</u>. Vampirella must find and <u>kill</u> her siblings, year after year, century after <u>century</u>.

BELIAL: So that their strength flows <u>through</u> her and returns to <u>you</u>.

PANEL 3
Reverse POV, so that we're looking past Belial from behind towards Vampi as he pulls the covers away from the Eidolon and reveals it. This means that we're not seeing the mirror surface at all—just the back of the frame. Vampi and Lilith both stare at it, nonplussed.

BELIAL: And for <u>that</u> she needs a reason. An <u>explanation</u> that she'll never question.

BELIAL: <u>Look</u>, Vampirella.

BELIAL: Look into the <u>Eidolon</u>.

PANEL 4
Tight on Vampi's hand as she tentatively reaches forward and touches the edge of the mirror's frame. This is the exact same moment that we've seen three times before, seen from the identical POV so that we get the shock of recognition.

PANEL 5
Close-up on Vampi's face, her eyes wide in surprise and alarm.

PANEL 6
Looking past Vampi from behind into the mirror—but instead of her own face reflected there, we can see the face of Peter Glass. He is animated and excited.

GLASS: This—

GLASS: —this is <u>amazing</u>.

PAGE 18
Mike, this page is a regular grid, two panels across and three tiers high. All three left-hand panels are cut-aways to Glass's house: all three right-hand panels remain in the mystical remembered/relived hallucination that Vampirella and Glass are currently sharing.

PANEL 1
Wide shot of Glass's conservatory, with the birds looking broody and uneasy.

PANEL 2
Close-up on Glass's face in the mirror. He speaks urgently, quickly, full of excitement at this amazing intellectual puzzle.

GLASS: Before—one stream of memories, strong and steady.

GLASS: After—a cat's <u>cradle</u>. Twisted. Tangled. Curdled.

GLASS: Something <u>happens</u> when you look into this mirror.

PANEL 3
Back to Glass's conservatory, but in tighter on the birds. They all look towards us, startled and agitated.

PANEL 4
Close-up on the face of the child Vampirella with the phantom outline of the adult Vampirella superimposed. The child looks startled and wondering, the adult angry and afraid.

GLASS: Something—<u>wraps</u> itself around your mind. Your <u>soul</u>.

GLASS: But perhaps, if I <u>cut</u>—here—and here—

PANEL 5
Back to the conservatory—in even tighter on the birds. They hunker down and squawk in loud, gape-mouthed protest, all staring straight ahead and down at us—or rather at something corresponding to our POV. Pandemonium is breaking loose here.

PANEL 6
Close-up on Glass's face. He looks off, taken by surprise, as the faint echoes of the distant squawking reach his ears.

GLASS: —I can find a way <u>through</u> to—

GLASS: ...

PAGE 19
PANEL 1
Back to the conservatory. Out wide. The birds scatter in panic flight.

PANEL 2
Tight on Glass—in his body now, rather than in the skein of memories. He comes out of his trance, sitting bolt upright: he's irritable and shaken.

GLASS: Stay <u>still</u>, you feathered vermin!

GLASS: Let me <u>see</u>—

PANEL 3
Close-up on Glass's face. He turns as a shadow falls across him—turns not at the shadow but at the sound of a voice from close by. He's hugely surprised and alarmed.

ATHALTOR: You.

ATHALTOR: You've <u>meddled</u> with what you don't <u>understand</u>.

PANEL 4
Out wide. Glass is surrounded by demons—really foul and scary-looking ones. The scariest of all, Athaltor, has lifted him bodily out of the chair and dangles him by his lapels so that his feet don't touch the ground. Glass is terrified, close to hysteria.

ATHALTOR: And you've made our <u>master</u> very angry.

GLASS: N—no!

GLASS: God, <u>no</u>! I was only—

PANEL 5
In tight, looking past Glass from behind towards Athaltor. Athaltor makes a raking swipe across Glass's face, removing most of it in a single clotted swathe of flesh. Glass sags, head lolling back, dead on the instant.

PAGE 20
PANEL 1
Out wide, high angle. The demons all advance on the suspended cage in which Vampirella dangles helplessly. This could be a high angle shot looking down. Vampi's head is

bowed, and if we can see her face her eyes are closed: she's still in the trance state.

ATHALTOR: This is her?

SECOND DEMON: Oh yes.

ATHALTOR: Bring her down, Grivarr, and let's see what Lilith's fabled daughter looks like in the flesh.

PANEL 2
Rotate POV, but stay out wide. One of the demons loosens the chain, and the gibbet comes crashing heavily to the ground.

SFX: SFLANGGG

PANEL 3
Tight two shot on Vampi and Athaltor. The gibbet, with Vampi in it, is now lying full-length on the floor. Athaltor crouches on top of it on all fours, leering in at Vampi. Her eyes have snapped open and she's staring at him at point blank range.

ATHALTOR: Mmmm! A meal fit for a king. Nothing to say, Vampirella?

ATHALTOR: No pleas? No threats? Quite lost for words?

PANEL 4
Close-up on Vampi's face, seen through the bars of the gibbet. Her lower lip crumples as she starts to dissolve into helpless, despairing, child-like tears.

VAMPIRELLA: I—I want to go home now. Please.

VAMPIRELLA: I want my mommy.

To be continued

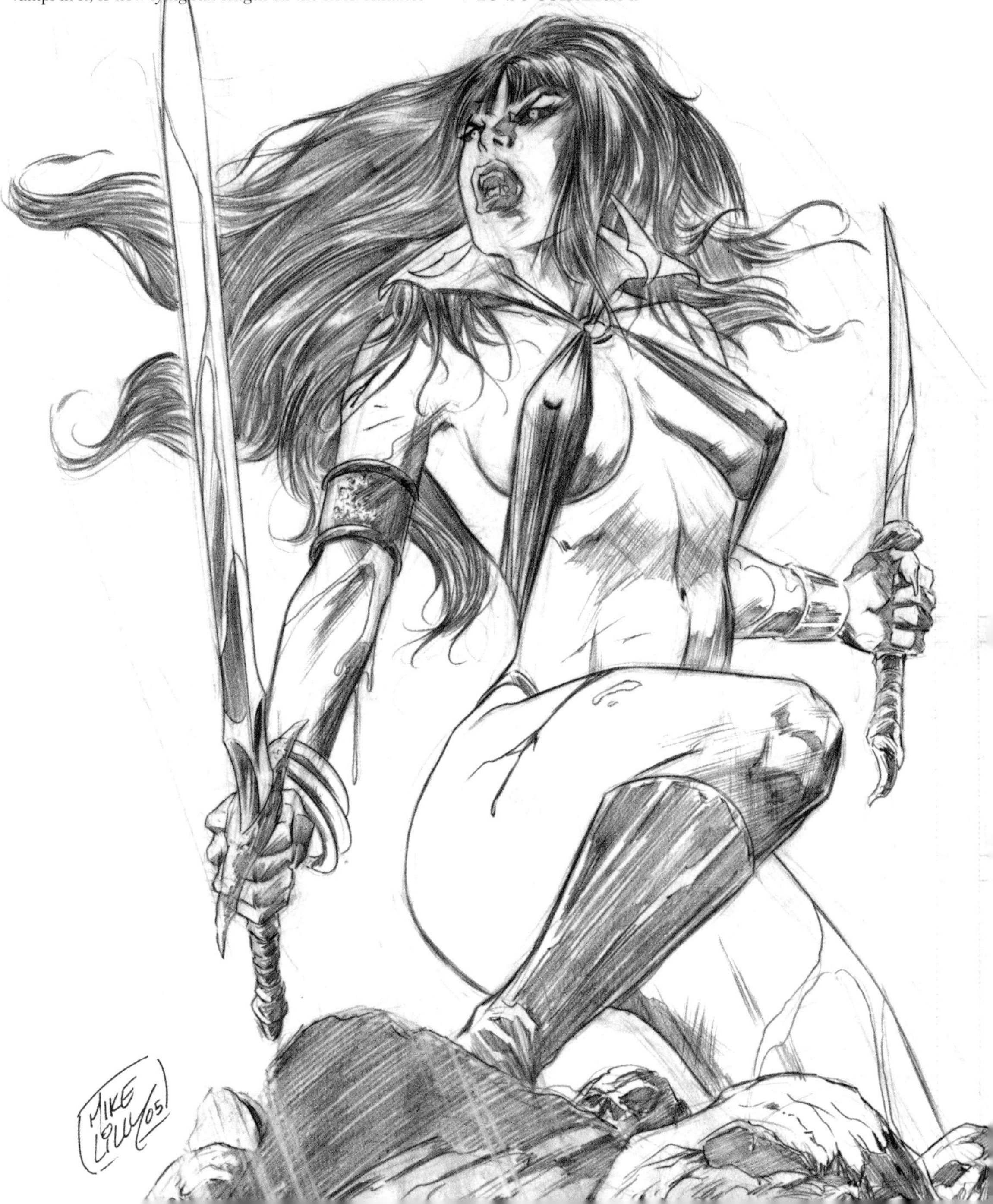
MIKE LILLY 05

Vampirella Quarterly – Fall Issue 2007
by Joshua Hale Fialkov
for Stephen Segovia

PAGE 1

PANEL 1
A business district in Washington, D.C., we should be able to see some of the DC architecture in the distant background. It's nighttime, and the city's lights are lit.

CAPTION: And so... we accomplish.

CAPTION: We succeed.

PANEL 2
Push in on a building; it's the warehouse from the end of the previous issue.

CAPTION: We set out to do things, and sometimes... even without meaning to...

PANEL 3
The building starts to glow, an explosion brewing inside.

CAPTION: We succeed.

PANEL 4
EXPLOSION!

CAPTION: Even though we meant to fail.

PAGE 2-3

PANEL 1
HUGE PANEL ACROSS THE TOP HALF OF BOTH PAGES - It's the apocalypse. From that mushroom cloud, all of Washington, D.C. is being showered with fire.

CAPTION: The journey of our lives is all that we have... all that we can stand by.

CHAOS (O.P.): And so, by the hand of his greatest enemy, CHAOS was set free.

CHAOS (O.P.): And through the body of his enemy's true love, CHAOS shall rule the Earth.

PANEL 2 (Bottom Left Corner of Page 2)
CHAOS, the emblem burning on the chest that was once Adam Van Helsing, the CHAOS aura blooming from him, his tongue licking at his lips. He's laughing, as the BRQ holds on to him lustfully.

CAPTION: My journey has led me here. To this day. To face the greatest evil this world has ever known.

CHAOS: I don't suppose the irony is lost on you, Vampirella.

PANEL 3
Vampirella is beaten and bruised, pushing herself up from the dust and rubble. She's ready for a fight though.

CAPTION: If that's my destiny, so be it.

VAMPIRELLA: This ends now, Chaos.

PANEL 4
Chaos rises up, the aura pulls a swirl of debris around him, as though it's 'filling itself in' and becoming solid.

CAPTION: I just wish I wasn't scared to death.

CHAOS: I couldn't agree more.

PANEL 5
Chaos raises his now giant fist and SMASHES VAMPIRELLA!

TITLE BOX: VENGEANCE OF VAMPIRELLA, Part 3 of 4
Written by Joshua Hale Fialkov
Art by Stephen Segovia
Colors by Jay David Ramos
Letters by Ed Dukeshire

PAGE 4

PANEL 1
Vampi is left, crushed into the street battered and broken, as CHAOS motions to the Queen.

CHAOS: Come, my Queen... let's have some fun.

PANEL 2
The Queen is giddy as a schoolgirl.

BRQ: Of course, my Lord.

PANEL 3
She spits on Vampirella as she passes by.

BRQ: Take that you blood-sucking bitch.

PANEL 4
Vampi's arm juts out, and grabs the Queen's leg.

PANEL 5
The Queen is on the ground as Vampi rises up; she's like a wild animal, the look of a hungry predator on her face.

VAMPIRELLA: Blood sucking is right.

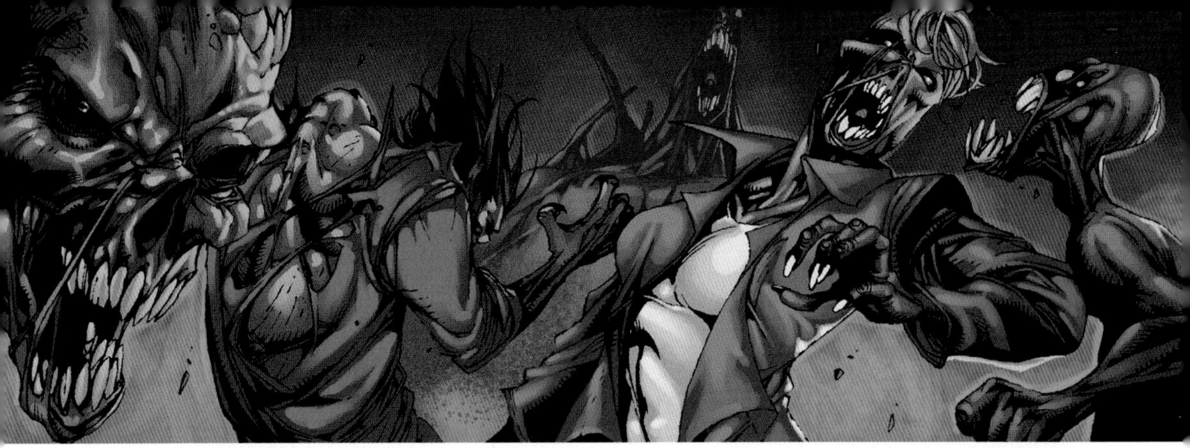

JOSHUA HALE FIALKOV: In this third part of my Vengeance of Vampirella story, knowing that it would be Stephen Segovia's last time drawing one of my scripts, I really wanted to make sure I got to see everything I've always wanted to see from him. From the amazing **design work on the transforming demon humans**, to the **fluid action of this gigantic battle,** he managed to take what could've been melodramatic and made a remarkable piece of work that I think transcends my writing.

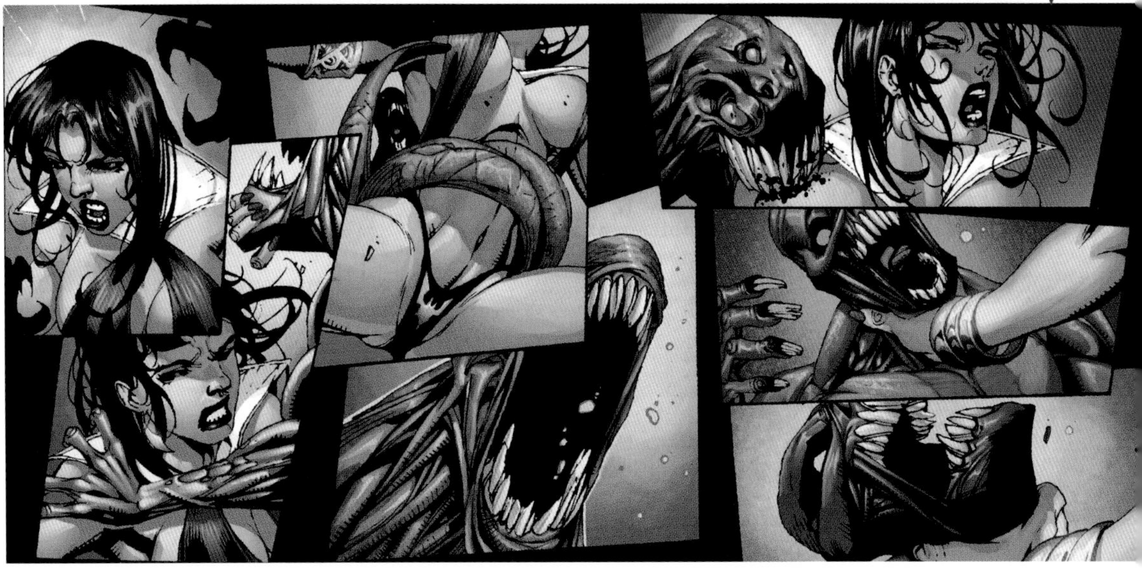

PAGE 5

PANEL 1
Chaos rises up in the middle of the city, the Washington Monument hanging like a broken twig in the background. Still the debris swirls, making him ever larger and more threatening.

CHAOS: I call on you, my armies of darkness, my hounds of hell, my cursed and broken masses... COME FORTH!

PANEL 2
From Chaos a wave of energy pours forth, through all of the civilians, it's as though they're being electrocuted.

CHAOS: Yes... my victory... OUR victory, my love... where...

VAMPIRELLA (O.P.): OVER HERE, CHAOS.

PANEL 3
Vampirella holds the nearly dead corpse of the Blood Red Queen, the blood dripping from her neck matching the blood on Vampi's face.

VAMPIRELLA: You let them go... now. Or she dies.

PANEL 4
CHAOS smiles as he releases the people.

CHAOS: As you wish.

PANEL 5
But the people are not right... they're transforming before Vampi's horrified eyes into hideous monsters and demons. Twisted soulless monsters with barely a touch of humanity left in them.

PAGE 6 and 7

PANEL 1
Top 2/3rds of the two pages, we see the army of Hell piling on Vampirella. The Blood Red Queen cackles, still in Vampi's hand.

CAPTION: I know I'm beginning to sound like a broken record here, but this is all my fault.

CAPTION: Adam's going to give me hell when I get him back.

CAPTION: Notice, I said 'when' and not 'if.'

CAPTION: That's the power of positive thinking.

BRQ: NOW, FINALLY, YOU DIE!

PANEL 2 - 10
Small, Square Panels lining the bottom of the page, each filled with extreme close-ups of Vampi.

First she slashes the BRQ down

The BRQ's Energy disperses, her body killed.

Vampi tries to dispense with the attacking monsters... but she can't use deadly force... they're still people.

In the final two panels one of them grabs Vampi and bites down on her. She's forced to snap its neck.

If you can do more panels, or lay it out differently, feel free.

BRQ: HAHAHAHAHAHAHAHAHAHAHAH!

CAPTION: I can't kill them... they're still people.

CAPTION: And CHAOS knows that.

CAPTION: I can't do this...

CAPTION: I have to do this.

PAGE 8

PANEL 1
Vampi holds the dead Monster who's slowly transforming back into a human.

VAMPI: Is that what you want Chaos? You want to see me kill? You want to see me destroy these innocents?

VAMPI: FINE.

PANEL 2
Vampi's grabbed another of the hellspawn. She holds him with a death grip.

VAMPI: They're all cursed anyways, right? Every one of them a monster on the inside.

VAMPI: RIGHT?

PANEL 3
CHAOS smiles. He's ruined her...

CHAOS: Something like that... yes.

PANEL 4
Vampirella tosses the creature away, alive, and unscathed.

VAMPI: I'm done playing your games, Chaos.

PANEL 5
Chaos watches, his hands on his hips, the massive junk filled aura turning him into a towering monster, and I'm talking Godzilla size... at his feet, flocking towards Vampi are literally thousands of transformed humans flooding towards her.

CHAOS: I don't think so, my dear.

PAGE 9

PANEL 1
As the horde is pouring at Vampi, Chaos grabs a nearby building and tears it up...

VAMPIRELLA: Don't you get it?

VAMPIRELLA: You can throw ANYTHING at me.

PANEL 2
Vampi launches herself over the horde.

VAMPIRELLA: And until you're back in hell, and I have my Adam back...

PANEL 3
She's crowd surfing, jumping from creature to creature as Chaos wields the building like a gigantic baseball bat.

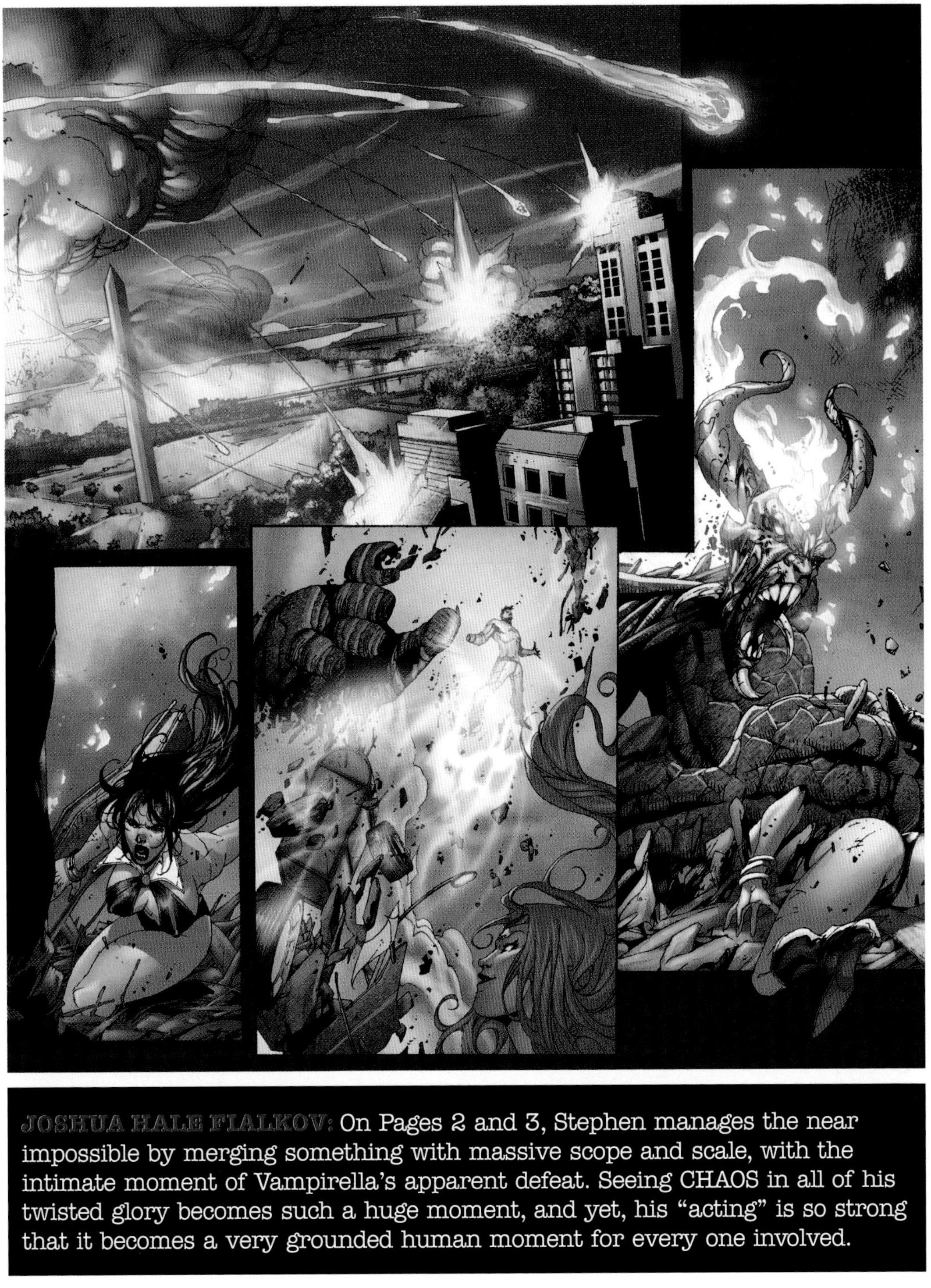

JOSHUA HALE FIALKOV: On Pages 2 and 3, Stephen manages the near impossible by merging something with massive scope and scale, with the intimate moment of Vampirella's apparent defeat. Seeing CHAOS in all of his twisted glory becomes such a huge moment, and yet, his "acting" is so strong that it becomes a very grounded human moment for every one involved.

VAMPIRELLA: I will not stop.

VAMPIRELLA: I will not surrender.

PANEL 5
Vampi pushes herself off, launching to attack CHAOS who...

PAGE 10

Panel 1
FULL PAGE SPLASH
CHAOS bats Vampirella with the building like she's nothing but a slow ball pitch... it's as though she's a fly, tiny before the mighty rubble body of CHAOS.

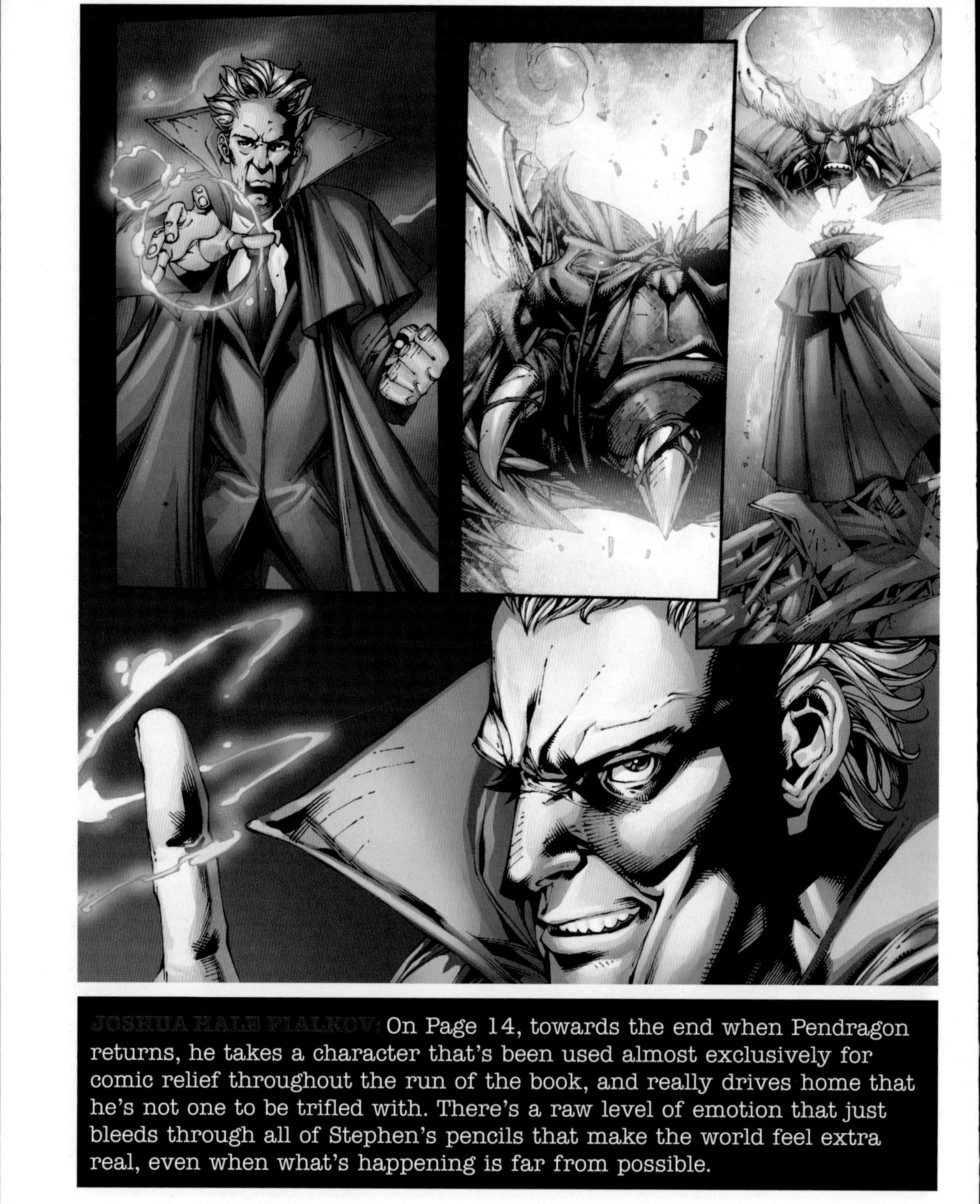

JOSHUA HALE FIALKOV: On Page 14, towards the end when Pendragon returns, he takes a character that's been used almost exclusively for comic relief throughout the run of the book, and really drives home that he's not one to be trifled with. There's a raw level of emotion that just bleeds through all of Stephen's pencils that make the world feel extra real, even when what's happening is far from possible.

PAGE 11

PANEL 1
Vampi is just plain CREAMED. She's blood soaked, and bruised... lying prone in a pile of rubble.

CHAOS (O.P.): You could've had the world, Vampirella...

CHAOS (O.P.): Together we could've ruled this dimension...

PANEL 2
Vampi starts pushing herself up... but it's tough going.

CHAOS (O.P.): But... oh no... you wouldn't be the Bride of Chaos.

PANEL 3
The Blood Red Queen is looking down at Vampi.
BRQ: You don't need this... thing... anyways, my love.

BRQ: She's nothing.

PANEL 4
Vampirella struggles pushing herself up to her knees, trying to ready herself to fight.

BRQ: Look at her! Look how cute!

BRQ: She thinks she can still win...

PANEL 5
Close on Vampi... anger in her eyes.

BRQ: Look around you, you fool.

BRQ: We already won.

PAGE 12

PANEL 1
We pull back... Earth already looks like Hell. The sky is burning red, the buildings are crumbling, and the Demon/People are running amok.

CHAOS: And so easy... look at them, Vampirella... the ones you want to save...

CHAOS: Not twenty minutes and they're already devolving...

PANEL 2
Push in on two of the Demon/People fighting...

CHAOS: They're nothing but mindless, soulless cattle.

CHAOS: Devoid of value.

PANEL 3
One of the monsters rips out the throat of the other, who starts becoming human again...

CHAOS: And for these beasts you risk YOUR life.

CHAOS: The life of the one you love.

PANEL 4
In the midst of CHAOS's body, Adam's body still sits... it looks like he's sleeping.

CHAOS: Your beloved Adam can't contain my life force for much longer, Vampirella. Soon, he'll become just another piece of me.

PANEL 5
XCU on Vampi's face, she looks ready to cry...

VAMPI: Adam... I'm coming...

PAGE 13

PANEL 1-3
(Should be one wide panel, split into three smaller panels, with Vampi moving through them)

Wide, cinematic motion shots, Vampi running and leaping from her perch of rubble up towards CHAOS's chest, where Adam's body sits.

PANEL 4
One of CHAOS's giant rubble hands grabs Vampi out of the air.

PANEL 5
Vampi squirms trying to escape, straining with all of her might.

CHAOS: Is that it? Is that ALL you have? You're going to run and jump and hit and slash at ME?

PANEL 6
The CHAOS 'construct' so to speak, towering over Vampi... he's in full on Mad God mode now.

CHAOS: I AM GOD.

CHAOS: And you... are nothing.

PAGE 14

PANEL 1
CHAOS gets blasted by a HUGE plume of magical energy, dropping Vampi in the process.

PANEL 2
We see the origin of that bolt of magic. Pendragon.

PENDRAGON: Get the hell away from my assistant.

PANEL 3
Chaos laughs.

CHAOS: YOU?!? Mordecai Pendragon... drunk and deviant... the man who would sell his own soul for a glass of bourbon.

CHAOS: Are you so inebriated that you think you're a REAL magician.

PANEL 4
Pendragon stands on a crest facing CHAOS.

PENDRAGON: No, you ancient fool... I know I'm barely a match for a flea, let alone you.

PANEL 5
Pendragon cracks a mischievous smile.

PENDRAGON: That's why I bought some friends along.

PAGE 15

PANEL 1
From around Pendragon come magicians of all kinds. Their hands all glow with the energy that Pen used to save the civilians earlier.

PENDRAGON: Y'see, Chaos... I did a lot of touring.

PENDRAGON: And met a LOT of other magicians.

PANEL 2
Two particularly menacing looking warlocks step forward.

PENDRAGON: And, well, as my lovely assistant would say...

PENDRAGON: I'm nothing if not charming.

PANEL 3
The magicians have formed a circle around Pendragon and CHAOS.

PENDRAGON: And over the past god knows how many years, you and your cult have pissed off the wrong bunch of magic users.

PANEL 4
Chaos readies himself for battle.

CHAOS: So it shall be.

CHAOS: Now, we fight.

PANEL 5
Pendragon gives a knowing wink.

PENDRAGON: You HONESTLY think I would fight you? After all this time?

PENDRAGON: There's only one fight for you, big guy.

PANEL 6
High, wide shot, the magician's energy channels into a spot in the rubble.

PAGE 16

PANEL 1
Small Thin Wide panel - A hand pulls out of the rubble.

PANEL 2
Small Thin Wide Panel - Another hand starts to pull the rest of her out of the rubble. The hands are glowing with the Good Magical energy.

PANEL 3
REST OF PAGE
Vampirella, a battle Aura formed around her, and she looks totally f***g juiced up. It's like she has the power of all 300 of the wussy Spartan boys powering her.**

VAMPIRELLA: Now.

VAMPIRELLA: Can we just end this already?

TO BE CONCLUDED!

JOSHUA HALE FIALKOV:
It's pretty rare, as a writer, to find an artist like Stephen. He manages to cross so many lines with his work. Most guys are either architecture guys, or character guys, or they do great designs but are inexpressive, or vice versa. Stephen can literally do it all. As you've seen throughout the rest of the book, there's just nothing you can throw at him that he can't execute the hell out of.

It's been an honor and a great learning experience for me to work with Stephen. I can only hope it's not the last time we collaborate.

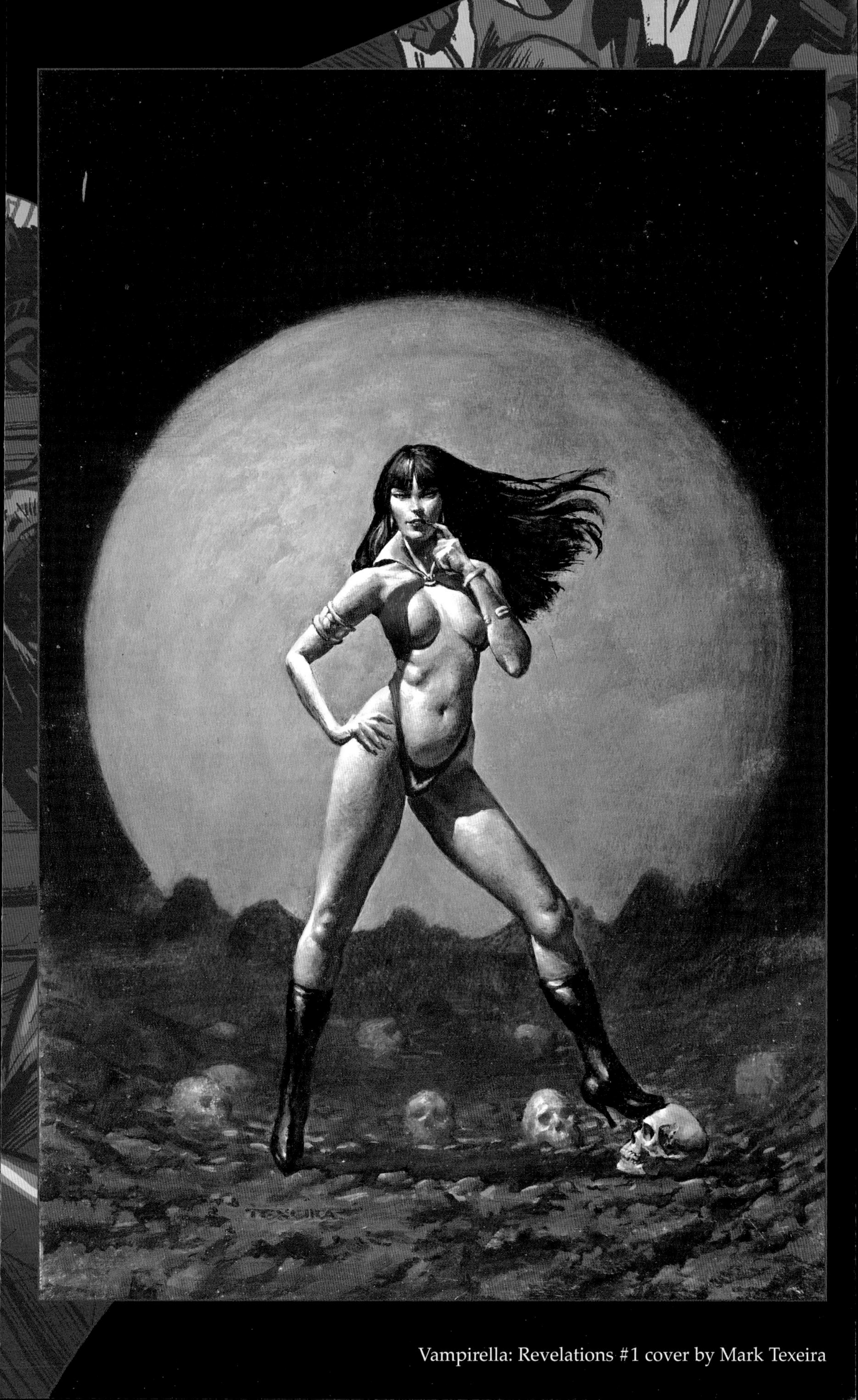
TEXEIRA

Vampirella: Revelations #1 cover by Mark Texeira

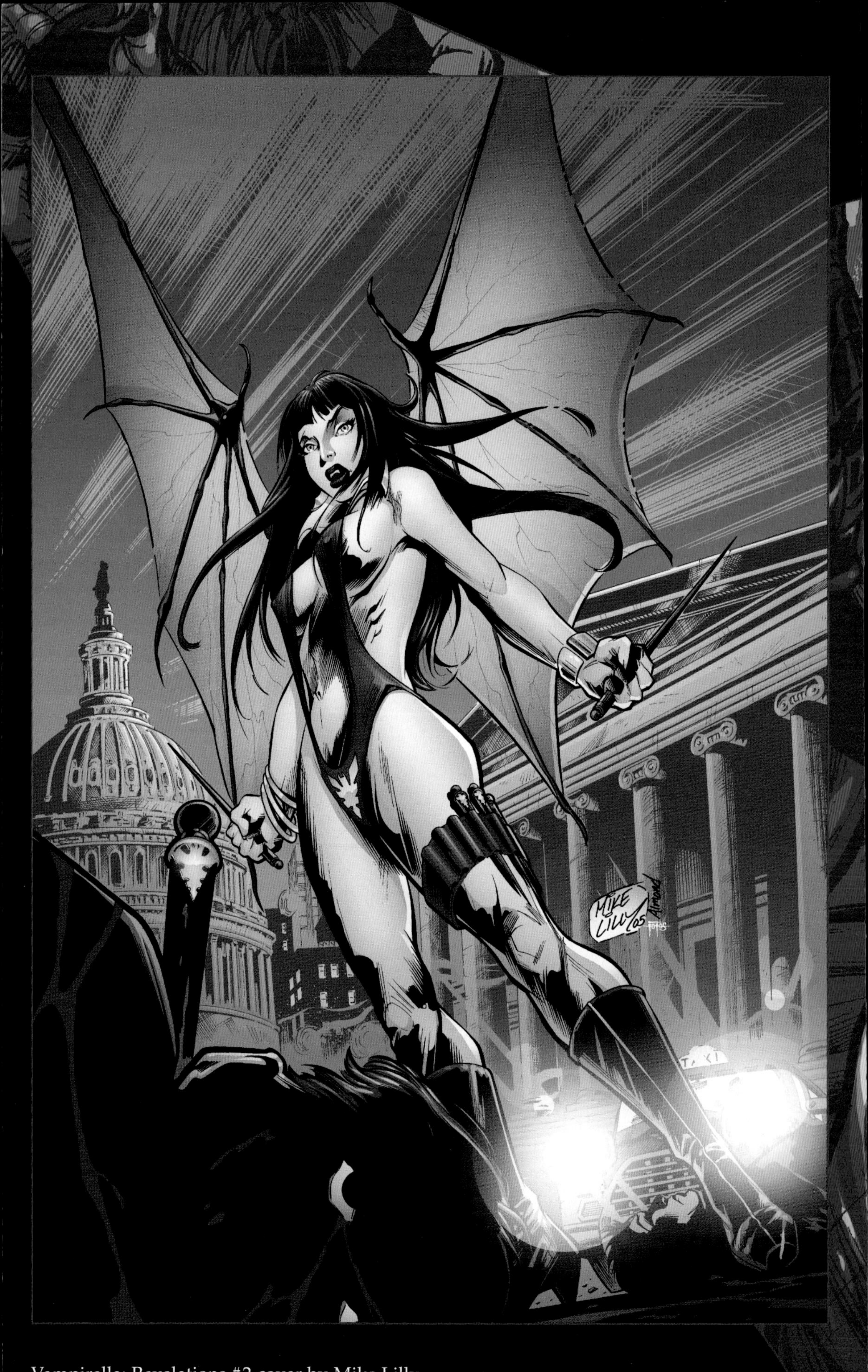
TAXI

Vampirella: Revelations #2 cover by Mike Lilly

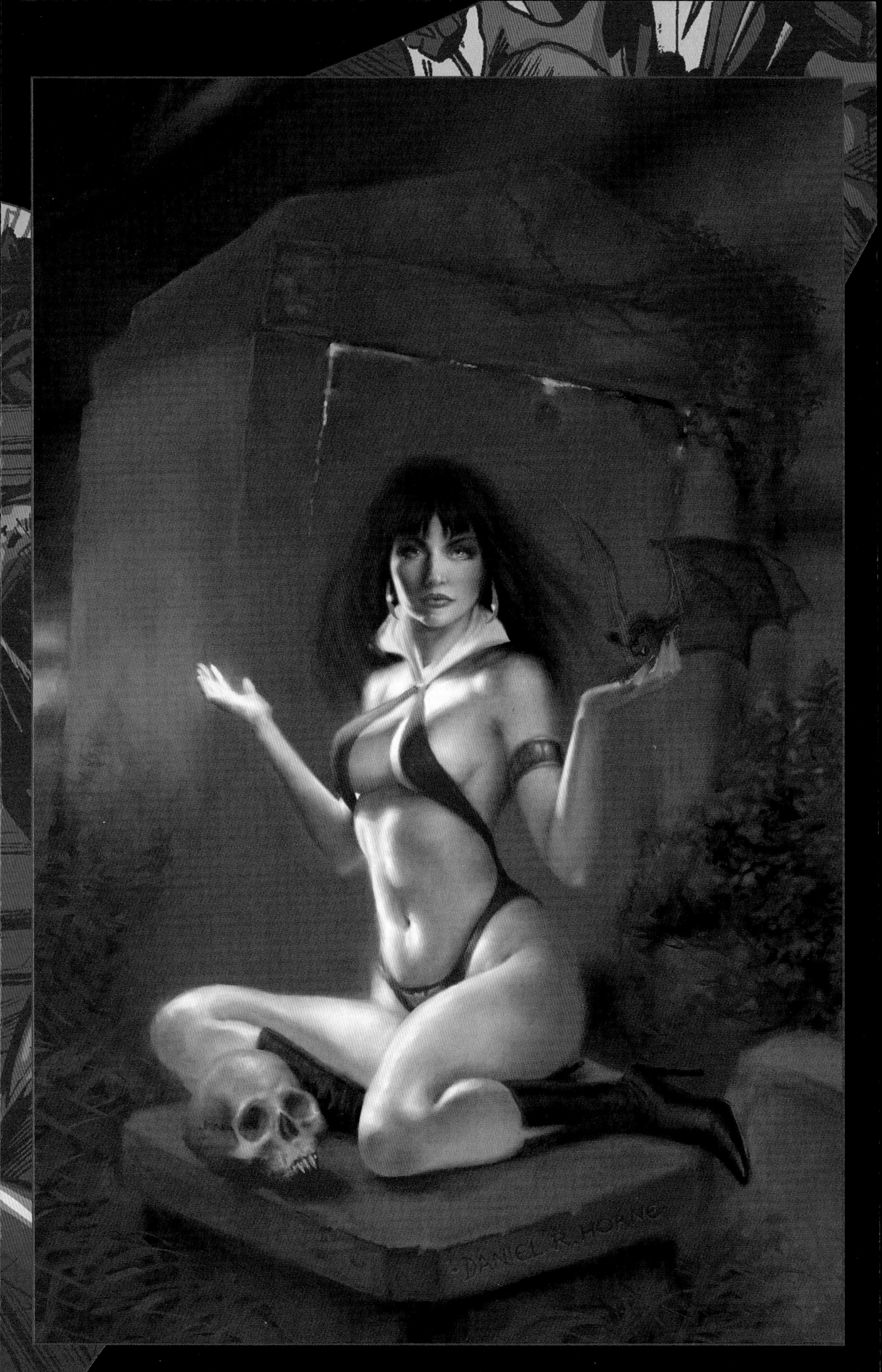
DANIEL R. HORNE

Vampirella: Revelations #3 cover by Daniel R. Horne

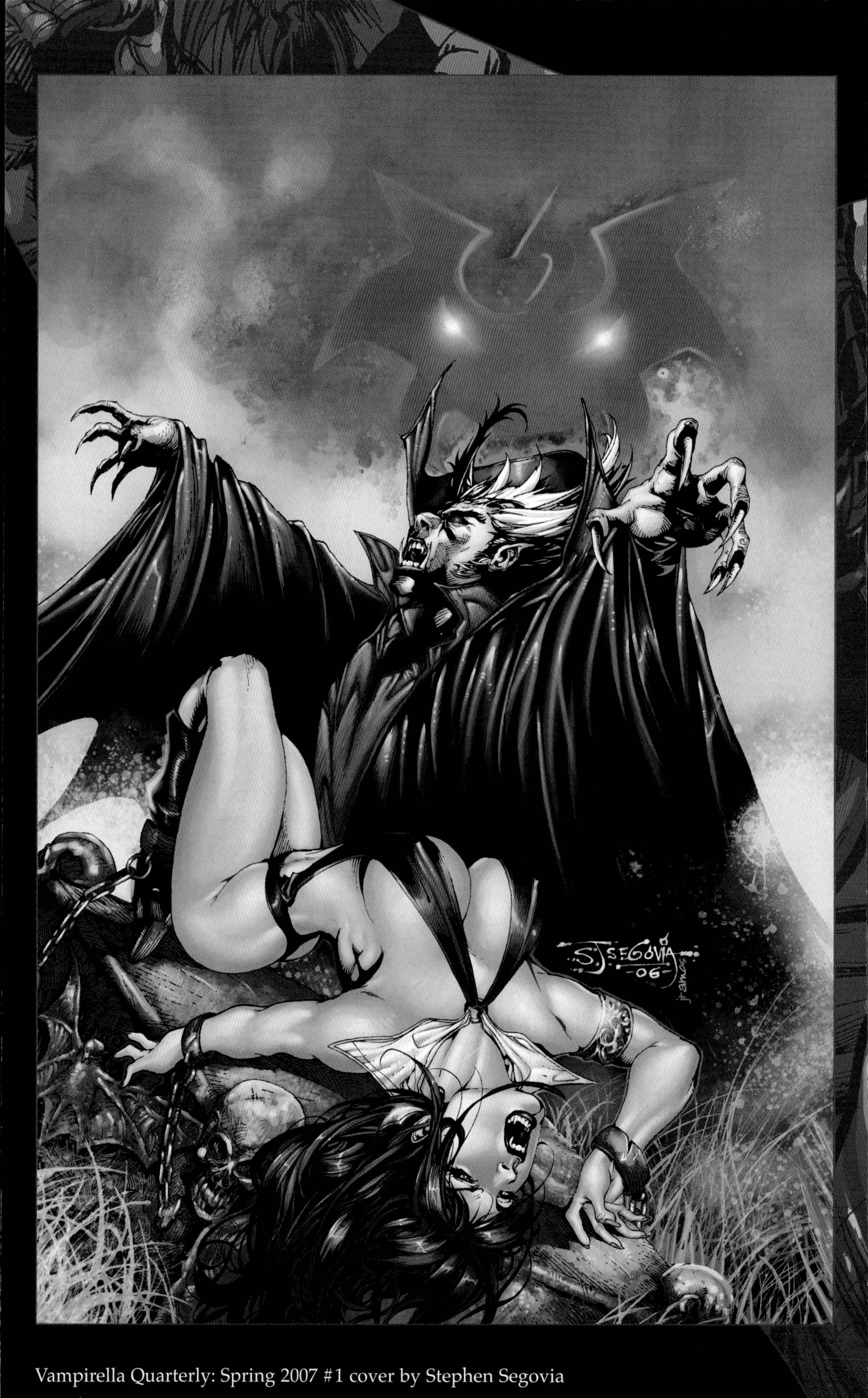

Vampirella Quarterly: Spring 2007 #1 cover by Stephen Segovia

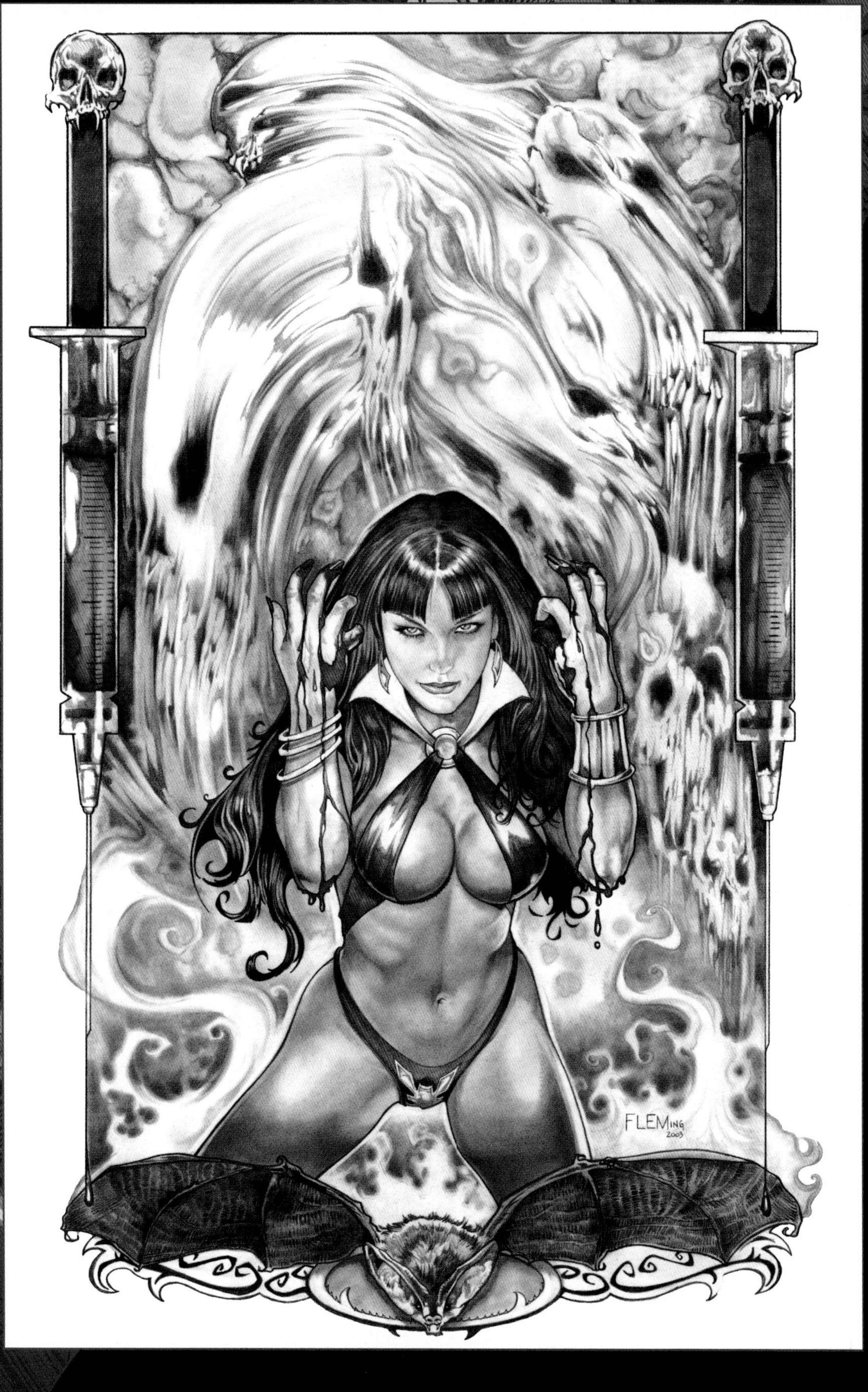
FLEMing
2003

Vampirella Quarterly: Spring 2007 #1 cover by Tom Flemming

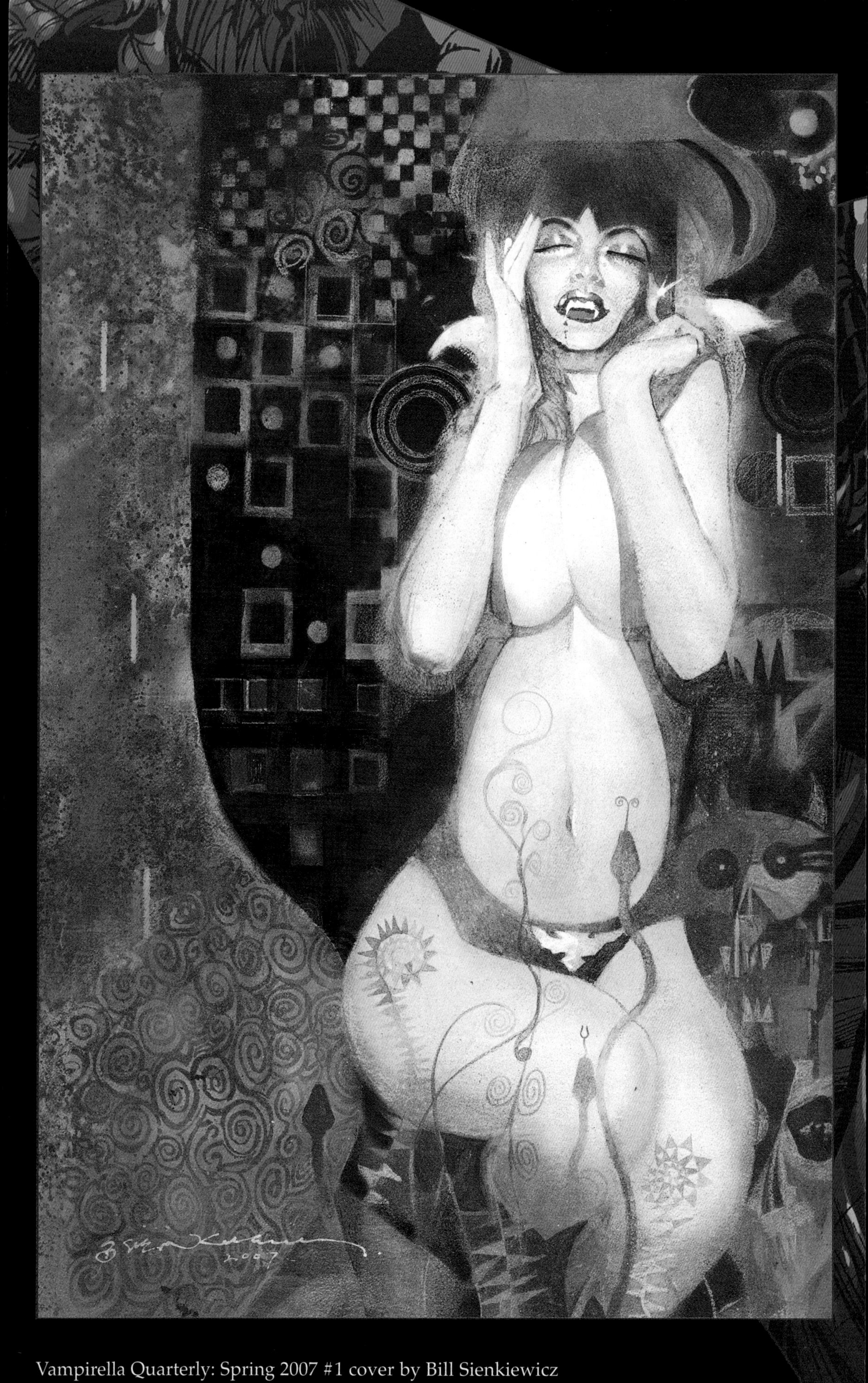

Vampirella Quarterly: Spring 2007 #1 cover by Bill Sienkiewicz

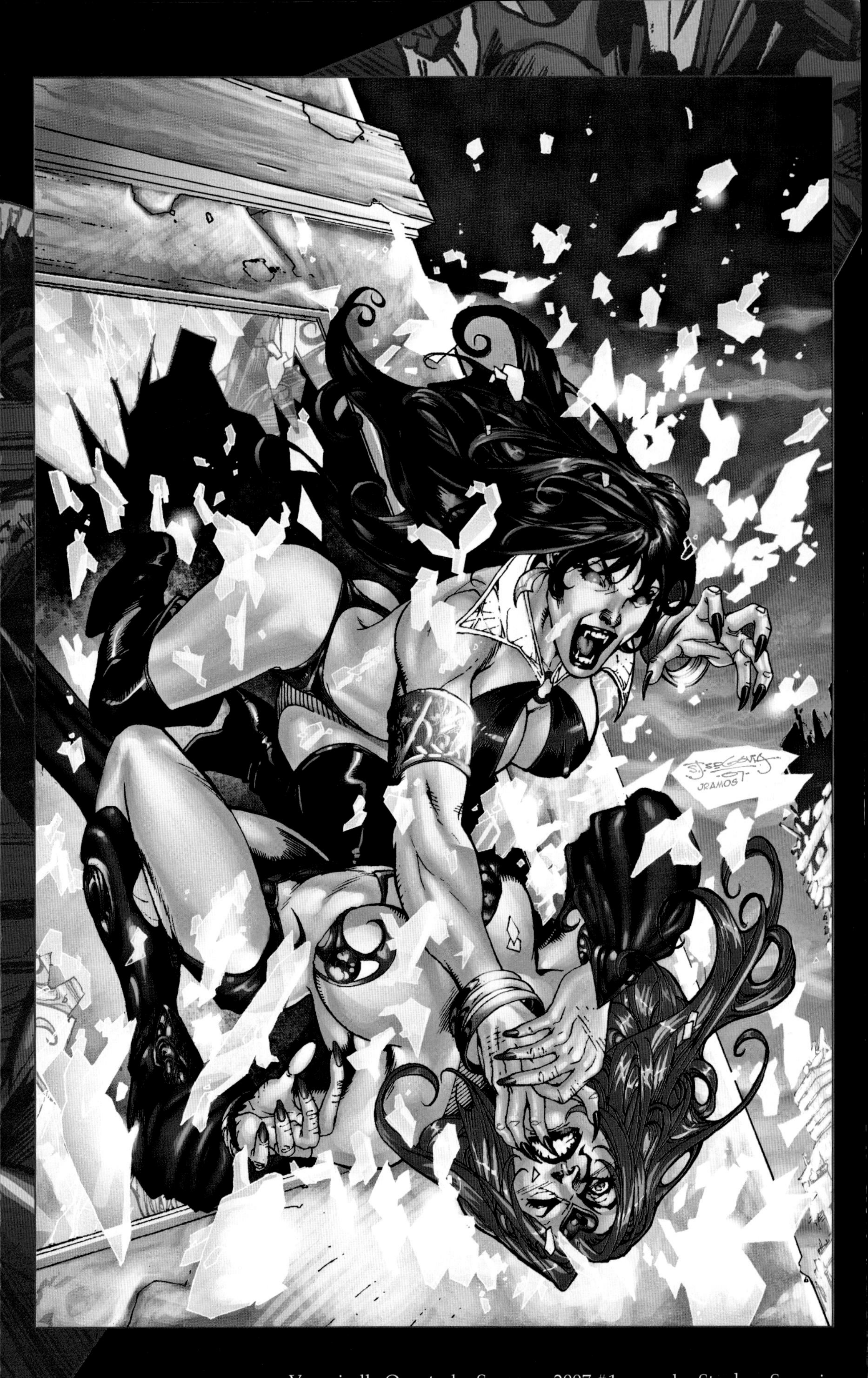

Vampirella Quarterly: Summer 2007 #1 cover by Stephen Segovia

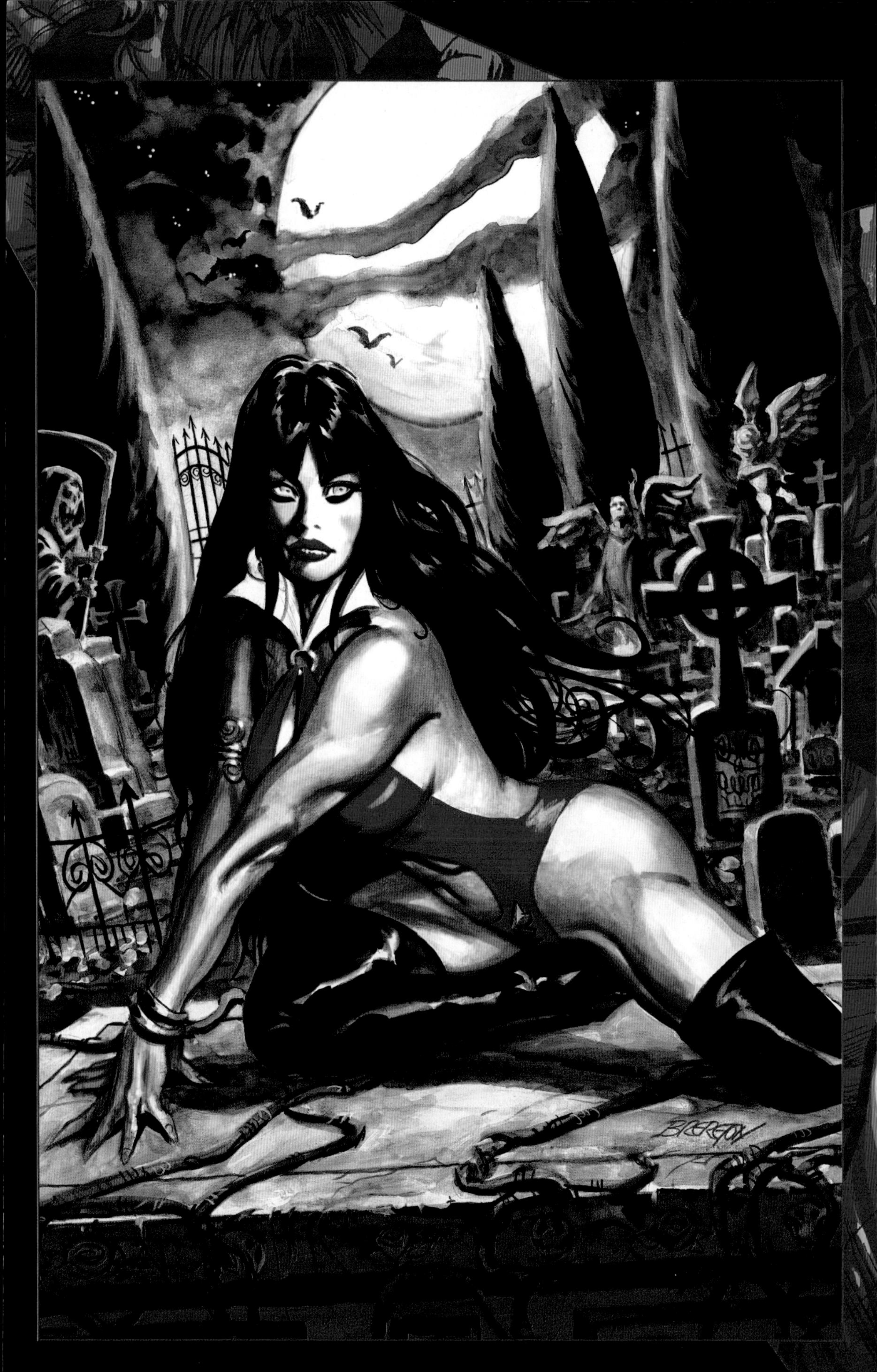

Vampirella Quarterly: Summer 2007 #1 cover by Dan Brereton

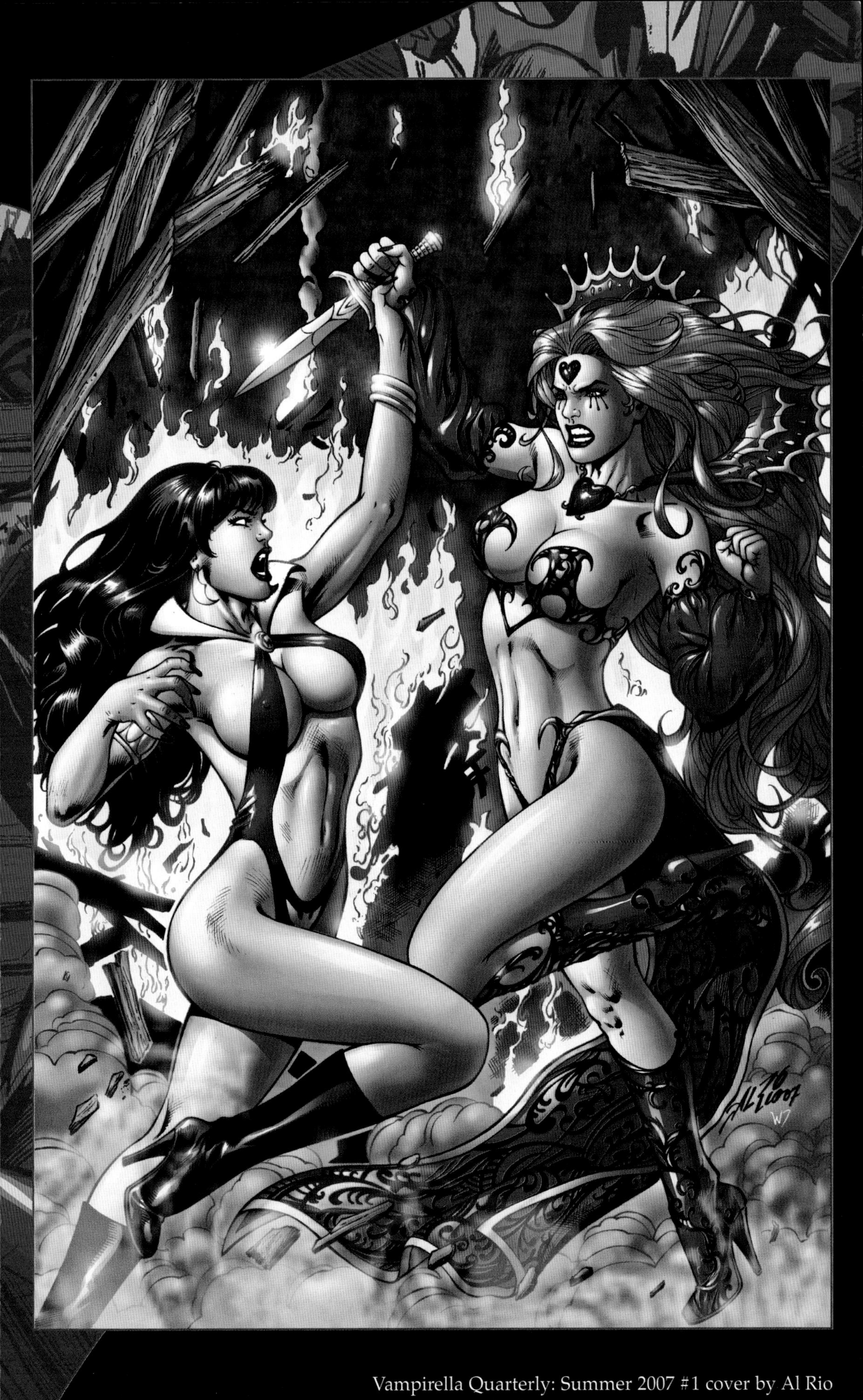

Vampirella Quarterly: Summer 2007 #1 cover by Al Rio

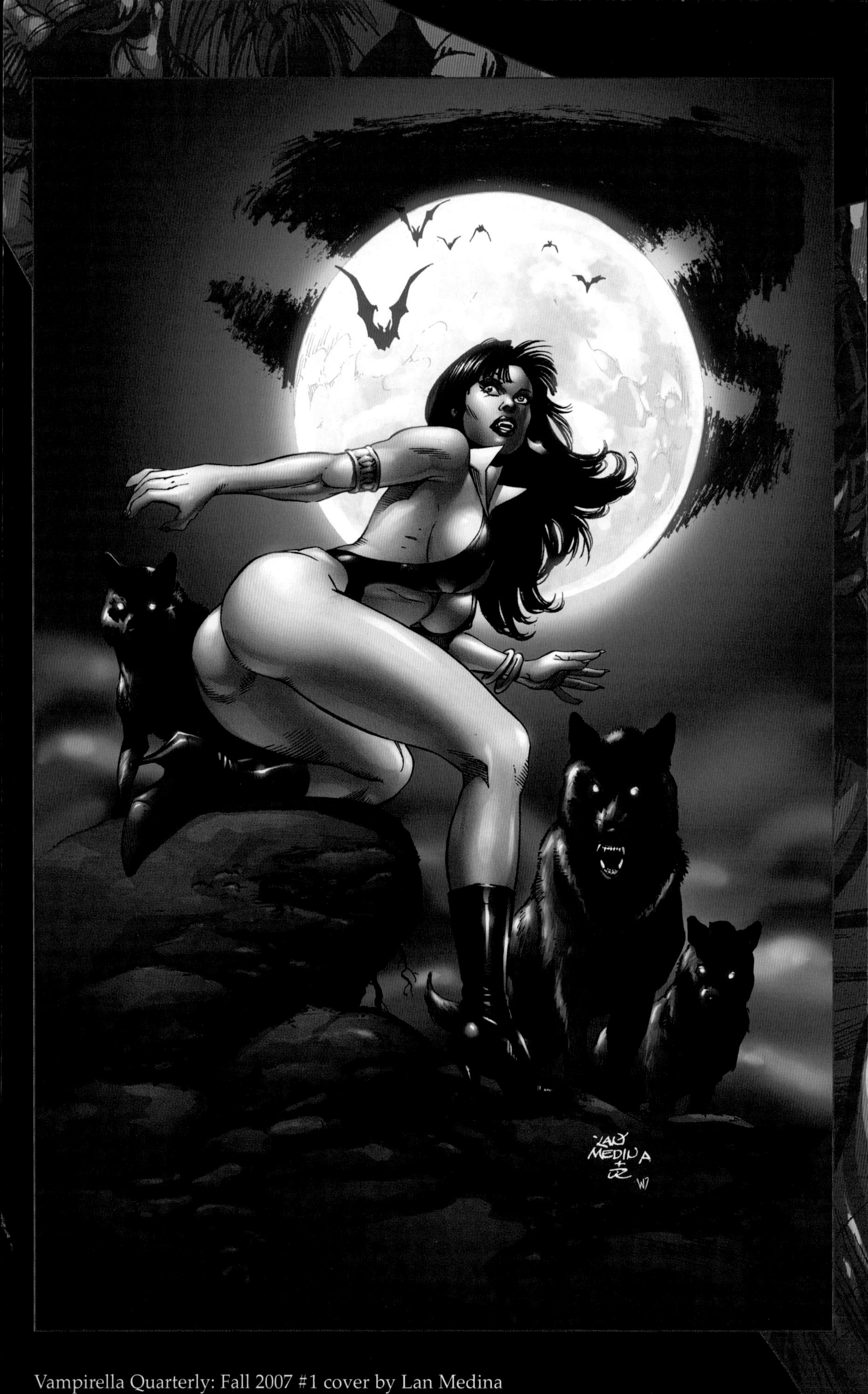

Vampirella Quarterly: Fall 2007 #1 cover by Lan Medina

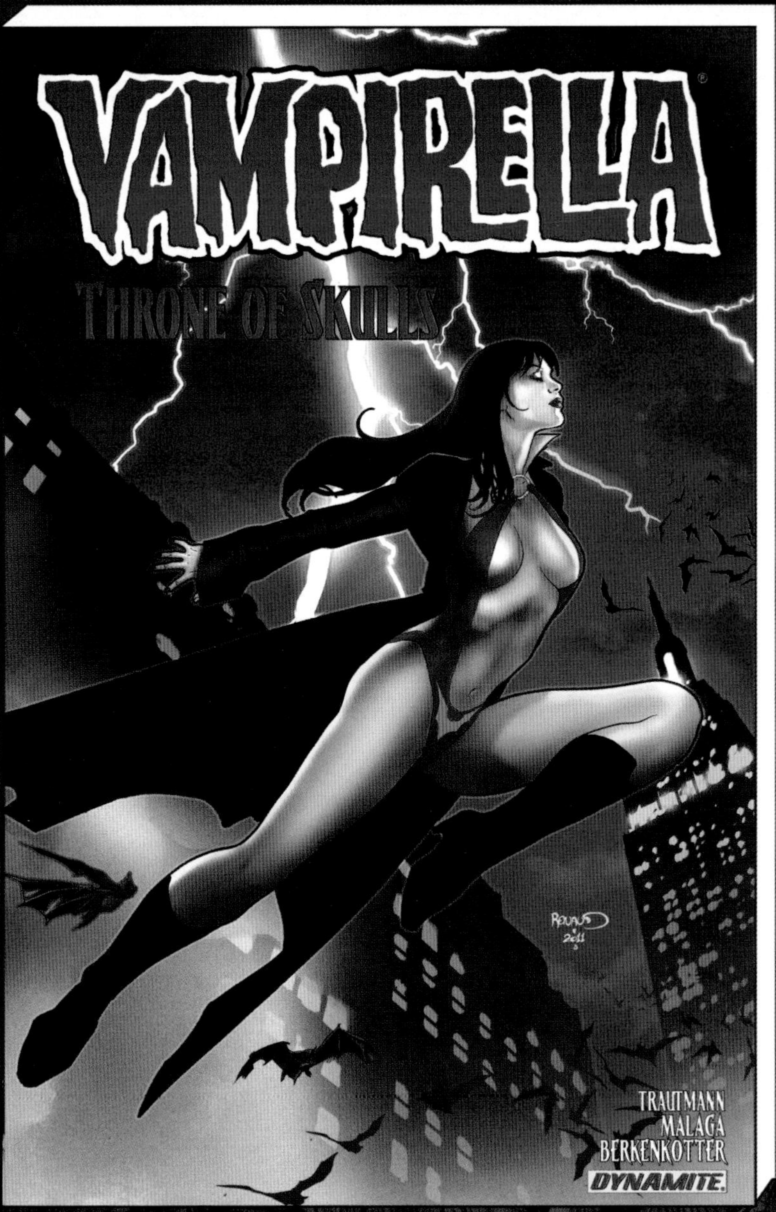

VAMPIRELLA
THRONE OF SKULLS
TRAUTMANN
MALAGA
BERKENKOTTER
DYNAMITE

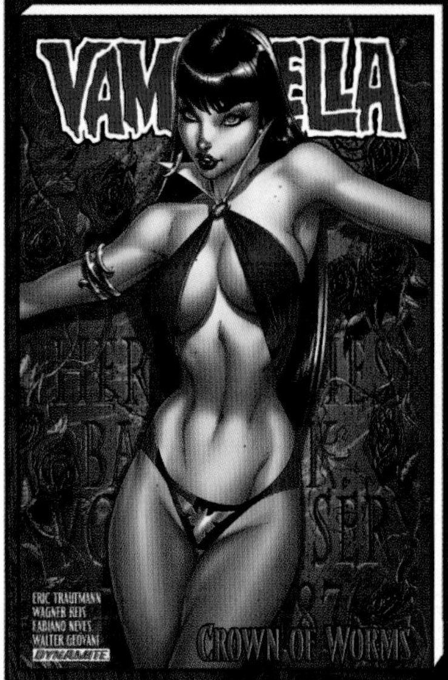

VAMPIRELLA
ERIC TRAUTMANN
WAGNER REIS
FABIANO NEVES
WALTER GEOVANI
DYNAMITE
CROWN OF WORMS

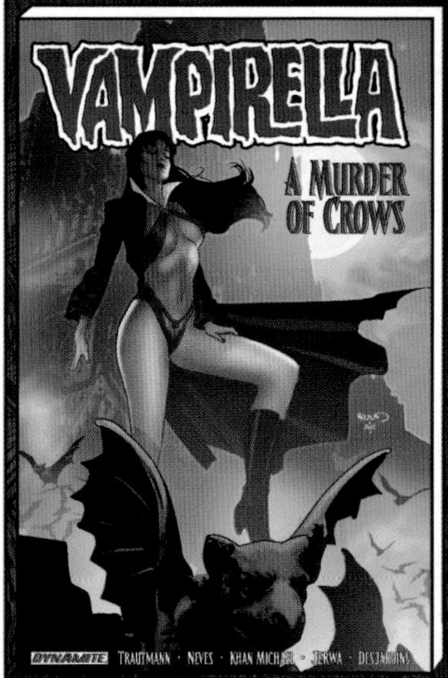

VAMPIRELLA
A MURDER OF CROWS
DYNAMITE
TRAUTMANN · NEVES

In Stores Now From Dynamite!

VAMPIRELLA VOL. ONE: "CROWN OF WORMS"

written by ERIC TRAUTMANN art by WAGNER REIS & WALTER GEOVANI cover by J. SCOTT CAMPBELL

Collects issues 1-7

VAMPIRELLA VOL. TWO: "A MURDER OF CROWS"

written by ERIC TRAUTMANN & BRANDON JERWA

art by FABIANO NEVES, HEUBERT KHAN MICHAEL & JOHNNY DESJARDINS cover by PAUL RENAUD

Collects issues 8-11

VAMPIRELLA VOL. THREE: "THRONE OF SKULLS"

written by ERIC TRAUTMANN art by JOSE MALAGA & PATRICK BERKENKOTTER cover by PAUL RENAUD

Collects issues 12 through 20 of the hit series!

WWW.DYNAMITE.COM FOLLOW US ON TWITTER: #DYNAMITECOMICS LIKE US ON FACEBOOK: /DYNAMITECOMICS

LOOK FOR THESE DYNAMITE GREATEST HITS!

**GARTH ENNIS
THE BOYS & MORE!**

**(Garth Ennis') Battlefields V1:
The Night Witches**
Ennis, Braun

**(Garth Ennis') Battlefields V2:
Dear Billy**
Ennis, Snejbjerg

**(Garth Ennis') Battlefields V3:
The Tankies**
Ennis, Ezquerra

**(Garth Ennis') The Complete
Battlefields V1**
Ennis, Braun, Ezquerra, more

**(Garth Ennis') Battlefields V4:
Happy Valley**
Ennis, Holden

**(Garth Ennis') Battlefields V5:
The Firefly and His Majesty**
Ennis, Ezquerra

**(Garth Ennis') Battlefields V6:
Motherland**
Ennis, Braun

**(Garth Ennis') The Complete
Battlefields V2**
Ennis, Braun, Holden, more

**The Boys V1 The Name of
the Game**
Ennis, Robertson

The Boys V2 Get Some
Ennis, Robertson, Snejbjerg

The Boys V3 Good For The Soul
Ennis, Robertson

The Boys V4 We Gotta Go Now
Ennis, Robertson

The Boys V5 Herogasm
Ennis, McCrea

**The Boys V6
The Self-Preservation Society**
Ennis, Robertson, Ezquerra

The Boys V7 The Innocents
Ennis, Robertson, Braun

The Boys V8 Highland Laddie
Ennis, McCrea

The Boys V9 The Big Ride
Ennis, Braun

**The Boys V10: Butcher, Baker,
Candlestickmaker**
Ennis, Robertson

**The Boys V11 Over the Hill
With the Swords of a
Thousand Men**
Ennis, Braun

The Boys Definitive Edition V1
Ennis, Robertson

The Boys Definitive Edition V2
Ennis, Robertson

The Boys Definitive Edition V3
Ennis, Robertson, more

The Boys Definitive Edition V4
Ennis, Robertson, more

Dan Dare Omnibus
Ennis, Erskine

**Jennifer Blood V1 A Woman's
Work Is Never Done**
Ennis, Batista, Baal, more

**Jennifer Blood V2 Beautiful
People**
Ewing, Baal, more

Just A Pilgrim
Ennis, Ezquerra

The Ninjettes
Ewing, Casallos

Seven Brothers Omnibus
Ennis, Diggle, Kang, more

**The Shadow V1 The Fire of
Creation**
Ennis, Campbell

**GREEN HORNET
KEVIN SMITH & MORE!**

**(Kevin Smith's) Green Hornet
V1 Sins of the Father**
Smith, Hester, Lau

**(Kevin Smith's) Green Hornet
V2 Wearing 'o the Green**
Smith, Hester, Lau

Green Hornet V3 Idols
Hester, Lau

Green Hornet V4 Red Hand
Hester, Smith, Vitorino, more

Green Hornet: Blood Ties
Parks, Desjardins

**The Green Hornet: Year One V1
The Sting of Justice**
Wagner, Campbell

**The Green Hornet: Year One V2
The Biggest of All Game**
Wagner, Campbell

The Green Hornet Parallel Lives
Nitz, Raynor

**The Green Hornet Golden Age
Re-Mastered**
Various

**Kato V1 Not My Father's
Daughter**
Parks, Garza, Bernard

Kato V2 Living in America
Parks, Bernard

Kato Origins V1 Way of the Ninja
Nitz, Worley

**Kato Origins V2 The Hellfire
Club**
Nitz, Worley

VAMPIRELLA!

**Vampirella Masters Series V1
Grant Morrison & Mark Millar**
Morrison, Millar, more

**Vampirella Masters Series V2
Warren Ellis**
Ellis, Conner Palmiotti, more

Vampi Omnibus V1
Conway, Lau

**Vampirella Masters Series V3
Mark Millar**
Millar, Mayhew

**Vampirella Masters Series V4
Visionaries**
Moore, Busiek, Loeb, more

**Vampirella Masters Series V5
Kurt Busiek**
Busiek, Sniegoski, more

**Vampirella Masters Series V6
James Robinson**
Robinson, Jusko, more

Vampirella Archives V1
Various

Vampirella Archives V2
Various

Vampirella Archives V3
Various

Vampirella Archives V4
Various

Vampirella Archives V5
Various

Vampirella V1 Crown of Worms
Trautman, Reis, Geovani

**Vampirella V2 A Murder of
Crows**
Trautman, Neves, more

Vampirella V3 Throne of Skulls
Trautman, Malaga, more

**Vampirella And The Scarlet
Legion**
Harris, Malaga

Vampirella vs. Dracula
Harris, Rodriguez

RED SONJA!

Adventures of Red Sonja V1
Thomas, Thorne, More

Adventures of Red Sonja V2
Thomas, Thorne, More

Adventures of Red Sonja V3
Thomas, Thorne, More

Queen Sonja V1
Ortega, Rubi

Queen Sonja V2 The Red Queen
Nelson, Herbert

Queen Sonja V3 Coming of Age
Lieberman, Rubi

Queen Sonja V4 Son of Set
Nelson, Salazar

**Red Sonja She-Devil With a
Sword V1**
Oeming, Carey, Rubi

**Red Sonja She-Devil With a
Sword V2: Arrowsmiths**
Oeming, Rubi, more

**Red Sonja She-Devil With a
Sword V3: The Rise of
Kulan Gath**
Oeming, Rubi, more

**Red Sonja She-Devil With a
Sword V4: Animals & More**
Oeming, Homs, more

**Red Sonja She-Devil With a
Sword V5: World On Fire**
Oeming, Reed, Homs

**Red Sonja She-Devil With a
Sword V6: Death**
Marz, Ortega, Reed, more

**Red Sonja She-Devil With a
Sword V7: Born Again**
Reed, Geovani

**Red Sonja She-Devil With a
Sword V8: Blood
Dynasty**
Reed, Geovani

**Red Sonja She-Devil With a
Sword V9: War Season**
Trautmann, Geovani, more

**Red Sonja She-Devil With a
Sword V10: Machines
of Empire**
Trautmann, Geovani, more

**Red Sonja She-Devil With a
Sword Omnibus V1**
Oeming, Carey, Rubi, more

**Red Sonja She-Devil With a
Sword Omnibus V2**
Oeming, Reed, Homs, more

**Red Sonja She-Devil With a
Sword Omnibus V3**
Reed, Geovani

Red Sonja vs. Thulsa Doom V1
David, Lieberman, Conrad

**Savage Red Sonja: Queen of
the Frozen Wastes**
Cho, Murray, Homs

Red Sonja: Travels
Marz, Ortega, Thomas, more

**Sword of Red Sonja: Doom of
the Gods (Red Sonja vs. Thulsa
Doom 2)**
Lieberman, Antonio

Red Sonja: Wrath of the Gods
Lieberman, Geovani

**Red Sonja: Revenge of the
Gods**
Lieberman, Sampere

Savage Tales of Red Sonja
Marz, Gage, Ortega, more

ART BOOKS!

**The Art of Howard Chaykin
The Art of Painted Comics
The Art of Ramona Fradon
The Art of Red Sonja
The Art of Vampirella
The Dynamite Art of Alex Ross
George Pérez: Storyteller
The Romita Legacy**

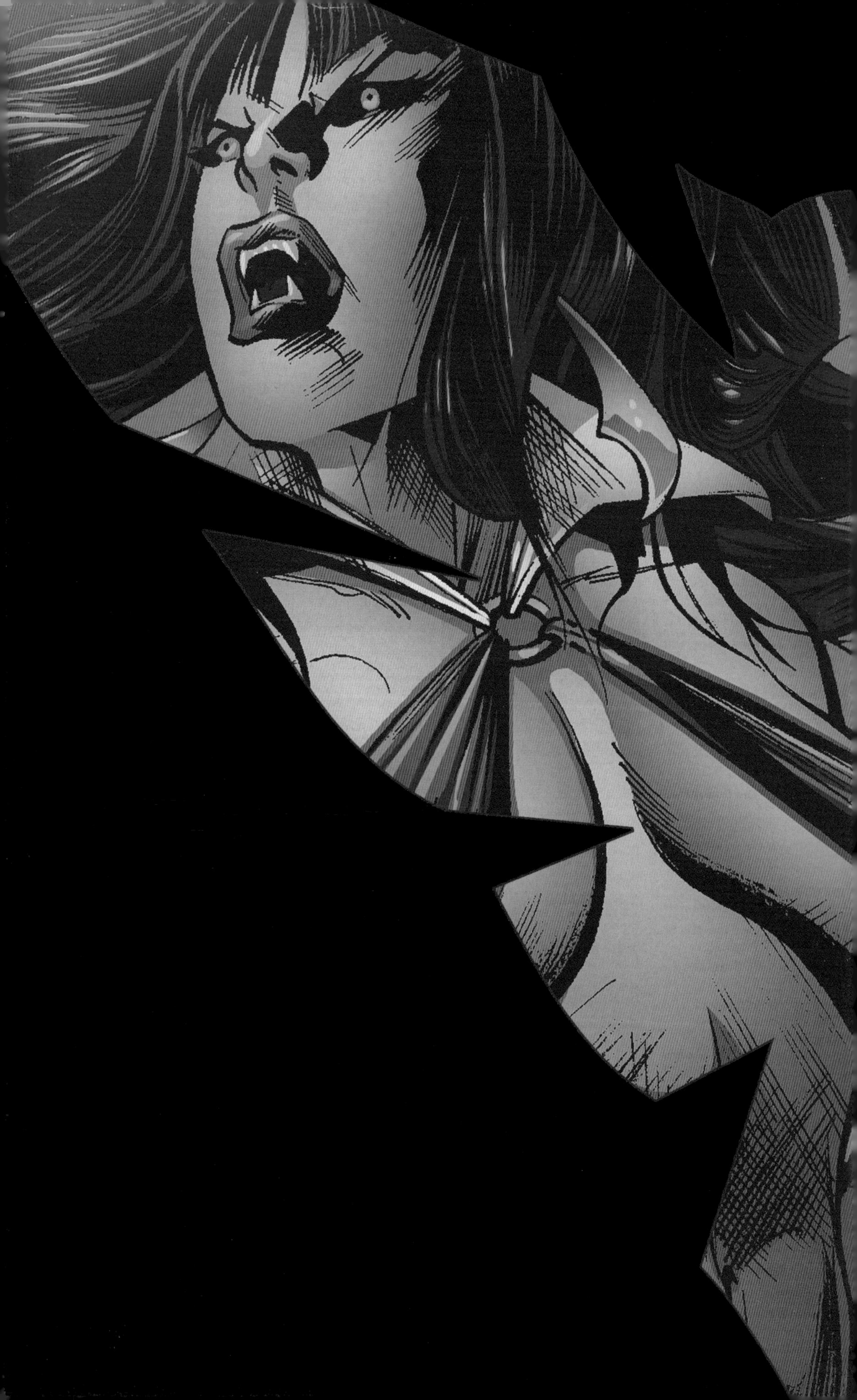